AUTOBIOGRAPHY OF SEVENTY YEARS

SENATOR GEORGE F. HOAR
From a photograph taken in 1897
Copyright 1897, by H. Schervee, Worcester, Mass.

SENATOR GEORGE F. HOAR
From a photograph taken in 1897
Copyright, 1897, by H. Schervee, Worcester, Mass.

AUTOBIOGRAPHY
OF SEVENTY YEARS

BY

GEORGE F. HOAR

WITH PORTRAITS

VOLUME I.

NEW YORK
CHARLES SCRIBNER'S SONS
1903

COPYRIGHT 1903
BY CHARLES SCRIBNER'S SONS

Published November, 1903

PRESS OF
THE NEW ERA PRINTING COMPANY,
LANCASTER, PA.

TO

MY WIFE AND CHILDREN

THIS RECORD OF A LIFE WHICH

THEY HAVE MADE HAPPY

IS AFFECTIONATELY DEDICATED

CONTENTS

CHAPTER I
INTRODUCTORY 1

CHAPTER II
ROGER SHERMAN AND HIS FAMILY 7

CHAPTER III
SAMUEL HOAR 20

CHAPTER IV
BOYHOOD IN CONCORD 40

CHAPTER V
FAMOUS CONCORD MEN 60

CHAPTER VI
FARM AND SCHOOL 81

CHAPTER VII
HARVARD SIXTY YEARS AGO 86

CHAPTER VIII
1846 TO 1850—FOUNDATION OF THE REPUBLICAN PARTY—
DANIEL WEBSTER 131

CHAPTER IX
LIFE IN WORCESTER 158

CHAPTER X
POLITICAL HISTORY IN MASSACHUSETTS FROM 1848 TO 1869.... 170

CHAPTER XI
THE KNOW NOTHING PARTY AND ITS OVERTHROW 188

CONTENTS

CHAPTER XII
ELECTION TO CONGRESS.................................. 192

CHAPTER XIII
SUMNER AND WILSON.................................... 213

CHAPTER XIV
PERSONALITIES IN DEBATE................................ 220

CHAPTER XV
THE NATIONAL HOUSE OF REPRESENTATIVES IN 1869.......... 222

CHAPTER XVI
POLITICAL CONDITION IN 1869............................ 245

CHAPTER XVII
RECONSTRUCTION 254

CHAPTER XVIII
COMMITTEE SERVICE IN THE HOUSE....................... 262

CHAPTER XIX
SALMON P. CHASE...................................... 282

CHAPTER XX
ADIN THAYER.. 289

CHAPTER XXI
POLITICAL CORRUPTION................................. 305

CHAPTER XXII
CREDIT MOBILIER....................................... 314

CHAPTER XXIII
THE SANBORN CONTRACTS............................... 325

CHAPTER XXIV
BENJAMIN F. BUTLER................................... 329

CHAPTER XXV
BELKNAP IMPEACHMENT................................. 364

CHAPTER XXVI
Electoral Commission.................................. 369

CHAPTER XXVII
Four National Conventions, 1876........................ 375

CHAPTER XXVIII
Four National Conventions, 1880........................ 384

CHAPTER XXIX
Four National Conventions, 1884........................ 405

CHAPTER XXX
Four National Conventions, 1888........................ 409

CHAPTER XXXI
Saturday Club... 422

CHAPTER XXXII
The Worcester Fire Society............................ 426

Appendix I.. 431

Appendix II... 432

AUTOBIOGRAPHY OF SEVENTY YEARS

CHAPTER I

INTRODUCTORY

EVERYBODY who reads this book through will wonder that a man who ought to be able to tell so much has really told so little.

I have known personally and quite intimately, or have known intelligent and trustworthy persons who have known personally and quite intimately, many men who have had a great share in the history of this country and in its literature for a hundred and thirty years.

In my younger days there were among my kindred and near friends persons who knew the great actors of the Revolutionary time and the time which followed till I came to manhood myself. But I did not know enough to ask questions. If I had, and had recorded the answers, I could write a very large part of the political and literary history of the United States. I never kept a diary, except for a few and brief periods. So for what I have to say, I must trust to my memory. I have no doubt that after these volumes are published, there will come up in my mind matter enough to make a dozen better ones.

I invoke for this book that kindly judgment of my countrymen which has attended everything I have done in my life so far. I have tried to guard against the dangers and the besetting infirmities of men who write their own biography. An autobiography, as the word implies, will be egotistical. An old man's autobiography is pretty certain to be garrulous. If the writer set forth therein his own ideals, he is likely to be judged by them, even when he may fall far short of them. Men are likely to think that he claims or pretends to have lived up to them, however painfully conscious he may be that they are only dreams which even if he have done his best have had little reality for him.

There is another danger for a man who tells the story of great transactions, in which he has taken part, whether legislative, executive, military, or political, or any other, in which the combined action of many persons was required for the result. He is apt to claim, consciously or unconsciously, that he himself brought the whole thing about.

"Papa," said the little boy to the veteran of the Civil War, "Did anybody help you to put down the Rebellion?"

This peril specially besets narrators in their old age. I am afraid that I can hardly escape it.

I once heard General George H. Thomas relate to a brilliant company at a supper party, among whom were Chief Justice Chase, General Eaton, Commissary General in two wars, Senator Trumbull, William M. Evarts, Joseph Henry, John Sherman, his brother the General, and several other gentlemen of equal distinction, the story of the battles of Nashville and Franklin. The story was full of dramatic interest. Yet no one who heard it would have known that the speaker himself had taken part in the great achievement, until, just at the end, he said of the Battle of Nashville that he thought of sending a detachment to cut off Hood's army at a ford by which he escaped after they were defeated, but he concluded that it was not safe to spare that force from immediate use in the battle. "If I had done it," he added, with great simplicity, "I should have captured his whole army. There is where I made my mistake."

The recollections of the actors in important political transactions are doubtless of great historic value. But I ought to say frankly that my experience has taught me that the memory of men, even of good and true men, as to matters in which they have been personal actors, is frequently most dangerous and misleading. I could recount many curious stories which have been told me by friends who have been writers of history and biography, of the contradictory statements they have received from the best men in regard to scenes in which they have been present.

If any critic think this book lacking in dignity, or wisdom, or modesty, it is hoped that it may, by way of offset, make up for it in sincerity. I have so far lived in this world without secrets. If my countrymen, or the people of Massachusetts, have trusted me, they have fully known what they were doing. "They had eyes and chose me."

I have never lifted my finger or spoken a word to any man to secure or to promote my own election to any office. I do not mean to criticise other men who advance their honorable ambition for public service or exert themselves to get office for which they think themselves fit. It was the "high Roman fashion." It has been the fashion in England always. English gentlemen do not disdain a personal solicitation for political support, and think no harm in it, to which no American gentleman would for a moment stoop.

It has been the custom in other parts of the country almost from the beginning of the Government. But what I think a better custom has prevailed in Massachusetts. I arrogate to myself no virtue in this respect. I only say that it has been my supreme good fortune to be the son of a Commonwealth among whose noble and high-minded people a better and more fastidious habit has prevailed.

The lesson which I have learned in life, which is impressed on me daily, and more deeply as I grow old, is the lesson of Good Will and Good Hope. I believe that to-day is better than yesterday, and that to-morrow will be better than to-day. I believe that in spite of so many errors and wrongs and even crimes, my countrymen of all classes desire what is good, and not what is evil. I repeat what I said to the State Convention of Massachusetts after the death of President McKinley:

"When I first came to manhood and began to take part in public affairs, that greatest of crimes, human slavery, was entrenched everywhere in power in this Republic. Congress and Supreme Court, Commerce and Trade and Social

Life alike submitted to its imperious and arrogant sway. Mr. Webster declared that there was no North, and that the South went clear up to the Canada line. The hope of many wise and conservative and, as I now believe, patriotic men, of saving this country from being rent into fragments was in leaving to slavery forever the great territory between the Mississippi and the Pacific, in the Fugitive Slave Law, a law under which freemen were taken from the soil of Massachusetts to be delivered into perpetual bondage, and in the judgment of the Supreme Court which declared it as the lesson of our history that the Negro had no rights that a white man was bound to respect.

"Last week at Dartmouth, at the great celebration in honor of Daniel Webster, that famous college gave the highest honor in its power to a Negro, amid the applause of the brilliant assembly. And there was no applause more earnest or hearty than that of the successor of Taney, the Democratic Chief Justice of the United States. I know that the people of that race are still the victims of outrages which all good men deplore. But I also believe that the rising sense of justice and of manhood in the South is already finding expression in indignant remonstrance from the lips of governors and of preachers, and that the justice and manhood of the South will surely make their way.

"Ah, Fellow Citizens, amid the sorrow and the mourning and the tears, amid the horror and the disappointment and the baffled hope, there comes to us from the open grave of William McKinley a voice of good omen! What pride and love must we feel for the republic that calls such men to her high places? What hope and confidence in the future of a people, where all men and all women of all parties and sections, of all faiths and creeds, of all classes and conditions, are ready to respond as ours have responded to this emotion of a mighty love.

"You and I are Republicans. You and I are men of the North. Most of us are Protestants in religion. We are men of native birth. Yet if every Republican were to-day to fall in his place, as William McKinley has fallen, I believe our countrymen of the other party, in spite of what we deem their errors, would take the Republic and bear on the flag to liberty and glory. I believe if every Protestant were to be stricken down by a lightning-stroke, that our brethren of the Catholic faith would still carry on the Republic in the spirit of a true and liberal freedom. I believe if every man of native birth within our borders were to die this day, the men of foreign birth, who have come here to seek homes and liberty under the shadow of the Republic, would carry it on in God's appointed way. I believe if every man of the North were to die, the new and chastened South, with the virtues it has cherished from the beginning, of love of home and love of State, and love of freedom, with its courage and its constancy, would take the country and bear it on to the achievement of its lofty destiny. The Anarchist must slay 75,000,000 Americans before he can slay the Republic.

"Of course there would be mistakes. Of course there would be disappointments and grievous errors. Of course there would be many things for which the lovers of liberty would mourn. But America would survive them all, and the nation our fathers planted would endure in perennial life.

"William McKinley has fallen in his high place. The spirit of Anarchy, always the servant of the spirit of Despotism, aimed its shaft at him, and his life for this world is over. But there comes from his fresh grave a voice of lofty triumph: 'Be of good cheer. It is God's way.'"

I account it my supreme good fortune that my public life has been spent in the service of Massachusetts. No man can know better than I do how unworthy I have been of a place in the great line of public men who have adorned her history for nearly three hundred years. What a succession it has been. What royal house, what empire or monarchy, can show a catalogue like that of the men whom in every generation she has called to her high places—Bradford, and Winthrop, and Sir Henry Vane, Leverett, and Sam Adams and John Adams and his illustrious son, and Cabot and Dexter, Webster and Everett and Sumner and Andrew. Nothing better can be said in praise of either than that they have been worthy of her, and she has been worthy of them. They have given her always brave and honest service, brave and honest counsel. She has never asked of them obsequiousness, or flattery, or even obedience to her will, unless it had the approval of their own judgment and conscience. That relation has been alike most honorable and most advantageous to both sides. They have never been afraid to trust the people and they have never been afraid to withstand the people. They knew well the great secret of all statesmanship, that he that withstands the people on fit occasions is commonly the man who trusts them most and always in the end the man they trust most.

CHAPTER II

ROGER SHERMAN AND HIS FAMILY

My mother, who died in 1866, at the age of eighty-three, was the daughter of Roger Sherman of Connecticut. Her father died when she was ten years old. She lived in her mother's house, opposite the College in New Haven, until her marriage in 1812. New Haven was one of the capital cities of New England. Its society had the special attraction which belonged to the seat of a famous college. Her mother's house was visited by the survivors of the great period of the Revolution and the framing of the Constitution, whom her father had known during an eminent public service of nearly forty years.

My mother was the most perfect democrat, in the best sense of the word, that I ever knew. It was a democracy which was the logical result of the doctrines of the Old Testament and of the New. It recognized the dignity of the individual soul, without regard to the accident of birth or wealth or power or color of the skin. If she were in the company of a Queen, it would never have occurred to her that they did not meet as equals. And if the Queen were a woman of sense, and knew her, it would never occur to the Queen. The poorest people in the town, the paupers in the poorhouse, thought of her as a personal friend to whom they could turn for sympathy and help. Not long before her death, an old black woman died in the poorhouse. She died in the night. An old man who had been a town pauper a good part of his life sat up with her and ministered to her wants as well as he could. Just before she died, the old woman thanked him for his kindness. She told him she should like to give him something to show her gratitude, but that she had nothing in the world; but she thought that if he would go to Mrs. Hoar and ask her to give him a dollar, as a favor to her she would do it. The draft on the bank of kindness was duly honored. And I think the legacy was valued as highly by her who paid it as if it had been a costly gem or a work of art from an emperor's gallery.

Mr. Calhoun was very intimate in my grandmother's household when he was in college, and always inquired with great interest after the young ladies of the family when he met anybody who knew them. He had a special liking for my mother, who was about his own age, and always inquired for her.

William M. Evarts visited Washington in his youth and called upon Mr. Calhoun, who received him with great consideration, went with him in person to see the President and what was worth seeing in Washington. Mr. Calhoun spoke in the highest terms of Roger Sherman to Mr. Evarts, said that he regarded him as one of the greatest of our statesmen, and that he had seen the true interests of the South when Southern statesmen were blind to them. This Mr. Calhoun afterward said in a speech in the Senate, including, however, Mr. Paterson of New Jersey and Oliver Ellsworth in his eulogy.

The story of Roger Sherman's life has never been told at length. There is an excellent memoir of him in Sanderson's "Lives of the Signers," written by Jeremiah Evarts, with the assistance of the late Governor and Senator Roger S. Baldwin of Connecticut. But when that was written the correspondence of the great actors of his time, and indeed the journals of the Continental Congress and the Constitutional Convention and the Madison Papers, were none of them accessible to the public.

An excellent though brief memoir of Mr. Sherman was published a few years ago by L. H. Boutell, Esq., of Chicago. Mr. Sherman was a man who seemed to care nothing for fame. He was content to cause great things to be done for his country, and cared nothing for the pride and glory of having done them. The personal pronoun I is seldom found in any speech or writing of his. He had a large share in the public events that led to the Revolution, in the conduct of the War, in the proceedings of the Continental Congress, in the framing of the Constitution, in securing its adoption by Connecticut, and in the action of the House and Senate in Washington's first Administration. He was also for many years Judge of the highest court of his State. He was a man of indefatigable industry. An accomplished lady employed to make investigations in the public archives of the Department of State, reported that she did not see how he could ever have gone to bed.

He had a most affectionate and tender heart. He was very fond of his family and friends. Although reserved and silent in ordinary company, he was very agreeable in conversation, and had a delightful wit. Some of the very greatest men of his time have left on record their estimate of his greatness.

Thomas Jefferson said of him: "There is old Roger Sherman, who never said a foolish thing in his life."

Theodore Sedgwick said: "He was a man of the selectest wisdom. His influence was such that no measure, or part of a measure which he advocated, ever failed to pass."

Fisher Ames said that if he were absent through a debate and came in before the vote was taken he always voted with Roger Sherman, as he always voted right.

Patrick Henry said that the first men in the Continental Congress were Washington, Richard Henry Lee, and Roger Sherman, and, later in life, that Roger Sherman and George Mason were the greatest statesmen he ever knew. This statement, published in the life of Mason, was carefully verified for me by my friend, the late William Wirt Henry, grandson and biographer of Patrick Henry, as appears by a letter from him in my possession.*

* I attach a passage from Mr. William Wirt Henry's letter, dated December 28, 1892.

"I am glad to be able to say that you may rely on the correctness of the passage at page 221 of Howe's Historical Collections of Va. giving Patrick Henry's estimate of Roger Sherman. It was furnished the author by my father and though a youth I well remember Mr. Howe's visit to Red Hill, my father's residence. My father, John Henry, was about three years of age when his

John Adams, in a letter to his wife, speaks of Sherman as "That old Puritan, as honest as an angel, and as firm in the cause of Independence as Mt. Atlas."

But perhaps the most remarkable testimony to his character, one almost unexampled in the history of public men, is that paid to him by Oliver Ellsworth, himself one of the greatest men of his time,—Chief Justice of the United States, Envoy to France, leader in the Senate for the first twelve years of the Constitution, and author of the Judiciary Act. He had been on the Bench of the Superior Court of Connecticut, with Mr. Sherman, for many years. They served together in the Continental Congress, and in the Senate of the United States. They were together members of the Convention that framed the Constitution, and of the State Convention in Connecticut that adopted it. Chief Justice Ellsworth told John Adams that he had made Mr. Sherman his model in his youth. Mr. Adams adds: "Indeed I never knew two men more alike, except that the Chief Justice had the advantage of a liberal education, and somewhat more extensive reading. Mr. Sherman was born in the State of Massachusetts, and was one of the strongest and soundest pillars of the Revolution." It would be hard to find another case of life-long and intimate companionship between two public men where such a declaration by either of the other would not seem ludicrous.

He was the only person who signed all four of the great State Papers, to which the signatures of the delegates of the different Colonies were attached:

The Association of 1774;

The Articles of Confederation;

The Declaration of Independence, and

The Constitution of the United States.

Robert Morris signed three of them.

father died, but his mother long survived Patrick Henry, as did several of the older children. From his mother, brothers and sisters my father learned many personal reminiscences of his father and his exceptionally retentive memory enabled him to relate them accurately. I have often heard him relate the reminiscences given on that page by Mr. Howe."

His tenacity, the independence of his judgment, and his influence over the great men with whom he was associated, is shown by four striking instances among many others where he succeeded in impressing his opinion on his associates.

First: It is well known that the dispute between the large States, who desired to have their votes in the National Legislature counted in proportion to numbers, and the small States, who desired to vote by States as equals, a dispute which nearly wrecked the attempt to frame a Constitution of the United States, arose in the Continental Congress, and gave rise to great controversy there when the Articles of Confederation were framed. Mr. Sherman was one of the Committee that framed those Articles, as he was afterward one of the Committee who reported the Declaration of Independence.

John Adams writes in his diary, that Mr. Sherman, in Committee of the Whole, moved August 1, 1776, that the vote be taken both ways, once according to numbers, and a second time, when the States should vote as equals.

This was, in substance, so far as the arrangement of political power was concerned, the plan of the Constitution. In the Constitutional Convention, Mr. Sherman first moved this plan, known as the Connecticut Compromise, and made the first argument in its support, to which his colleague, Oliver Ellsworth, afterward gave the weight of his powerful influence. The Convention afterward, almost in despair of any settlement of this vexed question, referred the matter to a grand committee, on which Mr. Ellsworth was originally named. But he withdrew from the committee, and Mr. Sherman took his place. Mr. Sherman had the parliamentary charge of the matter from the beginning, and at the close of the Convention, moved the provision that no State should be deprived of its equal vote without its consent.

When Mr. Sherman's known tenacity, and his influence over the great men with whom he was associated, testified to by so many of them, is borne in mind, it seems there can be no doubt that he is entitled to the chief credit of carrying out the scheme which he himself devised, and which, years before the Convention met, he himself first moved in the Continental Congress for which he made the first argument, and which was reported from the committee of which he was a member, representing the State which gave the name to the Compromise. His motion, which was adopted, that no State should be deprived of its equal vote in the Senate without its consent, made the equality secure.*

Second: In 1774, when Mr. Adams was on his way to the Continental Congress in Philadelphia, he records in his diary that he met Roger Sherman at New Haven, who, he says, "is a solid and sensible man." Mr. Sherman said to him that he thought the Massachusetts patriots, especially Mr. Otis, in his argument for the Writs of Assistance, had given up the whole case when they admitted that Parliament had the power to legislate for the Colonies under any circumstances whatever. He lived to join in the report from the committee, and to sign the Declaration of Independence, which put the case on his ground. The Declaration of Independence does not recognize Parliament at all, except indirectly, when it says the King "has combined with others" to do the wrongs which are complained of.

Third: In 1752 the whole country was overrun with paper money. Mr. Sherman published in that year a little pamphlet, entitled, "A Caveat Against Injustice, or An Inquiry Into the Evil Consequences of a Fluctuating Medium of Exchange." He stated with great clearness and force the arguments which, unhappily, we have been compelled to repeat more than once in later generations. He denounced paper money as "a cheat, vexation, and snare, a medium whereby we are continually cheating and wronging one another in our dealings and commerce." He adds, "So long as we import so much more foreign goods than are necessary, and keep so many merchants and traders employed to procure and deal them out to us: a great part of which we might as well make among ourselves; and another great part

---

* See Boutell's "Life of Roger Sherman," Lodge's "Flying Frigate,—Address on Ellsworth," Proceedings Am. Ant. Soc., October, 1902.

of which we had much better be without, especially the spiritous liquors, of which vast quantities are consumed in this colony every year, unnecessarily, to the great destruction of estates, morals, healths and even the lives of many of the inhabitants,—I say, so long as these things are so, we shall spend a great part of our labor and substance for that which will not profit us. Whereas, if these things were reformed, the provisions and other commodities which we might have to export yearly, and which other governments are dependent upon us for, would procure us gold and silver abundantly sufficient for a medium of trade. And we might be as independent, flourishing and happy a colony as any in the British Dominions."

He lived to move in the Convention, and to procure its insertion in the Constitution, the clause that no State should make anything but gold and silver legal tender.

Fourth: Mr. Sherman took his seat in the Federal Convention May 30, 1787. Mr. Randolph's resolution, submitted on the 29th day of May, being before the Convention the next day, included the proposition that the National Legislature ought to be empowered to enjoy the legislative rights vested in Congress by the confederation, "and moreover to legislate in all cases in which the separate States are incompetent,"—the question being whether the clause authorizing Congress to legislate in all cases in which the separate States are incompetent should be retained, every State in the Convention voted Aye, except Connecticut. Connecticut was divided. Ellsworth voted Aye, and Sherman, No.

Mr. Sherman lived, not only to sign a Constitution of limited powers, but himself to support the Tenth Article of Amendment thereto, which is as follows:

"The powers not delegated to the United States by the Constitution, nor prohibited by it to the States, are reserved to the States respectively, or to the people." The words "or to the people" were moved by Mr. Sherman after the original article was reported. So he saw clearly in the beginning, what no other member saw, the two great American principles, first that the National Government should be a Government of limited and delegated powers, and next, that there is a domain of legislation which the people have not delegated either to the National Government or to the States, and upon which no legislative power may rightfully enter.

I surely am not mistaken in thinking that even without the other services of a life devoted to the public, these four contributions to the Constitutional history of the country entitle Mr. Sherman to an honorable place in the grateful memory of his countrymen, and vindicate the tributes which I have cited from his illustrious contemporaries.

My grandmother, the daughter of Benjamin Prescott of Salem, was a woman of great intelligence and a great beauty in her time. She was once taken out to dinner by General Washington when he was President. Madam Hancock, whose husband had been President of the Continental Congress and Governor of Massachusetts, complained to General Washington's Secretary, Mr. Lear, that that honor belonged to her. The Secretary told General Washington, the next day, what she said. The General answered that it was his privilege to give his arm to the handsomest woman in the room. Whether the reply was communicated to Mrs. Hancock, or whether she was comforted by it, does not appear. General Washington had been a guest at my grandfather's house in my mother's childhood, and she had sat on his knee. She was then six years old. But she always remembered the occasion very vividly.

My grandfather was a friend of Lafayette, who mentions him in one of his letters, the original of which is in my possession. One of my mother's brothers, Lt. Colonel Isaac Sherman, led the advance at Princeton, and was himself intimate with Washington and Lafayette. He was a very brave officer and commanded a Connecticut regiment at the storming of Stony Point. He is honorably mentioned in Gen. Wayne's report of the action. Washington alludes to him in one of his letters to Lafayette, as one of his friends whom Lafayette will be glad to see if he will visit this country once more. There is, in the State Department, an amusing correspondence between Col. Sherman and Gen. Wayne, in which he complains that Mad Anthony does great injustice in his report to the soldiers from other States than Pennsylvania. Mad Anthony was mad at the letter. But after a rather significant request from Gen. Washington, he repaired the wrong.

Another of her brothers who died at the age of eighty-eight, when I was thirty years old, and at whose house I was often a visitor, spent three weeks as Washington's guest at Mount Vernon. Old Deacon Beers of New Haven, whom I knew in his old age, was one of the guard who had Andre in custody. During his captivity, Andre made a pen-and-ink likeness of himself, which he gave to Deacon Beers. It is now in the possession of Yale College.

I had from my mother the story of General Washington taking Chief Justice Ellsworth's twin children, one on each knee, and reciting to them the ballad of the Derbyshire Ram. This tradition has remained in the Ellsworth family. I have confirmed it by inquiry of the Rev. Mr. Wood, a grandson of Oliver Ellsworth, who died in Washington a few years ago.

Besides the uncle to whom I allude, who died in 1856, Judge Simeon Baldwin, who married two of my aunts, died in 1851, aged ninety. He was a Member of Congress in 1803-5, and was an intimate friend of Chancellor Kent, who was his classmate and chum in Yale, and was intimate with the Federalist leaders of the Hamilton party. I several times made visits in his household before his death. President Jeremiah Day, another uncle by marriage, was at the head of Yale for thirty years. He died in 1867, at the age of 94.

My mother's sister, Mrs. Jeremiah Evarts, was born January 28, 1774, and died in 1851, at the age of seventy-seven. She knew intimately many famous men and women of the Revolutionary period. Her husband was an intimate friend of John Jay. She had a great deal of the sprightly wit for which her son, William, was so famous. She was at home at the time of Washington's visit, then a child eleven years old, and opened the door for him when he took his leave. The General, who was very fond of children, put his hand on her head and said, "My little lady, I wish you a better office." She dropped a courtesy and answered, quick as lightning, "Yes, sir; to let you in."

Mrs. Evarts was a woman not only of sprightly wit, but of great beauty. She liked to tell in her old age of a dinner which John Hancock gave for her father and her, in Boston, when she was a girl. She described her dress with great minuteness, and added naïvely, "Didn't I look pretty?"

My mother, who was married in 1812, knew very intimately many of her father's and mother's old friends who had been distinguished in the public service in the Revolutionary period and the Administration of Washington and John Adams and Thomas Jefferson. She knew very well the family of John Jay. He and his wife were visitors at my grandmother's after their return from Spain. My mother was intimate in the household of Oliver Ellsworth as in a second home. His children were her playmates. She was also very intimate indeed with the family of Senator Hillhouse, whose daughter Mary was one of her dearest friends.

Senator Hillhouse held a very high place in the public life of Connecticut in his day. He was one of the friends of Hamilton, and one of the group of Federal statesmen of whom Hamilton was the leader. He was United States Senator for Connecticut from 1796 to 1810.

After she became a young lady, my mother, with Fanny Ellsworth, afterward Mrs. Wood, and Mary Hillhouse, daughter of the Senator, established a school to teach young colored children to read and sew. The colored people in New Haven were in a sad condition in those days. The law of the State made it a penal offence to teach a colored child to read. These girls violated the law. The public authorities interfered and threatened them with prosecution. But the young women were resolute. They insisted that they were performing a religious duty, and declared that they should disobey the law and take the consequences. A good deal of sympathy was aroused in their behalf. The New Haven authorities had to face the question whether they would imprison the daughter of a Signer of the Declaration of Independence, who had affixed his signature to the great affirmation that all men are created equal, the daughters of two Framers of the Constitution, and the daughter of James Hillhouse, then the foremost citizen of Connecticut, for teaching little children to read the Bible. They gave up the attempt. The school kept on and flourished. President Dwight raised a considerable fund for it by a course of lectures, and it continued down to within my own recollection. What became of the fund which was raised for its support I cannot tell.

Jeremiah Evarts was born February 13, 1781. He died May 10, 1831. He was the founder and Secretary of the American Board of Commissioners for Foreign Missions. He was one of the thirteen men who met in Samuel Dexter's office in 1812, to inaugurate the Temperance Reformation. The habit of excessive drinking was then almost universal in this country. Liquors and wines were freely used on social occasions, at weddings and at funerals. The clergyman staggered home from his round of pastoral calls, and the bearers partook of brandy or gin or rum in the room adjoining that where the coffin was placed ready for the funeral. A gentleman present said it was utterly impracticable to try to wean the American people from the habit of drinking. Jeremiah Evarts answered, "It is right, therefore practicable."

He was a Puritan of the old school. He made a vigorous but ineffectual attempt in Connecticut to enforce the Sunday laws. His death was caused by his exertions in resisting the removal of the Cherokee Indians from Georgia, a removal accomplished in violation of the Constitution and of public faith. The Supreme Court of the United States declared the law of Georgia unconstitutional. But Georgia defied the mandate of the Court, and it was never executed. The missionary agent was imprisoned and died of his confinement. Mr. Evarts said, "There is a court that has power to execute its judgments."

I told this story to Horace Maynard, an eminent member of Congress and member of the Cabinet. Mr. Maynard said, "There was never a prophecy more terribly accomplished. The territory from which those Indians were unlawfully removed was the scene of the Battle of Missionary Ridge, which is not far from the grave of Worcester, the missionary who died in prison. That land was fairly drenched with blood and honeycombed with graves."

Mr. Evarts edited the *Panoplist,* a very able magazine, which powerfully defended the old theology against the Unitarian movement, then at its height.

A well-known writer, Rev. Leonard W. Bacon, published a short time ago a sketch entitled, "The Greater Evarts," in which he contrasted the career of Jeremiah Evarts with that of his brilliant and delightful son. Whether that judgment shall stand we may know when the question is settled, which is to be answered in every generation, whether martyrdom be a failure.

Among the inmates of my grandfather's household in my mother's childhood and youth was Roger Minott Sherman. He was the son of the Reverend Josiah Sherman, my grandfather's brother, a clergyman of Woburn, Massachusetts, where Roger Minott was born. His father died in 1789. My grandfather took the boy into his household and educated him and treated him as a son, and just before his death gave him his watch, which is now in the possession of a son of General Sherman.

Roger Minott Sherman was unquestionably the ablest lawyer in New England who never obtained distinction in political life, and, with the exception of Daniel Webster and Jeremiah Mason and Rufus Choate, the ablest New England ever produced.*

Roger Minott Sherman's father died in 1789. The widow wrote to some of her friends to see what assistance could be obtained to enable her son to continue his studies at Yale.

* See Appendix.

It was apparently in response to this appeal that Mr. Sherman wrote the following letter to his nephew.

NEW YORK, April 28, 1790.

Dear Nephew,—I would have you continue your studies and remain at my house as you have done hitherto. I hope you will be provided for so as to complete your education at College, and lay a foundation for future usefulness. When I return home I shall take such further order respecting it as may be proper. I shall afford you as much assistance as under my circumstances may be prudent.

I am your affectionate uncle,
ROGER SHERMAN.

Mr. Sherman died a year after his nephew graduated; but before he died he doubtless saw the promise of that distinguished career which added new lustre to the Sherman name.

It is a rather remarkable fact that my mother had such close relations to so many eminent lawyers. Her father, though his public duties prevented him from practising law very long, was a very great lawyer and judge. Her brother-in-law, Judge Baldwin, was an eminent Judge of the Connecticut Supreme Court. Her cousin, Roger Minott Sherman, as has just been said, was an inmate of her father's household in her childhood, and was to her as a brother. She had, after his mother's death, the care of Senator Roger Sherman Baldwin, her nephew, who was for many years at the head of the Connecticut Bar. To her nephew, William M. Evarts, my father's house was as another home in his boyhood. He was the leading advocate of his time. Her son, E. R. Hoar, was Attorney General of the United States. And her husband was in his day one of the foremost advocates of Massachusetts. So, with a little alteration, the Greek epitaph of the woman who was the daughter, wife, sister and mother of princes, might apply to her, if, as I like to think, a first-rate American lawyer is entitled to as much respect as a petty Greek prince.

CHAPTER III

SAMUEL HOAR

I WAS born in Concord August 29, 1826. My grandfather, two great-grandfathers, and three of my father's uncles were at Concord Bridge in the Lincoln Company, of which my grandfather, Samuel Hoar, whom I well remember, was lieutenant, on the 19th of April, 1775. The deposition of my great-grandfather, John Hoar, with a few others, relating to the events of that day, was taken by the patriots and sent to England by a fast-sailing ship, which reached London before the official news of the battle at Concord came from the British commander. John had previously been a soldier in the old French War and was a prisoner among the Indians for three months. His life was not a very conspicuous one. He had been a Selectman of Lexington, dwelling in the part of the town afterward incorporated with Lincoln. There is in existence a document manumitting his slave, which, I am happy to say, is the only existing evidence that any ancestor of mine ever owned one.

My father's grandfather, on the mother's side, was Colonel Abijah Peirce, of Lincoln. He was prominent in Middlesex County from a time preceding the Revolutionary War down to his death. He was one of the Committee of the Town who had charge of corresponding with other towns and with the Committee of Safety in Boston. The day before the battle at Concord Bridge, he had been chosen Colonel of a regiment of Minute Men. But he had not got his commission, taken the oath, or got his equipments. So he went into the battle as a private in the company in which his son-in-law was lieutenant, armed with nothing but a cane. After the first volley was exchanged he crossed the bridge and took the cartridge-box and musket of one of the two British soldiers who were killed, which he used during the day. The gun was preserved for a long time in his family, and came to my grandfather, after his death. It was the first trophy of the Revolutionary War taken in battle. Such things, however, were not prized in those days as they are now. One of my uncles lent the musket to one of his neighbors for the celebration of the taking of Cornwallis, and it never was brought back. We would give its weight in gold to get it back.

I will put on record two stories about Colonel Peirce, which have something of a superstitious quality in them. I have no doubt of their truth, as they come from persons absolutely truthful and not superstitious or credulous themselves.

When Colonel Peirce was seventy years old, he told his wife and my aunt, her granddaughter, from whom I heard the story, who was then a grown-up young woman, that he was going out to the barn and going up to the high beams. In those days the farmers' barns had the hay in bays on each side, and over the floor in the middle rails were laid across from one side to the other, on which corn-stalks, for bedding the cattle, and other light things were put. They urged him not to go, and said an old man like him should not take such risks; to which he replied by dancing a hornpipe in the room in their presence, showing something of that exhilaration of spirit which the Scotch called being "fey" and which they regard as a presage of approaching misfortune. He went out, and within a few minutes fell from the high beams down to the floor and was instantly killed.

The other story is that a little while before this happened he said that he thought he saw the dim and misty figure of a ship pass slowly from one side of the barn to the other, under the roof.

A like story is told of Abraham Lincoln; that he used to see a vision of a ship before any great event, and that it came to him the night before he died.

I asked Mr. Secretary Hay about the Lincoln anecdote and give his reply.

DEPARTMENT OF STATE, WASHINGTON, April 18, 1903.
Dear Senator Hoar:

You will find on page 281 of Volume 10 of "The Life of Lincoln," by Nicolay and Hay, all I know about the story.

General Grant, in an interview with the President, on the 14th of April—the day he was shot—expressed some anxiety as to the news from Sherman. "The President answered him in that singular vein of poetic mysticism, which, though constantly held in check by his strong common sense, formed a remarkable element in his character. He assured Grant that the news would come soon and come favorable, for he had last night had his usual dream which preceded great events. He seemed to be, he said, in a singular and indescribable vessel, but always the same, moving with great rapidity towards a dark and indefinite shore. He had had this dream before Antietam, Murfreesboro, Gettysburg and Vicksburg."

The story is also found in George Eliot's Life (Vol. 3, 113), as related by Charles Dickens on the authority of Stanton, with characteristic amplifications.

Yours faithfully,
JOHN HAY.

The Honorable
George F. Hoar
United States Senate.

My father, Samuel Hoar of Concord, was born in 1778 and died in 1856. He was one of the most eminent lawyers at the Massachusetts Bar. To this statement I can give better testimony than my own, in the following letter from the Honorable Eben F. Stone, late member of Congress from the Essex District.

WASHINGTON 9 March, '84.
My dear Mr. Hoar:

When I was a law student, I dined at Ipswich in our county, with the Judges of the Supreme Court and the members of the Essex Bar, who then had a room and a table by themselves. The conversation took a professional turn, and a good deal was said about Mr. Choate's great skill and success as an advocate. Judge Shaw then remarked that, sitting at nisi prius in different parts of the State, he had had an opportunity to compare the different lawyers who were distinguished for their success with juries, and that there was no man in the State, in his opinion, who had so much influence with a jury as Sam Hoar of Concord. This he ascribed not simply to his legal ability, but largely to the confidence the people had in his integrity and moral character.

Yours truly,
E. F. Stone.

Mr. Hoar was associated with Mr. Webster in the defence of Judge Prescott when he was impeached before the Senate of Massachusetts. He encountered Webster, and Choate, and Jeremiah Mason, and John Davis, and the elder Marcus Morton, and other giants of the Bar, in many a hard battle. Mr. Webster makes affectionate reference to him in a letter to my brother, now in existence. He was a member of the Harrisburg Convention which nominated General Harrison for the Presidency in 1839. He represented Concord in the Massachusetts Convention to Revise the Constitution, in 1820, in which convention his father, Samuel Hoar, represented Lincoln. When he first rose to speak in that body, John Adams said, "That young man reminds me of my old friend, Roger Sherman." He was a Federalist, afterward a Whig, and in the last years of his life a Republican.

Mr. Hoar succeeded Edward Everett as Representative in Congress from the Middlesex District in 1835. He served there but a single term. He made one speech, a Constitutional argument in support of the power of Congress to abolish slavery in the District of Columbia. He also took rather a prominent part in a discussion in which the Whig members complained of one of the rulings of the Democratic speaker.

His service was not long enough to gain for him any considerable national distinction. But that he made a good impression on the House appears from an extract of a letter I lately received from my classmate, Rev. Walter Mitchell, the author of the spirited and famous poem, "Tacking Ship off Fire Island." He says: "I heard my uncle, Mr. Eliot, say that when your father went to Congress the Southern members said, 'Where has this man been all his life, and why have we never heard of him? With us a man of his ability would be known all over the South.' "

My father retired from active practice at the Bar shortly after his return from Congress in 1837. In 1844 an event occurred which contributed largely to the bitter feeling between the two sections of the country, which brought on the Civil War.

As is well known, under the laws of South Carolina, colored seamen on ships that went into the port of Charleston were imprisoned during the stay of the ship, and sold to pay their jail fees if the ship went off and left them, or if the fees were not paid.

The Legislature of Massachusetts directed the Governor to employ counsel to test the constitutionality of these laws. No Southern lawyer of sufficient ability and distinction could be found who would undertake the duty. The Governor found it difficult to procure counsel who were in active practice. Mr. Hoar was led by a strong sense of duty to leave his retirement in his old age and undertake the delicate and dangerous mission. When he arrived in South Carolina and made known his errand, the people of the State, especially of the city of Charleston, were deeply excited. The Legislature passed angry resolutions, directing the Governor to expel from the State "the Northern emissary" whose presence was deemed an insult. The mob of Charleston threatened to destroy the hotel where Mr. Hoar was staying. He was urged to leave the city, which he firmly and steadfastly refused to do. The mob were quieted by the assurances of leading gentlemen that Mr. Hoar would be removed. A deputation of seventy principal citizens waited upon him at his hotel and requested him to consent to depart. He had already declined the urgent request of Dr. Whittredge, an eminent physician, to withdraw and take refuge at his plantation, saying he was too old to run and could not go back to Massachusetts if he had returned without an attempt to discharge his duty. The committee told him that they had assured the people that he should be removed, and that he must choose between stepping voluntarily into a carriage and being taken to the boat, or being dragged by force. He then, and not till then, said he would go. He was taken by the committee to the boat, which sailed for Wilmington.

It has been generally said that Mr. Hoar was driven from Charleston by a mob. This I suppose to be technically true. But it is not true in the popular sense of the words. The committee of seventy, although they had no purpose of personal violence, other than to place one old gentleman in a carriage and take him to a boat, were, of course, in every legal sense a mob. But when that committee waited upon him the personal danger was over.

A solitary negative vote against the resolve of the Legislature directing Mr. Hoar to be expelled was cast by C. S. Memmenger, afterward Secretary of the Treasury of the Southern Confederacy. He is said to have been a Union man in 1832.

I was told by General Hurlburt of Illinois, a distinguished officer in the Civil War, and member of the national House of Representatives, that at the time of my father's mission to South Carolina, he was a law student in the office of James L. Petigru. Mr. Petigru, as is well known, was a Union man during the Civil War. Such, however, was the respect for his great ability and character that he was permitted to live in Charleston throughout the War. It is said that on one occasion while this strife was going on, a stranger in Charleston met Mr. Petigru in the street and asked him the way to the Insane Hospital. To this the old man answered by pointing north, south, east and west, and said, "You will find the Insane Hospital in every direction here."

According to General Hurlburt, Mr. Petigru had quietly organized a company of young men whom he could trust, who were ready, under his lead, to rescue Mr. Hoar and insure his personal safety if he were attacked by the mob.

John Quincy Adams says in his diary, speaking of the transaction: "I approved the whole of his conduct." Governor Briggs, in communicating the facts to the Legislature, says in a special message: "The conduct of Mr. Hoar under the circumstances seems to have been marked by that prudence, firmness and wisdom which have distinguished his character through his life." Mr. Emerson says, in a letter dated December 17, 1844:

"Mr. Hoar has just come home from Carolina, and gave me this morning a narrative of his visit. He has behaved admirably well, I judge, and there were fine heroic points in his story. One expression struck me, which, he said, he regretted a little afterward, as it might sound a little vapouring. A gentleman who was very much his friend called him into a private room to say that the danger from the populace had increased to such a degree that he must now insist on Mr. Hoar's leaving the city at once, and he showed him where he might procure a carriage and where he might safely stop on the way to his plantation, which he would reach the next morning. Mr. Hoar thanked him, but told him again that he could not and would not go, and that he had rather his broken skull should be carried to Massachusetts by somebody else, than to carry it home safe himself whilst his duty required him to remain. The newspapers say, following the Charleston papers, that he consented to depart: this he did not, but in every instance refused,—to the Sheriff, and acting Mayor, to his friends, and to the committee of the S. C. Association, and only went when they came in crowds with carriages to conduct him to the boat, and go he must,—then he got into the coach himself, not thinking it proper to be dragged."

I add this letter from Dr. Edward Everett Hale.

39 HIGHLAND ST., ROXBURY, MASS., Mar. 13, 1884.
Dear Hoar:

Thank you very much for your memoir of your father. I was in Washington the day he and your sister came home from Charleston. I remember that Grinnell told me the news—and my first real feeling *in life* that there must be a war, was when Grinnell said on the Avenue: "I do not know but we may as well head the thing off now—and fight it out." The first public intelligence the North had of the matter was in my letter to the *Daily Advertiser,* which was reprinted in New York, their own correspondents not knowing of the expulsion. Always yours,

EDW. E. HALE.

I have Dr. Vedder's permission to publish the accompanying correspondence, which so happily turns into a means of delightful reconciliation what has been so long, but can be no longer, a painful memory. I was received in Charleston with the delightful hospitality of which no other people in the world so fully understand the secret.

CHARLESTON, S. C., Oct. 20, 1898.
THE HONORABLE GEORGE F. HOAR.
Dear Sir:

We have a New England Society in Charleston which is now seventy-six years old. It has had a notable history, Daniel Webster having been among its annual orators. Its Forefathers' Anniversary is the social and literary event of our year. I write to extend the warm greeting of the Society to yourself, and the earnest request that you will be our guest at the banquet on Forefathers' Day Dec. 22, and speak to the sentiment—"The Day we Celebrate," or any other that you would prefer. Of course, it will be our privilege to make your coming wholly without cost to yourself.

May I venture to urge that your presence with us will have a beautiful significance in its relation to the good feeling which so happily obtains in all our land, and a past event which associates your honored Father's name so memorably and sadly with our City? Charleston would fain give the honored Son a welcome which shall obliterate the past.

Hoping for a favorable and early reply, I remain,
Yours with great respect,
CHARLES S. VEDDER, *President*.

WORCESTER, MASS., October 26, 1898.

My Dear Sir:

I am sure you will not doubt that I feel myself highly honored by your invitation in behalf of the New England Society of Charleston, as I am deeply touched and gratified by what you say in the letter which conveys it. I thank God that I have lived to behold this day, and that my eyes have been spared to see the people of the whole country united again in affection as in the early time.

I hope and expect to be able to attend your banquet next Forefathers' Day. I will do so if the condition of the public business shall permit. I have the charge of the business of the Committee on the Judiciary, two of whose important members are now absent in Paris, and it is of course possible that some of the great questions which are before us may require constant attendance in their places of all the Senators during the next session without the possibility of an interruption for a Christmas holiday. Subject to that possibility, I will accept your invitation, and am, with high regard, Faithfully yours,

GEO. F. HOAR.

In 1850, after he had withdrawn from professional and public life, being then seventy-two years old, Mr. Hoar was sent to the House of Representatives, by the town of Concord, to oppose the removal of the courts from Concord. He was successful in the opposition. He had, during the winter, an opportunity to render a very important service to Harvard College. There was a vigorous and dangerous attempt to abolish the existing Corporation, and transfer the property and control of the College to a board of fifteen persons, to be chosen by the Legislature by joint ballot, one third to go out of office every second year. This measure was recommended in an elaborate report by Mr. Boutwell, an influential member of the House, chosen Governor at the next election, and advocated by Henry Wilson, afterward Senator and Vice-President, and by other gentlemen of great influence. All the members of the Corporation were Whigs in politics and Unitarians, a sect containing a very small proportion of the people of the State. The project to take the College from their control was very popular. The House listened willingly to the able arguments with which the measure was introduced, and before Mr. Hoar spoke its opinion was unmistakably for the bill. He argued that the measure was in conflict with the Constitution of the United States, and defended the College with great earnestness from the charge that it had "failed to answer the just expectations of the public." The Boston *Daily Atlas,* edited by General Schouler, then a member of the House, said the next day of this speech: "The argument of Mr. Hoar was of transcendent excellence, and had a most overpowering effect upon the House. We regret that no report was made of it. It is a pity that so much learning, argument and eloquence should be lost."

This speech caused a revolution in the opinion of the body. The measure was referred to the next General Court. Mr. Hoar was employed by the Corporation as counsel to appear before the Legislature the next winter in its behalf. But the measure was never heard of afterward. Dr. Walker said of this occurrence, after his sententious fashion: "Other men have served the College; Samuel Hoar saved it."

The Board of Overseers, who have visitorial powers over the College, and whose concurrence is necessary to the election or appointment of officers, Professors and members of the Corporation, and who included for a long time the Governor, Lieutenant-Governor, and members of the Senate, had always been held to be the representative of the Commonwealth, although the members of the body who were not members *ex-officio* were elected by the Board itself.

A bill passed in 1851, to which no objection was made, vested the election of this body in the Legislature. But, after a few years' trial, that was abandoned, and the members of the Overseers are now chosen by the Alumni of the College.

I shall speak in a later chapter of the foundation of the Free Soil Party. The call for the Convention held at Worcester on the 28th of June, 1848, addressed to all persons opposed to the election of Cass and Taylor, written by his son, E. R. Hoar, was headed by Mr. Hoar. He presided over the meeting, and delegates were elected to a National Convention to be held at Buffalo, which nominated Van Buren and Adams for President and Vice-President. This was the origin of the Republican party.

After 1848, Mr. Hoar did not relax his efforts to bring about a union of all parties in the North, in opposition to further encroachments of the slave power. In accomplishing this end, his age, the regard in which he was held by all classes of people, his known disinterestedness and independence, fitted him to exert a large influence. The Free Soil movement had led to the formation of a party in Massachusetts, small in numbers, but zealous, active, in earnest, containing many able leaders, eloquent orators, and vigorous writers. They had sent Charles Allen to the lower House of Congress, and Sumner and Rantoul to the Senate. But they had apparently made little impression on the national strength of either of the old parties.

In 1854, the passage of the measure known as the Kansas-Nebraska Bill afforded a new opportunity. A meeting of citizens of Concord appointed a committee, of which Mr. Hoar was Chairman, and A. G. Fay, Secretary, who called a meeting of prominent persons from different parts of the State to meet at the American House in Boston, to take measures for forming a new party and calling a State Convention. This Convention was held at Worcester on the 7th of September, and formed a party under the name of Republican, and nominated candidates for State officers. Its meeting has been claimed to be the foundation of the Republican party of Massachusetts, and its twenty-fifth anniversary was celebrated accordingly in 1879. But it effected little more than to change the name of the Free Soil party. Few Whigs or Democrats united in the movement. A secret organization called Americans, or Know-Nothings, swept the Commonwealth like a wave, electing all the State officers, and, with scarcely an exception, the entire Legislature.

The candidate for Governor nominated by the Republicans at Worcester, himself joined the Know-Nothings, and labored to defeat his own election.

The next year the attempt was more successful. On the 10th of August, 1855, a meeting without distinction of party was held at Chapman Hall, in Boston, which was addressed by Mr. Hoar, George Bliss, Franklin Dexter, William Brigham, Lyman Beecher, Richard H. Dana, Jr., Charles F. Adams, Henry Wilson, Stephen C. Phillips, and others. On the 30th of the same month, a meeting of conference committees was held, representing the American or Know-Nothing party, the Know-Somethings, an antislavery organization which had held a National Convention at Cleveland in June, and the Chapman Hall Convention. This conference appointed a committee of twenty-six to call a State Convention, at the head of which they placed Mr. Hoar. This State Convention was held at Worcester, nominated Julius Rockwell for Governor, and the organization which it created has constituted the Republican party of Massachusetts to the present day.

The part taken in calling this Convention, and in promoting the union which gave it birth, was Mr. Hoar's last important public service. His failing health prevented his taking an active share in the Presidential campaign of 1856.

I prefer, in putting on record this brief estimate of a character which has been to me the principal object of reverence and honor in my life, to use the language of others, and not my own. From many tributes to my father's character, from persons more impartial than I can be, I have selected two or three.

I cannot quote at length Ralph Waldo Emerson's sketches of Mr. Hoar, who was his near neighbor and intimate personal friend for many years. They are noble and faithful as portraits of Van Dyke or Titian. One of them is a speech made in Concord town-meeting on the third day of November, 1856, the day after Mr. Hoar's death. The other was contributed to the *Unitarian Monthly Religious Magazine*, then edited by Rev. Dr. Huntington, afterward Bishop of New York. Mr. Emerson says in one of them: "His head, with singular grace in its lines, had a resemblance to the bust of Dante. He retained to the last the erectness of his tall but slender form, and not less the full strength of his mind. Such was, in old age, the beauty of his person and carriage, as if his mind radiated, and made the same impression of probity on all beholders."

He ends the other with this quatrain:

> With beams December planets dart,
> His cold eye truth and conduct scanned;
> July was in his sunny heart,
> October in his liberal hand.

The following is from a letter of Sherman Day, a man whose reputation for wisdom and integrity is among the treasures of California:

"BERKELEY, 23d May, 1884.

HON. GEO. FRISBIE HOAR,
  U. S. Senate, Washington, D. C.

My Dear Sir:

I was very much gratified to receive, some weeks since, a copy of your biographical sketch of your venerable father. It was the more precious to me because it awakened memories of my own early life; while it recalls the tall, the gentle and dignified figure and courteous demeanor of your father in his prime of life. I can remember being at your father's wedding at my grandmother's house when I was about 6½ years old. Several years before you were born, I was at the Phillips Academy at Andover, and used occasionally to spend a vacation with my beloved aunt, who was a sort of mother to me in my earliest childhood. It was at her house that I first read Washington Irving's Sketch Book, then just appearing in separate numbers. I believe the book belonged to a law student of your father's, as your father had not yet taken to the reading of romances.

"My memory extends back to the organization of the Constitutional Convention of 1820. I well remember the venerable figure of John Adams, as he took the seat of honor at the right hand of the president, and I remember the sonorous voice of Josiah Quincy, the Secretary. I was staying at the house of Mr. Evarts, and remember your father's dining there, and discussing the deportment and characteristics of several of the more prominent members. Among them was the tall member from Worcester, Levi Lincoln, conspicuous by his drab overcoat, by his frequent speaking, and by his constantly moving about among the members. The member who made the most lasting impression on my memory was Daniel Webster. He was not yet forty years old, stalwart, black haired and black eyed, with a somewhat swarthy complexion; his manly beauty and his eloquence being alike objects of admiration. He had not attained that stoutness which his form assumed in later years. I could illustrate his appearance better to your brother, Edward, by asking him to recall Don Pablo de la Guerra of Santa Barbara, whom I deemed a very good type, *in appearance,* of Webster in the Convention of 1820."

George William Curtis came to know Mr. Hoar very well during his own life in Concord. He and his brother, Burrill, were almost daily visitors at our house:

WEST NEW BRIGHTON, STATEN ISLAND, N. Y.,
March 19, 1884.
My dear Mr. Hoar:
I thank you very much for a copy of your sketch of your father which vividly recalls him to me as I remember him in my Concord days long ago. I recollect that when I saw in Paris Couture's famous picture of the Decadence of the Romans, it was your father that I thought of as I saw the

figures of the older Romans gazing reproachfully upon the revels. So he may have felt of his country as he died.

With great regard, very truly yours,

GEORGE WILLIAM CURTIS.

The following is from J. Evarts Greene, formerly editor of the Worcester *Spy,* and one of the ablest members of his profession in New England:

WORCESTER, Mar. 10, 1884.

My dear Mr. Hoar:

I want to thank you especially for the copy of the Memoir of your father, which I received to-day. I am exceedingly glad to have it on your account and his. He is the most venerable figure in my memory. He was always spoken of in our family with the highest respect, and few things have ever gratified me so much as his kindness to me on the occasion of my last visit to Concord during his lifetime. It was in 1850, I think, while I was in college and about fifteen years old. I had always held him in awe as the greatest and wisest man within my knowledge, and should no more have thought of familiar conversation with him than with the Pope. But his grave and kindly courtesy, as he sat down with me after supper, though it did not quite put me at my ease, gave me courage to talk more freely than I had ever thought possible; and while my veneration for him was not diminished, I felt that there was no one now on earth that I need be afraid of.

Faithfully yours,

J. EVARTS GREENE.

The Hon. Geo. F. Hoar.

The following letter is from Professor Thatcher, the eminent Latin Professor of Yale:

NEW HAVEN, 14th March, 1884.

HONORABLE GEORGE F. HOAR.

My dear Senator:

I write simply but cordially to thank you for the copy of your venerated Father's Memoir which you have been so kind as to send to your cousin, Elizabeth. I have read it with the delight which must be common to all who read it. A life so qualified with the selectest traits of a great and gentle soul, so substantial with continual but full and unembarrassed labor, and so constantly influential for elevated and beneficent ends, with nothing discoverable in it to check its great drift and power,—such a life is an almost unequalled gift of God to such a community as his.

There is a rare charm in the narrative, and one cannot help rejoicing that you have been able to gather together the recorded judgments of so many men whose judgments are worthy to be recorded.

I am, ever,
Very truly yours,
THOMAS A. THATCHER.

SENATE, WASHINGTON, March 9, 1884.
My dear Mr. Hoar:

I thank you very much for a copy of the Memoir of your father. It is a tribute to his worth and his fame worthy of him and of yourself. I hardly know which most to admire, the character it portrays, or the filial piety it evinces.

It brings back very vividly the venerable form and the lovely character I met and revered in the Massachusetts Legislature when I was a young man, and have ever since held among the safest and best of the land.

Permit me to count it my own best fortune that I can subscribe myself the colleague and friend of the son and biographer of Samuel Hoar.

Truly yours,
H. L. DAWES.
The Honorable Geo. F. Hoar,
Senate.

HONORABLE GEO. F. HOAR
Dear Sir

Thanks for the "Memoir of Samuel Hoar, by his Son, George F. Hoar."

For years the character of this true man, as a noble, courageous, self-sacrificing and independent American citizen has commanded my profound admiration and respect, and I am greatly pleased to become more familiar with his life. Fortunately the facts of it need no ornamentation or partial painting by the Son, for the modesty of the latter would never have responded to any such necessity.

I am,
Very truly
Yours, etc.
Wm. P. Frye.

Dear Mr. Hoar: Leicester, March 13/84.
I cannot too much thank you for sending me the memoir —tho' so brief and exceeding temperate—of your father. He was one of the few men who kept Massachusetts and New England from rushing down the steep place and perishing in the waters, as the herd of swine was doing,—a son worthy of the Fathers of New England. I think of him as a kind of tall pillar, on a foundation of such granite solidity as to quiet all fears of possible moving therefrom. He was an example—and became by his S. Carolina mission a conspicuous one; by his attitude and demeanor, opposing the whole moral power of the North to the despotic and insolent assumptions of Slavery.

Yours very truly,
Saml May.

My father, in everything that related to his own conduct, was controlled by a more than Puritan austerity. He seemed to live for nothing but duty. Yet he was a man of strong affections, unlike what is generally deemed to be the character of the Puritan. He was gentle, tolerant, kindly and affectionate. He had all his life a large professional income. But he never seemed to care for money. In that respect he was like one who dwelt by the side of a pond, ready to dip up and to give its waters to any man who might thirst. He never wasted money, or spent it for any self-indulgence. But he was ready to share it with any deserving object. Starr King said of him that "he lived all the beatitudes daily."

Mr. Hoar was, I suppose, beyond all question, the highest authority in New England, indeed in the whole country, on the difficult and abstruse questions belonging to the law of water privileges and running streams. He was declared to be such by the late Judge Benjamin R. Curtis. The great Locks and Canals Company was organized and all the arrangements for the ownership, management and control of the water-power of Lowell were made under his advice and direction. The same methods have been followed in substance at Lawrence and Woonsocket and other manufacturing places.

He preserved his vigor of body until he entered his seventy-seventh year, taking walks of five or six miles without fatigue. About that time he took a severe cold at a neighbor's funeral. An illness followed which seriously impaired his strength. He died, November 2, 1856, two days before the Presidential election.

He was six feet three inches in height, erect, with fine gray hair, blue eyes, of graceful and dignified deportment, and of great courtesy, especially to women and children.

He held a few simple beliefs with undoubting faith. He submitted himself to the rule of life which followed from these, and rigorously exacted obedience to it from all for whom he was responsible. He accepted the exposition of Christian doctrine given by Dr. Channing. The Massachusetts Constitution of 1780 seemed to him a nearly perfect system of government. He earnestly resisted, in the Convention of 1820, the abolition of the property qualification for voters, and of the obligation of all citizens to be taxed for the support of religious worship. He took early and deep interest in the temperance reform, and gave much time, labor, and money to promote it. "The strength and beauty of the man," says Mr. Emerson, "lay in the natural goodness and justice of his mind, which in manhood and in old age, after dealing all his life with weighty private and public interests, left an infantile innocence of which we have no second or third example,—the strength of a chief united to the modesty of a child. He returned from courts and Congresses to sit down with unaltered humility, in the church, or in the town-house, on the plain wooden bench, where Honor came and sat down beside him. He was a man in whom so rare a spirit of justice visibly dwelt, that, if one had met him in a cabin or in a court, he must still seem a public man answering as sovereign state to sovereign state; and might easily suggest Milton's picture of John Bradshaw,—'that he was a consul from whom the fasces did not depart with the year, but in private seemed ever sitting in judgment on kings.'"

But he would have liked better than anything else what was said of him in his official report by the President of the College he loved with that deep affection which her children felt for her in his time. President Walker closes his annual report of December 31, 1856, as follows: "The undersigned could not conclude his report without allusion to the recent lamented death of the Honorable Samuel Hoar, a distinguished and justly influential member of this board, —venerable alike for his age and his virtues,—a devoted friend of the College which he has been able to serve in a thousand ways by the wisdom of his counsels and the weight of his character."

Mr. Hoar was naturally conservative, as would be expected of an old Federalist who was educated at Harvard in the beginning of the nineteenth century. His rules of public and private conduct were strict and austere. He applied them more strictly to himself than to others. His classmates in college used to call him Cato. He favored the suppression of the sale and use of intoxicating liquors, and desired that the whole force of the State should be brought to bear to accomplish that end. He was the inveterate foe of oppression, and in his later years, opposed every compromise with slavery. But he had no sympathy with reforms which seemed to him to be devised merely as political instruments to advance the fortunes of persons or parties.

He had a huge respect for John Quincy Adams, a respect which I have good reason to know was reciprocated. But he was by no means Mr. Adams's blind follower. The ex-President, I think about the year 1832, published a pamphlet in which he savagely attacked the Masonic Order. He met Mr. Hoar in Boston and asked him what he thought of it. Mr. Hoar answered: "It seems to me, Mr. Adams, there is but one thing in the world sillier than Masonry. That is Anti-Masonry."

Mr. Hoar used to relate with some amusement a dialogue he had with a shrewd and witty old lawyer named Josiah Adams, who shared the old Federalist dislike of his namesake, John Quincy Adams. My father was talking quite earnestly in a gathering of Middlesex lawyers and said: "I believe John Quincy Adams means to be a Christian." "When?" inquired Josiah.

But I cannot draw the portraiture of this noble and stately figure. George Herbert did it perfectly, long ago, in his poem, "Constancy."

Old Dr. Lyman Beecher, the foremost champion in his day of the old Orthodoxy, spent his life in combating what he deemed the pestilent Unitarian heresy. He was the most famous preacher in the country. Mr. Hoar was a pillar of Unitarianism. Yet the Doctor came to know and honor his old antagonist. He read in the Boston papers, late Saturday evening, that Mr. Hoar was dying at Concord. Early Sunday morning before daybreak he started, with his son-in-law, Professor Stowe, and drove twenty miles to Concord. He got there just after Mr. Hoar's death. He asked to go into the chamber where his old friend lay. My sister said: "Father would have been glad to see you, if he were alive." The Doctor gazed a moment, and then said: "He's passed safe over, I haven't a doubt of it. He was an Israelite indeed, in whom there was no guile."

CHAPTER IV

BOYHOOD IN CONCORD

I HAVE never got over being a boy. It does not seem likely that I ever shall. I have to-day, at the age of three score and sixteen, less sense of my own dignity than I had when at sixteen I walked for the first time into the College Chapel at Harvard, clad as the statute required, in a "black or black-mixed coat, with buttons of the same color," and the admiring world, with its eyes on the venerable freshman, seemed to me to be saying to itself, "Ecce caudam!" Behold the tail!

Most men are apt to exaggerate the merits of their birthplace. But I think everybody who knew the town will agree with me that there never was in the world a better example of a pure and beautiful democracy, in the highest sense of the term, than the town of Concord from 1826 to the close of the war. If there were any aristocracy, it was an aristocracy of personal worth. There was little wealth and little poverty. There were no costly dwellings and no hovels. There was no pride of wealth or of family. The richest man in town took an interest in the affairs of the poorest, as in those of a kinsman. It never occurred to the poorest that he must, for that reason, doff his hat to any man.

The population was permanent, I suppose, as could have been found in any spot in Europe. Ninety-three of the inhabitants of the town, in 1654, signed a paper pledging their persons and estates to support the General Court in the contest with King Charles II. for the preservation of the Charter. Fourteen of their descendants, bearing the same name, were present at the Centennial Celebration in 1885, dwelling on the land which their ancestors occupied nearly 230 years before. There were 23 others whose descendants of the same name were dwelling at the time of the Centennial within the original limits of the town. A good many others were represented by female descendants. So that at least 50 of the 93 signers of the paper were represented in the assembly. A list of the names of the principal inhabitants of the town to-day would contain the names of a large number of the principal inhabitants of any generation since its foundation.

They were of good English stock. Many of them were of gentle blood and entitled to bear coat armor at home. It is interesting to observe how little the character of the gentleman and gentlewoman in our New England people is affected by the pursuit, for generations, of humble occupations, which in other countries are deemed degrading. Our ancestors, during nearly two centuries of poverty which followed the first settlement, turned their hands to the humblest ways of getting a livelihood, became shoemakers, or blacksmiths or tailors, or did the hardest and most menial and rudest work of the farm, shoveled gravel or chopped wood, without any of the effect on their character which would be likely to be felt from the permanent pursuit of such an occupation in England or Germany. It was like a fishing party or a hunting party in the woods. When the necessity was over, and the man or the boy in any generation got a college education, or was called to take part in public affairs, he rose at once and easily to the demands of an exalted station. What is true of New England people in this respect is, I suppose, true of the whole country.

I wrote, a few years ago, an account of so much of my boyhood as elapsed before I went to college. Through the kindness of the proprietors of *The Youth's Companion,* I am permitted to print it here. I think, on the whole, that is better than to undertake to tell the story in other phraseology adapted to maturer readers. Indeed, I am not sure that the best examples of good English are not to be found in books written for children. When we have to tell a story to a small boy or girl, we avoid little pomposities, and seek for the plainest, clearest and most direct phrase.

I believe that boys nowadays are more manly and mature than they were in my time. Perhaps this is partly because the boys show more gravity in my presence, now I am an old man, than they did when I was a boy myself. But in giving an account of the life of a boy sixty years ago, I must describe it as I saw it, even if it appear altogether childish and undignified.

The life and character of a country are determined in a large degree by the sports of its boys. The Duke of Wellington used to say that the victory at Waterloo was won on the playing-fields at Eton. That is the best people where the boys are manly and where the men have a good deal of the boy in them.

Perhaps all my younger readers do not know how much that makes up, not only the luxury, but the comfort of life, has first come in within the memory of persons now living. The household life of my childhood was not much better in those respects than that of a well-to-do Roman or Greek. It had not improved a great deal for two thousand years. There were no house-warming furnaces, and stoves were almost unknown. There were no double windows, and the houses were warmed by open fires. There were no matches.

There were no water-pipes in the houses, and no provision was made for discharging sewage. There were no railroads, telegraphs or telephones. Letter postage to New York from Boston was twenty-five cents. None of the modern agricultural machinery then existed, not even good modern plows. Crops were planted by hand and cultivated with the hoe and spade. Vegetables were dug with the hoe, and hay and grain cut with the sickle or scythe. There were no ice-houses. The use of ice for keeping provisions or cooling water was unknown.

My father was well-to-do, and his household lived certainly as well as any family in the town of Concord, where I was born. I have no doubt a Roman boy two hundred years before Christ, or an Athenian boy four hundred years before Christ, lived quite as well as I did, if not better.

The boy got up in the morning and dressed himself in a room into which the cold air came through the cracks in the window. If the temperature were twenty degrees below zero outside, it was very little higher inside. If he were big enough to make the fires, he made his way down-stairs in the dark of a winter morning and found, if the fire had been properly raked up the night before, a few coals in the ashes in the kitchen fireplace. The last person who went to bed the night before had done exactly what Homer describes as the practice in Ulysses's time, when he tells us that Ulysses covered himself with leaves after he was washed ashore in Phaiakia:

"He lay down in the midst, heaping the fallen leaves above, as a man hides a brand in a dark bed of ashes, at some outlying farm where neighbors are not near, hoarding a seed of fire to save his seeking elsewhere."

But first he must get a light. Matches are not yet invented. So he takes from the shelf over the mantelpiece an old tin or brass candlestick with a piece of tallow candle in it, and with the tongs takes a coal from the ashes, and holds the candle wick against the coal and gives a few puffs with his breath. If he have good luck, he lights the wick, probably after many failures.

My mother had a very entertaining story connected with the old-fashioned way of getting a light. Old Jeremiah Mason, who was probably the greatest lawyer we ever had in New England, unless we except Daniel Webster, studied law in my uncle's office and shared a room in his house with another law student. One April Fool's day the two young gentlemen went out late in the afternoon, and my aunt, a young unmarried girl who lived with her sister, and another girl, went into the room and took the old half-burnt candle out of the candlestick, cut a piece of turnip to resemble it, cut out a little piece like a wick at the end, blackened it with ink, and put it in the candlestick.

When Mr. Mason came in in the dark, he took a coal up with the tongs and put it against the wick, and puffed and puffed, until after a long and vexatious trial he discovered what was the matter. He said nothing but waited for his chum to come in, who went through the same trial. When they discovered the hoax they framed an elaborate complaint in legal jargon against the two roguish girls, and brought them to trial before a young lawyer of their acquaintance. The young ladies were found guilty and sentenced to pay as a fine a bowl of eggnog.

After getting his candle lighted, the boy takes dry kindling, which has been gathered the night before, and starts a fire. The next thing is to get some water. He is lucky if the water in the old cast-iron kettle which hangs on the crane in the fireplace be not frozen. As soon as the fire is started he goes outdoors to thaw out the pump, if they have a wooden pump. But that is all frozen up, and he has to get some hot water from his kettle to pour down over the piston till he can thaw it out. Sometimes he would have an old-fashioned well, sunk too low in the ground for the frost to reach it, and could get water with the old oaken bucket.

He brings in from out-of-doors a pail or two of water. If there has been a snow-storm the night before, he has to shovel a path to the wood-shed, where he can get the day's supply of wood from outside, and then from the doors of the house out to the street. Meantime the woman whose duty it is to get breakfast makes her appearance.

The wooden pump, which took the place of the old well in many dooryards, was considered a great invention. We all looked with huge respect upon Sanford Adams of Concord, who invented it, and was known all over the country.

He was quite original in his way. The story used to be told of him that he called at my father's house one day to get some advice as to a matter of law. Father was at dinner and went to the door himself. Mr. Adams stated his case in a word or two as he stood on the door-step, to which father gave him his answer, the whole conversation not lasting more than two minutes.

He asked Mr. Hoar what he should pay, and father said, "Five dollars." Mr. Adams paid it at once, and father said, "By the way, there is a little trouble with my pump. It does not draw. Will you just look at it?" So Mr. Adams went around the corner of the shed, moved the handle of the pump, and put his hand down and fixed a little spigot which was in the side, which had got loose, and the pump worked perfectly. Father said, "Thank you, sir." To which Adams replied: "It will be five dollars, Mr. Hoar," and father gave him back the same bill he had just taken.

I am afraid that the sympathy of the people who told the story was with the pump-maker and not with the lawyer.

The great kitchen fireplace presented a very cheerful appearance compared with the black range or stove of to-day. It was from six to eight or ten feet wide, with a great chimney. In many houses you could stand on the hearth and look up the chimney and see the stars on a winter night. Across the fireplace hung an iron crane, which swung on a hinge or pivot, from which hung a large number of what were called pothooks and trammels. From these were suspended the great kettles and little kettles and the griddles and pots and boilers for the cooking processes.

The roasting was done in a big "tin kitchen," which stood before the fire, in which meats or poultry were held by a large iron spit, which pierced them and which could be revolved to present one side after the other to the blaze. Sometimes there was a little clockwork which turned the spit automatically, but usually it was turned round from time to time by the cook. As you know, they used to have in England little dogs called turnspits, trained to turn a wheel for this purpose. A little door in the rear of this tin kitchen gave access for basting the meat. In the large trough at the bottom the gravy was caught.

No boy of that day will think there is any flavor like that of roast turkey and chicken or of the doughnuts and pancakes or griddle-cakes which were cooked by these open fires.

By the side of the fireplace, with a flue entering the chimney, was a great brick oven, big enough to bake all the bread needed by a large family for a week or ten days. The oven was heated by a brisk fire made of birch or maple or some very rapidly burning wood. When the coals were taken out, the bread was put in, and the oven was shut with two iron doors. The baking-day was commonly Saturday.

When the bread was taken out Saturday afternoon it was usual to put in a large pot of beans for the Sunday dinner.

They were left there all night and the oven was opened in the morning and enough came out for breakfast, when there was put into the oven a pot of Indian pudding, which was left with the rest of the beans for the Sunday dinner.

The parlor fire was a very beautiful sight, with the big logs and the sparkling walnut or oak wood blazing up. Some of the housekeepers of that time had a good deal of skill in arranging the wood in a fireplace so as to make of it a beautiful piece of architecture. Lowell describes these old fires very well in his ballad, "The Courtin' ":

> A fireplace filled the room's one side
> With half a cord o' wood in—
> There warn't no stoves (tell comfort died)
> To bake ye to a puddin'.
>
> The wannut logs shot sparkles out
> Towards the pootiest, bless her!
> An' leetle flames danced all about
> The chiny on the dresser.
>
> Agin' the chimbley crooknecks hung,
> An' in amongst 'em rusted
> The ole queen's arm thet Gran'ther Young
> Fetched back from Concord busted.

We did not have fireplaces quite as large as this in my father's house, although they were common in the farmers' houses round about.

In the coldest weather the heat did not come out a great way from the hearth, and the whole family gathered close about the fire to keep warm. It was regarded as a great breach of good manners to go between any person and the fire. The fireplace was the centre of the household, and was regarded as the type and symbol of the home. The boys all understood the force of the line:

> Strike for your altars and your fires!

I wonder if any of my readers nowadays would be stirred by an appeal to strike for his furnace or his air-tight stove.

Sunday was kept with Jewish strictness. The boys were not allowed to go out-of-doors except to church. They could not play at any game or talk about matters not pertaining to religion. They were not permitted to read any books except such as were "good for Sunday." There were very few religious story-books in those days, and what we had were of a dreary kind; so the boy's time hung heavy on his hands.

"Pilgrim's Progress," with its rude prints, was, however, a great resource. We conned it over and over again, and knew it by heart. An elder brother of mine who was very precocious was extremely fond of it, especially of the picture of the fight between Apollyon and Christian, where the fiend with his head covered with stiff, sharp bristles "straddled clear across the road" to stop Christian in his way. Old Dr. Lyman Beecher, who had his stiff gray hair cropped short all over his head, made a call at our house one afternoon. While he was waiting for my mother to come down, the little fellow came into the room and took a look up at the doctor, and then trotted round to the other side and looked up at him again. He said, "I think, sir, you look like Apollyon."

The doctor was infinitely amused at being compared to the personage of whom, in his own opinion and that of a good many other good people, he was then the most distinguished living antagonist.

The church was an old-fashioned wooden building, painted yellow, of Dutch architecture, with galleries on three sides, and on the fourth a pulpit with a great sounding-board over it, into which the minister got by quite a high flight of stairs. Just below the pulpit was the deacons' seat, where the four deacons sat in a row. The pews were old-fashioned square, high pews, reaching up almost to the top of the head of a boy ten years old when he was standing up.

The seats were without cushions and with hinges. When the people stood up for prayer the seats were turned up for greater convenience of standing, and when the prayer ended they came down all over the church with a slam, like a small cannonade.

One Sunday, in the middle of the sermon, the old minister, Doctor Ripley, stood up in the pulpit and said in a loud voice, "Simeon, come here. Take your hat and come here." Simeon was a small boy who lived in the doctor's family and sat in the gallery. We boys all supposed that Simeon had been playing in church, or had committed some terrible offence for which he was to be punished in sight of the whole congregation.

Simeon came down trembling and abashed, and the doctor told him to go home as fast as he could and get the Thanksgiving Proclamation. The doctor filled up the time as well as he could with an enormously long prayer, until the boy got back. Simeon confessed to some of the boys that he had been engaged in some mischief just before he was called, and he was terribly afraid the doctor had caught him.

This old church with its tower, yellow spire, old clock and weathercock, seems to me as I look back on it to have been a very attractive piece of architecture. It was that church which suggested to Emerson the leading thought in one of his most famous poems, "The Problem."

In those days, when people were to be married the law required notice to be given of their intention by proclaiming it aloud in the church three Sundays in succession. So just before the service began, the old town clerk would get up and proclaim: "There is a marriage intended between Mr. John Brown of this town and Miss Sarah Smith of Sudbury," and there was great curiosity in the congregation to hear the announcement. The town clerk in my boyhood had been a wealthy old bachelor for whom the young ladies had set their caps in vain for two generations. One day he astonished the congregation by proclaiming: "There is a marriage intended between Dr. Abiel Keywood"—which was his own name—"and Miss Lucy P. Fay, both of Concord." That was before I can remember, as his boys were about my age.

Doctor Ripley, the minister in Concord, was an old man who had been settled there during the Revolutionary War, and was over the parish sixty-two years. He was an excellent preacher and scholar, and his kindly despotism was submitted to by the whole town. His way of pronouncing would sound very queer now, though it was common then. I well remember his reading the lines of the hymn—

> Let every critter jine
> To praise the eternal God.

Scattered about the church were the good gray heads of many survivors of the Revolution—the men who had been at the bridge on the 19th of April, and who made the first armed resistance to the British power. They were very striking and venerable figures, with their queues and knee-breeches and shoes with shining buckles. Men were more particular about their apparel in those days than we are now. They had great stateliness of behavior, and admitted of little familiarity.

They had heard John Buttrick's order to fire, which marked the moment when our country was born. The order was given to British subjects. It was obeyed by American citizens. Among them was old Master Blood, who saw a ball strike the water when the British fired their first volley. I heard many of the old men tell their stories of the Battle of Concord, and of the capture of Burgoyne.

I lay down on the grass one summer afternoon, when old Amos Baker of Lincoln, who was in the Lincoln Company on the 19th of April, told me the whole story. He was very indignant at the claim that the Acton men marched first to attack the British because the others hesitated. He said, "It was because they had bagnets [bayonets]. The rest of us hadn't no bagnets."

One day a few years later, when I was in college, I walked up from Cambridge to Concord, through Lexington, and had a chat with old Jonathan Harrington by the roadside. He told me he was on the Common when the British Regulars fired upon the Lexington men. He did not tell me then the story which he told afterward at the great celebration at Concord in 1850. He and Amos Baker were the only survivors who were there that day. He said he was a boy about fifteen years old on April 19, 1775. He was a fifer in the company. He had been up the greater part of the night helping get the stores out of the way of the British, who were expected, and went to bed about three o'clock, very tired and sleepy. His mother came and pounded with her fist on the door of his chamber, and said, "Git up, Jonathan! The Reg'lars are comin' and somethin' must be done!"

Governor Briggs repeated this anecdote in the old man's presence at the Concord celebration in 1850. Charles Storey, a noted wit, father of the eminent lawyer, Moorfield Storey, sent up to the chair this toast: "When Jonathan Harrington got up in the morning on April 19, 1775, a near relative and namesake of his got up about the same time—Brother Jonathan. But his mother didn't call him."

A very curious and amusing incident is said, and I have no doubt truly, to have happened at this celebration. It shows how carefully the great orator, Edward Everett, looked out for the striking effects in his speech. He turned in the midst of his speech to the seat where Amos Baker and Jonathan Harrington sat, and addressed them. At once they both stood up, and Mr. Everett said, with fine dramatic effect, "Sit, venerable friends. It is for us to stand in your presence."

After the proceedings were over, old Amos Baker was heard to say to somebody, "What do you suppose Squire Everett meant? He came to us before his speech and told us to stand up when he spoke to us, and when we stood up, he told us to sit down."

So you will understand how few lives separate you from the time when our country was born, and the time when all our people were British subjects.

But to come back to our old meeting-house. The windows rattled in the winter, and the cold wind came in through the cracks. There was a stove which was rather a modern innovation; but it did little to temper the coldness of a day in midwinter. We used to carry to church a little foot-stove with a little tin pan in it, which we filled with coal from the stove in the meeting-house, and the ladies of the family would pass it round to each other to keep their toes from freezing; but the boys did not get much benefit from it.

They had good schools in Concord, and the boys generally were good scholars and read good books. So whenever they thought fit they could use as good language as anybody; but their speech with one another was in the racy, pithy Yankee dialect, which Lowell has made immortal in the "Biglow Papers." It was not always grammatical, but as well adapted for conveying wit and humor and shrewd sense as the Scotch of Burns.

The boys knew very well how to take the conceit or vanity out of their comrades. In the summer days all the boys of the village used to gather at a place on the river, known as Thayer's swimming-place, about half a mile from the town pump, which was the centre from which all distances were measured in those days. There was a little gravel beach where you could wade out a rod or two, and then for a rod or two the water was over the boy's head. It then became shallow again near the opposite bank. So it was a capital place to learn to swim.

After they came out, the boys would sit down on the bank and have a sort of boys' exchange, in which all matters of interest were talked over, and a great deal of good-natured chaff was exchanged. Any newcomer had to pass through an ordeal of this character, in which his temper and quality were thoroughly tried. I remember now an occasion which must have happened when I was not more than eight or ten years old, when a rather awkward-looking greenhorn had come down from New Hampshire and made his appearance at the swimming-place. The boys, one after another, tried him by putting mocking questions or attempting to humbug him with some large story. He received it all with patience and good nature until one remark seemed to sting him from his propriety. He turned with great dignity upon the offender, and said, "Was that you that spoke, or was it a punkin busted?" We all thought that it was well said, and took him into high favor.

I suppose the outdoor winter sports have not changed much since my childhood. The sluggish Concord River used to overflow its banks and cover the broad meadows for miles, where we found excellent skating, and where the water would be only a foot or two in depth. The boys could skate for ten miles to Billerica and ten miles back, hardly going over deep water, except at the bridges, the whole way.

Sleigh-riding was not then what it is now. There were a few large sleighs owned in the town which would hold thirty or forty persons, and once or twice in the winter the boys and girls would take a ride to some neighboring town when the sleighing was good.

The indoor games were marbles, checkers, backgammon, dominoes, hunt-the-slipper, blind-man's-buff, and in some houses, where they were not too strict, they played cards. High-low-jack, sometimes called all-fours or seven-up, everlasting and old maid were the chief games of cards. Most of these games have come down from a very early antiquity.

The summer outdoor games were mumble-the-peg, high-spy, snap-the-whip, a rather dangerous performance, in which a long row of boys, with the biggest boy at one end, and tapering down to the smallest at the other end, would run over a field or open space until suddenly the big boy would stop, turn half around, and stand still and hold fast with all his might. The result was that the boy next to him had to move a very little distance, but the little fellow at the end was compelled to describe a half-circle with great rapidity, and was sometimes hurled across the field, and brought up with a heavy fall. There were thread-the-needle, hunt-the-red-lion and football, played very much as it is now, except with less system and discipline, and various games of ball. These games of ball were much less scientific and difficult than the modern games. Chief were four-old-cat, three-old-cat, two-old-cat and base.

We had fewer studies at our school than now. The boys who did not go to college learned to read and write, perhaps an elementary history of the United States, and arithmetic, and occasionally made some little progress in algebra. On Saturdays we used to "speak pieces." Our favorites were some spirited lyric, like "Scots Wha Hae" or Pierpont's "Stand, the ground's your own, my braves," "The boy stood on the burning deck," and "Bernardo del Carpio."

Sometimes, though not often, some comic piece was chosen, like Jack Downing's "Tax on Old Bachelors."

Those who fitted for college added Latin and Greek to these studies. The children were sent to school earlier than is the present fashion, and had long school hours and few vacations. There were four vacations in the year, of a week each, and three days at Thanksgiving time. Little account was made of Christmas. The fashion of Christmas presents was almost wholly unknown. The boys used to be allowed to go out of school to study in the warm summer days, and would find some place in a field, and sometimes up in the belfry of the little schoolhouse. I remember studying Cæsar there with George Brooks, afterward judge, and reading with him an account of some battle where Cæsar barely escaped being killed, on which Brooks's comment was, "I wish to thunder he had been!"

I am afraid the boys did not respect the property of the owners of the neighboring apple orchards, as undoubtedly the better-trained boys of modern times do now. We understood the law to be that all apples that grew on the branches extending over the highway were public property, and I am afraid that when the owner was not about we were not very particular as to the boundary-line. This seems to have been a trait of boy nature for generations. You know Sidney Smith's account of the habit of boys at his school to rob a neighboring orchard, until the farmer bought a large, savage bulldog for his protection. Some of the big boys told Sidney that if a boy would get down on his hands and knees and go backward toward the dog, the dog would be frightened, and he could get the apples. He tried the experiment unsuccessfully, and with the result that he concluded, as he says, that "it makes no difference to a bulldog which end of a boy he gets hold of, if he only gets a good hold."

The discipline of the schoolmaster in those days was pretty severe. For slight offences the boys were deprived of their recess or compelled to study for an hour after the school was dismissed. The chief weapon of torture was the ferule, to the efficacy of which I can testify from much personal knowledge. The master had in his desk, however, a cowhide for gross cases. I do not remember knowing how that felt from personal experience, but I remember very well seeing it applied occasionally to the big boys.

In the infant schools, which were kept by women, of course the discipline was not expected to be so severe. The schoolmistress in those days wore what was called a busk— a flat piece of lancewood, hornbeam, or some other like tough and elastic wood, thrust into a sort of pocket or sheath in her dress, which came up almost to the chin and came down below the waist. This was intended to preserve the straightness and grace of her figure. When the small boy misbehaved, the schoolma'am would unsheath this weapon, and for some time thereafter the culprit found sitting down exceedingly uncomfortable.

Sometimes the sole of the schoolmistress's slipper answered the same purpose, and sometimes a stick from some neighboring birch-tree. It all came to pretty much the same thing in the end. The schoolmistress knew well how to accomplish her purpose. There was a diversity of gifts but the same spirit.

We were put to school much earlier than children are now, and were more advanced in our studies on the whole. I began to study Latin on my sixth birthday. When I was nine years old I was studying Greek, and had read several books of Virgil. We were not very thorough Latin scholars, even when we entered college, but could translate Virgil and Cicero and Cæsar and easy Greek like Xenophon.

The boys occasionally formed military companies and played soldier, but these did not, so far as I remember, last very long. There was also a company of Indians, who dressed in long white shirts, with pieces of red flannel sewed on them. They had wooden spears. That was more successful, and lasted some time.

They were exceedingly fond of seeing the real soldiers. There were two full companies in Concord, the artillery and the light infantry. The artillery had two cannon captured from the British, which had been presented to the company by the legislature in honor of April 19, 1775. When these two companies paraded, they were followed by an admiring train of small boys all day long, if the boys could get out of school. I remember on one occasion there was a great rivalry between the companies, and one of them got the famous Brigade Band from Boston, and the other an equally famous band, called the Boston Brass Band, in which Edward Kendall, the great musician, was the player on the bugle. A very great day indeed was the muster-day, when sometimes an entire brigade would be called out for drill. These muster-days happened three or four times in my boyhood at Concord.

But the great day of all was what was called "Cornwallis," which was the anniversary of the capture of Cornwallis at Yorktown. There were organized companies in uniform representing the British army and an equally large number of volunteers, generally in old-fashioned dress, and with such muskets and other accoutrements as they could pick up, who represented the American army. There was a parade and a sham fight which ended as all such fights, whether sham or real, should end, in a victory for the Americans, and Cornwallis and his troops were paraded, captive and ignominious. I quite agree with Hosea Biglow when he says, "There is fun to a Cornwallis, though; I aint agoin' to deny it."

The boys cared little for politics, though they used to profess the faith of their fathers; but every boy sometimes imagined himself a soldier, and his highest conception of glory was to "lick the British." I remember walking home from school with a squad of little fellows at the time Andrew Jackson issued his famous message, when he threatened war if the French did not pay us our debt. We discussed the situation with great gravity, and concluded that if the French beat us, we should have a king to rule over us.

Besides the two military companies, there was another called the "Old Shad." The law required every able-bodied man of military age to turn out for military training and inspection on the last Wednesday in May; they turned out just to save the penalty of the law, and used to dress in old clothes, and their awkward evolutions were the object of great scorn to the small boy of the time.

The streets of Concord were made lively by the stage-coaches and numerous teams. There were four taverns in the town, all well patronized, with numerous sleeping-rooms. Two of them had large halls for dancing. A great many balls were given, to which persons came from the neighboring towns.

There was an excellent fiddler named John Wesson, who continued to give the benefit of his talent to all parties, public and private, down to the time of the war, when he said he would not play a dancing tune till the boys came home. He died soon after, and I do not know whether his music was ever heard again. These taverns were crowded with guests. One principal route for stages and teams to New Hampshire, Vermont and Canada passed through Concord.

There were several lines of stages, one from Lowell to Framingham, and two at least from Boston. The number of passengers, which now are all carried by rail, was so large that extras were frequently necessary. The teams were very often more than the barns of the taverns in the town could accommodate, and on summer nights the wagons would extend for long distances along the village street with horses tied behind them.

The sound of the toddy stick was hardly interrupted in the barroom inside from morning till night. The temperance reform had not made great headway in my youthful days. It was not uncommon to see farmers, bearing names highly respected in the town, lying drunk by the roadside on a summer afternoon, or staggering along the streets. The unpainted farmhouses and barns had their broken windows stuffed with old hats or garments. I have heard Nathan Brooks, who delivered the first temperance lecture in the town, at the request of the selectmen, say that after it was over he and the selectmen and some of the principal citizens went over to the tavern, and each took a mug of flip.

There were great quantities of huckleberries in the pastures about Concord, and the sweet high blackberries abounded by the roadside. There were plenty of chestnuts in the woods, and the walnut, or pig-nut, also abounded; so that berrying and nutting were favorite pastimes.

When I was a small boy a party of us went down to Walden woods, afterward so famous as the residence of Henry Thoreau. There was an old fellow named Tommy Wyman, who lived in a hut near the pond, who did not like the idea of having the huckleberry-fields near him invaded by the boys. He told us it was not safe for us to go there. He said there was an Indian doctor in the woods who caught small boys and cut out their livers to make medicine. We were terribly frightened, and all went home in a hurry.

When we got near the town, we met old John Thoreau, with his son Henry, and I remember his amusement when I told him the story. He said, "If I meet him, I will run this key down his throat," producing a key from his pocket. We reported the occurrence at the village store, but were unable to excite any interest in the subject.

Thanksgiving was then, as it is and ought to be now, the great day of the year. All the children were at home. The ambition of the head of the house was to get the largest turkey that money could buy. No Thanksgiving dinner was quite complete unless there were a baby on hand belonging to some branch of the family, no bigger than the turkey. The preparation for Thanksgiving was very interesting to the small boy mind. A boiled or roasted turkey, a pair of chickens, chicken pie, wonderful cranberry sauce, a plum pudding, and all manner of apple pies, mince pies, squash pies, pumpkin pies, and nuts, raisins, figs and noble apples made part of the feast. I suppose Thanksgiving customs have changed less than most others, except in one particular. I do not believe there is a small boy's stomach in this generation that can hold a tenth part of what used to go into mine, not only on Thanksgiving day, but on the days before and after. The raisins were to be picked over, the nuts and citron got ready, when Thanksgiving was coming on, of all which we took abundant tolls. The cold and warmed-over dishes lasted through the rest of the week. I do not know what the Jewish festival or the old Roman banquets might have been, but they could not have equalled a New England Thanksgiving week in a house in the country.

The doctor in those days was a terror to the small boy. The horrible and nasty castor oil, ipecac and calomel, and the salts and senna, sulphur and molasses taken three mornings in succession and then missed three mornings, were worse than any sickness. Of the last I speak only from hearsay, not from personal knowledge. Then the cupping and bleeding were fearful things to go through or look upon. We had none of the sweet patent medicines that the children now cry for, and none of the smooth capsules or the pleasant comfits that turn medicine into confectionery nowadays.

The boys were not allowed in most families to read novels, even on week-days. My father had a great dislike to fiction of all sorts, and for a good while would not tolerate any novels in the house; but one winter day he went to Pepperell, in the northern part of the county, to try a case before a sheriff's jury. About the time the case got through there came a sudden and violent snowstorm, which blocked up the roads with deep drifts so that he could not get home for two or three days. He had to stay at a small country tavern, and the time hung very heavily on his hands.

He asked the landlord if he had any books. The only one he could find was a first volume of Scott's "Redgauntlet," which was then just published in Boston by a bookseller named Parker, in what was called Parker's revised edition. Father read it with infinite delight. His eyes were opened to the excellence of Scott. He got home the next day at about noon, and immediately sent one of the children down to the circulating library to get the second volume. He subscribed to Parker's edition, and was a great lover of Scott ever after.

We were permitted, however, to read the "Tales of a Grandfather." I hope if any boy reads this book he will read the "Tales of a Grandfather," especially the parts which give the history of Scotland. It is a most interesting and noble story. I can remember now how the tears ran down my cheeks as I read Scott's description of finding the bones of Robert Bruce in the old abbey at Dunfermline:

"As the church would not hold half the numbers, the people were allowed to pass through it one after another, that each one, the poorest as well as the richest, might see all that remained of the great king, Robert Bruce. Many people shed tears; for there was the wasted skull which once was the head, that thought so wisely and boldly for his country's deliverance; and there was the dry bone which had once been the sturdy arm that killed Sir Henry de Bohun, between the two armies, at a single blow on the evening before the Battle of Bannockburn."

I account it one of the chief blessings of my life that my boyhood was spent in the pure, noble and simple society of the people of Concord. I am afraid I did not do it much credit then. Old Dr. Bartlett, one of the worthiest and kindliest of men, but who always uttered what was in his heart, said after my two oldest brothers and I had grown up, that Samuel Hoar's boys used to be the three biggest rascals in Concord, but they all seemed to have turned out pretty well. I have so far kept this statement strictly from the knowledge of the Democratic papers. But I suppose it is too late to do any harm now.

CHAPTER V

FAMOUS CONCORD MEN

THERE were in Concord in my boyhood three writers who afterward became very famous indeed—Emerson, Hawthorne and Thoreau. Mr. Lowell said that these three names shine among all others in American literature as the three blazing stars in the belt of Orion shine in the sky.

The town is represented in the beautiful building of the Congressional Library at Washington by busts of Emerson and Hawthorne on the outside front of the building; by Emerson's name on the mosaic ceiling in the entrance pavilion, and by three sentences from his writings inscribed on the walls. These are two out of eight such busts. It is also represented by two figures, a symbolic Statue of History, and a bronze Statue of Herodotus, both by Daniel Chester French, the sculptor, a Concord man.

Emerson came to live in Concord in the summer of 1835. Although he was born in Boston and went to school there, he belonged to the town by virtue of his descent from a race of Concord ministers who held the pulpit, with very brief intervals, from 1635 to 1841. But I do not think his influence upon the town was very great for the first fifteen or twenty years of his life there. Indeed, I think he would have said that the town had more influence upon him than he had upon it. The Concord people, like the general public, were slow in coming to know his great genius. He was highly respected always. But the people were at first puzzled by him. His life was somewhat secluded. He spent his days in study and in solitary walks. Until Mrs. Ripley came to the old manse, about 1846, Emerson had, I think, no intimate friend outside of his own household, except my sister Elizabeth, who had been betrothed to his brother, Charles, and was as a sister to Emerson until her death in

1878. A good many allusions to her will be found in his life and in his letters to Carlyle. After she died and shortly before his own death he appeared at my brother's house one day with a manuscript which he had handed to the Judge. He had gone over his diary for a great many years and extracted and copied everything in it which related to her.

He used to read lectures to the Lyceum, and in reading his books now I find a great many passages which I remember to have heard him read in my youthful days. In one of his lectures upon Plato, he said that he turned everything to the use of his philosophy, that "wife, children and friends were all ground into paint"—alluding to Washington Allston's story of the Paint King who married a lovely maiden that he might make paint of the beautiful color of her cheeks.

A worthy farmer's wife in the audience took this literally, and left the room in high dudgeon. She said she thought Waldo Emerson might be in better business than holding up to the people of Concord the example of a wicked man who ground his wife and children into paint.

In Emerson's later days he was undoubtedly a powerful educational influence in the town. He was a man of much public spirit. In his philosophy his "soul was like a star and dwelt apart."

But he had a heart full of human affections. He loved the town. He loved his country. He loved his family. He loved his neighbors and friends. He could be stirred deeply on fit occasions by righteous indignation. Some of the men who frequented the tavern, posted in the barroom a scurrilous libel upon old Dr. Bartlett, the venerable physician, who had incurred their hostility by his zeal in enforcing the prohibitory laws. Emerson heard of it and repaired to the spot and tore down the offensive paper with his own hand. After Wendell Phillips made an equally scurrilous attack on Judge Hoar, Emerson refused to take his hand.

In his lament for his beautiful boy he uttered the voice of parental sorrow in immortal accents. In the poems, "In Memoriam," and in "The Dirge," he records how lonely the lovely Concord Valley is to him since his brothers are gone, as he wanders there in the long sunny afternoon:

> Harken to yon pine warbler,
> Singing aloft in the tree!
> Hearest thou, O, traveller,
> What he singeth to me?
>
> Not unless God made sharp thine ear
> With sorrow such as mine,
> Out of that delicate lay couldst thou
> Its heavy tale divine.

But I think that the life of his younger brother Charles, though he died so early, was felt as an even greater force in Concord than that of Waldo.

I hope I may be pardoned if I put on record here a slight and imperfect tribute to the memory of Charles Emerson, who was betrothed to my eldest sister. It is nearly seventy years ago. Yet the sweet and tender romance is still fresh in my heart. He was a descendant of a race of Concord clergymen, including Peter Bulkeley, the founder of the town. He was born in Boston, but spent much of his youth in Concord in the household of Dr. Ripley, who was the second husband of the grandmother of the Emersons. He studied law partly at Cambridge Law School, partly in Daniel Webster's office in Boston, and afterward with my father in Concord. When my father took his seat in Congress, in 1835, Emerson succeeded to his office, and if he had lived would have succeeded to his practice. Waldo Emerson has left it on record that he was led to choose Concord as his dwelling-place to be near his brother. Waldo's house had been enlarged to make room for Charles and his bride under the same roof. The house was ready and the wedding near at hand when, in riding from Boston to Concord on top of the stage, Charles took a violent cold, which was followed by pleurisy and death. He was of a very sociable nature, knew all the town people, lectured before the Lyceum, had a class in the Sunday-school and used to speak in the Lyceum debates. He had a very pleasant wit. He was on the committee for the celebration of the settlement of the town in 1835, at the end of two hundred years, and about the same time was on a committee to attend the celebration at Acton, where the people claimed for themselves all the glory of the Concord Fight. He had thought it likely the Acton people would ask him to speak. But they did not. As he was riding back in the chaise, he said if they had asked him to speak, he had it in mind to give as a toast, "The blessed Memory of the Pilgrim Fathers, who first landed at Acton."

He was especially fond of boys, and they of him. When he died, every schoolboy thought he had lost a friend. One had a knife and another a book or a picture which he prized, and another a pair of skates which Charles Emerson had given him. It may be a fond exaggeration, but I think he was the most brilliant intellect ever born in Massachusetts.

Mr. Webster, who was consulted as to where Emerson should settle, said, "Settle! Let him settle anywhere. Let him settle in the midst of the back woods of Maine, the clients will throng after him." Mr. Everett delivered an eloquent eulogy after his death, at the Phi Beta Kappa dinner at Harvard.

Dr. Holmes's exquisite tribute in his Phi Beta poems is well known:

> Thou calm, chaste scholar! I can see thee now,
> The first young laurels on thy pallid brow,
> O'er thy slight figure floating lightly down
> In graceful folds the academic gown,
> On thy curled lip the classic lines that taught
> Now nice the mind that sculptured them with thought,
> And triumph glistening in the clear blue eye,
> Too bright to live,—but Oh! too fair to die.

Dr. Holmes also says in his last tribute to Waldo:

"Of Charles Chauncey, the youngest brother, I knew something in my college days. A beautiful, high-souled, pure, exquisitely delicate nature in a slight but finely wrought mortal frame, he was for me the very ideal of an embodied celestial intelligence. I may venture to mention a trivial circumstance, because it points to the character of his favorite reading, which was likely to be guided by the same tastes as his brother's, and may have been specially directed by him. Coming into my room one day, he took up a copy of Hazlitt's British Poets. He opened it to the poem of Andrew Marvell's, entitled 'The Nymph Complaining for the Death of her Fawn,' which he read to me with delight irradiating his expressive features. The lines remained with me, or many of them, from that hour,—

> Had it lived long, it would have been
> Lilies without, roses within.

"I felt as many have felt after being with his brother, Ralph Waldo, that I had entertained an angel visitant. The fawn of Marvell's imagination survives in my memory as the fitting image to recall this beautiful youth; a soul glowing like the rose of morning with enthusiasm, a character white as the lilies in its purity."

The late Samuel May, who was in the class after Emerson's at Harvard, told me that the impression his character and person made upon the students of his time was so great that when he passed through the college yard, everybody turned to look after him, as in later days men looked after Webster when he passed down State Street.

The Rev. Joseph H. Cross, now (1903) still living, the oldest graduate of Harvard, was his classmate. I received this letter from him a few years ago:

66 Bradford St., Lawrence,
January 8, 1897.

Hon. G. F. Hoar,
Dear Sir:
Yours of 5th inst. is before me; and I am glad to remember my classmate Emerson and answer your inquiries. I knew that he studied law in your Honored Father's office, and was betrothed to your eldest sister.

Your first inquiry is "as to his looks." He was about medium height, well proportioned and straight as an arrow, brown hair and clear blue eyes, with fair complexion and handsome features. "His scholarship and talents," both of the highest order. The class regarded him as the first and best scholar, dignified and refined in manners, courteous and amiable in spirit. He had great influence in his own class, and was much esteemed and beloved by all.

I think the impression he made upon all who knew him was that of a classical scholar and a perfect gentleman.

Dr. Channing said when he died that all New England mourned his loss.

Although Charles was seven years the younger, his brother Waldo speaks of him as his own master and teacher. The following letter was written by Waldo to his aunt Mary just after Charles's death. A part of it is printed in Cabot's Biography. Waldo and my sister, Elizabeth, heard of the extremity of his danger, and were on their way to see him, but arrived too late to find him alive.

"12 May.

"You have already heard that E. and I arrived too late to see Charles. He died on Monday afternoon, immediately after returning from a ride with Mother. He got out of the coach alone, walked up the steps and into the house without assistance, then sat down upon the stairs, fainted and never recovered. Yesterday afternoon we attended his funeral, and that is the end on this side Heaven, of his extraordinary promise, the union of such shining gifts,—grace and genius, and sense and virtue. What a loss is this to us all—to Elizabeth and Mother and you and me. In him I have lost all my society. I sought no other and formed my habits to live with him. I deferred to him on so many questions and trusted him more than myself, that I feel as if I had lost the best part of myself. In him were the foundations of so solid a confidence and friendship that all the years of life leaned upon him. His genius too was a fountain inexhaustible of thoughts and kept me ever curious and expectant. Nothing was too great, nothing too beautiful for his grasp or his expression, and as brilliant as his power of illustration was, he stuck like a mathematician to his truth and never added a syllable for display. I cannot tell you how much I have valued his conversation for these last two or three years, and he has never stopped growing, but has ripened from month to month. Indeed, the weight of his thoughts and the fresh and various forms in which he instantly clothed them has made Shakespeare more conceivable to me, as Shakespeare was almost the only genius whom he wholly loved. His taste was unerring. What he called good was good, but so severe was it that very few works and very few men could satisfy him, and this because his standard was a pure ideal beauty and he never forgot himself so far as to accept any lower actual one in lieu of it. But I must not begin yet to enumerate his perfections. I shall not know where to stop, and what would be bare truth to me would sound on paper like the fondest exaggeration.

"I mourn for the Commonwealth, which has lost before it yet had learned his name the promise of his eloquence and rare public gifts. He blessed himself that he had been bred from infancy as it were in the public eye, and he looked forward to the debates in the Senate on great political questions as to his fit and native element. And with reason, for in extempore debate his speech was music, and the precision, the flow and the elegance of his discourse equally excellent. Familiar as I was with his powers, when a year ago I first heard him take part in a debate, he surprised me with his success. He spoke so well that he was impatient of writing as not being a fit medium for him. I never shall hear such speaking as his, for his memory was a garden of immortal flowers, and all his reading came up to him as he talked, to clear, elevate and decorate the subject of his present thought. But I shall never have done describing, as I see well I shall never cease grieving as long as I am on the earth that he has left it. It seems no longer worth living in, if whatever delights us in it departs. He has quitted forever the apparent, the partial. He has gone to make acquaintance with the real, the good, the divine, and to find mates and coöperators such as we could not offer him."

Charles Emerson entered with zeal and sympathy into the daily life of the people of Concord. He delivered a few lectures, which were quite celebrated. Some of his manuscripts are in existence, and there is a boyish essay or two in the *Harvard Magazine,* one on Conversation and one on Friendship, which show a singular charm and simplicity of style. He wrote the epitaph on the tomb of Professor Ashmun at Mount Auburn, and a tribute to his friend, James Jackson, Jr., which is preserved in Jackson's memoir by his father.

Miss Martineau, in a chapter of her autobiography written in 1836, describes the feeling in Boston in regard to the opposition to slavery, which seems now incredible even to those who remember it. She says:

"The Emersons, for the adored Charles Emerson was living then, were not men to join an association for any object. . . . But at the time of the hubbub against me in Boston, Charles Emerson stood alone of a large company in defence of free thought and speech, and declared that he had rather see Boston in ashes than that I or anybody should be debarred in any way from perfectly free speech."

Robert C. Winthrop, who was Charles Emerson's intimate friend in boyhood, wrote for the *Advertizer* a beautiful obituary notice. He says: "Emerson was eminently a man of genius. We know not that in his riper years he ever wrote a line of poetry, but no one could have listened to him, either in private or public without feeling that he had a poet's power; while his prose composition was of so pure and finished a style as to show plainly that close perusal of the English Classics in which he so much delighted. . . . One opinion which Mr. Emerson had early formed, and which had he been spared to mature life might have contributed much to his eminence may, in the sad event which has occurred, have contracted the circle of his fame. . . . He had formed in his own mind a standard of education far beyond that which can be completed, even by the most faithful application, within the ordinary rounds of school and college—an education in which every man must be mainly his own master. In the work of this enlarged self-education he was engaged, and, until it was finished, he shrunk from the appearance of attempting to instruct others. He had in him all the elements which would have insured the success of early efforts at display—a fluent speech, a fine elocution, quick conception, a brilliant fancy. But his ambition, . . . while it aspired to a lofty eminence, was content to see that eminence still in the distance." Mr. Winthrop adds, "Principle, unyielding and uncompromising principle, was the very breath of his soul, and pervaded and animated his whole intellectual system. . . . He openly professed what he believed, and he acted up to his professions. He not only held conscience the guide of his life, but he took care to school and discipline that conscience so that its dictates should always conform to truth, to duty, to the laws of God. He was an honorable, high-minded, virtuous man—a sincere and devout Christian. . . . He has fallen at the very gate of an honorable and eminent career, and a thousand hopes are buried in his grave."

A few years before Mr. Winthrop died I met him in Cambridge, at the Peabody Museum, of which we were both trustees. The trustees were gathered in their room waiting for the meeting to be called to order. Mr. Winthrop was talking about his college days. I asked him how it happened that there were so many distinguished persons, in various departments of excellence, who were graduated from Harvard about his time, in his class and in the few classes following and preceding. I said that sometimes there would be several orators, or eminent men of science, or eminent classical scholars, or eminent teachers, graduated about the same time, and their excellence would be attributed to some one instructor; but that in his time there seemed to be a crop of great men in all departments of life—in natural history, in the pulpit, the bar, in oratory, in literature, and in public life. Mr. Winthrop rose to his feet from his chair and brought his hand down with great emphasis on the table as he answered: "It was the influence of Charles Emerson, Sir."

Charles Emerson delivered just before his death a very beautiful and impressive lecture on Socrates. It was long remembered by the people of Concord. It is said that they who heard it never forgot his beautiful figure and glowing countenance as he ended a passage of great eloquence at the close of the lecture with the words,

"God for thee has done His part. Do thine."

Mr. Hawthorne had published some short stories which had already made his name quite celebrated, but his great fame was still to be gained. He was poor and had a good deal of difficulty in gaining a decent living for himself and his young wife. I will not undertake to repeat the story of his life which Hawthorne has told so beautifully in his "Mosses from an Old Manse." I knew Mrs. Hawthorne very well indeed. She was a great friend of my oldest sister and used to visit my father's house when I was a boy, before she was married. It was owing to that circumstance that the Hawthornes came to live in Concord. She was quite fond of me. I used to get strawberries and wild flowers for her, and she did me the great honor to draw my portrait, which now, fortunately or unfortunately, is lost. I went up to the house while they were absent on their wedding journey when I was a boy of fourteen or fifteen to help put things in order for the reception of the young couple.

The furniture was very cheap; a good deal of it was made of common maple. But Mrs. Hawthorne, who was an artist, had decorated it by drawings and paintings on the backs of the chairs and on the bureaus and bedsteads. On the headboard of her bed was a beautiful copy, painted by herself, of Guido's Aurora, with its exquisite light figures and horses and youths and maidens flying through the air.

I never knew Hawthorne except as a stately figure, whom I saw sometimes in Concord streets and sometimes in his own home. He rarely, if ever, opened his lips in my hearing. He was always very silent, hardly spoke in the presence of any visitor with whom he was not very intimate. So far as I know he never visited at the houses of his neighbors and never went to town-meeting. The latter was a deadly sin in the eyes of his democratic neighbors. Mr. Emerson induced him, one evening, to be one of a small company at his house. But Hawthorne kept silent and at last went to the window and looked out at the stars. One of the ladies said to the person next her: "How well he rides his horses of the night." He was very fond of long walks, and of rowing on the river with Thoreau and Ellery Channing.

The Old Manse was built in 1759 by the Rev. Daniel Bliss for his daughter Phoebe on her marriage to the Rev. William Emerson. She was grandmother of Waldo Emerson. Her second husband was the Rev. Dr. Ripley.

I knew Henry Thoreau very intimately. I went to school with him when I was a little boy and he was a big one. Afterward I was a scholar in his school.

He was very fond of small boys, and used to take them out with him in his boat, and make bows and arrows for them, and take part in their games. He liked also to get a number of the little chaps of a Saturday afternoon and take them out in his boat, or for a long walk in the woods.

He knew the best places to find huckleberries and blackberries and chestnuts and lilies and cardinal and other rare flowers. We used to call him Trainer Thoreau, because the boys called the soldiers the "trainers," and he had a long, measured stride and an erect carriage which made him seem something like a soldier, although he was short and rather ungainly in figure. He had a curved nose which reminded one a little of the beak of a parrot.

His real name was David Henry Thoreau, although he changed the order of his first two names afterward. He was a great finder of Indian arrow-heads, spear-heads, pestles, and other stone implements which the Indians had left behind them, of which there was great abundance in the Concord fields and meadows.

He knew the rare forest birds and all the ways of birds and wild animals. Naturalists commonly know birds and beasts and flowers as a surgeon who has dissected the human body, or perhaps sometimes a painter who has made pictures of them knows men and women. But he knew birds and beasts as one boy knows another—all their delightful little habits and fashions. He had the most wonderful good fortune. We used to say that if anything happened in the deep woods which only came about once in a hundred years, Henry Thoreau would be sure to be on the spot at the time and know the whole story.

> It seemed that Nature could not raise
> A plant in any secret place,
> In quaking bog or snowy hill,
> Beneath the grass that shades the rill,
> Under the snow, between the rocks,
> In damp fields known to bird and fox,
> But he would come in the very hour
> It opened in its virgin bower,
> As if a sunbeam showed the place,
> And tell its long-descended race.
> It seemed as if the breezes brought him;
> It seemed as if the sparrows taught him;
> As if by secret sight he knew
> Where, in far fields, the orchis grew.
> Many haps fall in the field
> Seldom seen by wishful eyes,
> But all her shows did Nature yield,
> To please and win this pilgrim wise.
> He saw the partridge drum in the woods;
> He heard the woodcock's evening hymn;
> He found the tawny thrushes' broods;
> And the shy hawk did wait for him;
> What others did at distance hear,
> And guessed within the thicket's gloom,
> Was shown to this philosopher,
> And at his bidding seemed to come.

These lines fit Henry Thoreau exactly. Most people think Emerson had him in mind when he wrote them. But as a matter of fact, they were written before he knew Henry Thoreau.

I wonder how many know the woodcock's evening hymn. I have known many sportsmen and naturalists who never heard it or heard of it. When the female is on her nest the male woodcock flies straight up into the sky, folds his wings and falls down through the air, coming down within a foot or two of the nest from which he ascended, pouring out a beautiful song, which he never sings at any other time. He is said to be one of the best and sweetest of our song-birds.

It is a singular fact that Emerson did not know Henry Thoreau until after Thoreau had been some years out of college. Henry walked to Boston, eighteen miles, to hear one of Emerson's lectures, and walked home again in the night after the lecture was over. Emerson heard of it, and invited him to come to his house and hear the lectures read there, which he did. People used to say that Thoreau imitated Emerson, and Lowell has made this charge in his satire, "A Fable for Critics":

> There comes ——, for instance; to see him's rare sport,
> Tread in Emerson's tracks with legs painfully short.

I think there is nothing in it. Thoreau's style is certainly fresh and original. His tastes and thoughts are his own. His peculiarities of bearing and behavior came to him naturally from his ancestors of the isle of Guernsey.

I retained his friendship to his death. I have taken many a long walk with him. I used to go down to see him in the winter days in my vacations in his hut near Walden. He was capital company. He was a capital guide in the wood. He liked to take out the boys in his boat. He was fond of discoursing. I do not think he was vain. But he liked to do his thinking out loud, and expected that you should be an auditor rather than a companion.

I have heard Thoreau say in private a good many things which afterward appeared in his writings. One day when we were walking, he leaned his back against a rail fence and discoursed of the shortness of the time since the date fixed for the creation, measured by human lives. "Why," he said, "sixty old women like Nabby Kettle" (a very old woman in Concord), "taking hold of hands, would span the whole of it." He repeats this in one of his books, adding, "They would be but a small tea-party, but their gossip would make universal history."

Another man who was famous as a writer went to school, and afterward tended store in Concord in my childhood.

This was George H. Derby, better known as John Phœnix. He was also very fond of small boys. I remember his making me what I thought a wonderful and beautiful work of art, by taking a sheet of stiff paper of what was called elephant foolscap, and folding it into a very small square, and then with a penknife cutting out small figures of birds and beasts. When the sheet was opened again these were repeated all over the sheet, and made it appear like a piece of handsome lace.

He did not get along very well with his employer, who was a snug and avaricious person. He would go to Boston once a week to make his purchases, leaving Derby in charge of the store. Derby would lie down at full length on the counter, get a novel, and was then very unwilling to be disturbed to wait on customers. If a little girl came in with a tin kettle to get some molasses, he would say the molasses was all out, and they would have some more next week. So the employer found that some of his customers were a good deal annoyed.

Another rather famous writer who lived in Concord in my time was Mr. A. Bronson Alcott. He used to talk to the children in the Sunday-school, and occasionally would gather them together in an evening for a long discourse. I am ashamed to say that we thought Mr. Alcott rather stupid. He did not make any converts to his theories among the boys.

He once told us that it was wicked to eat animal food; that the animal had the same right to his life that we had to ours, and we had no right to destroy the lives of any of God's creatures for our own purposes. He lived only on vegetable food, as he told us. But he had on at the time a very comfortable pair of calfskin boots, and the boys could not reconcile his notion that it was wicked to kill animals to eat, with killing animals that he might wear their hides. When such inconsistencies were pointed out to him he gave a look of mild rebuke at the audacious offender, and went on with his discourse as if nothing had happened.

The people who do not think very much of Alcott ought to speak with a good deal of modesty when they remember how highly Emerson valued him, and how sure was Emerson's judgment; but certainly nobody will attribute to Alcott much of the logical faculty. Emerson told me once:

"I got together some people a little while ago to meet Alcott and to hear him converse. I wanted them to know what a rare fellow he was. But we did not get along very well. Poor Alcott had a hard time. Theodore Parker came all stuck full of knives. He wound himself round Alcott like an anaconda; you could hear poor Alcott's bones crunch."

Margaret Fuller used to visit Concord a good deal, and at one time boarded in the village for several months.

She was very peculiar in her ways, and made people whom she did not like feel very uncomfortable in her presence. She was not generally popular, although the persons who knew her best valued her genius highly. But old Doctor Bartlett, a very excellent and kind old doctor, though rather gruff in manner, could not abide her.

About midnight one very dark, stormy night the doctor was called out of bed by a sharp knocking at the door. He got up and put his head out of the window, and said, "Who's there? What do you want?" He was answered by a voice in the darkness below, "Doctor, how much camphire can anybody take by mistake without its killing them?" To which the reply was, "Who's taken it?" And the answer was, "Margaret Fuller." The doctor answered, in great wrath, as he slammed down the window, and returned to bed: "A peck."

William Ellery Channing, the poet, was a constant visitor of my sister, and later of my brother Edward. He was a moody and solitary person, except in the company of a few close friends who testified to the charming and delightful quality of his companionship. I suppose his poems will outlast a great many greater reputations. But they will always find very few readers in any generation.

Channing visited my elder sister almost every day or evening for a good while, but rarely remained more than two or three minutes if he found anybody else in the room.

George William Curtis, afterward the famous orator, and his brother, Burrill, occupied for a year or two a small farmhouse or hut, with one or two rooms in it, in Concord, on the Lincoln road. They had been at Brook Farm and came to Concord, I suppose attracted by Emerson. They came to my father's house during their stay there every afternoon, and their call was as much a regular incident of the day as any stated meal. Each of them was a boy of a very pleasant and delightful nature. I think if George Curtis had dwelt almost anywhere but in New York city, he would have been a very powerful influence in the public life of his generation. But he did not find any congenial associates in the men in New York who had any capacity to effect much good. His pure and lofty counsel fell unheeded upon the ears of his near neighbors, and the people of Massachusetts did not listen very patiently to lectures on political purity or reform in civil service from New York city.

I never maintained any considerable intimacy with Curtis, although I have a few letters from him, expressing his regard for some of my kindred or his interest and sympathy in something I had said or done. These I value exceedingly. One of the very last articles he wrote for *Harper's Weekly*, written just before his death, contains a far too kind estimate of my public service.

The Concord quality has come down with its people from the first settlement. The town was founded by Peter Bulkeley. He was a clergyman at Odell in Bedfordshire, where the church over which he was settled is still standing. He was a gentleman of good family and of a considerable estate which he spent for the benefit of the people whom he led into the wilderness. He encountered the hostility of Laud and, to use the phrase of that time, was "silenced for nonconformity." With Major Simon Willard, he made a bargain with the Indians, just to both parties, and with which both parties were perfectly satisfied, which rendered the name of Concord so appropriate, although in fact the name was given to the settlement before the company left Boston. That pulpit was occupied by Bulkeley and his descendants either by blood or marriage, from 1635 to 1696; from 1738 to 1841; and from 1882 to 1893.

I was able some forty years ago to settle in Concord a matter which had puzzled English historians, as to the legitimacy of the famous statesman and Chief Justice, Oliver St. John. Lord Campbell, in his "Lives of the Chief Justices," says: "It is a curious circumstance that there should be a dispute about the parentage of such a distinguished individual, who flourished so recently. Lord Clarendon, who knew him intimately from his youth, who practised with him in the Court of King's Bench, who sat in the House of Commons with him, and who was both associated with him and opposed to him in party strife, repeatedly represents him as illegitimate; and states that he was 'a natural son of the house of Bolingbroke.' Lord Bacon's account of his origin is equivocal—calling him 'a gentleman as it seems of an ancient house and name.' By genealogists and heralds a legitimate pedigree is assigned to him, deducing his descent in the right male line from William St. John, who came in with the Conqueror; but some of them describe him as the son of Sir John St. John, of Lydiard Tregose in Wiltshire, and others as the son of Oliver St. John of Cagshoe in Bedfordshire, and they differ equally respecting his mother. Lord Clarendon could hardly be mistaken on such a point, and I cannot help suspecting that the contrary assertions proceed from a desire to remove the bar sinister from the shield of a Chief Justice."

Lord Campbell has had diligent search made in the archives of Oxford and Lincoln's Inn, but does not find anything to change his opinion.

Fortunately we are able to settle the question about which Lord Campbell and Lord Bacon and Lord Clarendon were misled, in Old Concord. Peter Bulkeley was the uncle of Oliver St. John. He speaks of him in his will, and leaves him his Bible. Bulkeley's Gospel-Covenant, a book the substance of which was originally preached to his congregation, is dedicated to Oliver St. John. In the Epistle Dedicatory, he speaks of the pious and godly lives of St. John's parents, and alludes to the dying words of St. John's father as something which he and St. John had heard, but which was not known to other men. "I speak a mystery to others but not unto your Lordship."

So it is quite clear that St. John could not have been born out of wedlock, and the son of a man who had seduced the sister of this eminent and pious clergyman.

In Noble's "Memoirs of the Cromwell Family," published about seventy-five years after the death of St. John, he is said to be the son of Oliver St. John of Cagshoe in Bedfordshire.

When the "Lives of the Chief Justices" was first published, I wrote to Lord Campbell, telling him these facts, and received the following letter in reply:

LONDON, Jany 9th, 1861.
Sir

I thank you very sincerely for your interesting letter of December 13th, respecting Lord Chief Justice St. John.

I think you establish his legitimacy quite satisfactorily and in any future edition of my Lives of the Chief Justices I shall certainly avail myself of your researches.

I have the honor to be
Sir
Your obliged and obedient Servant
CAMPBELL.

The Honorable
Geo. F. Hoar.

Something of Bulkeley's character may be gathered from this extract from the Gospel-Covenant, which Mr. Emerson, who was his descendant, loved to quote. Think of these words, uttered to his little congregation in the wilderness; the only company of white men in the Western Hemisphere who dwelt away from tide-water:

"And for ourselves, the people of New England, wee should in a speciall manner, labour to shine forth in holinesse above other people; we have that plenty and abundance of ordinances and meanes of grace as few people enjoy the like; wee are as a City set upon a hill, in the open view of all the earth, the eyes of the world are upon us, because wee professe ourselves to be a people in Covenant with God, and therefore not only the Lord our God, with whom we have made Covenant, but heaven and earth, Angels and men, that are witnesses of our profession, will cry shame upon us, if we walk contrary to the Covenant which we have professed to walk in; if we open the mouths of men against our profession, by reason of the scandalousnesse of our lives, wee (of all men) shall have the greater sinne.

"To conclude, let us study so to walk, that this may be our excellency and dignity among the Nations of the world, among which we live; That they may be constrained to say of us, onely this people is wise, an holy and blessed people: that all that see us, may see and know that the name of the Lord is called upon us: and that we are the seed which the Lord hath blessed. Deut. 28. 10 Esay. 61. 9. There is no people but will strive to excell in something: what can we excell in if not in holinesse? If we look to number, we are the fewest; If to strength, we are the weakest; If to wealth and riches, we are the poorest of all the people of God throughout the whole world, we cannot excell (nor so much as equall) other people in these things; and if we come short in grace and holiness too, we are the most despicable people under heaven; our worldy dignitie is gone, if we lose the glory of grace too, then is the glory wholly departed from our Israel, and we are become vile; strive we therefore herein to excell, and suffer not this crown to be taken away from us: Be we an holy people, so shall we be honorable before God and precious in the eyes of his Saints."

To these eminent Concord authors should be added the name of William S. Robinson. He was one of the brightest and wittiest men of his time. He very seldom had praise for anybody, although for a few of his old Anti-Slavery friends he had a huge liking. When I was a little boy he was in a newspaper office in Concord, where he got most of his education. Afterward he was associated with William

Schouler in editing the Lowell *Courier,* a Whig paper. When Schouler became editor of the *Atlas,* Robinson succeeded to the paper. But when the Free Soil movement came in, he would not flinch or abate a jot in his radical Anti-Slavery principles, which were not very agreeable to the proprietors of the cotton mills in Lowell, who depended both for their material and their market largely upon the South. Sumner described their alliance with their Southern customers as an alliance between the Lords of the Loom and the Lords of the Lash. So Robinson was compelled to give up his paper, in doing which he voluntarily embraced poverty instead of a certain and lucrative employment. He started an Anti-Slavery weekly paper in Lowell known as the Lowell *American.* That afforded him a bare and difficult living for a few years. After the Anti-Slavery people got into power he was made Clerk of the Massachusetts House of Representatives. Then he began to write his famous letters to the Springfield *Republican,* which he signed Warrington. They were full of wit and wisdom and displayed great knowledge of the best English literature. He made many enemies and finally, by a concert among them, was turned out of office. He lost his health not long after, and died prematurely.

He was quite unsparing in his attacks on anybody who offended him, or against whom he took a dislike; and he seemed to dislike everybody whom he did not know. It was said of him that, like the rain of Heaven, he "fell alike on the just and on the unjust." He attacked some of the most venerable and worthy citizens of the Commonwealth without any apparent reason. He used to call Chief Justice Chapman, one of the worthiest and kindest of men, Chief Justice Wheelgrease. He had a controversy in his paper of long standing with a man named Piper, a pompous and self-important little personage, who edited the Fitchburg *Reveille.* That was a Whig paper which circulated in the country towns where Robinson's paper was chiefly taken. He made poor Piper's life unhappy. One of the issues of his paper contained a life of Piper. It begun by saying that Piper began life as the driver of a fish-cart in Marblehead, and that he was discharged by his employer on account of the diffuseness of his style. He quoted with great effect on Otis P. Lord the toast given by the Court Jester of Archbishop Laud's time: "Great Laud be to God, and Little Lord to the Devil."

When he was clerk of the House of Representatives there was a story in the newspapers that he was preparing a treatise on Parliamentary law. He published a letter denying the statement. But he added, that if he did write such a treatise, he should sum it up in one sentence: "Never have an ass in the chair."

I was associated with him one day on the Committee on Resolutions of the Republican State Convention, held in Worcester. The Committee went over to my office to consult. While we were talking together Robinson broke out with his accustomed objurgations levelled at several very worthy and excellent men. I said: "William, it is fortunate you did not live in the Revolutionary time. How you would have hated General Washington." He replied, with a smile which indicated the gratification he would have had if he could have got at him: "He was an old humbug, wasn't he?"

But Robinson was always on the righteous side of any question involving righteousness. He was kind, generous, absolutely disinterested, and a great and beneficent power in the Commonwealth.

CHAPTER VI

FARM AND SCHOOL

I SPENT my life in Concord until I entered college except one year when I lived on a farm in Lincoln. There I had an opportunity to see at its best the character of the New England farmer, a character which has impressed itself so strongly and so beneficently on our history. Deacon James Farrar, for whom I worked, was, I believe, the fifth in descent from George Farrar, one of the founders of the town of Lincoln. All these generations dwelt on the same farm and under the same roof. An ancient forest came to a point not far from the house. That, with a large river meadow and some fertile upland fields, made up the farm. In every generation one or more of the family had gone to college and had become eminent in professional life, while one of them had stayed at home and carried on the farm. An uncle of the Deacon with whom I lived was Timothy Farrar of New Ipswich, an eminent judge who died considerably more than a hundred years old, and who was the oldest graduate of Harvard. Deacon James's own brother was Professor John Farrar of Harvard, a famous mathematician in his day, thought by his pupils to be the most eloquent man of his time, although Webster and Everett and Channing were his cotemporaries. It was a healthy and simple life of plain living and high thinking. But I think I got more good out of it in learning how the best intelligence of the State of Massachusetts was likely to judge of the questions of morals and duty than I got afterward from my four years in college. Two of the Deacon's sons succeeded him on the farm. One was his successor in his office in the church. Another son, George Farrar, graduated at Amherst where he was cotemporary with Dr. Storrs and Henry Ward Beecher. He died a few years after his admission to the

Bar. But he had already given proof that he would, if he had lived, have taken rank among the foremost at the Bar in Massachusetts.

Before entering college I was for about six months a pupil of Mrs. Sarah Ripley of Waltham. She removed to Concord with her husband afterward. She was one of the most wonderful scholars of her time, or indeed of any time. President Everett said she could fill any professor's chair at Harvard. She was an admirable mathematician. She read the "Mécanique Céleste" of Laplace in the original without the aid of Dr. Bowditch's translation. She was a fine German and Italian scholar. She had a great fondness for Greek literature, especially for Plato and Æschylus. She was an accomplished naturalist. She was simple as a child, an admirable wife and mother, performing perfectly all the commonest duties of the household. The authorities of Harvard used to send boys to her who were rusticated for some offence. She would keep them along in all their studies, in most cases better instructed than they would have been if they had stayed in Cambridge. I remember her now with the strongest feeling of reverence, affection and gratitude. In that I say what every other pupil of hers would say. I do not think she ever knew how much her boys loved her.

In 1876 the Directors of the Centennial Exposition at Philadelphia took steps to have the lives of three or four of the foremost women of the century that had just passed written as the best examples of American womanhood for our first century. Mrs. Schuyler was selected from New York, Mrs. Livermore from New Hampshire, and Mrs. Randolph from Virginia. Mrs. Ripley was chosen as the representative of Massachusetts. If anybody doubt the capacity of the intellect of woman to rival that of man in any calling requiring the highest intellectual capacity, without in the least forfeiting any quality of a delicate womanhood, let him read the "Life of Sarah Ripley."

After her death Mr. Emerson wrote the following notice of her. It is not found in his collected works.

"Died in Concord, Massachusetts, on the 26th of July, 1867, Mrs. Sarah Alden Ripley, aged seventy-four years. The death of this lady, widely known and beloved, will be sincerely deplored by many persons scattered in distant parts of the country, who have known her rare accomplishments and the singular loveliness of her character. A lineal descendant of the first governor of Plymouth Colony, she was happily born and bred. Her father, Gamaliel Bradford, was a sea-captain of marked ability, with heroic traits which old men will still remember, and though a man of action yet adding a taste for letters. Her brothers, younger than herself, were scholars, but her own taste for study was even more decided. At a time when perhaps no other young woman read Greek, she acquired the language with ease and read Plato,—adding soon the advantage of German commentators.

"After her marriage, when her husband, the well-known clergyman of Waltham, received boys in his house to be fitted for college, she assumed the advanced instruction in Greek and Latin, and did not fail to turn it to account by extending her studies in both languages. It soon happened that students from Cambridge were put under her private instruction and oversight. If the young men shared her delight in the book, she was interested at once to lead them to higher steps and more difficult but not less engaging authors, and they soon learned to prize the new world of thought and history thus opened. Her best pupils became her lasting friends. She became one of the best Greek scholars in the country, and continued, in her latest years, the habit of reading Homer, the tragedians, and Plato. But her studies took a wide range in mathematics, in natural philosophy, in psychology, in theology, as well as in ancient and modern literature. She had always a keen ear open to whatever new facts astronomy, chemistry, of the theories of light and heat had to furnish. Any knowledge, all knowledge, was welcome. Her stores increased day by day. She was absolutely without pedantry. Nobody ever heard of her learning until a necessity came for its use, and then nothing could be more simple than her solution of the problem proposed to her. The most intellectual gladly conversed with one whose knowledge, however rich and varied, was always with her only the means of new acquisition. Meantime her mind was purely receptive. She had no ambition to propound a theory, or to write her own name on any book, or plant, or opinion. Her delight in books was not tainted by any wish to shine, or any appetite for praise or influence. She seldom and unwillingly used a pen, and only for necessity or affection.

"But this wide and successful study was, during all the hours of middle life, only the work of hours stolen from sleep, or was combined with some household task which occupied the hands and left the eyes free. She was faithful to all the duties of wife and mother in a well-ordered and eminently hospitable household, wherein she was dearly loved, and where

'her heart
Life's lowliest duties on itself did lay.'

She was not only the most amiable, but the tenderest of women, wholly sincere, thoughtful for others, and, though careless of appearances, submitting with docility to the better arrangements with which her children or friends insisted on supplementing her own negligence of dress; for her own part indulging her children in the greatest freedom, assured that their own reflection, as it opened, would supply all needed checks. She was absolutely without appetite for luxury, or display, or praise, or influence, with entire indifference to trifles. Not long before her marriage, one of her intimate friends in the city, whose family were removing, proposed to her to go with her to the new house, and, taking some articles in her own hand, by way of trial artfully put into her hand a broom, whilst she kept her in free conversation on some speculative points, and this she faithfully carried across Boston Common, from Summer Street to Hancock Street, without hesitation or remark.

"Though entirely domestic in her habit and inclination, she was everywhere a welcome visitor, and a favorite of society, when she rarely entered it. The elegance of her tastes recommended her to the elegant, who were swift to distinguish her as they found her simple manners faultless. With her singular simplicity and purity, such as society could not spoil, nor much affect, she was only entertained by it, and really went into it as children into a theatre,—to be diverted,—while her ready sympathy enjoyed whatever beauty of person, manners, or ornament it had to show. If there was conversation, if there were thought or learning, her interest was commanded, and she gave herself up to the happiness of the hour.

"As she advanced in life, her personal beauty, not remarked in her youth, drew the notice of all, and age brought no fault but the brief decay and eclipse of her intellectual powers."

In 1833, three years before Emerson wrote "Nature," Mrs. Ripley said of him: "We regard him still, more than ever, as the apostle of the Eternal Reason. We do not like to hear the crows, as Pindar says, caw at the bird of Jove."*

* On the stone which marks Mrs. Ripley's grave in the beautiful cemetery at Concord, her children placed an inscription containing a part of the passage with which Tacitus ends his Life of Agricola. "It was a passage which was specially dear to her," says her biographer; "many of her friends will recall the fine glow of feeling with which she read or quoted it; and to these it will always be associated with her memory. I cannot better close this imperfect sketch of her life than by giving the whole of it: of no one was it ever more worthily spoken than of her. The words enclosed in brackets are those which are on her gravestone."

"Si quis piorum manibus locus; si, ut sapientibus placet, non cum corpore exstinguuntur magnae animae; (placide quiescas, nosque, domum tuam, ab infirmo desiderio et mulieribus lamentis ad contemplationem virtutum tuarum voces, quas neque lugeri neque plangi fas est: admiratione te potius, temporalibus laudibus, et, si natura suppedit, similitudine decoremus.) Is verus honos, ea conjunctissimi cujusque pietas. Id filiae quoque uxorique praeceperim, sic patris, sic mariti memoriam venerari, ut omnia facta dictaque ejus secum revolvant; famamque ac figuram animi magis quam corporis complectantur: non quia intercedendum putem imaginibus, quae marmore aut aere finguntur, sed ut vultus hominum, ita simulacra vultus imbecilla ac mortalia sunt, forma mentis aeterna, quam tenere et exprimere non per alienam materiam et artem, sed tuis ipse moribus possis. Quidquid ex Agricola amavimus, quidquid mirati sumus, manet mansurumque est in animis hominum, in aeternitate temporum, fama rerum. Nam multos veterum, velut inglorios et ignobiles oblivio obruet: Agricola posteritati narratus et superstes erit."

CHAPTER VII
HARVARD SIXTY YEARS AGO

I DO not think Harvard College had changed very much when I entered it on my sixteenth birthday in the year 1842 either in manners, character of students or teachers, or the course of instruction, for nearly a century. There were some elementary lectures and recitations in astronomy and mechanics. There was a short course of lectures on chemistry, accompanied by exhibiting a few experiments. But the students had no opportunity for laboratory work. There was a delightful course of instruction from Dr. Walker in ethics and metaphysics. The college had rejected the old Calvinistic creed of New England and substituted in its stead the strict Unitarianism of Dr. Ware and Andrews Norton,—a creed in its substance hardly more tolerant or liberal than that which it had supplanted. There was also some instruction in modern languages,—German, French and Italian,—all of very slight value. But the substance of the instruction consisted in learning to translate rather easy Latin and Greek, writing Latin, and courses in algebra and geometry not very far advanced.

The conditions of admission were quite easy. They were such as a boy of fourteen of good capacity, who could read and write the English language and had gone through some simple book of arithmetic, could easily master in two years. There were three or four schools where the boys were pretty well fitted, so that they could translate Cicero and Virgil, Nepos and Sallust and Cæsar and Xenophon and Homer. The Boston Latin School, the Roxbury Latin School, Phillips Academy at Exeter and Phillips Academy at Andover and Mrs. Ripley's school at Waltham were the best schools for this purpose. The boys from the Boston Latin School generally took their places at the head of the class when they entered. Next came the best scholars from the other schools I have named. But the bulk of the pupils were very poorly fitted.

There was, as it seems to me in looking back, little instruction of much value. The good scholars and the bad went to the recitation together. The good ones lost the hour, and the poor scholars got the benefit of hearing the good ones recite. Their mistakes were corrected by the professor. They handed in written exercises in Latin and Greek which were examined by the instructor and the faults corrected, and returned. There were, during the last three years, declamations once a month, where the boy recited some piece of prose or poetry in the presence of the class, but got very little instruction or criticism from the professor. Then, in the last three years, English themes were required. The subjects were given out by Professor Channing, himself a most accomplished and admirable scholar in his line. He seemed to choose his subjects with a view of taxing the ingenuity of the boy to find anything to say about them instead of taking something which the boy knew about and devoting himself to improve his English style in expressing his thought. Channing was a good critic. His published lectures on rhetoric and oratory, now almost wholly forgotten, remind one of Matthew Arnold in their delicate and discriminating touch. He had a face and figure something like that of Punch in the frontispiece of that magazine. His method was to take the themes which the boys handed in one week, look them over himself, then, a week after, meet the class, call the boys in succession to sit down in a chair by the side of his table, read out passages from the theme, and ridicule them before the others. It was a terrible ordeal for a bashful and awkward boy. Those of a more robust nature, or whose performance had nothing ridiculous in it, profited by the discipline. But it certainly took all the starch and courage out of me. I never sat down to write my theme without fancying that grinning and scornful countenance looking at my work. So I used to write as few sentences as I thought would answer so that I should not be punished for failure to bring in any theme at all, and never attempted to do my best.

But the Faculty themselves were certainly an assemblage of very able men. Making all the allowance for the point of view, and that I was then a youth looking at my elders who had become famous, and that I am now looking as an old man at young men, I still think there can be no comparison between the college administrators of fifty years ago and those of to-day. It was then the policy of the college to call into its service great men who had achieved eminent distinction in the world without. It is now its policy to select for its service promising youth, in the hope that they will become great. Perhaps the last method is the best where it succeeds. But the effect of failure is most mischievous. Presidents Quincy, Everett, Walker and Sparks administered in succession the office of President during my connection with the Academic Department and the Law School, although Dr. Walker's inauguration was not until later. Each of them in his own way was among the first men of his time. Quincy had been an eminent statesman, a famous orator, and a most successful mayor of Boston. Edward Everett had been in his early youth one of the most famous pulpit orators of the country, afterward a distinguished Member of Congress, Governor of the Commonwealth, Minister to England, and Senator of the United States. He was a consummate orator, on whose lips thousands and thousands of his countrymen had hung entranced. He was, what is less generally remembered now, perhaps the ablest and most accomplished diplomatist ever in the public service of the United States. Jared Sparks was a profound student of history, somewhat dull as a narrator, but of unerring historic judgment. I suppose he would be placed by all our writers of history with great unanimity at the head of American historic investigators. James Walker was a great preacher and a profound thinker. In the judgment of his hearers, young and old, he was probably deemed nearly or quite the foremost of American preachers.

That I may not be supposed to imply any disparagement of the present accomplished head of Harvard, let me say that while each of the men I have named had done a great work in life and achieved a great fame before he came to the Presidency, President Eliot has, in my opinion, achieved an equal fame and performed an equal work since he came to it.

A like policy prevailed in those days in the choice of instructors in the Law School. Judge Story, the senior professor, died just before I graduated from the College. His fame as a jurist was known throughout Europe. He was undoubtedly the most learned judge in the United States. Chief Justice Marshall and Chief Justice Shaw of Massachusetts doubtless excelled him in intellectual vigor. Chancellor Kent rivalled him as a writer upon law. But he had no other rival among judges or commentators in this country,—few anywhere. He was unquestionably, at the time of his death, the most famous teacher of law in the civilized world. His associate professor, Greenleaf, was an admirable lawyer, who, before he went to Harvard, had had a great practice in Maine, and made some good arguments in the Supreme Court of the United States. Judge Story was succeeded by Chief Justice Joel Parker of New Hampshire, a very eminent jurist, who was saturated with the old learning of special pleading and real property. He would have been a fit associate for Coke or Saunders, and would have held his own anywhere with either.

There was nothing in the teaching of Latin or Greek to inspire the student with any love of Greek or Latin literature. The professor never pointed out its beauties or illustrated the text in any way. The students, in succession, were called upon to construe a few lines, reading one or two Greek words and then giving their English equivalents. The time of the good scholar was taken up in hearing the recitation of the poor scholar and so very largely wasted. I had four or five persons in my class who became afterward eminent classical scholars. I do not believe that when we graduated there were more than four men in the class who could write a decent Latin sentence without the laborious use of grammar and dictionary. I doubt whether there was more than one, certainly there were not more than three, who could do the same thing in Greek. I do not suppose there was a man in the class who could have spoken either language with ease.

Yet, somehow, the graduates of Harvard got a good intellectual training from the University. The rough country boy, if he had it in him, came out at his graduation a gentleman in behavior and in character. He was able to take hold of life with great vigor. The average age of graduation I suppose was twenty. Not more than three years were spent in studying a profession. In some few cases, the graduate got a little money by teaching for a year. But the graduates of Harvard College and Harvard Law School were apt to take quite rapidly the high places of the profession. That was true then much more than it is now.

There were many persons who graduated before my time or shortly afterward whose high place in the public life of the Commonwealth and of the country was assured before they were thirty years old. Edward Everett was called to the pulpit of Brattle Street Church at the age of nineteen. He succeeded in that pulpit Joseph Stevens Buckminster, who was himself settled over that important parish at the age of twenty-one and was a wonderful pulpit orator. Edward Everett preached a sermon when he was twenty-four years old before a large audience in the Representatives Chamber at Washington which was heard with breathless silence. Rufus King said it was the best sermon he ever heard, and Harrison Gray Otis was affected to tears. Benjamin R. Curtis was admitted to the bar in Boston when he was twenty-two years old and shortly after was retained in a very important case. It is said that an old deputy sheriff, who had just heard Curtis's opening argument, was met in the street and asked if anything was going on in court. "Going on?" was the reply. "There's a young chap named Curtis up there has just opened a case so all Hell can't close it." I suppose Edward Everett Hale and James Freeman Clarke were almost as famous in the pulpit when they were twenty-five or twenty-six years old as they ever were afterward. I might extend the catalogue indefinitely. Where is there to be found to-day at the New England bar or in the New England pulpit a man under thirty of whom it can be said that his place among the great men of his profession is assured? It will not do to say in answer to this that it takes a greater man in this generation to fill such a place than it took in other days. That is not true. The men of those generations have left their work behind them. It does not suffer in comparison with that of their successors. There was something in the college training of that day, imperfect as were its instruments, and slender as were its resources, from which more intellectual strength in the pupil was begotten than there is in the college training of the present generation. I will not undertake to account for it. But I think it was due in large part to the personality of the instructors. A youth who contemplated with a near and intimate knowledge the large manhood of Josiah Quincy; who listened to the eloquence of James Walker, or heard his expositions of the principal systems of ethics or metaphysics; or who sat at the feet of Judge Story, as he poured forth the lessons of jurisprudence in a clear and inexhaustible stream, caught an inspiration which transfigured the very soul of the pupil.

Josiah Quincy, "old Quin" as we loved to call him, was a very simple and a very high character. He was born in Boston, February 4, 1772, just before the Revolutionary War. It was said, I have no doubt truly, that the nurse who attended his mother at his birth went from that house to the wife of Copley, the painter, when her son, Lord Lyndhurst, was born. Copley was a Tory, though a patriot and an ardent lover of his country. His departure from Boston made Lord Lyndhurst an Englishman. Quincy entered early into politics. He was a candidate for Congress in the last century before he was twenty-five years old. I heard him say once that the Democrats called for a cradle to rock the Federal candidate. He was a good type of the old Massachusetts Federalist,—brave, manly, sincere, of a broad and courageous statesmanship, but distrustful of the people and not understanding their temper. He made some very powerful speeches in the House of Representatives, attacking the greed and office-seeking of that time. His eloquence was something of the style of the famous Irish orators. One of his passages describing the office-seekers tumbling over each other like pigs to a trough will be long remembered. He hated Jefferson and moved his impeachment in the House of Representatives,—a motion for which he got no vote but his own. He retired disgusted from National public life, became Mayor of Boston, an office which he filled with much distinction, and then was called to the Presidency of Harvard, mainly because of his business capacity. The finances of the University were then in a sad condition. He put them on an excellent footing. He was very fond of the boys and they of him, although he was rough and hasty in his manners. While I was in college (although I happened to be at home that day and did not see the affair) some of the boys had got into some serious rows in Boston one Saturday. They had undertaken to wear the Oxford cap and gown. They were ridiculed by the populace in Boston, and a good many fights were the consequence. They were driven from the streets, and in the afternoon a lot of roughs took hold of a long rope, as if they belonged to an engine company, ran out to Cambridge across the bridge, and proposed to attack the college buildings. Old Quin gathered the students together at the gate and told the boys to keep within the yard and not to attack anybody unless they were attacked, but to permit none of those men to come within the gate. The old fellow was ready to head the students and a fight was expected. But the police gathered, and finally the Boston roughs were persuaded to depart in peace.

The old gentleman's heart always warmed to the son of an old Federalist. I had to visit his study a good many times, I regret to say, to receive some well-deserved admonitions. But the interview always ended in an inquiry after my father and some jolly, or at least kindly utterance about myself. One of my classmates gave an account in rhyme of one of these interviews which I wish I could repeat. I can only remember two lines:

> Quin deigned a grin, perforce,
> And Hoar a roar, of course.

He died in 1864 at the age of ninety-two, preserving to the last his mental vigor and his ardent interest in public affairs. During the darkest period of the War he never lost his hope or faith. He fell on the ice and broke his hip a little while before his death. He was treated by the somewhat savage method of the surgery of the time. Dr. George E. Ellis, from whom I had the story, went to see him one day at his house on Park Street and found the old man lying on his bed with a weight hanging from his foot, which projected over the bed, to keep the bones in their place and the muscles from contracting. He said to Mr. Quincy's daughter: "You have been shut up here a long time. Now go and take a walk round the Common and let me stay with your father." Miss Quincy went out and the old man kept Dr. Ellis so full of interest by his cheerful and lively talk that he never once thought to ask him how he was getting along. When Miss Quincy returned, he took his leave and had got downstairs when the omission occurred to him. He went back to the chamber and said to Mr. Quincy: "I forgot to ask you how your leg is." The old fellow brought his hand down with a slap upon the limb and said: "Damn the leg. I want to see this business settled."

When Felton was inaugurated as President, Gov. Banks in performing his part of the ceremony of presenting the charter and the keys to the new officer alluded in his somewhat grandiloquent way to four of Felton's predecessors, Everett, Sparks, Walker and Quincy, who were upon the stage. Speaking of Quincy he said: "He would be reckoned among honorable men, though their number were reduced to that of the mouths of the Nile or the gates of Thebes."

Felton, the Greek professor, was the heartiest and jolliest of men. He was certainly one of the best examples of a fully rounded scholarship which this country or perhaps any country ever produced. He gave before the Lowell Institute a course of lectures on Greece Ancient and Modern, into which is compressed learning enough to fill a large encyclopædia. He also edited two or three Greek plays and an edition of Homer, which was extensively used as a text-book.

Professor Felton was a very impulsive man, though of great dignity and propriety in his general bearing. He had some theories of his own as to the matter of pure and correct English and was very much disgusted if anybody transgressed them. His brother, John Felton, of the class of 1847, afterward the foremost lawyer on the Pacific Coast, was altogether the best and most brilliant scholar in his class. He was reported to the Faculty just before his graduation for the offence of swearing in the College Yard, an offence which was punished by what was called a public admonition which involved a considerable loss of rank and a letter to the parent or guardian of the offender. The Faculty, in consideration of John Felton's excellent scholarship, instead of the ordinary punishment directed that Professor Felton should admonish his brother of his fault in private. The professor was some eighteen or twenty years the elder and was respected by his brother rather as a father than as a brother. He sent for John to his study and told him the nature of the complaint, and proceeded: "I cannot tell you how mortified I am that my brother, in whose character and scholarship I had taken so much pride, who stood so high in his class, should have been reported to the Faculty for this vulgar and wicked offence." John said, with great contrition: "I am exceedingly sorry. It was under circumstances of great provocation. I have never been guilty of such a thing before. I never in my life have been addicted to profanity." "Damnation, John," interposed the professor, "how often have I told you the word is profaneness and not profanity?" It is needless to say that the sermon ended at that point.

But the most interesting single figure in the Harvard Faculty in my day was James Walker. He was a man of quiet dignity, and of modest bearing. He appeared rather awkward when he walked, as if there were some want of strength in the feet or ankles. He heard the classes in my time in Jouffroy and Cousin and in Butler's "Analogy." His method was to require the boy to get into his mind some account of a system or special course of reasoning of the author and to state it at considerable length in his own language. I think all that I got out of college that was of much use to me came from this training in James Walker's recitation-room, except that I think I got some capacity for cross-examining witnesses which was very useful to me afterward from reading Plato's dialogues and getting familiar with Socrates's method of reducing a sophist ad absurdum. But Dr. Walker's throne was the pulpit of the College Chapel. He used to preach four Sundays in each of the two terms. He had a beautiful head, a deep but clear voice, a deliberate manner and a power of emphasizing his weighty thoughts which I have never seen surpassed by any orator. He had a small and beautiful hand of which it is said, though such a thing is hard to believe of him, he was somewhat vain. But his only gesture was to bring very infrequently the back of his hand down upon the cushion of the pulpit before him. The ticking of the clock in the College Chapel was inaudible when the chapel was empty. But it ticked out clear and loud upon the strained ears of the auditors who were waiting in the pauses of his sentences. I can remember his sermons now. They are admirable to read, although, like other eloquence, their life and spirit is lost without the effect of speech. There was one on the text, "Thou shalt say no," which no hearer, I venture to say, ever forgot to the day of his death. There was another, on the control of the thoughts, from the text, "Leading into captivity every thought." This made a deep impression on the students. I seem to hear the tones of his voice now. The Doctor described with a terrific effect the thinking over in imagination scenes of vice by the youth who seemed to the world outside to fall suddenly from virtue. He said there was no such thing as a sudden fall from virtue. The scene had been enacted in thought and the man had become rotten before the time of the outward act.

"Sometimes the novice in crime thinks himself ready to act when he is not; as appears from his hesitancy and reluctance when the moment for action arrives. If, however, this unexpected recoil of his nature does not induce him to change his purpose altogether, he knows but too well how to supply the defect in his training for sin. If we could look into his heart, we should find him at his accursed rehearsals again. A few more lessons, and the blush and the shudder will pass away, never to return."

This is tame enough in the recital. But I dare say there are old men who will read these pages to whom it will bring back the never-forgotten scenes of more than fifty years ago. The Doctor had a great gift of sententious speech, not only in his written discourses, but in his ordinary conversation or his instruction from the professor's chair. He was speaking one day of Combe and of something disrespectful he had said about the English metaphysicians. "What does Mr. Combe mean?" said the Doctor. "I make no apology for the English metaphysicians. They have made their mistakes. They have their shortcomings. But they are surely entitled to the common privilege of Englishmen—to be judged by their peers." He was speaking one day of some rulers who had tried to check the rising tide of some reform by persecuting its leaders. "Fools!" said the Doctor. "They thought if they could but wring the neck of the crowing cock it would never be day."

One of the delightful characters and humorists connected with Harvard was Evangelinus Apostolides Sophocles, tutor in Greek. He was a native of Thessaly, born near Mount Pelion and educated in the convent of the Greek Church on Mount Sinai. It is said, although such instances are rare, that he was of the purest Greek blood. At any rate, his face and head were of the Greek type. He was a man of wonderful learning,—I dare say the best Greek scholar of his generation, whether in Europe or America. He was a very simple-hearted person in dealing with ordinary affairs. But his conversation and his instruction in the class-room were full of wit and sense. He used to tell a story, whether of his father or his grandfather I am not sure, that one night very late he was sitting in his warehouse alone when two men entered and told him they were come to kill him. He asked them why they wished to kill him, and they told him that they had been hired by an enemy of his. "Well," said the old man, "what are you to be paid?" They told him the sum. He said: "I will give you twice as much to kill him." Accordingly they accepted the offer and went away, leaving the old fellow alive, kept their bargain with him and killed his enemy.

Sophocles had a great love of little children and a curious love of chickens which he treated as pets and liked to tame and to play with, squatting down on the ground among them as if he were a rooster himself. It is said that during his last sickness the doctor directed that he should have chicken broth. He indignantly rejected it, and declared he would not eat a creature that he loved.

In what I have said about Professor Channing I am describing him and his method of instruction faithfully as it seemed to me at the time. It is quite possible I may be wrong. I am sure that the better scholars and the youths who were much better in every way than I was at that time of my life who were his pupils will dissent from my opinion and be shocked at what I say. So it is quite likely that I am in fault and not he. I have read again lately his book on Rhetoric and Oratory since what I said a little while ago was dedicated, and I wish to reaffirm my high opinion of the book. For fresh, racy and correct style, for clear perception and exquisite literary taste, it is one of the best books on the subject, as it is one of the best books on any subject ever written by an American. His mistake was, in large measure, the prevalent mistake of the College in his time,—the use of ridicule and severity instead of sympathy as a means of correcting the faults incident to youth. It was the fault of the College, both of instructors and of the students. Dr. Walker in one of his public addresses speaks with commendation of "the storm of merciless ridicule" which overwhelms young men who are addicted to certain errors which he is criticising.

The Latin professor was Charles Beck, Ph.D. He was a native of Heidelberg. He had been compelled to leave Prussia because of his love of liberty. He had studied theology, and had published a treatise on gymnastics, in which he was accomplished. We read with him Terence and Plautus, the Medea of Seneca, Horace, and probably some Latin prose, which I have forgotten. He was a very learned Latin scholar. I do not know whether he cared anything about poetry or eloquence or the philosophy of the Roman authors or no. Certainly he did nothing to indicate to us that he had any such interest or to stimulate any such interest in his pupils. He was strict to harshness in dealing with his class. The only evidence of enthusiasm I ever witnessed in Dr. Beck was this: He brought into the classroom one day an old fat German with very dirty hands and a dirty shirt. He had a low forehead and a large head with coarse curling hair which looked as if it had not seen a comb or brush for a quarter of a century. We looked with amazement at this figure. He went out before the recitation was over. But Dr. Beck said to us: "This is Dr. —————, gentlemen. He is a most admiwable scholar." (This was the Doctor's pronunciation of the r.) "He has wead Cicewo through every year for nearly fifty years for the sake of settling some important questions. He has discovered that while necesse est may be used indifferently either with the accusative and infinitive, or with ut with the subjunctive, necesse ewat can only be used before ut with the subjunctive. I should think it well worth living for to have made that discovewy."

I suppose we all thought when we graduated that Dr. Beck was a man of harsh and cold nature. But I got acquainted with him later in life and found him one of the most genial and kind-hearted of men. He was a member of the Legislature. He was a Free Soiler and an Abolitionist, liberally contributing to the Sanitary Commission, and to all agencies for the benefit of the soldiers and the successful prosecution of the war.

He came vigorously to the support of Horace Mann in his famous controversy with Mr. Webster. Mann had vigorously attacked Webster, and Webster in return had spoken of Mann as one of that class of persons known among the Romans as Captatores Verborum, which he supposed to mean one of those nice persons who catch up other person's words for the sake of small criticism and fault-finding. Mr.

Mann replied that Webster was wrong in his Latin, and the words Captatores Verborum meant toad-eaters, or men who hang on the words of great men to praise and flatter them, of which he found some conspicuous modern examples among Webster's supporters. Professor Felton, the Greek professor, who was a staunch friend of Webster, attacked Mann and charged him with ignorance of Latin. But Dr. Beck came to the rescue, and his authority as a Latin scholar was generally conceded to outweigh that of Webster and Felton put together.

One of the most brilliant men among the Faculty was Professor Benjamin Peirce. Undoubtedly he was the foremost American mathematician of his time. He dwelt without a companion in the lofty domain of the higher mathematics.

A privacy of glorious light is thine.

He was afterward the head of the Coast Survey. He had little respect for pupils who had not a genius for mathematics, and paid little attention to them. He got out an edition of Peirce's Algebra while I was in college. He distributed the sheets among the students and would accept, instead of a successful recitation, the discovery of a misprint on its pages. The boys generally sadly neglected his department, which was made elective, I think, after the sophomore year. At the examinations, which were held by committees appointed by the Board of Overseers, he always gave to the pupil the same problem that had been given to him in the last preceding recitation. So the boys were prepared to make a decent appearance. He used to dress in a very peculiar fashion, wearing a queer little sack and striped trousers which made him look sometimes as if he were a salesman in a Jew clothing-store. He had a remarkably clear and piercing black eye. One night one of the students got into the belfry and attached a slender thread to the tongue of the bell, contrived to lock the door which led to the tower and carry off the key, then went to his room in the fourth story of Massachusetts Hall and began to toll the bell. The students and the Faculty and proctors gathered, but nobody could explain the mysterious ringing of the bell until Peirce came upon the scene. His sharp eye perceived the slender line and it was traced to the room where the roguish fellow who was doing the mischief thought himself secure. He was detected and punished.

Peirce gained great fame in the scientific world by his controversy with Leverrier. Leverrier, as is well known, discovered some perturbations in the movement of the planet Herschel, now more commonly called Uranus, which were not accounted for by known conditions. From that he reasoned that there must be another planet in the neighborhood and, on turning his glass to the point where his calculations told him the disturbing body must be, he discovered the planet sometimes called by his name and sometimes called Neptune. This discovery created a great sensation and a burst of admiration for the fortunate discoverer. Peirce maintained the astounding proposition that there was an error in Leverrier's calculations, and that the discovery was a fortunate accident. I believe that astronomers finally came to his conclusion. I remember once going into Boston in the omnibus when Peirce got in with a letter in his hand that he had just got from abroad and saying with great exultation to Professor Felton, who happened to be there, "Gauss says I am right."

I got well acquainted with Professor Peirce after I left College. He used to come to Washington after I came into public life. I found him one of the most delightful of men. His treatise "Ideality in the Physical Sciences," and one or two treatises of a religious character which he published, are full of a lofty and glowing eloquence. He gave a few lectures in mathematics to the class which, I believe, were totally incomprehensible to every one of his listeners with the possible exception of Child. He would take the chalk in his hand and begin in his shrill voice, "If we take," then he would write an equation in algebraic characters, "then we have," following it by another equation or formula. By the time he had got his blackboard half covered, he would get into an enthusiasm of delight. He would rub the legs of his pantaloons with his chalky hands and proceed on his lofty pathway, apparently unconscious of his auditors. What has become of all those wonderful results of genius I do not know. He was invited to a banquet by the Harvard Alumni in New York where he was the guest of honor. Mr. Choate expressed a grave doubt whether the professor could dine comfortably without a blackboard.

John W. Webster gave lectures to the boys on chemistry and geology which they were compelled to attend. I think the latter the most tedious human compositions to which I ever listened. The doctor seemed a kind-hearted, fussy person. He was known to the students by the sobriquet of Sky-rocket Jack, owing to his great interest in having some fireworks at the illumination when President Everett was inaugurated. There was no person among the Faculty at Cambridge who seemed less likely to commit such a bloody and cruel crime as that for which he was executed. The only thing that I know which indicated insensibility was that when he was lecturing one day in chemistry he told us that in performing the experiment which he was then showing us a year or two before with some highly explosive gas a copper vessel had burst and a part of it had been thrown with great violence into the back of the bench where a row of students were sitting, but fortunately the student who sat in that place was absent that day and nobody was hurt. He added drily: "The President sent for me and told me I must be more careful. He said I should feel very badly indeed if I had killed one of the students. And I should."

There was nothing in my time equivalent to what used to be called a rebellion in the older days, and I believe no such event has occurred for the last fifty years. The nearest to it was a case which arose in the senior class when I was a freshman. One of the seniors, who was a rather dull-witted but well-meaning youth, concluded that it was his duty to inform the Faculty of offences committed by his classmates, a proceeding it is needless to say contrary to all the boys' sentiments as to honorable conduct. Some windows had been broken, including his. He informed the Faculty of the person who had broken them, who was rusticated for a short time as a punishment. The next day being

Saturday, this informer, dressed up in his best, was starting for Boston, when he was seized by six of his classmates and held under the College pump until he received a sound ducking. He seized the finger of one of them with his teeth and bit it severely, though it was protected somewhat by a ring. He complained of five of the six, who were forthwith suspended until the next Commencement, losing, of course, their rank in the class and their chances for taking part in the Commencement exercises. One of them, of whom he omitted to tell, was much disturbed by the omission and demanded of the informer why he left him out. He said that he had rather a pity for him, as he had already been suspended once and he supposed the new offence would lead to his being expelled. Whereupon he said, "I will give you some reason to tell of me," and proceeded to administer a sound caning. That was at once reported to the Faculty. The offender was expelled, and criminal proceedings had which resulted in a fine.

We had some delightful lectures from Longfellow on the literature of the Middle Ages. He read us some of his own original poems and some beautiful translations. All the substance of these lectures I think is to be found in his book entitled "The Poets and Poetry of the Middle Ages." I do not see that we gained anything of solid instruction by having them read to us that we could not have got as well by reading them. We had also a course of lectures from Jared Sparks on American history. They were generally dull and heavy, but occasionally made intensely interesting when he described some stirring event of the Revolutionary War. We hung breathless on his account of the treason of Arnold and its detection and the class burst out into applause when he ended,—a thing the like of which never happened in my time in College. There was a little smattering of instruction in modern languages, but it was not of much value. We had a French teacher named Viau whom the boys tormented unmercifully. He spoke English very imperfectly, and his ludicrous mistakes destroyed all his dignity and rendered it impossible to maintain any discipline in the class. He would break out occasionally in despair, "Young zhentlemen, you do not respect me and I have not given you any reason to." A usual punishment for misconduct in those days was to deduct a certain number of the marks which determined rank from the scale of the offending student. M. Viau used to hold over us this threat, which, I believe, he never executed, "Young zhentlemen, I shall be obliged to deduce from you."

He was followed by the Comte de la Porte, a gentleman in bearing and of a good deal of dignity. The Count was asked one day by Nat Perry, a member of the class from New Hampshire who was very proud of his native State and always boasting of the exploits in war and peace of the people of New Hampshire, what sort of a French scholar M. Viau, his predecessor, was. The Count replied: "He was not a fit teacher for young gentlemen. He was an ignorant person from the Provinces. He did not have the Parisian accent. He did not know the French language in its purity. It would be as if somebody were to undertake to teach English who came from New Hampshire or some such place." The Count said this in entire innocence. It was received with a roar of laughter by the class, and the indignation and wrath of Perry may be well imagined.

Another instructor in modern languages was Dr. Bachi. He was a very accomplished gentleman. His translations of Italian poetry, especially of Dante and Tasso, were exquisite. It was like hearing a sweet and soft music to hear him read his beloved poets, and he had a singular gift of getting hold of the most sweet and mellifluous English words for his rendering. "And he did open his mouth, and from it there did come out words sweeter than honey." He once translated to us a passage in the Inferno where the damned are suspended, head downwards, with the burning flames resting upon the soles of their feet. "Ah," exclaimed Bachi, "they do curl up their toes."

My class is not one of the very famous classes of the College. Certainly it does not equal the class of 1802 or the class of 1829. But I think it was, on the whole, very considerably above the average. In it were several persons who became eminent scholars and teachers, and some who have been eminent in other walks of life. I think, on the whole, its two most distinguished members, entitled to hold a greater place than any others in the memory of future generations, were Dr. Calvin Ellis, Dean of the Medical Faculty of Harvard, who died in 1883, and Judge Nathan Webb, of the United States District Court of Maine, who died in 1902. Neither of these had very high rank in the class. The first half of the class used to have parts assigned at Commencement in those days. Ellis's part was very nearly the lowest of the first half. Webb's was higher. Webb entered college very young. He was quite small in stature and was known all through college as "little Webb." He grew to a stature of about six feet after he left college. He did, I believe, some very hard work indeed in his senior year. Although universally liked and respected by his classmates, he was not regarded as among the eminent scholars. Ellis performed all his duties in College very fairly but did not seem to care much for rank or for scholarship until, in the senior year, some lectures on anatomy were delivered by old Dr. John C. Warren. Ellis was filled with enthusiasm, as were some of the other members of the class. He and I got a skull somewhere and studied bones, processes, and sutures, both meaning to be physicians. My zeal lasted but a few weeks. Ellis's never abated until his death. He was at the head of his profession in the country in his own department, became Dean of the Harvard Medical School, and was loved and revered by his numerous pupils as by the members of his profession. He was one of the most simple-hearted, affectionate, spotless and lovable of men. He died of a lingering and painful disease, never losing his courage and patience, or his devoted interest in science. Webb was exceedingly fond of his home, not being very ambitious of higher office, but content to discharge ably and faithfully and to the universal satisfaction of the profession and the public, the duty of the important place he held. I have seen a good many public men from Maine of both parties. They all unite in this estimate of Judge Webb. There is no doubt that if he had been willing he would long ago have been made Judge of the Circuit Court, and then if the seat on the

Supreme Court of the United States held by Mr. Justice Gray of the New England Circuit had become vacant, I suppose he would have been called from the Circuit Bench to that Court by almost universal consent.

Three persons, Child, Lane and Short, all very distinguished scholars in after life, took their place at the head of the class in the beginning. Two of them held the same place when they graduated. Short was outstripped by Edwin Moses Bigelow, who is now living, a lawyer, in Boston. He entered college from the country not so well fitted when he entered as most of the class. But he made his way by an indefatigable diligence until he graduated with great distinction, the third scholar, going a little above Short.

Child was a man of great genius. He seems to me now, as I look back upon him, to have been as great a man at seventeen when he entered college, as he was when he died. He was the best writer, the best speaker and the best mathematician, the most accomplished person in his knowledge of general literature in the class,—indeed, I suppose, in college,—in his day. He was probably equaled, and I dare say more lately excelled, by Lane as a Latin scholar, and by Short as a Greek scholar. He was a great favorite with the class. He delivered a very beautiful class oration when we graduated. He spent his life in the service of the College. He was tutor for a short time and soon succeeded Channing as Professor of Rhetoric and Oratory. He became one of the most eminent scholars in the country in early English literature and language. He edited a collection of ballads, Little & Brown's edition of the British Poets, and was a thorough student of Shakespeare and Chaucer. To the elucidation of the text of Chaucer he made some admirable contributions. He was shy and diffident, full of kindness toward persons whom he knew and to children, and of sympathy with persons who were in sorrow, but whimsical, grotesque, and apt to take strong prejudices against persons whom he did not know. I suppose some of the best of our American men of letters of late years would have submitted their productions to the criticism of Child as to a master.

Next to him stood Lane, the learned Latin scholar. I do not believe that anybody ever went through Harvard College who performed four years of such constant and strenuous labor. What he did in his vacations I do not know, but there was no minute lost in the term time. It is said that he never missed attendance on morning and evening prayers but once. The class were determined that Lane should not go through college without missing prayers once. So one night a cord was fastened to the handle of his door and attached to the rail of the staircase. But Lane succeeded in wrenching open the door and got to morning prayers in time. He was the monitor, whose duty it was to mark the students who were absent from prayers and who were punished for absence by a deduction from their rank and, if the absences were frequent enough, by a more severe penalty. The next time the measures were more effective. Lane's chum, Ellis, was in the conspiracy. The students bored holes carefully into the door and into the jamb by the side and took a quantity of hinges and screwed them carefully on to the door and the jamb. When Lane got ready to start for prayers in the morning, he found it impossible to open the door. As soon as he discovered what was the trouble, he seized his hatchet and undertook to cut his way out. His chum, Ellis, who had remained quietly in bed, sprang out of bed and placed his back against the door and declared that the door of his room should not be hewn down in that manner. Lane was obliged to desist. He however took his monitor's book, marked himself and his chum absent, and submitted. There were a good many such pranks played by the boys in those days, in the spirit of a harmless and good-natured mischief. I do not know whether the College has improved in that particular or no. I do not think anybody in my day would have defaced the statue of John Harvard.

Whether Lane will go farther down on the path to immortality as the author of the admirable Latin Grammar to which he gave so much of his life or as author of the song, "The Lone Fish Ball," posterity alone will determine.

Charles Short, the third of the three whom I named as standing at the head of the class, became President of Kenyon College and afterward Professor of Latin in Columbia College. He was one of the committee to prepare the revised version of the Scriptures, and contributed largely to the Harpers' excellent Latin Dictionary.

Another of our famous scholars was Fitzedward Hall, who died lately in England. He was a very respectable scholar in the ordinary college studies, but he attained no special distinction in them as compared with the others whom I have mentioned. He became, however, quite early, interested in Arabic and other Oriental languages, a study which he pursued, I think, without the help of an instructor. He had a very remarkable career. After graduating, he sailed for the East Indies with a view to pursue there the study of the Oriental languages and literature. He took with him letters of introduction to influential persons in Calcutta, and, of course, a sufficient supply of funds. But the vessel on which he was a passenger was wrecked as it approached the shore. He got ashore with difficulty, drenched with sea-water, having lost his letters of introduction and of credit, and with no resources but a few coins which happened to be in his pockets. He knew nobody in Calcutta. He disliked very much to present himself to the persons to whom he had been commended by his friends in America in that sorry plight with the possibility that he might be suspected of being an impostor. Accordingly, he determined that he would take care of himself. He walked about the street to see what he could find to do. As he went along he saw the sign of the *Oriental Quarterly Review*. He went in and inquired for the editor and asked him if he would accept an article. The editor said that he would consider it if it were brought in. Hall then went out and found a bookstore. Going in he spied a copy of Griswold's "Poets and Poetry of America." With a pencil and some sheets of paper, he wrote an article on American literature, filled up with pretty copious extracts. He took it to the editor of the *Review* who paid him for it, I think five pounds, and told him that he should be happy to have him make other contributions. Hall supported himself by writing for that review and some other periodicals published by the same concern until he could send home, get new letters of introduction and credit and support himself as a gentleman. He spent three years in Calcutta studying Hindostanee and Persian, and afterward, Bengalee and Sanscrit. Later he removed to Benares, where he was appointed to a tutorship in the Government College. Then he became professor and afterward Inspector of Schools for Ajmere and Mairwara. He was in a besieged fort for seven months during the Indian Mutiny. He received the degree of D.C.L. from Oxford in 1860. He went to London afterward to promote the election of Max Müller as professor at Oxford. While there he was himself made professor of Sanscrit and of Indian jurisprudence in London University. I saw him in England, I think in 1871, when he was librarian of the great library of the East India Company, having in charge not only a vast library, but the archives of the East India Company going back beyond the time of Cromwell. He showed me many interesting letters and documents in manuscript of Cromwell, Nelson and other famous persons. Professor Edward B. Whitney once told me that with the exception of Max Müller he considered Hall the foremost Oriental scholar in the world. I suppose Hall would have said the same of Professor Whitney.

Hall maintained his sturdy Americanism throughout his long life in England. He was ready at all times to do battle, in public or in private, when his countrymen were attacked. I think, in many cases, if he had been at home, he would have attacked the same things with which the Englishmen found fault. He could not bear Ruskin. He thought he, himself, as an American had to endure much contempt and injury from Englishmen because of Ruskin's bitter and contemptuous speech. But when we consider that he was an American we must admit that England treated him very well. He had, I suppose, the most welcome admission to all their scientific journals. In his time he was employed on the very best and most important work done in England in his line. He was professor of Hindostanee and of Hindoo law and Indian jurisprudence in King's College in London, also of the Sanscrit language and literature, and Indian history and geography. In April, 1865, he was made Librarian of the India Office, having in his charge the best collection of Oriental manuscripts in the world, twenty thousand in number.

While the catalogues of the libraries show a large number of books published under his name, he said that the greater part of his work had been anonymous.

In 1893 he wrote to a London magazine: "Although I have lived away from America upwards of forty-six years, I feel to this hour, that in writing English I am writing a foreign language."

Next in rank to Child, Lane, Bigelow and Short was Judge Soule. Next to him came George Cheyne Shattuck Choate, one of the well-known family of brothers of that name, sons of a Salem physician. Choate became a physician himself. He was at the head of the Massachusetts Institution for the Insane at Taunton. He afterward had an establishment of his own near New York, where Horace Greeley was under his care. I saw little of him after we graduated. But he was nearly or quite at the head of his department in the country. It is said that his testimony in court involving questions of medical jurisprudence was wonderful for its beauty, its precision and its profound analysis.

But I am inclined to think that the one member of our class whose fame will last to remote posterity, a fame which he will owe to a single poem, is Walter Mitchell. He was a very bright and accomplished person in college and a great favorite with his friends. He studied law, but afterward determined to become a clergyman and took orders in the Episcopal Church. I have never heard him preach, but I have no doubt from his distinction as a writer and scholar in college that he is an excellent preacher. But his poem of the sea entitled "Tacking the Ship off Fire Island" is one of the most spirited and perfect of its kind in literature. You can hear the wind blow and feel the salt in your hair as you read it. I once heard it read by Richard Dana to the Phi

Beta Kappa Society at Harvard, and again by that most accomplished elocutionist, E. Harlow Russell. I never read it or hear it without a renewed admiration.

But the brightest, raciest, wittiest, liveliest, spunkiest of all the youths was Daniel Sargent Curtis, one of the race of that name so well known in Boston for excellence in various departments. Curtis was the son, I believe, of Thomas B. Curtis, the merchant, a nephew of Charles P. Curtis, the eminent lawyer, and a cousin of Judge Benjamin R. Curtis. I do not know what he would not have made of himself if he had cultivated his great literary capacity. Certainly if he had performed the promise of his boyhood he would have been one of the foremost men in American literature. He studied law but pretty soon became a banker. Soon after he took up his residence in Italy, where I suppose he is living now. He produced some serious poetry which he read to some college societies. I hope for the credit of the class and for the country and his name he may have done something in later years which will be given to the world. It is said, I know not how truly, that he was for many years a near neighbor and intimate friend of Browning. When he was in college and in the Law School the boys used to enliven all social gatherings by repeating his good jests as, in later years, the lawyers did those of Rufus Choate, or the people in public life in Washington still later, those of Evarts. Such things lose nine-tenths of their flavor in the repetition and nine parts of the other tenth when they are put in writing. Curtis was quite small in stature but he was plucky as a gamecock, and a little dandyish in his dress. It is said that when he was a freshman, the boys at the Cambridge High School, a good many of whom were much bigger than he was, undertook to throw snowballs at him one day as he went by. Whereupon Curtis marched up to the biggest boy and told him if another snowball were thrown at him he would thrash him and he might pass it over to the boy who did it. The result was that Curtis was not troubled again.

You could not attack or rally him without some bright reply. Horace Gray, afterward the judge, went shooting one day and met Curtis as he was coming back with his gun over West Boston Bridge. Curtis asked him if he had shot anything. Gray said, "No, nothing but a hawk in Watertown. I stopped at the Museum as I came by, and gave it to Agassiz." "I suppose Agassiz said 'Accipiter,' " said Curtis.

When Professor Greenleaf resigned his place at the Dane Law School, much to the regret of the students, it was proposed to secure a likeness of him for the lecture room. There was some discussion whether it should be a bust or a picture, and if a bust what should be the material. Curtis said: "Better make it Verd Antique. That means Old Green."

Dr. Beck once required his class each to bring a Latin epigram. Dan Curtis, who was not very fond of work unless it was in the line of his own tastes, sent in the following:

Fugiunt. Qui fugiunt? Galli; tunc moriar contentus.

"What is that, Curtis?" said the Doctor. "Dying words of Wolfe, sir," replied Curtis. "Ah," said the Doctor with great satisfaction. He thought it was Wolf the famous Greek scholar, and thought the epigram highly to Curtis's credit.

I have still in my memory a very bright poem of his. I do not think I ever saw or read it written or in print. But I remember hearing it read in one of the college clubs more than fifty years ago. He has Longfellow's style very happily, including the dropping from a bright and sometimes a sublime line to one which is flat and commonplace, as for instance in the ode on the death of the Duke of Wellington.

> Meantime without the surly cannon waited,
>   The sky gleamed overhead.
> Nothing in Nature's aspect indicated
>   That a great man was dead.

This is Curtis's poem:

> Wrapped in musings dim and misty,
>   Sit I by the fitful flame;
> And my thoughts steal down the vista
>   Of old time, as in a dream.

Here the hero held his quarters,
Whom America holds dear;
He beloved of all her daughters,
Formerly resided here.

Here you often might have seen him,
Silvery white his reverend scalp,
Frowned above a mighty chapeau
Like a storm-cap o'er the Alp.

Up and down these rooms the hero
Oftentimes would thoughtful stray,
Walking now toward the window,
Stalking then again away.

By the fireside, quaintly moulded
Oft his humid boots would lie;
And his queer surtout was folded
On some strange old chair to dry.

In the yard where now before me
Underclothes, wind-wafted hang,
Waved the banners of an army,
Warriors strode with martial clang.

These things now are all departed,
With us on the earth no more,
But the chieftain, noble-hearted,
Comes to visit me once more.

In he comes without permission,
Sits him down before mine eyes,
Then I tremble, and demnition
Curious thoughts within me rise.

Slow he speaks in accents solemn,
Life is all an empty hum,
Man, by adulation only
Can'st thou ever great become.

I ought perhaps to mention a young man of most brilliant promise, an excellent scholar and a great favorite, who died before the class graduated, on a voyage to the East Indies which he undertook in the hope of restoring his health,—

Augustus Enoch Daniels. He left behind him one *bon mot* which is worth recording. We were translating one day one of the choruses in Æschylus, I think in the Agamemnon, where the phrase occurs νήνεμοι λέχοι, meaning "couches unvisited by the wind," which he most felicitously rendered "windlass bedsteads." Such is the vanity of human life that it is not uncommon that some hardworking, faithful and bright scholar is remembered only for one single saying, as Hamilton in the House of Commons was remembered for his single speech. Another instance of this is that worthy and excellent teacher of Latin and Professor of History, Henry W. Torrey. He was an instructor in college in our time, afterward left the college to teach a young ladies' school and came back again later as Professor. I presume if any member of the class of 1846 were asked about Torrey he would say: "Oh, yes. He was an excellent Latin scholar, an excellent teacher in elocution and in history. But all I remember of him is that on one occasion a man who professed to be learned in Egyptian antiquities advertised a course of lectures, one of which was to be illustrated by unrolling from a mummy the bandages which had been untouched since its interment, many centuries before Christ. The savant claimed to be able to read the inscription on the cloth in which the mummy was wrapped and declared that it was the corpse of an Egyptian princess, whose name and history he related. Having given this narrative and excited the expectation of his auditors, the wrappers were taken off and, alas, it turned out to be the body of a man. The poor professor was, of course, much disconcerted and his lectures, I believe, came to a sudden ending. Mr. Torrey said that 'it was undoubtedly the corpse of Spurius Mummius.'"

But no account of my class ought to omit the name of Henry Whitney. He was a universal favorite. In all the disputes which arose in all the divisions of sets or sections, Whitney maintained the regard and affection of the whole class.

After graduating he was a very successful and influential business man in Boston and was President of the Boston & Providence Railroad, which under his masterly administration, attained a very high degree of prosperity. I think he corresponded with every member of the class, and did more to preserve and create a kindly class feeling than any other member. It seemed when he died as if half the college had died. He was a man of great refinement and scholarship, and fond of collecting rare books. He had a great many editions of Milton which he liked to exhibit to his friends. He had a most delightful wit, and was the author of some very good songs and other humorous poetry.

I do not of course undertake to give sketches of all my classmates, either the living or the dead, or those who have attained distinction as useful and honorable members of society. So far as I know their career since they left college, there is none of them of whom the class or the college need be ashamed.

The different classes had not much intercourse with each other unless it happened in the case of boys who came from the same town, or who came from the same school, until late in the college course, when the members of the Hasty Pudding Club and the Porcellian, the two principal secret societies, formed intimacies beyond their own class in the meetings of those clubs. There were some persons in the classes near mine, both below and above me, with whom I had an acquaintance in college which grew into a cordial friendship in the Law School or in later life. Perhaps, taking him all together, the most brilliant man in Harvard in my time was John Felton. He went to California and became afterward unquestionably the greatest lawyer they have ever had on the Pacific Coast. He was in the class after mine. I knew him slightly in our undergraduate days. But when I went to the Law School in September, 1847, we boarded together in the same house. We speedily became intimate and used to take long walks together of three or four hours every day. We rambled about Watertown and Brighton and Somerville and West Cambridge and had long discussions about law and politics and poetry and metaphysics and literature and our own ambitions and desires. We were constantly in each other's rooms, and often sat up together, sometimes until the constellations set, with the wasteful, time-consuming habits of boyhood.

> Say, for you saw us, ye immortal lights,
> How oft, unwearied, have we spent the nights
> In search of deep philosophy,
> Wit, eloquence and poetry,—
> Arts which I loved, for they, my friend, were thine.

John came of a distinguished family. His brother Cornelius was a famous Greek professor, one of the most striking figures about Cambridge. Another brother was Samuel M. Felton, the most distinguished civil engineer in the country of his time; builder of the Fitchburg Railroad, afterward builder and President of the Pennsylvania Railroad; the man who conceived the plan of getting the New England troops into Washington by the way of Annapolis when Baltimore was in the power of the Rebels. Another brother was quite distinguished in college in the class of 1851. John after he graduated went to California and never came back from the Pacific Coast or kept up his communication with his old friends, although he received them with great hospitality, I am told, when they went out there. I think he had a fancy that he would keep to himself until he could come back in some great place, like that of Senator or Judge of the Supreme Court of the United States. He was a candidate for the Senate at one time, but was defeated by a much inferior man. He was fond of argument; never was contented without challenging somebody and was a very tough customer to encounter, whatever side of a question he chose to take. He liked, however, nothing better than a sturdy resistance. To yield to him was never the way to win his good will. The first day when we went to live at the same boarding-house, I got into a hot dispute with him at dinner over the Wilmot Proviso, and the constitutional power of Congress to legislate against slavery in the territories, which was then a burning question. John took the Southern side of that question, although I dare say he would have taken the other if a Southerner had introduced it, and we got pretty zealous on both sides and walked home together continuing the argument as we walked. As we separated, Felton said: "We will continue this discussion tomorrow. Meantime, won't you look up the history of the matter a little?" "Yes," said I, "and won't you study up a little on Whately's Logic?" The answer seemed to delight Felton, and he took me into high favor. I never knew a man of such ready wit, although I have known a good many famous wits in my day. But all these things evaporate with time. Or, if you remember them, they are vapid and tasteless in the telling, like champagne which has been uncorked for a week. We were one day discussing some question of law at the table, and John, who had not yet begun to study law himself, put in his oar as usual, when Charles Allen, afterward Judge of the Massachusetts Supreme Court, turned on him with some indignation. "What do you know about it, Johnny? You don't know what a quantum meruit is." "If you had it, 't would kill you," said Felton. He was invited to the dinner given by the people of Nevada in honor of their admission as a State, and there was some discussion about a device for a State seal. Felton suggested that the Irish emblem would be the most appropriate, the "Lyre and shamrock." Once after deciding a case in his favor, Mr. Justice Field said to him: "Felton, I have made great use of your brief in my opinion." "Always do that, Judge," said Felton. He possessed considerable capacity for poetry, although I do not know that he cultivated it much after he left college. He delivered a very successful poem at Commencement, and gave the Phi Beta Kappa poem the next year and read some very witty verses at the Society's dinner the same day. He was much distressed over choosing a subject, and put off and put off writing his poem till within a few days of the time when it was to be delivered. And he finally resolved, in a fit of desperation, that he would go into his room, shut his eyes, turn round three times and take for his subject the first object on which they rested when he opened them. That happened to be a horseshoe which he had picked up in the street and hung over his fireplace for luck. He made a charming poem from this subject, on Superstition. The opening lines are:

Just over the way, with its front to the street,
Up one flight of stairs, is a room snug and neat,
With a prospect Mark Tapley right jolly would call;—
Two churches, one graveyard, one bulging brick wall,
Where, raven-like, Science gloats over its wealth,
And the skeleton grins at the lectures on health.
The tree by the window has twice hailed the Spring
Since we circled its trunk our last chorus to sing.
Maidens laughed at our shouts, they knew better than we;
And the world clanked its chains as we cried, "We are free."
On the wall hangs a Horseshoe I found in the street;
'Tis the shoe that to-day sets in motion my feet
'Tis a comfort, while Europe to freedom awoke
Is peeping like chickens just free from their yolk
To think Pope and Monarch their kingdoms may lose;
Yet I hang my subject wherever I choose.

He goes on in a more serious strain to sketch the history of superstition and ends with an eloquent aspiration for a day of universal peace:

As now my thoughts like clustering bees have clung
To thee, my Horseshoe, o'er the lintel hung,
The future bard, with song more richly fraught,—
Some reverenced wrong the nucleus of his thought,
Some relic crown or virtuoso's gun,
Some nation's banner when all earth is one,—
Back through the past in mournful strain shall wind
Where demon fancies vex the darkling mind,
Where light but faintly streaks the dappled sky,
Nor Morn has shot his glittering shafts on high;
Trembling with grief and hope, his lyre shall thrill
To twilight times of blending good and ill,
Where whizz of bullets, and the clanking chain,
Jar on the praise of Peace and Freedom's reign.
In louder strains shall burst the exulting close,
That sounds the triumph o'er the struggling foes,—
The slave unbound, War's iron tongues all dumb,—
His glorious Present, our all hail To Come,

All hail To Come, when East and West shall be—
While rolls between the undividing sea—
Two, like the brain, whose halves ne'er think apart,
But beat and tremble to one throbbing heart!

He took what was then an unusual method of making himself a good lawyer. That was to begin to deal with a legal principle in historic order, going back to the first case where it was announced and tracing it down through the reports, making no use of text-books. That was the way the old lawyers before Blackstone got their training. I have been told, though that happened after I left Cambridge, that he and Professor Langdell, the eminent teacher at Harvard who has introduced that method with so much success, studied together. Whether it was Felton's plan or Langdell's I do not know.

John Felton died suddenly in May, 1877. Everybody who comes to Washington from California who is old enough speaks with pleasure of his knowledge of Felton and is full of stories of his brilliant wit. He had probably the largest fees ever received by an American lawyer. He is said by his biographer to have received a fee of a million dollars in one case. His death was received with universal sorrow. All the places of business and amusement were closed and the flags displayed at half mast on the day of his funeral.

Another rather interesting figure among the men of the classes above me was Thomas Hill, afterward President of the College. He was a good mathematician and a good preacher. But he was not as successful in the Presidency as his friends hoped. The only thing I remember about him of any importance is highly to his credit. One winter's day a little gaunt-looking and unhappy pig that had strayed away from a drove wandered into the College Yard just as the boys were coming out of evening prayers. The whole surface of the yard was covered with a sheet of thin and very slippery ice. It was rather hard to stand up on it. The boys came across the pig, which was frightened and attempted to run. After running a little, he would slip on the ice and slide and tumble over, and then gather himself up again and try once more. There was a general shout and a general chase. Poor piggy strove to elude his pursuers. His own tail was a little slippery, so that if a boy caught it he did not hold it long. The whole college, pretty much, engaged in the pursuit, which certainly seemed to be great fun. But, on a sudden, there was a loud, angry shout from a stentorian voice as Tom Hill jumped in among the pursuers, who were just on the point of conquering the bewildered animal. "For shame. Take one of your size." The boys saw the point, were filled with mortification, desisted, and allowed the poor creature to go in peace.

The boys generally boarded in the College Commons, where they could board for $2.25 a week on one side, and on the other called "starvation commons" for $1.75 a week. In the latter they had meat only every other day. A few of the sons of the wealthier families boarded in private houses where the rate of board varied from $3 to $3.50 a week. The rooms were furnished very simply, almost always without carpets, though in rare instances the floors would be covered with a cheap carpet which did not last very well under the wear and tear of boyish occupation. The students generally made their own fires and blacked their own boots and drew their own water. But there was a family of negroes named Lewis who performed those services for such boys as desired, at a compensation of $5 or $6 a term. The patriarch of this race was a very interesting old character. He was said to be one hundred years old. He was undoubtedly very near it. One morning, just as we were coming out of morning prayers, shortly after six o'clock, old Mr. Lewis drove by with a horse which he was said to have bought for $5, and a wagon of about the same value. He had a load of all sorts of vegetables which he had raised in his little garden near where the Arsenal stood and was carrying into Boston to market. One of his old wheels broke and the wagon came down, spilling the old fellow himself and his load of vegetables. He lay there flat on his back, unable to get up, surrounded by turnips and squashes and onions and potatoes, etc. As he lay with his black face and his white, grizzled poll, he was a most ludicrous spectacle. One of us asked him: "Why, Mr. Lewis, what is the matter?" "Well," he said with a mournful tone, "I laid eaout to go into Boston."

I suppose there was more turbulence and what would be called rowdyism in my day than now. At any rate I do not hear of such things very often nowadays. But it was usually of a harmless character. There were very few instances indeed of what would be called dissipation, still fewer of actual vice. The only game which was much in vogue was foot-ball. There was a little attempt to start the English game of cricket and occasionally, in the spring, an old-fashioned, simple game which we called base was played. But the chief game was foot-ball, which was played from the beginning of the September term until the cold weather set in, and sometimes, I believe, in the spring. It was very unlike the game as at present carried on. After evening prayers, which were over about five or ten minutes after six, the boys repaired to the foot-ball ground and ranged themselves on sides nearly equal in number. If one side thought they were not fairly matched they would shout, "More, more," until enough went over to them from the other side to make it about equal. Then one of the best kickers gave the ball a kick toward the other side of the field, and there was a rush and an attempt to get it past the goal. Nobody was allowed to pick up the foot-ball, or to run with it in his hand. A fast runner and good kicker who could get the ball a little outside of the line of his antagonists could often make a great progress with it across the field before he was intercepted. It was allowable to trip up one of the other side by thrusting the foot before him. But touching an opponent with the hand would have been resented as an assault and insult. The best foot-ball players were not the strongest men but the swiftest runners, as a rule.

The practice of hazing freshmen during a few weeks after their entering was carried on sometimes under circumstances of a good deal of cruelty. One boy in my class was visited by a party of sophomores, treated with a good deal of indignity, and his feelings extremely outraged. He was attacked by a fever shortly afterward of which he died. During his last hours, in his delirium, he was repeating the scenes of this visit to his room. His father thought that the indignity caused his death. Another was taken out from his room in his night clothes, tied into a chair and left on the public common in the cold. It was a long time before he was discovered and rescued. A heavy cold and a fit of sickness were the consequence.

There was an entertaining custom of giving out what were called mock parts when the real parts for the exhibitions or Commencement were announced. They were read out from a second-story window to an assemblage of students in the yard, and after the real parts had been given some mock parts were read. Usually some peculiarity of the person to whom they were assigned was made the object of good-natured ridicule in the selection of the subject. For example, one boy, who was rather famous for smoking other fellows' cigars and never having any of his own, had assigned to him as a subject "The Friendships of this Life all Smoke."

When the parts were assigned for Commencement, which were given usually to the first half of the class, there was a procession of what was called the Navy Club and an assignment of honors which were in the reverse order of excellence to that observed in the regular parts. The Lord High Admiral was supposed to be the worst scholar in the class,—if possible, one who had been rusticated twice during the college course. The laziest man in the class was Rear Admiral. Then there was a Powder Monkey and a Coxswain, and other naval officers, who were generally famous for what used to be called demerits. The members of the class to whom parts were assigned were called "digs" and marched in the procession, each with a spade on his shoulder, the first scholar, who in our class was Child, as the "dig of digs," having a spade of huge dimensions. I believe James Russell Lowell was the Lord High Admiral in his class. The Rear Admiral in mine was borne about on a couch or litter, supported by four men, having another one marching by his side to carry his pipe, which he was supposed to be too lazy to put into his mouth or take out of his mouth himself. The procession had banners bearing various devices and went around to take leave of the President and the different professors, giving them cheers at their houses. President Everett, who was a serious-minded person, was much offended by the whole proceeding. He sent for some members of the class and remonstrated; told them he had been obliged to apologize to his English servant-girl for such an exhibition. I believe our class was the last one which performed this harmless and highly entertaining ceremony.

One of my classmates, afterward a worthy physician, was a tall man, older considerably than the rest of the class. He used to wear an old-fashioned blue, straight-bodied coat with brass buttons, a buff vest, and nankeen pantaloons which were said to have come down as an heirloom in his family from a remote generation. He was addicted to rather a pompous style of speech. He was very fond of playing the bass-viol, of which he was by no means a very skilful master. He had, as a subject for his mock part, "The Base Violation of all Rules of Harmony." One Sunday evening he had a few friends with him who were singing psalm tunes to the accompaniment of his bass-viol. They made a prodigious noise, not at all to the liking of the proctor who had the care of the discipline of that entry, which was in Holworthy. He went to the room from which the noise issued. It was locked and he had some difficulty in getting in. The persons assembled, instead of maintaining their place, betook themselves to hiding places in the inner rooms. My classmate, however, stood his ground like a Roman and told the officer that his room was his castle and that he had no right to come in. The matter was reported to the Faculty and the musician sent for. Instead of submitting himself, however, he maintained very sturdily that the visit of the official to his room was an outrage which he ought not to be asked to endure. He made quite an oration to the Faculty. Thereupon he was sentenced, more for his contumacy than for the original offence, to suspension from the college for two or three months. The class were very indignant and determined to manifest their indignation in a way that should be understood. They got a chariot with six white horses which drove up to his door in Holworthy at midday. Nearly the whole college assembled to see him off. He came out and took his seat in solitary state in the chariot. Some eight or ten of the class on horseback accompanied him as outriders. They drove into Boston to the front door of the Tremont House in great state. It was just at the time the Governor-General of Canada, I think Lord Elgin, was expected in Boston on a great occasion in the history of the city. The waiters and landlord at the Tremont House thought the English nobleman had arrived and hurried down the steps to open the door and meet him. But he got out of his carriage with his carpet-bag in his hand and disappeared in a humble fashion round the corner. The Faculty were very indignant and thought of disciplining severely the members of the class who had got up the burlesque, especially the outriders. Edward Everett then had under consideration the question whether he would accept the Presidency of the College. It was thought that if a rebellion occurred then he would decide against undertaking the responsibility. So they let the whole matter pass.

The principal figure in this scene used to be a thorn in the flesh of Professor Channing. He used to insert very pompous and magniloquent sentences in his themes, much to Channing's disgust. One day Channing took up a theme and held it up and called out, X. X. came to the chair by the Professor's side, and the Professor read, in his shrill voice: " 'The sable sons of Afric's burning coast.' You mean negroes, I suppose." He admitted that he did. The Professor took his pen and drew a line over the sentence he had read and substituted the word "negroes" above the line, much to X.'s mortification.

I was guilty of one practical joke of which I have repented all my days, but for which the poetical justice of Providence administered to me, many years afterward, a punishment in kind. There was a classmate who sat next to me in the recitation in the sophomore year, whom everybody knew and liked, but who was not very much interested in study. He got along as he best could by his native wits and such little application as he found absolutely necessary. One day we were reciting in Lowth's Grammar. The Bishop says that in English the substantive singular is made plural for the most part by adding s. Professor Channing called up this classmate of mine, who stated this as follows: "The author says that the distinction between nouns in the singular and plural is that the latter end in s." "Is that a good distinction?" asked the Professor. My neighbor answered with great confidence, "No, sir," as he was well warranted in doing from the form of the question. "Can't you give us some instance of words in the singular number that end in s?" said the Professor. My friend, who was considerably embarrassed, stammered, was staggered, and hesitated a moment. I whispered in his ear, "Hoss," on which he, without any reflection, blurted out, "Hoss." There was a roar of laughter from the class, and the poor fellow sat down, much distressed at his blunder. Channing dismissed the class, and the next day gave us a lecture. He said our uproarious laughter had disturbed Dr. Walker's recitation in the neighboring room, "especially you, Curtis, with your pit laugh." I ought to have risen up instantly and avowed myself the guilty cause of my classmate's innocent blunder. But, much to my own shame and disgrace, I did not do it. But some forty years afterward, I was engaged in an earnest discussion in the Senate Chamber with Butler of South Carolina, at the time of the passage of the first Civil Service law. Butler favored the law and his whole bearing in the discussion was exceedingly proper and creditable. We were talking of some prohibition, of some clause forbidding the imposing assessments upon office-holders for political purposes, and it was proposed to except from the prohibition voluntary contributions for proper election purposes. Butler asked me what I should consider improper election purposes. I hesitated a moment when Miller of California, who was a man of a good deal of fun, whispered in my ear, "Buying shotguns to shoot negroes with," which I, without reflecting and indeed hardly conscious of what I was saying, repeated aloud. Butler, who was a man of high spirit, and quick temper, was furious. He came down upon me with a burst of wrath. I tried to interrupt him. But he was so angry that it was impossible to interrupt him and said something which made it seem to me impossible either to explain or apologize. But I regretted the transaction exceedingly, and have always considered that I was well punished for my joke at the expense of my unhappy classmate.

An anecdote came down from a class before my time which I think ought not to be lost. One of the boys when the cold weather came on in the first term of his freshman year took out from the college library a book which was nearly the largest and thickest volume it contained. It was the works of Bishop Williams, who I think was one of the seven bishops persecuted by James II. The book contained an exceedingly dull treatise on theology. The youth had no special literary tastes, of which anybody knew, and that was the only book he was ever known to take out. He kept it out the six weeks which were allowed, and then renewed it, not taking it back to the library until the hot weather of the following summer. He repeated this in his sophomore and junior and senior years. Dr. Harris, the librarian, was very much puzzled and asked some of the boys if they could tell him why this young man kept Bishop Williams's works so constantly. None of the boys knew. They used to see it lying on his table, but never saw any signs of his reading it. At last one winter night late in the senior year something happened which caused a good deal of excitement. Several of the boys who were down in the yard rushed up in great haste to this classmate's room. It happened to be unlocked. They got in without knocking and found him undressed with nothing on but his nightgown. His bed happened to be near the fire, and standing up on the edge in front of the fire was Bishop Williams's works. It turned out that he was in the habit of thoroughly warming the book and then of putting it in the bed before he got in himself, so that it would serve the function of a warming-pan. The young gentleman turned out in after life to be a very distinguished

Bishop himself, an eminent champion of the doctrines of the Episcopal Church, which he had doubtless acquired by absorption.

The boys were always ready for mischief and always kind and easily moved to sympathy. One day just before prayers there was found on the square in front of Willard's Hotel a large load of straw. The owner had stopped and unhitched his horses to feed them at Willard's stable. Some mischievous boy set fire to the load and it burned with a blaze which illuminated the whole neighborhood. Pretty soon the owner appeared in a state of great distress; said he was a very poor man; that he was moving his household furniture and that his beds, chairs, and all the goods he had in the world were in the cart covered up with the straw. The boys immediately took up a subscription and sent the fellow off well satisfied with his sale. It was said he got about twice as much as the value he set on all his goods, and that about a week after he appeared with another load of straw which he left exposed in the same place at the same time in the afternoon. I believe that was not molested.

The people of Cambridge in those days were a quiet folk. The students did not go much into the society of the town unless they happened to have some kindred there. There were a great many old houses, some of which are standing now, built before the Revolutionary War. Some had been occupied by old Tories. Among them was the Craigie House still standing, having been Washington's headquarters, and now more famous still as the residence of Longfellow. There were a few old gentlemen wandering about the streets who were survivors of the generation which just followed the Revolutionary War, among them Dr. Jennison, the old physician, and Dr. Popkin, the old Greek professor, of whom a delightful life was written by President Felton. Mr. Sales, an old Spaniard, had given lessons in Spanish from time immemorial. He was a queer looking old gentleman, who had his gray hair carefully dressed every day by a barber, wearing an ancient style of dress, covered with snuff, but otherwise scrupulously neat. He had a curious bend and walk, which made him seem a little like a dog walking on his hind legs. He was very fond of the boys and they of him. He made full allowance for the exuberance of youth. Two careless students who were driving in a sleigh ran against him in the street and knocked him over and injured him severely. But the old fellow would not betray their names and had nothing to say when somebody talked severely of their carelessness but "Oh, oh, young blood, young blood." I never saw him in the least disturbed or angry with anything the boys said or did except on one occasion. Henry Whitney said, in reciting in Don Quixote, in the course of some discussion, "By Jingo, Mr. Sales." Sales was struck with horror. He said it was the most horrible phrase that ever came from the lips of mortal man, and he should think the walls of the building where they were would fall down on Whitney's head and overwhelm him. What awful and mysterious meaning the words "by Jingo" had for the old Spanish gentleman we never could discover. He declined to give any explanation and treated the subject as one to be avoided with horror ever after. I commend the question to the consideration of philologists.

The treatment of the students in general by the authorities and the college was stern, austere and distant. The students had little social intercourse with the families or the professors, except such of them as had relatives in Cambridge, which allowed intercourse with the families of the professors. The professors did nothing to encourage familiarity, or even to encourage any request for help in the difficulties of study. Indeed a boy who did that fell into disfavor with his companions, and was called a fish.

President Eliot in some speech, I think before the graduates of the Latin School, speaking of his life as a boy, said he had a great respect for his little self. I cannot say that of my young self at Harvard. My time was largely wasted in novel reading or reading books which had not much to do with the college studies, and lounging about in my own room or that of other students. I am not sure that the period of growth from sixteen to twenty is one when it is good for a youth to study hard. So far as my observation extends the poor scholars who have graduated at Harvard become as useful and eminent men in after life as the good scholars. I do not now think of any person, who has graduated first scholar since Edward Everett, who became in after life a very great man, although some of them have been very respectable. Judge Thomas Russell, who was first in the class before mine, was a very successful and brilliant man, performing admirably everything that he undertook. He was a good judge of the Superior Court, a good minister to Venezuela, a good advocate, and an excellent political speaker. But he never attained a place in the world equal to that of his classmate Gray, who, if I remember right, did not have a part at Commencement. Professor Child gained great distinction in his chosen field, but, I incline to think, would have gained the same distinction if he had devoted himself to the same pursuits and had never entered college at all. The first scholar in the class of 1843, the first class which graduated after I entered, was Horace Binney Sargent, a brave soldier, and the author of some beautiful and spirited war lyrics. But there were several of his classmates, including Thomas Hill, John Lowell and Octavius B. Frothingham, who attained much greater distinction. In the class of 1844 the first scholar was Shattuck Hartwell, a highly respectable and worthy gentleman, many years an officer in the Boston Custom House, who spent a large part of his life fitting pupils for college, while Francis Parkman, the historian, Benjamin Apthorp Gould, the mathematician, and Dr. John Call Dalton, the eminent physician, neither of whom had a very high record, became distinguished in after life. Among my own classmates, as I have already said, Judge Webb, Fitzedward Hall and Calvin Ellis attained very great distinction, although no one of them stood very high in rank. In the next class John Felton, Judge Endicott, Judge Charles Allen, and Tuckerman, the naturalist, were the persons who have been most famous in after life. I believe no one of them, except Felton who graduated the second scholar, ranked very high in college. I myself graduated with a fairly decent rank. I believe I was the nineteenth scholar in a class of sixty-six. When I graduated I looked back on my wasted four years with a good deal of chagrin and remorse. I set myself resolutely to make up for lost time. I think I can fairly say that I have had few idle moments since. I have probably put as much hard work into life as most men on this continent. Certainly I have put into it all the work that my physical powers, especially my eyes, would permit. I studied law in Concord the first year after graduation. I used to get up at six o'clock in the morning, go to the office, make a fire and read law until breakfast time, which was at seven in the summer and half-past in the winter. Then I went home to breakfast and got back in about three-quarters of an hour and spent the forenoon until one diligently reading law. After dinner, at two o'clock, I read history until four. I spent the next two hours in walking alone in the woods and roads of Concord and the neighboring towns, went back to the office at seven, read a little geometry and algebra, reviewing the slender mathematics which I had studied in college, and then spent two hours in reading Greek. I read through Thucydides, Homer and Xenophon's Hellenica and some other Greek books in that year. Sundays I went to church twice, but shut myself up in a room at home the rest of the day and read a great quantity of English literature, including Milton, Spencer, Chaucer, George Herbert, South's Sermons and other English classics, reading over again Butler's Analogy and Jouffroy. It has been said that if a man wish to acquire a pure English style he should give his days and nights to Addison. I say that if a law student wish to acquire a vigorous and manly English style, the fit vehicle for conveying weighty thoughts to courts or juries or popular assemblages, let him give his days and nights to Robert South.

I spent two years at the Law School after graduating from the College. I cannot state too strongly my great debt to it, and to Franklin Dexter, Simon Greenleaf, Joel Parker, and Theophilus Parsons. I have no remorse for wasted hours during those two years. The time in a Law School is never likely to be wasted if the youth have in him any spark of generous ambition. He sees the practical relation of what he is learning with what he has to do in life. The

Dane Law School was then, and I suppose it is even more true of it now, a most admirable place for learning the science of law and preparing for its practice. The youth breathed a legal atmosphere from morning till night all the year round. He had the advantage of most admirable instruction, and the resources of a complete library. He listened to the lectures, he studied the text-books, he was drilled in the recitations, he had practice in the moot courts and in the law clubs. He discussed points of law in the boarding-house and on his walks with his companions. He came to know thoroughly the great men who were his instructors, and to understand their mental processes, and the methods by which they had gained their success. The title of old Nathan Dane to a high place on the roll of his country's benefactors, and to the gratitude of the profession of the law, and of all lovers of jurisprudence throughout the country cannot be disputed.

CHAPTER VIII

1846 TO 1850. FOUNDATION OF THE REPUBLICAN PARTY. DANIEL WEBSTER

THE foundation of the Republican party, and my personal memories of Daniel Webster, belong to the same period. I will not try to separate them.

The story I am to tell may seem trivial enough to my readers. But it is to me a very tender and sacred memory. The time was ripe for the great movement that abolished slavery. If no one of the eminent men of that day had ever lived other men would have been found in abundance for the work. If Massachusetts had failed in her duty some other State would have taken her place. But in the Providence of God it was given to Massachusetts to lead in this great battle and it was given to these men whom I have to name to be leaders in Massachusetts. I thank God that it was given to my eyes to behold it. The American people have had many great affairs to deal with since that day. They have had great trials and great triumphs. They have won renown among the nations. They have grown in wealth and in power. They have subdued a mighty rebellion. They have carried their flag in triumph to the ends of the earth. They have wrested the last vestige of power in this hemisphere from an old and proud nation who once occupied the place that England has since occupied and which it seems likely we are to occupy hereafter. They have resisted many strong temptations and acquired much glory. I am afraid they have of late yielded for a time to one strong temptation and missed an opportunity for still greater glory, that never will come back. But there was something in that struggle with slavery which exalted the hearts of those who had a part in it, however humble, as no other political battle in history.

Bliss was it in that dawn to be alive.

And, surely, to be young was far nearer Heaven than Wordsworth found France in the opening of the French Revolution.

I became of age at just about the time when the Free Soil Party, which was the Republican party in another form, was born. In a very humble capacity I stood by its cradle. It awakened in my heart in early youth all the enthusiasm of which my nature was capable, an enthusiasm which from that day to this has never grown cold. No political party in history was ever formed for objects so great and noble. And no political party in history was ever so great in its accomplishment for liberty, progress and law.

I breathed a pure and bracing atmosphere in those days. It was a time of plain living and high thinking. It was a pretty good education, better than that of any university, to be a young Free Soiler in Massachusetts. I had pretty good company, not in the least due to any merit or standing of my own, but only because the men who were enlisted for the war in the great political battle against slavery were bound to each other by a tie to which no freemasonry could be compared. Samuel G. Howe used, when his duties brought him to Worcester on his monthly visit, to spend an hour or two of an afternoon in my office. I was always welcome to an hour's converse with Charles Allen, the man who gave the signal at Philadelphia for breaking away from the Whig Party. Erastus Hopkins occasionally spent a Sunday with me at my boarding house. When I went to Boston I often spent an hour in Richard Dana's office, and was sure of a kindly greeting if I chanced to encounter Sumner. The restless and ubiquitous Henry Wilson, who, as he gathered and inspired the sentiment of the people, seemed often to be in ten places at once, used to think it worth his while to visit me to find out what the boys were thinking of. In 1851 I was made Chairman of the Free Soil County Committee of Worcester County. I do not think there was ever so good a political organization in the country before, or that there ever has been a better one since. The Free Soilers carried all but six, I think, of the fifty-two towns in that county. I was in correspondence with the leading men in every one of them, and could at any time summon them to Worcester, if there were need.

We acquired by the Mexican War nearly six hundred thousand square miles of territory. When the treaty was signed, the struggle began between freedom and slavery for the control of this imperial domain. No reader of the history of Massachusetts will doubt her interest in such a struggle. Three things stood in the way of lovers of liberty in the Commonwealth.

First, the old attachment to the Whig party;

Second, her manufacturing interests; and

Third, her devotion to Daniel Webster.

Massachusetts was a Whig State. There were many things which tended to give that great political organization a permanent hold on her people. Its standard of personal character was of the highest. Its leading men—Saltonstall, Reed, Lawrence, Lincoln, Briggs, Allen, Ashmun, Choate, Winthrop, Davis, Everett, and their associates—were men whose private and public honor was without a stain. Its political managers were not its holders of office or its seekers of office. It contained a large body of able and influential men who wielded the power of absolute disinterestedness. They were satisfied if they could contribute, by counsel or labor, to the well-being of the State by the advancement of their cherished political principles. They asked no other reward. The Whigs were in favor of using wisely, but courageously, the forces of the Nation and State to accomplish public objects for which private powers or municipal powers were inadequate. The Whigs desired to develop manufacture by national protection; to foster internal improvements and commerce by liberal grants for rivers and harbors; to endow railroads and canals for public ways by grants of public lands and from the treasury; to maintain a sound currency; and to establish a uniform system for the collection of debts, and for relieving debtors by a National bankruptcy law.

The Whig policy had made Massachusetts known the world over as the model Commonwealth. It had lent the State's credit to railroads. It had established asylums for the blind and insane and deaf and dumb, and had made liberal gifts to schools. The Massachusetts courts were unsurpassed in the world. Her poor laws were humane. All her administrative policies were wise, sound, and economical.

They asked from the National Government only a system of protection that should foster home manufacture, and that they might pursue their commercial and manufacturing occupation in peace.

Daniel Webster was the idol of the people. He was at the fulness of his great intellectual power. The series of speeches and professional and political achievements which began with the oration at Plymouth in 1820 was still in progress. The Whigs of Massachusetts disliked slavery; but they loved the Union. Their political gospel was found in Webster's reply to Hayne and his great debates with Calhoun. It was the one heart's desire of the youth of Massachusetts that their beloved idol and leader should be crowned with the great office of the Presidency.

Mr. Webster tried to avert the conflict by voting against the treaty with Mexico, by which we acquired our great territory in the far West; but in vain. The Whigs feared the overthrow of the Whig Party. The manufacturer and the merchant dreaded an estrangement that would cause the loss of their southern trade, and with it all hope of a law that would protect their manufactures.

It was in this condition of things that I cast my first vote in November, 1847, shortly after I became of age. It was for the Whig Governor. The Whig Party was already divided into two sections, one known as "Cotton Whigs," and the other as "Conscience Whigs." These names had been suggested in a debate in the State Senate in which Mr. Thomas G. Carey, an eminent Boston merchant, had deprecated some proposed anti-slavery resolutions by saying that they were likely to make an unfavorable impression in the South, and to be an injury to business interests; to which Mr. E. R. Hoar of Middlesex answered, that "he thought it quite as desirable that the Legislature should represent the conscience as the cotton of the Commonwealth."

Both parties struggled for the possession of the Whig organization, and both parties hoped for the powerful support of Mr. Webster. The leader of the manufacturing interest was Mr. Abbott Lawrence, a successful, wealthy manufacturer of great business capacity, large generosity, and princely fortune. He had for some years chafed under Mr. Webster's imperious and arrogant bearing. He was on terms of personal intimacy with Henry Clay, and was understood to have inspired the resolutions of the Whig State Convention, a few years before, which by implication condemned Mr. Webster for remaining in President Tyler's Cabinet when his Whig colleagues resigned. But the people of Massachusetts stood by Webster. After the ratification of the Ashburton Treaty, he came home to reassert his old title to leadership and to receive an ovation in Faneuil Hall. In his speech he declared with a significant glance at Mr. Lawrence, then sitting upon the platform: "I am a Whig, a Massachusetts Whig, a Boston Whig, a Faneuil Hall Whig. If any man wishes to read me out of the pale of that communion, let him begin, here, now, on the spot, and we will see who goes out first."

The first time I remember seeing Daniel Webster was June 17, 1843, at Bunker Hill. The students of Harvard, where I was a freshman, had a place in the procession. We marched from Cambridge to Boston, three miles and a half, and stood in our places for hours, and then marched over to Charlestown. We were tired out when the oration began. There was a little wind which carried the sound of Mr. Webster's voice away from the place where we stood; so it was hard to hear him during the first part of his speech. He spoke slowly and with great deliberation. There was little in the greater part of that weighty discourse to excite a youthful auditor; but the great thing was to look at the great orator. Waldo Emerson, who was there, said of him:

"His countenance, his figure, and his manners were all in so grand a style that he was, without effort, as superior to his most eminent rivals as they were to the humblest. He alone of all men did not disappoint the eye and the ear, but was a fit figure in the landscape. There was the Monument, and there was Webster. He knew well that a little more or less of rhetoric signified nothing; he was only to say plain and equal things—grand things, if he had them; and if he had them not, only to abstain from saying unfit things—and the whole occasion was answered by his presence."

He went almost through his weighty discourse without much effect upon his auditors other than that which Emerson so well described. But the wind changed before he finished, and blew toward the other quarter where the boys stood; and he almost lifted them from their feet as his great organ tones rolled out his closing sentences:

"And when both we and our children shall have been consigned to the house appointed for all living, may love of country and pride of country glow with equal fervor among those to whom our names and our blood shall have descended! And then, when honored and decrepit age shall lean against the base of this monument, and troops of ingenuous youth shall be gathered around it, and when the one shall speak to the other of its objects, the purposes of its construction, and the great and glorious events with which it is connected, there shall rise from every youthful breast the ejaculation, 'Thank God, I also—AM AN AMERICAN!'"

Mr. Webster came to Concord in the summer of 1843 as counsel for William Wyman, President of the Phœnix Bank of Charlestown, who was indicted for embezzling the funds of the bank. This was one of the *causes célébres* of the day. Wyman had been a business man of high standing. Such offences were rare in those days, and the case would have attracted great attention whoever had been for the defence. But the defendant's counsel were Daniel Webster, Rufus Choate, Franklin Dexter, and my brother, E. R. Hoar, a young man lately admitted to the bar. Mr. Webster, notwithstanding his great fame as a statesman, is said never to have lost his eager interest in causes in which he was retained. When he found himself hard pressed, he put forth all his strength. He was extremely impatient of contradiction. The adulation to which he had been so long accustomed tended to increase a natural, and perhaps not wholly unjustifiable, haughtiness of manner.

The Government was represented by Asahel R. Huntington, of Salem, District Attorney for the district which included Essex and Middlesex. He was a man of great intellectual vigor, unquestioned honesty and courage, possessed of a high sense of the dignity and importance of his office, very plain spoken, and not at all likely to be overawed by any opposing counsel, whatever his fame or dignity. Yet he had a huge reverence for Daniel Webster, whom, like the other Massachusetts Whigs of that day, he probably thought as another described him—

The foremost living man of all the world!

The case was tried three times: The first time at Concord, the second time at Lowell, and the third time at Concord. Mr. Webster had several quite angry encounters with the court and with the prosecuting attorney. He was once exceedingly disrespectful to Judge Washburn, who replied with great mildness that he was sure the eminent counsel's respect for his own character would be enough to prevent him from any disrespect to the court. Mr. Webster was disarmed by the quiet courtesy of the judge, and gave him no further cause for complaint. At Lowell, where Wyman was convicted, Webster saw the case going against him, and interrupted the charge of the judge several times. At last Judge Allen, who was presiding, said: "Mr. Webster, I cannot suffer myself to be interrupted." Mr. Webster replied: "I cannot suffer my client to be misrepresented." To which the judge answered: "Sit down, sir." Mr. Webster resumed his seat. When the jury went out, Judge Allen turned to the Bar where Mr. Webster was sitting and said: "Mr. Webster." Mr. Webster rose with the unsurpassed courtesy and grace of manner of which he was master, and said: "Will the court pardon me a moment?" He then proceeded to express his regret for the zeal which had impelled him to a seeming disrespect to His Honor, and expressed his sorrow for what had occurred; and the incident was at an end.

At the first trial at Concord, Mr. Webster had frequent altercations with District Attorney Huntington. In his closing argument, which is said to have been one of great power, and which he began by an eloquent reference to the battle of Concord Bridge, which, he said, was fought by Concord farmers that their children might enjoy the blessings of an impartial administration of justice under the law, he said that it was unlikely that Wyman could have abstracted large sums from the bank and no trace of the money be found in his possession. He was a man of small property, living simply and plainly, without extravagant habits or anything which would have been likely to tempt him to such crime. When Huntington came to reply he said, very roughly: "They want to know what's become of the money. I can tell you what's become of the money. Five thousand dollars to one counsel, three thousand dollars to another, two thousand to another," waving his hand in succession toward Webster and Choate and Dexter. Such fees, though common enough now, seemed enormous in those days. Choate smiled in his peculiar fashion, and said nothing; Franklin Dexter looked up from a newspaper he was reading, and exclaimed: "This is beneath our notice"; but Mr. Webster rose to his feet and said with great indignation: "Am I to sit here to hear myself charged with sharing the spoils with a thief?" The presiding judge said: "The counsel for the Government will confine himself to the evidence." That was all. But Mr. Webster was deeply incensed. The jury disagreed. Mr. Webster came to the next trial prepared with an attack on Huntington, in writing, covering many pages, denouncing his method and conduct. This he read to my brother. But Huntington who, as I have said, adored Webster, was unwilling to have another encounter—not in the least from any dread of his antagonist, but solely from his dislike to have a quarrel with the man on earth he most reverenced. Accordingly, Mr. Wells, the District Attorney of Greenfield, was called in, who conducted the trial at Lowell and succeeded in getting a conviction. My brother, who was very fond of Huntington, took an occasion some time afterward to tell Mr. Webster how much Huntington regretted the transaction, and how great was his feeling of reverence and attachment for him. Mr. Webster was placated, and afterward, when an edition of his speeches was published, sent a copy to Huntington with an inscription testifying to his respect.

The general reader may not care for the legal history of the trial, but it may have a certain interest for lawyers. Mr. Wyman was indicted for embezzlement of the funds of the bank under the Revised Statutes of Massachusetts, which provided that "if any cashier or other officer, agent or servant of any incorporated bank shall embezzle or fraudulently convert to his own use the property of the bank, he shall be punished," etc. It was earnestly contended that a president of a bank was not an officer within the meaning of the statute; but this contention was overruled by the presiding judge, who was sustained in that view by the Supreme Court on exception. There was, however, no such offence as embezzlement known to the common law. So a person who fraudulently converted to his own use the property of another could only be convicted of larceny; and the offence of larceny could not be committed where the offender had been entrusted with the possession of the property converted, the essence of larceny being the felonious taking of the property from the possession of the owner. Further, nobody could be convicted of larceny except on an indictment or complaint which set forth the time and place of each single conversion. So, if a servant or agent appropriated the fund of his principal, the embezzlement extending over a long period of time, and it was not possible to set forth or to prove the time, place, and circumstance of any particular taking, the offender could not be convicted. The statute to which I have just referred was intended to cure both these difficulties; first, by making persons liable to punishment who fraudulently appropriated the property of others, notwithstanding they had come rightfully into possession; and next, the necessity of setting forth the particular transaction was obviated by an enactment that it should be enough to prove the embezzlement of any sum of money within six months of the time specified in the indictment.

After the conviction of Wyman, the case was carried to the Supreme Court, which held that the statute making bank officers liable included bank presidents. But the court held that the other part of the statute, providing for the mode of setting forth the offence in the indictment, did not apply to bank officers; and that they could only be held on an indictment which described the particular transaction, with time and place. So the verdict of guilty against Wyman was set aside, and a new trial ordered.

Before the new trial came on at Concord, a statute was passed by the Legislature for the purpose of meeting this very case, extending the provisions of the Revised Statutes as to the mode of pleading in such cases to officers of banks. It was claimed and argued by Mr. Choate, with great zeal, eloquence, and learning, that this was an *ex post facto* law, which could not, under the Constitution, be made applicable to transactions which happened before its passage. Mr. Choate argued this question for several hours. The court took time for consideration, and overruled his contention. There seemed nothing for it but to go to trial again on the facts, upon which one verdict of guilty had already been had. As they were going into the court-house in the morning, Mr. Choate said to Mr. Hoar, whose chief part in the trial, so far, had been finding law books, hunting up authorities, and taking notes of the evidence: "You made a suggestion to me at the last trial which I did not attend to much at the time; but I remember thinking afterward there was something in it." Mr. Hoar replied: "It seems to me that Wyman cannot be convicted of embezzlement unless the funds of the bank were entrusted to him. They must either have been in his actual possession or under his control. There is nothing in the office of president which involves such an authority. It cannot exist unless by the express action of the directors, or as the result of a course of business of the bank." The facts alleged against Wyman were that he had authorized the discount of the notes of some friends of his who were irresponsible, and that he had, in some way, shared the proceeds. Mr. Choate seized upon the suggestion. The Government witnesses, who were chiefly the directors of the bank, were asked in cross-examination whether they had not consented that Mr. Wyman should have the right to dispose of the funds of the bank, or to give him power or authority to dispose of them. They supposed the question was put with the intent of making them morally, if not legally, accomplices in his guilt, or of charging them with want of fidelity or gross carelessness in their office. Accordingly, each of them indignantly denied the imputation, and testified that Wyman had no power or authority to authorize the discount or to meddle with the funds. When the Government case closed, the counsel asked the court to rule that as the funds were never entrusted to the possession of Wyman he could not be convicted of embezzlement. The court so held and directed an acquittal. This is another instance, not unusual in trials in court, of the truth of the old rhyme, with which the readers of "Quentin Durward" are familiar:

> The page slew the boar,
> The peer had the gloire.

Mr. Webster always had a strong and kindly regard for my brother. When Mr. Hoar visited Washington in 1836, Webster received him with great kindness, showed him about the Capitol, and took him to the Supreme Court, where he argued a case. Mr. Webster began by alluding very impressively to the great changes which had taken place in that Tribunal since he first appeared as counsel before them. He said: "No one of the judges who were here then, remains. It has been my duty to pass upon the question of the confirmation of every member of the Bench; and I may say that I treated your honors with entire impartiality, for I voted against every one of you." After the argument was over Mr. Webster gave Mr. Hoar a very interesting sketch of the character of each of the judges, and told him the reasons which caused him to vote against confirmation in each case.

The next time I saw Daniel Webster was on July 4, 1844. He made a call at my father's house in Concord. I was near one of the front windows, and heard a shout from a little crowd that had gathered in the street, and looked out just as Mr. Webster was coming up the front steps. He turned, put his hand into his bosom under his waistcoat and made a stately salutation, and then turned and knocked at the door and was admitted. He was physically the most splendid specimen of noble manhood my eyes ever beheld. It is said, I suppose truly, that he was but a trifle over five feet nine inches high, and weighed one hundred and fifty-four pounds. But then, as on all other occasions that I saw him, I should have been prepared to affirm that he was over six feet high and weighed, at least, two hundred. The same glamour is said to have attended Louis XIV., whose majesty of bearing was such that it never was discovered that he was a man of short stature until he was measured for his coffin.

Mr. Webster was then in the very vigor of his magnificent manhood. He stood perfectly erect. His head was finely poised upon his shoulders. His beautiful black eyes shone out through the caverns of his deep brows like lustrous jewels. His teeth were white and regular, and his smile when he was in gracious mood, especially when talking to women, had an irresistible charm. I remember very little that he said. One thing was, when the backwardness or forwardness of the season was spoken of, that there was a day—I think it was June 15—when, in every year vegetation was at about the same condition of forwardness, whether the spring were early or late. A gentleman who was in the room said: "You have the cool breezes of the sea at Marshfield?" "There, as at other sea places," replied Mr. Webster. When he rose to go, he said: "I have the honor to be a member of the Young Men's Whig Club of Boston. I must be in my place in the ranks."

I heard him also in Faneuil Hall, in the autumn of 1844, after the elections in Maine and Pennsylvania and in the South had made certain the defeat of Mr. Clay. I remember little that he said, except from reading the speech since.

What chiefly impressed the audience was the quotation from Milton, so well known now:

> What though the field be lost?
> All is not lost; the unconquerable will,
> And study of revenge, immortal hate,
> And courage never to submit or yield,
> And what is else not to be overcome.

I also saw Mr. Webster at the inauguration of Edward Everett as President of Harvard, April 30, 1846. It was perhaps the proudest period of Webster's life. It was also, perhaps, the greatest day of the life of Edward Everett. Webster had been Everett's great over-shadower. Gov. Everett would have been, but for him, the chief public man and the orator of Massachusetts at that time. He had returned from the Court of St. James crowned with new laurels, and had been called to succeed Josiah Quincy as the head of the University. By a simple but impressive inaugural ceremony the Governor had just invested Mr. Everett with his office, and delivered to him the keys and the charter. Everett was stepping forward to deliver his inaugural address when Webster, who had come out from Boston a little late, came in upon the stage by a side door. President and orator and occasion were all forgotten. The whole assembly rose to greet him. It seemed as if the cheering and the clapping of hands and the waving of handkerchiefs would never leave off. The tears gushed down the cheeks of women and young men and old. Everything was forgotten but the one magnificent personality. When the din had subsided somewhat, Mr. Everett, with his never-failing readiness and grace, said: "I would I might anticipate a little the function of my office, and saying—*Expectatur oratio in vernacula*—call upon my illustrious friend who has just entered upon the stage to speak for me. But I suppose that the proprieties of the occasion require that I speak for myself."

It is to the credit of Mr. Everett and of that other Massachusetts orator, Rufus Choate, that no tinge of jealousy or of envy ever embittered in the smallest degree their hearty love and support of their friend. They were his pupils, his companions, his supporters, his lovers, while he lived, and were his best eulogists when he died.

I heard another speech of his, which I think was never reported. He appeared before a Committee of the Legislature as counsel for the remonstrants against the scheme to fill up the Back Bay lands.

I do not think the employment of a Senator of the United States as counsel before the Legislature would be approved by public opinion now.

I do not know what year it was, but probably 1849 or 1850. He had grown old. But I learned more of the fashion of his mental operations than could be learned from his speeches on great occasions, especially after they had been revised for publication. He spoke with much contempt of a petition signed by many of the foremost merchants and business men of Boston. He described with great sarcasm the process of carrying about such petitions, and the relief of the person to whom they were presented on finding he was not asked to give any money. "Oh, yes, I'll sign—I'll sign." He then read out one after another the names of men well known and honored in the city. He threw down the petition with contempt, and the long sheet fell and unrolled upon the floor.

He had a singular habit, which made it wearisome to listen to his ordinary speech, of groping after the most suitable word, and trying one synonym after another till he got that which suited him best. "Why is it, Mr. Chairman, that there has gathered, congregated, this great number of inhabitants, dwellers, here; that these roads, avenues, routes of travel, highways, converge, meet, come together, here? Is it not because we have here a sufficient, ample, safe, secure, convenient, commodious, port, harbor, haven?" Of course, when the speech came to be printed all the synonyms but the best one would be left out.

Mr. Webster seemed rather feeble at that time, and called upon his friend Mr. William Dehon to read for him the evidence and extracts from reports with which he had to deal. His tone was the tone of ordinary conversation, and his speech, while it would not be called hesitating, was exceedingly slow and deliberate. I have been told by persons who heard him in the Supreme Court in his later years that the same characteristic marked his arguments there, and that some of his passages made very little impression upon the auditors, although they seemed eloquent and powerful when they came to be read afterward.

His is frequently spoken of as a nervous Saxon style. That is a great mistake, except as to a few passages where he rose to a white heat. If any person will open a volume of his speeches at random, it will be found that the characteristic of his sentences is a somewhat ponderous Latinity.

A considerable number of Democrats joined the Free Soil movement in 1848. Conspicuous among them was Marcus Morton, who had been Governor and one of our ablest Supreme Court judges, and his son, afterward Chief Justice, then just rising into distinction as a lawyer. The members of the Liberty Party also, who had cast votes for Birney in 1844, were ready for the new movement. But the Free Soil Party derived its chief strength, both of numbers and influence, from the Whigs. The Anti-Slavery Whigs clung to Webster almost to the last. He had disappointed them by opposing the resolution they offered at the Whig State Convention, pledging the party to support no candidate not known by his acts or declared opinions to be opposed to the extension of slavery. But he had coupled his opposition with a declaration of his own unalterable opposition to that extension, and had said, speaking of those who were in favor of the declaration: "It is not their thunder."

He declared in the Senate, as late as 1848: "My opposition to the increase of slavery in this country, or to the increase of slave representation in Congress, is general and universal. It has no reference to lines of latitude or points of the compass. I shall oppose all such extension, and all such increase, at all times, under all circumstances, even against all inducements, against all combinations, against all compromises."

So the Anti-Slavery Whigs eagerly supported him as their candidate for the Whig nomination in 1848.

If Mr. Webster had been nominated for the Presidency in 1848, the Free Soil Party would not have come into existence that year. There would have been probably some increase in the numbers of the Liberty Party; yet the Anti-Slavery Whigs of Massachusetts would have trusted him. But the nomination of General Taylor, a Southerner, one of the largest slaveholders in the country, whose laurels had been gained in the odious Mexican War, upon a platform silent upon the engrossing subject of the extension of slavery, could not be borne. The temper of the Whig National Convention was exhibited in a way to irritate the lovers of freedom in Massachusetts. When some allusion was made to her expressed opinions, it was received with groans and cries of "Curse Massachusetts." But, on the whole, the Massachusetts Whigs shared the exultant anticipation of triumph, and of regaining the power from which they had been excluded since the time of John Quincy Adams, except for the month of Harrison's short official life. But as the convention was about to adjourn, intoxicated with hope and triumph, Charles Allen, a delegate from Massachusetts, a man of slender figure, rose, and with a quiet voice declared the Whig Party dissolved. Never was prediction received with more derision; never was prediction more surely fulfilled. He was reinforced by Henry Wilson, afterward Vice-President of the United States.

Immediately on their return from Philadelphia, a call was circulated for a convention to be held at Worcester of all persons opposed to the nomination of Cass and Taylor. The call was written by E. R. Hoar. My father, Samuel Hoar, was its first signer.

This is the call. It should be preserved in a form more enduring than the leaflet, of which I possess, perhaps, the only copy in existence.

"To the People of Massachusetts.

"The Whig National Convention have nominated General Taylor for President of the United States. In so doing they have exceeded their just authority, and have proposed a candidate whom no Northern Whig is bound to support.

"He is not a Whig, when tried by the standard of our party organization. He has never voted for a Whig candidate, has declared that the party must not look to him as an exponent of its principles, that he would accept the nomination of the Democratic Party, and that he would not submit his claims to the decision of the Whigs, acting through their regularly constituted Convention.

"He is not a Whig, if judged by the opinions he entertains upon questions of public policy. Upon the great questions of currency and Finance, of Internal Improvements, of Protection to American Industry, so far from agreeing with the Whigs, he has distinctly avowed that he has formed no opinion at all.

"He is not a Whig, if measured by the higher standard of principle, to which the Whigs of Massachusetts and of the North have pledged themselves solemnly, deliberately, and often. He is not opposed to the extension of Slavery over new territories, acquired, and to be acquired, by the United States. He is a Slave-holder, and has been selected because he could command votes which no Whig from the free States could receive.

"To make room for him, the trusted and faithful Champions of our cause have all been set aside.

"The Whigs of Massachusetts, by their Legislature, and in their popular assemblies, have resolved, that opposition to the extension of Slavery is a fundamental article in their political faith. They have spoken with scorn and upbraiding of those Northern Democrats who would sacrifice the rights and the interests of the Free States upon the altar of party subserviency.

"The Whigs of the Legislature have recently declared to the country, 'that if success can attend the party, only by the sacrifice of Whig principles, or some of them,' they do not mean to be thus successful; that they are determined 'to support a candidate who will not suffer us to be overbalanced by annexations of foreign territory, nor by the further extension of the institution of Slavery, which is equally repugnant to the feelings, and incompatible with the political rights of the Free States'; and that they 'believe it to be the resolute purpose of the Whig people of Massachusetts, to support these sentiments, and carry into effect the design which they manifest.'

"Believing that the support of General Taylor's nomination is required by no obligations of party fidelity, and that to acquiesce in it would be the abandonment of principles which we hold most dear, treachery to the cause of Freedom, and the utter prostration of the interests of Free Labor and the Rights of Freemen:

"The undersigned, Whigs of Massachusetts, call upon their fellow-citizens throughout the Commonwealth, who are opposed to the nomination of CASS and TAYLOR, to meet in Convention at Worcester, on *Wednesday,* the 28th day of June current, to take such steps as the occasion shall demand, in support of the PRINCIPLES to which they are pledged, and to co-operate with the other Free States in a Convention for this purpose."

My first political service was folding and directing these circulars. The Convention was held, and Samuel Hoar presided. It was addressed by men most of whom afterward became eminent in the public service. Among them were Charles Sumner, Charles Francis Adams, Henry Wilson, E. R. Hoar, Edward L. Keyes, Charles Allen, Lewis D. Campbell, of Ohio, and Abraham Payne, of Rhode Island. Richard H. Dana was present, but I think he did not speak. William Lloyd Garrison and Francis Jackson were present, but took no part whatever. I rode to Boston in a freight car after the convention was over, late at night. Garrison and Jackson were sitting together and talking to a group of friends. Garrison seemed much delighted with the day's work, but said he heard too much talk about the likelihood that some of the resolutions would be popular and bring large numbers of votes to the party. He said: "All you should ask is, what is the rightful position? and then take it." Among the resolutions was this:

"That Massachusetts looks to Daniel Webster to declare to the Senate and to uphold before the country the policy of the Free States; that she is relieved to know that he has not endorsed the nomination of General Taylor; and that she invokes him at this crisis to turn a deaf ear to 'optimists' and 'quietists,' and to speak and act as his heart and his great mind shall lead him."

Daniel Webster's son Fletcher was present, and heartily in accord with the meeting; and this resolution was passed with his full approval. It met great opposition from the men who had come into the movement from the Liberty Party and from the Democratic Party. The shouts of "No, no; too late" were nearly, if not quite, equal to the expressions of approval. But the president declared that it was passed.

Mr. Webster sulked in his tent during the summer, and at last, September 1, 1848, made a speech at Marshfield, in which he declared the nomination of Taylor not fit to be made, but gave it a half-hearted support. My brother, Judge E. R. Hoar, had been an enthusiastic admirer of Webster, who had treated him with great personal kindness; and, as I have said, he had been associated with Mr. Webster in the famous Wyman trial. Mr. Webster made a speech in the Senate in August, declaring his renewed opposition to the extension of slavery. Mr. Hoar wrote a letter expressing his satisfaction with that speech, and urging him to take his proper place at the head of the Northern Free Soil movement. This is Mr. Webster's reply. It is interesting as the last anti-slavery utterance of Daniel Webster.

MARSHFIELD, August 23, 1848.

My Dear Sir:

I am greatly obliged to you, for your kind and friendly letter. You overrate, I am sure, the value of my speech, it was quite unpremeditated and its merit, if any, consists I presume in its directness and its brevity. It mortified me to see that some of the newspaper writers speak of it as the "taking of a position"; as if it contained something new for me to say. You are not one of them, my dear sir, but there are those who will not believe that I am an anti-slavery man unless I repeat the declaration once a week. I expect they will soon require a periodical affidavit. You know, that as early as 1830 in my speech on Foote's resolutions, I drew upon me the anger of enemies, and a regret of friends by what I said against slavery, and I hope that from that day to this my conduct has been consistent. But nobody seems to be esteemed to be worthy of confidence who is not a new convert. And if the new convert be as yet but half converted, so much the better. This I confess a little tries one's patience. But I can assure you in my own case, it will not either change my principles or my conduct.

It is utterly impossible for me to support the Buffalo nomination. I have no confidence in Mr. Van Buren, not the slightest. I would much rather trust General Taylor than Mr. Van Buren even on this very question of slavery, for I believe that General Taylor is an honest man and I am sure he is not so much committed on the wrong side, as I know Mr. Van Buren to have been for fifteen years. I cannot concur even with my best friends in giving the lead in a great question to a notorious opponent to the cause. Besides; there are other great interests of the country in which you and I hold Mr. Van Buren to be essentially wrong, and it seems to me that in consenting to form a party under him Whigs must consent to bottom their party on one idea only, and also to adopt as the representative of that idea a head chosen on a strange emergency from among its steadiest opposers. It gives me pain to differ from Whig friends whom I know to be as much attached to universal liberty as I am, and they cannot be more so. I am grieved particularly to be obliged to differ in anything from yourself and your excellent father, for both of whom I have cherished such long and affectionate regards. But I cannot see it to be my duty to join in a secession from the Whig Party for the purpose of putting Mr. Van Buren at the head of the Government. I pray you to assure yourself, my dear Sir, of my continued esteem and attachment, and remember me kindly and cordially to your father.

Yours, etc.,
DANIEL WEBSTER.

Honorable E. Rockwood Hoar.

Mr. Hoar had before had a somewhat interesting interview with Mr. Webster to the same effect. Late in the winter, before the convention at Philadelphia, some young Whigs had a dinner at the Tremont House, to concert measures to support his candidacy. There were forty or fifty present. Mr. Webster was expected to speak to them, but his daughter Julia was very ill. He sent them a message that he would see them at the house in Summer Street where he was staying. So when the dinner was half over, the party walked in procession to Mr. Paige's house. As Judge Hoar described the interview, he seemed very glum. He shook hands with the young men as they passed by him, but said very little. There was an awkward silence, and they were about to take leave, when the absurdity of the position struck Mr. Hoar, who was the youngest of the party, rather forcibly. Just then he heard Mr. Webster say to somebody near him: "The day for eminent public men seems to have gone by." Whereupon Hoar stepped forward and made him a brief speech, which he began by saying that the object of their coming together was to show that, in their opinion, the day for eminent public men had not gone by, and some more to the same effect. Webster waked up and his eyes flashed and sparkled. He made a speech full of vigor and fire. He spoke of his name being brought before the Whig convention at Philadelphia, and of his fidelity to the party. He said that whether his own name should be in the judgment of the convention suitable or the best to present to the country the convention would determine, and added: "If the convention shall select anyone of our conspicuous leaders, trained and experienced in civil affairs, of national reputation as a statesman, he will receive my hearty support. But if I am asked whether I will advise the convention at Philadelphia to nominate, or if nominated I will recommend the people to support for the office of President of the United States, a swearing, fighting, frontier colonel, I only say that I shall not do it."

Many people think that if Mr. Webster would have supported General Taylor's policy of dealing with the questions relating to slavery it would have prevailed, and that the country would have been pacified and the Civil War avoided. I do not think so. The forces on both sides who were bringing on that conflict were too powerful to be subdued by the influence of any individual statesman. The irrepressible conflict had to be fought out. But Mr. Webster's attitude not only estranged him from the supporters of General Taylor in his own party, but, of course, made an irreparable breach between him and the anti-slavery men who had founded the Free Soil Party. He was the chief target for all anti-slavery arrows from March 7, 1850, to his death.

When I was in the Harvard Law School, Mr. Webster was counsel in a very interesting divorce case where Choate was upon the other side. The parties were in high social position and very well known. Mr. Choate's client, who was the wife, was charged with adultery. I did not hear the closing argument, but my classmates who did reported that Mr. Webster spoke of the woman with great severity and argued the case with a scriptural plainness of speech. He likened the case of the husband bound to an adulterous wife to the old Hebrew punishment of fastening a living man to a corpse. "Who shall deliver me from the body of this death?" But Judge Fletcher, who held the court, decided in favor of the wife.

The meeting which gathered at Worcester in pursuance of the above call, inaugurated for the first time a party for the sole object of resisting the extension of slavery. The Liberty Party, which had cast a few votes in the presidential election of 1840, and which, in 1844, had turned the scale in New York and so in the nation against Mr. Clay, was willing to support the candidates of other parties who were personally unobjectionable to them in this respect. But the Free Soil Party, of which the present Republican party is but the continuation under a change of name, determined that no person should receive its support for any national office, who himself continued his association with either of the old political organizations.

The Free Soil Party of Massachusetts cast in the presidential election of 1848 only about 37,000 votes, but it included among its supporters almost every man in the Commonwealth old enough to take part in politics who has since acquired any considerable national reputation. Charles Sumner who had become known to the public as an orator and scholar by three or four great orations, was just at the threshold of his brilliant career. Charles Francis Adams, who had served respectably but without great distinction, in each branch of the Legislature, brought to the cause his inflexible courage, his calm judgment, and the inspiration of his historic name. John A. Andrew, then a young lawyer in Boston, afterward to become illustrious as the greatest war Governor in the Union, devoted to the cause an eloquence stimulant and inspiring as a sermon of Paul. John G. Palfrey, then a Whig member of Congress from the Middlesex District, discussed the great issue in speeches singularly adapted to reach the understanding and gratify the taste of the people of Massachusetts, and in a series of essays whose vigor and compactness Junius might have envied, and with a moral power which Junius could never have reached. Anson Burlingame, afterward Minister to China, captivated large crowds with his inspiring eloquence.* Samuel G. Howe, famous in both hemispheres by his knightly service in the cause of Greek independence, famous also by his philanthropic work in behalf of the insane and blind, brought his great influence to the party. Henry Wilson, a mechanic, whose early training had been that of the shoemaker's shop, but who understood the path by which to reach the conscience and understanding of the workingmen of Massachusetts better than any other man,

---

* Shortly after Burlingame came into active life, he made a journey to Europe. The American Minister obtained for him a ticket of admission to the House of Commons. He was shown into a very comfortable seat in the gallery. In a few minutes an official came and told him he must leave that seat; that the gallery where he was was reserved for Peers. They are very particular about such things there. Burlingame got up to go out when an old Peer who happened to be sitting by and had heard what was said, interposed. "Let him stay, let him stay. He is a Peer in his own country." "I am a Sovereign in my own country, Sir," replied Burlingame, "and shall lose caste if I associate with Peers." And he went out.

had been also a delegate to the Convention at Philadelphia, and had united with Judge Allen in denunciation of its surrender of liberty. Stephen C. Phillips, a highly respected merchant of Salem, and formerly Whig Representative from the Essex District, gave the weight of his influence in the same direction. Samuel Hoar, who had been driven from South Carolina when he attempted to argue the case for the imprisoned colored seamen of Massachusetts before the courts of the United States, one of the most distinguished lawyers of the Massachusetts bar, came from his retirement in his old age to give his service in the same cause; of which his son, E. R. Hoar, was also a constant, untiring, and enthusiastic champion. Richard H. Dana, master of an exquisite English style, the only Massachusetts advocate who ever encountered Rufus Choate on equal terms, threw himself into the cause with all the ardor of his soul. On the Connecticut River, George Ashmun, the most powerful of the Whig champions in western Massachusetts, found more than his match in Erastus Hopkins. William Claflin, afterward Speaker, Lieutenant Governor, and Governor of Massachusetts, member of the National House of Representatives, and Chairman of the Republican National Committee, was then in early youth. But he had already gained a competent fortune by his business sagacity. He brought to the cause his sound judgment, his warm and affectionate heart, and his liberal hand. He was then, as he has ever since been, identified with every good and generous cause. His staunch friendship was then, as it has been ever since, the delight and comfort of the champions of freedom in strife and obloquy.

Each of these men would have been amply fitted in all respects for the leader of a great party in State or Nation. Each of them could have defended any cause in which he was a believer, by whatever champion assailed. They had also their allies and associates among the representatives of the press. Among these were Joseph T. Buckingham, of the Boston *Courier,* then the head of the editorial fraternity in Massachusetts; John Milton Earle, the veteran editor of the Worcester *Spy;* William S. Robinson, afterward so widely known as Warrington, whose wit and keen logic will cause his name to be long preserved among the classics of American literature.

I have spoken of some of these men more at length elsewhere. I knew them, all but two, very intimately. I only knew Joseph T. Buckingham by sight. He edited the Boston *Courier* with great ability. He was a member of both Houses of the Massachusetts Legislature. He was a member of the State Senate in 1850 and 1851. He left the *Courier* in June, 1848, about the time the Free Soil movement begun, and was not active in politics afterward.

I had no personal acquaintance with Charles Francis Adams. I have known his son, Charles Francis Adams, President of the Massachusetts Historical Society, pretty well. He inherits a great deal of the ability and independence which belongs to his race. He would undoubtedly have taken a very high place in the public and official life of his generation if he had found himself in accord with either of the great political parties.

I do not think anybody, except the very intimate friends of Charles Francis Adams, was aware of his great abilities until he manifested them amid the difficulties of the English Mission. They were known, however, to a few men who were intimate with him. I was quite astonished one day when I called on Dr. Palfrey, at his house in Cambridge in 1852, and he told me Mr. Adams was entirely competent for the office of President of the United States.

Mr. Adams was rather dull as a public speaker. He was apt to announce commonplaces slowly and deliberately, as if they were something he thought his audience was listening to for the first time. But the influence of his historic name was very great. His marvellous resemblance to his father and grandfather made a great impression. When he said at Worcester on the 28th of June, 1848: "I say, in words to which I have a hereditary right, 'Sink or Swim, Live or Die, Survive or Perish, I give my hand and my heart to this movement,'" it seemed to the audience as if old John Adams had stepped down from Trumbull's picture of the Signing of the Declaration of Independence to give his benediction.*

Besides these more conspicuous leaders, there was to be found, in almost every town and village in Massachusetts, some man eminent among his neighbors for purity of life, for philanthropy, and for large intelligence who was ready to join the new party. The glowing hopes and dreams and aspirations of youth were inspired by the muse of Whittier and Longfellow and Lowell and Bryant. The cause of free labor appealed to the strongest sympathies of the mechanics of Essex and the skilled laborers of Worcester.

Four years afterward Daniel Webster, as he lay dying at Marshfield, said to the friend who was by his side: "The Whig candidate will obtain but one or two States, and it is well; as a national party, the Whigs are ended."

* I like very much the epitaph which his sons placed over him in the burial place at Quincy. Every word of it is true.

THIS STONE
MARKS THE GRAVE OF
CHARLES FRANCIS ADAMS
SON OF JOHN QUINCY
AND LOUISA CATHERINE (JOHNSON)
ADAMS
BORN 18 AUGUST 1807
Trained from his youth in politics and letters
His manhood strengthened by the convictions
Which had inspired his fathers
He was among the first to serve
And among the most steadfast to support
That new revolution
Which restored the principles of liberty
To public law
And secured to his country
The freedom of its soil
During seven troubled and anxious years
Minister of the United States in England
afterward arbitrator at the tribunal of Geneva
He failed in no task which his Government imposed
Yet won the respect and confidence
of two great nations
Dying 21 November 1886
He left the example
of high powers nobly used
and the remembrance
of a spotless name.

FOUNDATION OF REPUBLICAN PARTY

The Whig Party retained its organization in Massachusetts until 1856; but its intellect and its moral power were gone. Mr. Winthrop, as appears from the excellent "Life" published by his son, had no sympathy with Mr. Webster's position. Mr. Webster died, a disappointed man, in the autumn of 1852. He took no part in political affairs in Massachusetts after 1850. Mr. Choate, who was to follow his great leader to the grave within a few years, transferred his allegiance to the Democrats. Mr. Everett, after a brief service in the Senate, a service most uncongenial to his own taste, resigned his seat in the midst of the angry conflict on the Nebraska bill, and devoted himself to literary pursuits until, when the war broke out, he threw himself with all his zeal, power, and eloquence into the cause of his country.

CHAPTER IX

LIFE IN WORCESTER

AFTER leaving college I studied for a year in my brother's office in Concord, then for two years at the Harvard Law School, and afterward for four months in the office of Judge Benjamin F. Thomas in Worcester. I was led to choose Worcester as a place to live in chiefly for the reason that that city and county were the stronghold of the new Anti-Slavery Party, to which cause I was devoted with all my heart and soul. I have never regretted the choice, and have spent my life there, except when in Washington, for considerably more than half a century. In that time Worcester has grown from a city of fifteen thousand to a city of one hundred and thirty thousand people. I can conceive of no life more delightful for a man of public spirit than to belong to a community like that which combines the youth and vigor and ambition of a western city with the refinement and conveniences, and the pride in a noble history, of an old American community. It is a delight to see it grow and a greater delight to help it grow,—to help improve its schools, and found its Public Library, and help lay the foundations of great institutions of learning. Worcester had an admirable Bar, admirable clergymen, and physicians of great skill and eminence. Among her clergymen was Edward Everett Hale, then in early youth, but already famous as a preacher throughout the country. There was no Unitarian pulpit where he was not gladly welcomed. So his congregation here, by way of exchange, heard the most famous pulpit orators of the country.

Among the physicians was Dr. Joseph Sargent, a man then without a superior in his profession in Massachusetts. The friendship I formed with him in 1849 lasted till his death, more than forty years afterward.

The mechanics of Worcester were unsurpassed for their ingenuity anywhere on the face of the earth. Worcester was the centre and home of invention. Within a circle of twelve miles radius was the home of Blanchard, the inventor of the machine for turning irregular forms; of Elias Howe, the inventor of the sewing machine; of Eli Whitney, the inventor of the cotton gin, which doubled the value of every acre of cotton-producing land in the country; of Erastus B. Bigelow, the inventor of the carpet machine; of Hawes, the inventor of the envelope machine; of Crompton and Knowles, the creators and perfectors of the modern loom; of Ruggles, Nourse and Mason, in whose establishment the modern plow was brought to perfection, and a great variety of other agricultural implements invented and improved. There were many other men whose inventive genius and public usefulness were entitled to rank with these. The first house-warming furnace was introduced here, and the second cupola furnace was set up near by.

These inventors and mechanics were all men of great public spirit, proud of Worcester, of its great achievements, and its great hope. They got rich rapidly. They and their households made social life most delightful. There was little pride of family or wealth. Men and women were welcomed everywhere on their merits.

The City of Worcester was the heart of one of the foremost agricultural counties in the country. The county stood fourth among American counties in the value of its agricultural products, and the proportion of the value of the product to the value of the lands. It was the spot on the face of the earth where labor got the largest proportion of the joint product of labor and capital. The farmers made an excellent living. They made excellent legislators, excellent town officers, excellent jurors, and excellent clients. I have been at some time or other in my life counsel for every one of the fifty-two towns in Worcester County. I had a large clientage among the farmers. In the intimacy of that relation I got a knowledge of the inmost soul and heart of a class of men who I think constituted what was best in American citizenship, a knowledge which has been a great educational advantage to me and valuable in a thousand ways in my public and professional life.

From the first of December, 1849, until the fourth of March, 1869, I was diligently employed in my profession, save for a single year's service in each house of the Massachusetts Legislature. But during all that time I kept a very zealous interest in political affairs. I was Chairman of the County Committee for several years, made political speeches occasionally, presided at political meetings, always attended the caucus and was in full sympathy and constant communication with the Free Soil and Republican leaders.

The Worcester Bar in my time afforded a delightful companionship. It was like a college class in the old days. My best and most cordial friends were the men whom I was constantly encountering in the courts. The leaders of the Bar when I was admitted to it,—Charles Allen, Emory Washburn, Pliny Merrick, Benjamin F. Thomas, Peter C. Bacon,—would have been great leaders at any Bar in the United States, or on any circuit in England. Study at a law school is invaluable to the youth if he is to rise in his profession; but there is no law school like a court-house when such men are conducting trials. The difficult art of cross-examination, the more difficult art of refraining from cross-examination, can only be learned by watching men who are skilled in the active conduct of trials.

The Supreme Court of Massachusetts at that day with Chief Justice Shaw at its head was without an equal in the country and not surpassed by the Supreme Court of the United States itself. I can conceive of no life more delightful than that of a lawyer in good health, and with good capacity, and with a sufficient clientage, spent in that manly emulation and honorable companionship.

The habit of giving dissenting opinions which has become so common both in the Supreme Court of the United States and of late in the Massachusetts Supreme Court did not then exist. If there were a division on an important question of law the statement of the result was usually "a majority of the Court is of opinion." That was all. I do not believe any court can long retain public confidence and respect when nearly all its opinions in important matters are accompanied by a powerful attack on the soundness of the opinion and the correctness of the judgment from the Bench itself. The Reporter of the Commonwealth of Massachusetts is, I believe, authorized to report the decisions of the court more or less at length at his discretion. If he would exercise that discretion by an absolute refusal to print dissenting opinions, except in a few very great and exceptional cases, he would have the thanks of the profession. It may be harder to put a stop to the practice in the Supreme Court of the United States. That will have to be done, if at all, by the good sense of the Judges. The recent opinions of the Court in what are known as the Insular Cases have shocked the country and greatly diminished the weight and authority of the tribunal. This was not because of public disapproval of the opinion of the Court. It was because upon one of the greatest questions of Constitutional law and Constitutional liberty that ever went to judgment, there could be found no single reason for the decision of the Court strong enough to convince any two judges.

The fact that I have been for nearly thirty-five years in public life, and likely to be, if I live, in public life a few years longer, is an instance of how—

>The best laid schemes o' mice and men
>Gang aft a-gley.

Down to the time I was admitted to the Bar, and indeed for a year later, my dream and highest ambition were to spend my life as what is called an office lawyer, making deeds and giving advice in small transactions. I supposed I was absolutely without capacity for public speaking. I expected never to be married; perhaps to earn twelve or fifteen hundred dollars a year, which would enable me to have a room of my own in some quiet house, and to earn enough to collect rare books that could be had without much cost. I can honestly say with George Herbert: "I protest and I vow I even study thrift, and yet I am scarce able, with much ado, to make one half year's allowance shake hands with the other. And yet if a book of four or five shillings come in my way, I buy it, though I fast for it; yea, sometimes of ten shillings."

But I happened one night in the autumn of 1850 to be at a great mass meeting in the City Hall, at Worcester, which Charles Allen was expected to address. It was the year of the Compromise Measures, including the Fugitive Slave Law, and of Daniel Webster's 7th of March speech. Judge Allen, as he was somewhat apt to do, came in late. A vast audience had gathered and were waiting. Nobody seemed ready to speak. Somebody started the cry, "Hoar! Hoar!" My father and brother were known as leaders in the Free Soil Party, and that I suppose made somebody call on me. I got up in my place in the middle of the hall in great confusion. There were shouts of "platform," "platform." I made my way to the platform, hoping only to make my excuses and get off without being detected. But the people were disposed to be good-natured, and liked what I said. Dr. Stone, the famous stenographic reporter, was present and took it down. It was printed in the Free Soil papers, and from that time I was in considerable demand as a public speaker. The coalition between the Free Soilers and Democrats carried the State of Massachusetts that year and elected Sumner Senator and Boutwell Governor. The next year Worcester failed to elect her representatives to the Legislature, which were voted for all on one ticket and required a majority, and there was to be a second election on the fourth Monday of November. There was a delegate convention to nominate representatives, of which I was a member. When the vote was announced, to my surprise and consternation, I was one of the persons nominated. Nobody had said a word to me about it beforehand. That was Friday night. I told the Convention I could not accept such a nomination without my father's approval. I was then twenty-five years old. It was proposed that the Convention adjourn until the next evening, and that meantime I should go down to Concord and see if I could get my father's leave. Accordingly the Convention adjourned to see if the infant candidate could get permission to accept. My father told me that he thought that to go to the Legislature once would be useful to me in my profession; I should learn how laws were made, and get acquainted with prominent men from different parts of the State. So he advised me to accept, if I would make up my mind that I would go only for one year, and would after that stick to the law, and would never look to politics as a profession or vocation. I accepted the nomination, was elected, and was made Chairman of one of the Law Committees in the House.

I declined a reelection and devoted myself to my profession, except that I served in the Massachusetts Senate one year, 1857, being nominated unexpectedly and under circumstances somewhat like those which attended my former nomination. I was Chairman of the Judiciary Committee that year. I devoted all my time, day and even far into the night, to my legislative duties. I was never absent a single day from my seat in the House in 1852, and was absent only one day from my seat in the Senate, in 1857, when I had to attend to an important law suit. It so happened that there was a severe snow storm that day, which blocked up the railroads, so that there was no quorum in the Senate. I could not myself have got to the State House, if I had tried. I suppose I may say without arrogance that I was the leader of the Free Soil Party in each House when I was a member of it. In 1852 I prepared, with the help of Horace Gray, afterward Judge, who was not a member of the Legislature, the Practice Act of 1852, which abolished the common law system of pleading, and has been in principle that on which the Massachusetts courts have acted in civil cases ever since. I studied the English Factory legislation, and read Macaulay's speeches on the subject. I became an earnest advocate for shortening the hours of labor by legislation. That was then called the ten-hour system. Later it has been called the eight-hour system. I made, in 1852, a speech in favor of reducing the time of labor in factories to ten hours a day which, so far as I know, was the first speech in any legislative body in this country on that subject. My speech was received with great derision. The House, usually very courteous and orderly, seemed unwilling to hear me through. One worthy old farmer got up in his seat and said: "Isn't the young man from Worcester going to let me get up in the morning and milk my caouws."

When a member of the Senate in 1857, I was Chairman of the Judiciary Committee. I made a very earnest and carefully prepared speech against the asserted right of the jury to judge of the law in criminal cases. It is a popular and specious doctrine. But it never seemed to me to be sound. Among others, there are two reasons against it, which seem to me conclusive, and to which I have never seen a plausible answer. One is that if the jury is to judge of the law, you will have as many different laws as you have juries. There is no revision of their conclusion. They are not obliged to tell, and there is no way in which the court can know, what their opinion was. So a man tried on one side of the court-house may be held guilty, and another man tried on the other side of the court-house may be held innocent for precisely the same act.

The other reason is that the court must always decide what evidence shall be admitted. So if the jury are to be the judges of the law, one authority must determine what evidence they shall consider, and another determine what law shall be applied to it. For instance, suppose a defendant charged with homicide offers to prove certain facts which as he claims justify the killing. The Judge says these facts do not, under the law, justify the killing and excludes the evidence. That may be the real point in the case, and the jury may believe that those facts fully justify the homicide; still they cannot be permitted to hear them. It is preposterous to suppose that so logical and reasonable a system as the Common Law could ever have tolerated such an absurdity. My friend, Mr. Justice Gray of the United States Supreme Court, an admirable judge and one of the great judges of the world, in his dissenting opinion in *Sparf et al. v. U. S., 156, U. S. Reports, page 51, etc.*, has little to say on this point, except that of course there must be some authority to regulate the conduct of trials.

I declined a reelection to the Senate. I was twice nominated for Mayor by the Republicans of Worcester, when the election of their candidate was sure; once by a Citizens' Convention, and once by a Committee authorized to nominate a candidate, and another year urged by prominent and influential citizens to accept such a nomination. But I preferred my profession. I never had any desire or taste for executive office, and I doubt if I had much capacity for it.

When Charles Allen declined reelection to Congress, in 1852, I have no doubt I could have succeeded him if I had been willing, although I was but twenty-six years old, only a year past the Constitutional age.

As I found myself getting a respectable place in the profession my early ambitions were so far changed and expanded that I hoped I might some day be appointed to the Supreme Court of the Commonwealth of Massachusetts. It seemed to me then, as it seems to me now, that there could be no more delightful life for a man competent to the service than one spent in discussing with the admirable lawyers, who have always adorned that Bench, the great questions of jurisprudence, involving the rights of citizens, and the welfare of the Commonwealth, and helping to settle them by authority. This ambition also was disappointed. I have twice received the offer of a seat on that Bench, under circumstances which rendered it out of the question that I should accept it, although on both occasions I longed exceedingly to do so.

Shortly after I was admitted to the Bar, good fortune brought me at once into the largest practice in the great County of Worcester, although that Bar had always been, before and since, one of the ablest in the country. Judge Emory Washburn, afterward Governor and Professor of Law at Harvard, and writer on jurisprudence, had the largest practice in the Commonwealth, west of Boston, and I suppose with one exception, the largest in the Commonwealth out of Boston. He asked me to become his partner in June, 1852. I had then got a considerable clientage of my own. Early in 1853 he sailed for Europe, intending to return in the fall. I was left in charge of his business during his six months' absence, talking with the clients about cases in which he was already retained, and receiving their statements as to cases in which they desired to retain him on his return. Before he reached home he was nominated for Governor by the Whig Convention, to which office he was elected by the Legislature in the following January. So he had but a few weeks to attend to his law business before entering upon the office of Governor. I kept on with it, I believe without losing a single client. That winter I had extraordinarily good fortune, due I think very largely to the kindly feeling of the juries toward so young a man attempting to undertake such great responsibilities.

My professional life from January 1, 1850, until the 4th of March, 1869, was a life of great and incessant labor. When the court was in session I was constantly engaged in jury trials. Day after day, and week after week, I had to pass from one side of the court-house to the other, being engaged in a very large part of the important actions that were tried in those days. The Court had long sessions. The judges who came from abroad were anxious to get their work done and go back to their homes. So the Courts sat from half past eight or nine o'clock in the morning until six in the afternoon with an intermission of an hour, or an hour and a quarter, for dinner. The parties to the suits came from all over Worcester County. Frequently it was impossible to see the witnesses until the trial came on, or just before. So the lawyer had to spend his evenings and often far into the night in seeing witnesses and making other preparations for the next day. General Devens and I had at one term of the Supreme Court held by Chief Justice Bigelow twenty trial actions. The term resulted in a serious injury to my eyes and in my being broken down with overwork. So I was compelled to go to Europe the following year for a vacation.

But I found time somehow, as I have said, to keep up a constant and active interest in politics. I was also able to contribute something to other things which were going on for the benefit of our growing city. I got up the first contribution for the Free Public Library, of which I was made

President. I took a great interest in the founding of the famous Worcester Polytechnic Institute, and I was the first person named in its Act of Incorporation. The first meeting of its Trustees was held in my office, and I am now the only surviving member of that Board, in which I have retained a warm interest ever since. In 1869 I made before the Massachusetts Legislature, on a petition which was successful for a legislative grant to that school, what I believe is the first public address ever made in behalf of Technical Education in this country. I was for some time President of the Board of Trustees of the City Library and while President planned the excellent reading room connected with the Library, for which I obtained a handsome endowment by personal solicitation.

I was also Trustee of Leicester Academy.

The Worcester Lyceum, which furnished the principal course of lectures in the city in those days, was in the hands of some very worthy and conservative old Whigs. They would not permit any politics or religion, or what was called Radicalism, either in religious or social matters, to be discussed on their platform. So we had to listen to very respectable and worthy, but rather dull and tame conservative gentlemen, or stay away, as we preferred. A few of the young men, of whom I was one, conspired to get possession of the Lyceum. They turned out in force for the election of officers, chose me President, and we got Wendell Phillips and Theodore Parker and Ralph Waldo Emerson and other shining lights of a newer philosophy, much to the indignation of the old Whig magnates. But the lectures were very successful, and at the end of my Presidency, which lasted two or three years, we had an ample balance in our treasury.

If I were to give an account of my professional life for twenty years, I must make another book. It was full of interest and romance. The client in those days used to lay bare his soul to his lawyer. Many of the cases were full of romantic interest. The lawyer followed them as he followed the plot of an exciting novel, from the time the plaintiff first opened his door and told his story till the time when he heard the sweetest of all sounds to a lawyer, the voice of the foreman saying: "The jury find for the plaintiff." Next to the "yes" of a woman, that is the sweetest sound, I think, that can fall on human ears.

I used to have eighteen or twenty law cases at the fall term every year. The judges gave their opinions orally in open Court, and the old judges like Shaw and Metcalf, used to enliven an opinion with anecdotes or quaint phrases, which lent great interest to the scene. If Walter Scott could have known and told the story of the life of an old Massachusetts lawyer from the close of the Revolution down to the beginning of the Rebellion, there is nothing in the great Scotch novels which would have surpassed it for romance and for humor.

I think I may fairly claim that I had a good deal to do with developing the equity system in the courts of Massachusetts, and with developing the admirable Insolvency system of Massachusetts, which is substantially an equity system, from which the United States Bankruptcy statutes have been so largely copied.

The great mass of the people of Massachusetts, Whigs and Democrats as well as Republicans, were loyal and patriotic and full of zeal when the war broke out. A very few of the old Whigs and Democrats, who were called "Hunkers" or "Copperheads," sympathized with the Rebellion, or if they did not, were so possessed with hatred for the men who were putting it down that they could find nothing to approve, but only cause for complaint and faultfinding. Andrew, the Governor, Sumner and Wilson, the Senators, most of the members of Congress, most of the leaders in the Legislature and in the military and political activities, were of the old Free Soil Party. There was a feeling, not wholly unreasonable, that the old Whigs had been somewhat neglected, and that their cooperation and help were received rather coldly. This feeling led to the movement, called the People's Party, which begun at a large public meeting in Cambridge, where my dear old friend and partner, ex-Governor Washburn, was one of the speakers. That party called a State Convention and nominated Charles Devens for Governor. Devens had been an old Whig. He had become a Republican in 1856, and had been one of the earliest to enlist in the War, in which he became afterward the most famous Massachusetts soldier. He was a man of spirit, very affectionate and generous, always ready to stand by his friends, especially if he suspected that anybody had treated them unjustly. The People's Party sent a Committee to the seat of war in September, 1862. The Committee found Devens in his tent, repeated to him the plans of his old Whig friends, and induced him to accept the nomination of the People's Party for Governor.

I was called to the battlefield of Antietam, where a near kinsman of mine had been mortally wounded, just about the same time. I entered Devens's tent just as this Committee was leaving it with his written acceptance in their hands. I told him the other side of the story, told him how the whole people were alive with enthusiasm, and that Governor Andrew was doing the very best possible, and that these petty jealousies, while there was some little reason for them, ought not to affect the public action of the people. Devens regretted very much what he had done. He told me that if he could recall the letter, he would do it. But it was too late.

Governor Andrew was triumphantly reelected, and Devens was ever after an earnest and loyal Republican.

CHAPTER X

POLITICAL HISTORY OF MASSACHUSETTS FROM 1848 TO 1869

IN 1848, the Free Soil Party in Massachusetts nominated candidates for State officers. It was made up of Whigs, Democrats and members of the Liberty Party. It had made no distinct issue with the Whig Party upon matters of State administration. Governor Briggs, the Whig Governor, was a wise and honest Chief Magistrate, highly respected by all the people. But the Free Soil leaders wisely determined that if they were to have a political party, they must have candidates for State officers as well as National. It is impossible to organize a political party with success whose members are acting together in their support of one candidate and striving with all their might against each other when another is concerned. My father was urged to be the Free Soil candidate for Governor. Charles Francis Adams and Edmund Jackson visited him at Concord to press it upon him as a duty. Charles Allen wrote him an earnest letter to the same effect. But he was an old friend of Governor Briggs and disliked very much to become his antagonist. He looked to the Whig Party for large accessions to the Free Soil ranks. A large plurality of the people of the community were still devoted to that party. He doubted very much the wisdom of widening the breach between them by a conflict on other questions than that of slavery. So he refused his consent. Stephen C. Phillips, an eminent Salem merchant, and a former Member of Congress, was nominated. The result was there was no choice of State officers by the people, and the election of the Whig candidates was made by the Legislature.

The next year it occurred to the leaders of the Free Soil and Democratic Parties that they had only to unite their forces to overthrow the Whigs. The Free Soil leaders thought the effect of this would be the eventual destruction of the Whig Party at the North,—as afterward proved to be the case,—and the building up in its place of a party founded on the principle of opposition to the extension of slavery. So in 1849 there was a coalition between the Free Soil and the Democratic Parties in some counties and towns, each supporting the candidates of the other not specially obnoxious to them, neither party committing itself to the principles of the other party or waiving its own. In the fall of the next year, 1850, this policy was pursued throughout the State and resulted in the election by the Legislature of a Democratic Governor, Mr. Boutwell, and of Charles Sumner as the successor of Daniel Webster in the Senate. The experiment was repeated with like success in the fall of 1851.

These two parties had little in common. They could not well act together in State matters without some principle or purpose on which they were agreed other than mere desire for office and opposition to the Whig Party. They found a common ground in the support of a law providing for secrecy in the ballot. There had been great complaint that the manufacturers, especially in Lowell, who were in general zealous Whig partisans, used an undue influence over their workmen. It was said that a man known to be a Democrat, or a Free Soiler, was pretty likely to get his discharge from the employ of any great manufacturing corporation that had occasion to reduce its force, and that he would have no chance to get an increase of wages. I do not now believe there was much foundation for this accusation. But it was believed by many people at the time. So a law requiring secrecy in the ballot was framed and enacted in spite of great resistance from the Whigs. This has undoubtedly proved a good policy, and has prevailed in Massachusetts ever since, and now prevails largely throughout the country.

But this one measure was not enough to hold together elements otherwise so discordant. So the Democratic and Free Soil leaders agreed to call a convention to revise the

Constitution of the Commonwealth, which had remained unchanged save in a few particulars since 1780. There had been a Convention for that purpose in 1820, made necessary by the separation of Maine. But the old Constitution had been little altered. The concentration of the population in large towns and cities had caused a demand for a new distribution of political power. Many people desired an elective judiciary. Others desired that the judges should hold office for brief terms instead of the old tenure for life. There was a great demand for the popular election of Sheriffs and District Attorneys, who under the existing system were appointed by the Governor. Others desired the choice of Senators, who had before been chosen by the several counties on a joint ticket, by single districts. A proposition for a Convention was submitted to the people by the Legislature of 1851. But the people were attached to the old Constitution. There was a special dread of any change in the independent tenure of the judiciary. So although the coalition had a majority in the State the proposition for a Constitutional Convention was defeated.

The scheme was renewed the next year in the Legislature of 1852, of which I was a member. Several of the Free Soilers, among whom I was included, were unwilling to have the matter tried again without a distinct assurance that there should be no meddling with the judiciary. This assurance was given in the report of a joint committee of the Legislature to whom the matter was committed, consisting of the leaders of the Democratic and Republican parties, who reported that there was no purpose to change the judicial tenure with which the people were well satisfied. Accordingly I voted for it. The measure got a bare majority in the House which it never would have had without that stipulation. The plan was submitted to the people again with a proposition that the choice of delegates to the Constitutional Convention should be by secret ballot. The people approved the plan by a substantial majority.

I have no doubt that the pledge above mentioned was made in good faith and that the men who made it meant to keep it. But before the Convention met two things happened which changed the conditions. The coalition was wrecked. There were two causes for its overthrow. One of them was the appointment by Governor Boutwell of Caleb Cushing to a seat on the Supreme Bench of Massachusetts. General Cushing was a man of great accomplishment, though never a great lawyer. He could collect with wonderful industry all the facts bearing on any historic question and everything that had been said on either side of any question of law. But he never had a gift of cogent argument that would convince any judge or jury. He owed his success in life largely to the personal favor of men who knew him and were charmed by his agreeable quality. He was regarded by the people of Massachusetts as a man without moral convictions and as utterly subservient to the slave power. So his appointment was a great shock to the Anti-Slavery men and made them believe that it was not safe to put political power in Democratic hands. General Cushing vindicated this opinion afterward by the letter written when he was Attorney-General in the Cabinet of President Pierce declaring that the Anti-Slavery movement in the North "must be crushed out," and also by a letter written to Jefferson Davis after the beginning of the Rebellion recommending some person to him for some service to the Confederacy. The discovery of this letter compelled President Grant who had been induced to nominate him for Chief Justice to withdraw the nomination. The other cause was the passage of the bill for the prohibition of the manufacture and sale of intoxicating liquors, known as the Maine law. This measure had passed the Legislature, containing a provision for its submission to the people. It was vetoed by Governor Boutwell. The reason assigned by him was his objection to the provision for its submission to the people, without the secret ballot. The referendum, a scheme by which men charged with political duties avoid responsibility by submitting to the people measures which they fear may be unpopular,—has never found much favor in Massachusetts. After many changes of sentiment, and after passing, modifying, and repealing many laws, the people of the Commonwealth seem to have settled down on a policy which permits each town or city to decide by vote whether the sale of liquor shall be permitted within their limits. The bill was then passed, without the reference to the people. But the measure sealed the fate of the coalition. Some of its provisions, especially that for seizing and destroying stocks of liquor kept for sale in violation of law, were very severe, and were held unconstitutional by the Court. The liquor sellers, almost all of them, were Democrats. They would not readily submit to a law which made their calling criminal.

So the Whigs were restored to power by the fall election in 1852. Their heads were turned by their success. They did not quite dare to repeal the law providing for a Constitutional Convention, but they undertook to repeal so much of it as required that the choice of delegates should be by secret ballot. The minority resisted this repeal with all their might. They alleged with great reason that it was not decent for the Legislature to repeal a provision which the people had expressly approved. But their resistance was in vain, and after a long and angry struggle which stirred the people of the Commonwealth profoundly the provision for the secret ballot was abrogated. But the result of the contest was that the Whigs were routed at the special election for delegates to the Convention. That body was controlled by the Coalition by a very large majority. Their triumph made them also lose their heads.

So when the Convention assembled in 1853, they disregarded the pledges which had enabled them to get the assent of the people to calling the convention, and provided that the tenure of office of the Judges of the Supreme Court should be for ten years only, and that the Judges of Probate should be elected by the people of the several counties once in three years. It is said, and, as I have good reason to know, very truly, that this action of the Convention was taken in consequence of a quarrel in Court between the late Judge Merrick and General Butler and Mr. Josiah G. Abbott, two eminent leaders of the Democrats, members of the Convention. They had neither of them agreed to the proposition to change the judicial tenure.

They were absent from the convention for several days in the trial of an important cause before Merrick, and returned angry with the Judge and determined to do something to curb the independent power of the Judges. The proposition was adopted.

These schemes were a distinct violation of the pledge which had been given when the Legislature submitted to the people the proposition for calling the Convention. Of course it was a fair answer to this complaint to say that the members of the committee who made that report could in such a matter bind nobody but themselves. That was true. But I think if the men who signed that report, and the men who joined them in giving the assurance to the people, had been earnest and zealous in the matter it is quite likely they could have prevented the action of the Convention.

The scheme for a new constitution passed the Convention by a large majority and was submitted to the people. The Whig leaders, who seemed to have had all their wisdom and energy taken out of them when the Free Soilers left them, were much alarmed by the strength of the discontent with the existing order of things manifested by the coalition victory in the election of the Constitutional Convention. Many of them concluded that it would be unwise to resist the popular feeling. One Saturday afternoon during that summer I was in the office of Francis Wayland, a great friend of mine, long Dean of the New Haven Law School, when Henry S. Washburn, a member of the Whig State Central Committee, came into Wayland's office and told me he had just attended a meeting of the Committee that day and that it determined to make no contest against the new Constitution. The Springfield *Republican,* then a Whig journal, had an article that day, or the following Monday, to the same effect. I was very much disturbed. I hurried to Concord by the first train Monday morning, and saw my brother, who was then a Judge of the Court of Common Pleas. He agreed with me in thinking the proposed scheme of government a very bad one. He went at once to Cambridge and saw John G. Palfrey, a very able and influential leader of the Free Soilers. Mr. Palfrey agreed that the Constitution ought to be defeated, if possible. Judge Hoar and he sat down together and prepared a pamphlet, the Judge furnishing the legal argument and Mr. Palfrey the rest, clothing it all in his inimitable style. It was published under Dr. Palfrey's name. Judge Hoar, being then upon the bench, did not think it becoming to take any more public action in the matter, although he made his opinion known to all persons who cared to know it. Charles Francis Adams and Marcus Morton also made powerful arguments on the same side. My father, Samuel Hoar, also made several speeches against the Constitution. At this defection of so many Free Soilers the Whig leaders took heart and made a vigorous and successful resistance.

The result was that the people voted down the whole constitution. Several of the most eminent leaders of the Free Soilers and Democrats separated themselves from their party and joined the Whigs in defeating it. Among them were Marcus Morton, formerly Governor and Judge of the Supreme Court; John G. Palfrey, who had been the Free Soil candidate for Governor; Charles Francis Adams, afterward member of Congress and Minister to England, and Samuel Hoar.

I was myself, at this time, an enthusiastic Free Soiler, and was, as I have said, Chairman of the Republican County Committee, but I joined the rebels against the dominant feeling of my party.

The defeat of the Constitution was aided, however, undoubtedly by a very just and righteous proposal which was submitted to a separate vote of the people, but which had its effect on the feeling in regard to the whole scheme, to prohibit the use of any money raised by taxation for sectarian schools. To this the Catholic clergy were opposed, and the Catholic vote, not however then very important in Massachusetts, was cast against the whole scheme.

But the Whigs did not entirely get over the feeling that something must be done to propitiate the desire for change. Accordingly they, through the Legislature, submitted to the people propositions for the election by the people of the counties of Sheriffs and District Attorneys who before that time had been appointed by the Governor. These proposals were ratified by the people and became part of the Constitution. I have always thought the change a bad one. I think the Governor likely to make quite as good if not a better choice of Sheriffs and District Attorneys than the people. But the objection to the new system is this. So long as the State makes the laws, the State, whether acting by a popular vote or through its executive, should have the power to enforce them and select the instrumentalities for that purpose. Now if the particular law which the State enacts be unpopular in a particular county, and the people be determined to defeat it, no Sheriff or District Attorney can be elected who will enforce it. That has been shown in the case of the legislation to prohibit or regulate the sale of intoxicating liquors in Suffolk County. Those laws have been always unpopular and since the change in the mode of appointment of District Attorneys and Sheriffs have not been enforced until they were modified to meet the popular objections. This difficulty applies also to the enforcing of the laws for the employment of children in factories. The Legislature undertook to meet this difficulty by creating officials, called State Constables, to be appointed by the Governor and to enforce the liquor laws and the laws regulating child labor. But that did not wholly cure the evil. The officials appointed solely to enforce a law against which there are strong objections in any quarter are always themselves unpopular. The Sheriffs have been from the beginning officials of great dignity, commanding popular respect and confidence. So if it were difficult to enforce the law the character of the Sheriff was a great force on its side. But in the case of these particular laws persons of less dignity and authority, often quite obscure when they are appointed, whose whole duty is odious to the persons to be affected by it, instead of giving dignity to the law tend to make it unpopular by their attempts to enforce it. Indeed in my opinion the Massachusetts Constitution of 1780 was as nearly a perfect system of government as was ever devised. Some changes in it were made necessary by the separation of Maine. I suppose the abrogation of the provision that every man should pay a tax for the support of public worship somewhere was demanded by a public sentiment it would have been impossible to resist, and undoubtedly the aggregation of population in the large cities and towns required a change in the system of representation. But I think the old method of electing Senators, where it was necessary that a man should have a reputation through an entire county to be chosen, to be better than the system of electing them by small single districts, and I think the slight property qualification was highly useful as a stimulant to saving and economy.

It is, however, a great pity that the labors of this Constitutional Convention were wasted. It was a very able body of men. With the exception of the Convention that framed the Constitution in the beginning, and the Convention which revised it in 1820, after the separation from Maine, I doubt whether so able a body of men ever assembled in the Commonwealth of Massachusetts, or, with very few exceptions indeed, in the entire country. The debates, which are preserved in three thick and almost forgotten volumes, are full of instructive and admirable essays on the theory of constitutional government. Among the members were Rufus Choate, Charles Sumner, Henry Wilson, George N. Briggs, Marcus Morton, Marcus Morton, Jr., Henry L. Dawes, Charles Allen, George S. Hillard, Richard H. Dana, George S. Boutwell, Otis P. Lord, Peleg Sprague, Simon Greenleaf, and Sidney Bartlett.

There were a good many interesting incidents not, I believe, recorded in the report of the debates, which are worth preserving.

One was a spirited reply made by George S. Hillard to Benjamin F. Butler, who had bitterly attacked Chief Justice Shaw, then an object of profound reverence to nearly the whole people of the Commonwealth. Butler spoke of his harsh and rough manner of dealing with counsel. To which Hillard replied, pointing at Butler: "While we have jackals and hyenas at the bar, we want the old lion upon the bench, with one blow of his huge paw to bring their scalps over their eyes."

Hillard was an accomplished and eloquent man, "of whom," Mr. Webster said in the Senate of the United States, "the best hopes are to be entertained." But he lacked vigor and courage to assert his own opinions against the social influences of Boston, which were brought to bear with great severity on the anti-slavery leaders.

Hillard was not so fortunate in another encounter. He undertook to attack Richard H. Dana, and to reproach him for voting for a scheme of representation which somewhat diminished the enormous political power of Boston. She elected all her representatives on one ballot, and had a power altogether disproportionate to that of the country. He said, speaking of Dana: "He should remember that the bread he and I both eat comes from the business men of Boston. He ought not, like an ungrateful child, to strike at the hand that feeds him." Dana replied with great indignation, ending with the sentence: "The hand that feeds me—the hand that feeds me, sir? No hand feeds me that has a right to control my opinions!"

A *bon mot* of Henry Wilson is also worth putting on record. Somebody, who was speaking of the importance of the Massachusetts town meeting, said that it was not merely a place for town government alone, but that it was a place where the people of the town met from scattered and sometimes secluded dwelling-places to cultivate each other's acquaintance, to talk over the news of the day and all matters of public interest; and that it was a sort of farmers' exchange, where they could compare notes on the state of agriculture, and even sometimes swap oxen. Governor Briggs, who had been beaten as a candidate for reelection by the Coalition, replied to this speech and said, referring to the Coalition, "that the gentlemen on the other side seemed to have carried their trading and swapping of oxen into politics, and into the high offices of the state." To which Henry Wilson answered, referring to Briggs's own loss of his office, "that so long as the people were satisfied with the trade, it did not become the oxen to complain."

Undoubtedly the ablest member of the Convention was Charles Allen. He spoke seldom and briefly, but always with great authority and power. Late in the proceedings of the Convention a rule was established limiting the speakers to thirty minutes each. Hillard, who was one of the delegates from Boston, made a very carefully prepared speech on some pending question. Allen closed the debate, making no reference whatever to Hillard's elaborate and most eloquent argument, until he was about to sit down, when he said: "Mr. President, I believe my time is up?" The President answered: "The gentleman from Worcester has two minutes more." "Two minutes!" exclaimed Allen. "Time enough to answer the gentleman from Boston." And he proceeded in that brief period to deal a few strokes with his keen scimitar, which effectually demolished Hillard's elaborate structure.

There is nothing in the political excitements of recent years which approaches in intensity that of the period from 1848 until the breaking out of the War. The people of Massachusetts felt the most profound interest in the great conflict between slavery and freedom for the possession of the vast territory between the Mississippi and the Pacific. But almost every man in Massachusetts felt the Fugitive Slave Law as a personal dishonor. I think no great public calamity, not the death of Webster, not the death of Sumner, not the loss of great battles during the War, brought such a sense of gloom over the whole State as the surrender of Anthony Burns and of Sims. Worcester, where I dwelt, was the centre and stronghold of the anti-slavery feeling in Massachusetts. This odious statute was, perhaps, the greatest single cause of the union of the people of the North in opposition to the further encroachments of slavery. Yet but two slaves were taken back into slavery from Massachusetts by reason of its provisions. I will not undertake to tell the story of those years which will form an important chapter in the history of the country. But I had a special knowledge of two occurrences which are alluded to by Colonel Higginson in his charming essay entitled, "Cheerful Yesterdays," in regard to which that most delightful writer and admirable gentleman has fallen into some slight errors of recollection.

The first person seized under the Fugitive Slave Law was a slave named Shadrach. He was brought to trial before George T. Curtis, United States Commissioner. One of the chief complaints against the Fugitive Slave Law was that it did not give the man claimed as a slave, where his liberty and that of his posterity were at stake, the right to a jury trial which the Constitution secured in all cases of property involving more than twenty dollars, or in all cases where he was charged with the slightest crime or offence. Further, the Commissioner was to receive twice as much if the man were surrendered into slavery as if he were discharged. Horace Mann, in one of his speeches, commented on this feature of the law with terrible severity. He also pointed out that the Commissioner was not a judicial officer with an independent tenure, but only the creature of the courts and removable at any time. He also dwelt upon what he conceived to be the unfair dealing of the Commissioners who had presided at the trial of the three slaves who had been tried in Massachusetts, and added: "Pilate, fellow-citizens, was at least a Judge, though he acted like a Commissioner."

Elizur Wright, a well-known Abolitionist, editor of the *Chronotype,* was indicted in the United States Court for aiding in the rescue of Shadrach. While the hearing before Geo. T. Curtis on the proceedings for the rendition of Shadrach was going on, a large number of men, chiefly negroes, made their way into the court-room by one door, swept through, taking the fugitive along with them, and out at the other, leaving the indignant Commissioner to telegraph to Mr. Webster in Washington that he thought it was a case of levying war. I went into the court-room during the trial of Mr. Wright, and saw seated in the front row of the jury, wearing a face of intense gravity, my old friend Francis Bigelow, always spoken of in Concord as "Mr. Bigelow, the blacksmith." He was a Free Soiler and his wife a Garrison Abolitionist. His house was a station on the underground railroad where fugitive slaves were harbored on their way to Canada. Shadrach had been put into a buggy and driven out as far as Concord, and kept over night by Bigelow at his house, and sent on his way toward the North Star the next morning. Richard H. Dana, who was counsel for Elizur Wright, asked Judge Hoar what sort of a man Bigelow was. To which the Judge replied: "He is a thoroughly honest man, and will decide the case according to the law and the evidence as he believes them to be. But I think it will take a good deal of evidence to convince him that one man owns another."

It is not, perhaps, pertinent to my personal recollections but it may be worth while to tell my readers that Theodore Parker, Wendell Phillips, and some others were indicted afterward for participation in an intended rescue of Anthony Burns, another fugitive slave. The indictment was quashed by Judge Curtis, who had probably got pretty sick of the whole thing. But Parker, while in jail awaiting trial, prepared a defence, which is printed, and which is one of the most marvellous examples of scathing and burning denunciation to be found in all literature. I commend it to young men as worth their study.

Some time after the Shadrach case, Asa O. Butman, a United States Deputy Marshal, who had been quite active and odious in the arrest and extradition of Burns, came to Worcester one Saturday afternoon, and stopped at the American Temperance House. This was October 30, 1854. It was believed that he was in search of information about some fugitive negroes who were supposed to be in Worcester, and I suppose that to be the fact, although it was claimed that his errand was to summon witnesses against persons concerned in the riot which took place when Burns was captured. The fact of his presence became known in the course of the day on Sunday, and a pretty angry crowd began to gather in the streets in the neighborhood of the American House. Butman learned his danger, and took refuge in the City Marshal's office in the City Hall, where the police force of the city were gathered for his protection. No attack was made during the night, but it was not deemed prudent to have Butman leave his shelter. I had been to Concord to spend Sunday with my kindred there. I got to Worcester at nine o'clock Monday morning, and was told at the station of the condition of things. I went immediately to the City Hall, made my way through the crowd to the building, and was admitted to the police office by the City Marshal, who was my client, and apt to depend on me for legal advice. I found Butman in a state of great terror. It was evident that the crowd was too large for any police force which the little city had in its service. Unless it should be pacified, something was likely to happen which we should all have much regretted. I accordingly went out and addressed the crowd from the steps of the City Hall. They listened to me respectfully enough. I was pretty well known through the city as an earnest Free Soiler, and as sharing the public feeling of indignation against the delivering up of fugitives. I reminded the crowd that my father and sister had been expelled from Charleston, S. C., where he had gone at the risk of his life to defend Massachusetts colored sailors who were imprisoned there, and appealed to them not to give the people of South Carolina the right to excuse their own conduct by citing the example of Massachusetts. There were shouts from the crowd: "Will he promise to leave Worcester and never come back?" Butman, who was inside, terribly frightened, said he would promise never to come to Worcester again as long as he lived. I did not, however, repeat Butman's promise to the crowd. I thought he ought to go without conditions. The time approached for the train to pass through Worcester for Boston. It went from a little wooden station near the site of the present Union Depot, about half a mile from the City Hall. It was determined, on consultation, to take advantage of an apparently pacific mood of the crowd, and to start Butman at once for the station in time to catch the train. I took one arm and I am quite sure Colonel Higginson took the other; a few policemen went ahead and a few behind; and we started from the back door of the City Hall. The mob soon found what we were after and thronged around us. It has been estimated that a crowd of two thousand people at least surrounded

Butman and his convoy. I suppose he had no friend or defender among the number. Most of them wanted to frighten him; some of them to injure him, though not to kill him. There were a few angry negroes, I suppose, excited and maddened by their not unnatural or unjustifiable resentment against the fellow who had been the ready and notorious tool of the slave-catchers, who would have killed him if they could. He was kicked several times by persons who succeeded in the swaying and surging of the crowd, in getting through his guard, and once knocked onto his knees by a heavy blow in the back of the neck which came from a powerful negro, who had a stone in his hand which increased the force of the blow. I believe he was hit also by some missiles. He reached the depot almost lifeless with terror. The train was standing there, and started just after we arrived. It was impossible to get him into it. It was then endeavored to put him into a buggy which was standing outside of the depot, but the owner, a young business man of Worcester, seized the bridle of his horse and stoutly refused to allow the horse to start. Butman was then thrust into a hack, into which one or two other persons also got, and the hack was driven rapidly through the crowd with no damage but the breaking of the windows. Mr. Higginson thought Butman was left at Westboro'; but my recollection, which is very distinct, and with which I think he now agrees, is that Lovell Baker, the City Marshal, followed with his own horse and buggy, and took Butman from the hack after he got a short distance out of Worcester. Butman implored him not to leave him at the way-station, fearing that the crowd would come down in an accommodation train, which went also about that time, and waylay him there. So Baker drove him the whole distance to Boston, forty miles. When Butman got to the city, he was afraid that the news of the Worcester riot might have reached Boston, and have excited the people there; and, by his earnest solicitation, Baker took Butman by unfrequented streets across the city to a place where he thought he could be concealed until the excitement abated. Baker, who died a short time ago in Worcester, aged over ninety, told me the whole story immediately on his return.

The proceeding undoubtedly was not to be justified; but it was a satisfaction to know that no slave-hunter came to Worcester after that occurrence. Five or six people—including, if I am not mistaken, Mr. Higginson himself, certainly including Joseph A. Howland, a well-known Abolitionist and non-resistant, and also including Martin Stowell, who was afterward indicted for killing Batchelder, a Marshal who took part in the rendition of Burns—were complained of before the police court, and bound over to await the action of the grand jury. The grand jury returned no indictment, except against one colored man. Mr. District Attorney Aldrich was quite disgusted at this, and promptly *nol prossed* that indictment. And so ended the famous Butman riot.

The Whigs were in a minority in Massachusetts after the year 1848. But the constitution required a majority of all the votes to elect a Governor; and, in case of no choice, the Governor, the Lieutenant Governor, the Executive Council, and the Senators from counties where there had been no election were chosen on joint ballot by the members elected to the two Houses. The Whigs were able to carry the Legislature, and in that way chose their Governor and Lieutenant Governor, elected Councillors, and filled vacancies in the Senate. But the Free Soil and Democratic leaders were not content to leave the power in the hands of the Whig minority. In 1849 a few Representatives and Senators were chosen to the Legislature by a union of the Free Soil and Democratic Parties. In the autumn of 1850 this arrangement was extended through the State. The Whigs were in a minority in the Legislature, and the coalition proceeded to elect a Democratic Governor and Lieutenant Governor and an Executive Council. In consideration of giving these offices to the Democrats, it was agreed that Mr. Sumner should be chosen Senator. A few of the Democrats, who desired to keep their party relations with the South, refused to agree to this arrangement. Mr. Winthrop was the Whig candidate. The Senate, on its part, promptly elected Mr. Sumner, but there was a long contest in the House of Representatives, extending through three months. Twenty-six ballots were cast, of which no candidate had a majority until the last. Mr. Sumner several times came within two or three votes of an election. At last it was apparent that some member had cast more than one vote; and an order was offered by Sidney Bartlett, an eminent Whig member from Boston, requiring the members to bring in their votes in sealed envelopes. This resulted in the choice of Sumner.

Another contribution to Mr. Sumner's election ought not to be forgotten. The town of Fall River was represented by Whigs; but it was a community where there was a strong anti-slavery feeling. A town-meeting was called by the friends of Mr. Sumner, and a motion made to instruct their representatives, according to the right of the people declared in the constitution of Massachusetts, to vote for Sumner. An earnest and eloquent speech in favor of the resolution was made by Robert T. Davis, a young Quaker, since a distinguished member of Congress. The resolution was carried, which Mr. Borden, one of the Representatives from Fall River, obeyed. The result was Sumner's election by a single vote.

As stated in the preceding chapter, I was a member in 1852 of the Massachusetts House of Representatives, then consisting of about four hundred and twenty members. It was, I think, as admirable a body of men for the training of a public speaker as I ever knew. The members were honest. The large majority was made up of sensible, strong-headed country farmers, rather slow in making up their minds, but making them up always on considerations of what was best for the Commonwealth. There was a time, when the opinion of the House seemed to be precipitating or crystallizing, not too early in the debate and not too late, when a vigorous and effective speech had great influence. I was made Chairman of the Committee of Probate and Chancery, the second law committee in the House; and I suppose it is not presumptuous to say that I did as much of the hard work of the body and had as much influence in leading its action and shaping its legislation as anybody.

In the year 1856 I was, with Eli Thayer, sent from Worcester as a delegate to a Convention held at Buffalo to concert measures to help the settlers from the Free States in their contest with slave owners led by Atchison and Stringfellow, of Missouri, for the possession of Kansas. Atchison had been President pro tempore of the Senate of the United States. The slave holders had organized a formidable body of men to drive out the Free State settlers from the Territories, which had just been opened after the repeal of the Missouri Compromise. We met at Buffalo some gentlemen, among whom was Zachariah Chandler, of Michigan, then in the vigor of early manhood. We made arrangements for getting large contributions of money and arms with which the Northern emigrants were equipped, and which undoubtedly enabled them to maintain successfully their resistance and establish their free State.

CHAPTER XI

THE KNOW NOTHING PARTY AND ITS OVERTHROW

THE political history of Massachusetts from 1846 to 1865 is, in general, the history of the share of the Commonwealth in the great National contest with Slavery; the beginning and growth of the Free Soil or Republican Party and the putting down of the Rebellion. The rise and dominion for three years, and final overthrow of the Know Nothing Party is an episode which should not be wholly omitted, although it is an episode which might be omitted without injury to the sense.

There have been, ever since the Irish immigration which begun somewhere about 1840 down to to-day, a great many worthy people who have been afraid of the Pope and the influence of Catholicism in this country, and have been exceedingly jealous of the influence of foreigners, especially of those of the Roman Catholic Church. Self-seeking political adventurers and demagogues have not been slow to take advantage of this feeling for their own purposes. They have, for some reason, always preferred to make their political movement in secret societies. The Catholic vote had generally been cast for the Democrats, and was supposed to be largely influenced by the Catholic clergy. It was thought that this influence had a good deal to do with defeating Mr. Clay in 1844. A movement of this kind swept over the country after the Presidential election of 1852. It had nearly spent its force by 1856. It made little headway at the South, except in two or three States. There was a struggle with it in Virginia, where it was defeated by the superhuman energy of Henry A. Wise. The party organized for the purpose of excluding men of foreign birth from any share in the Government, sometimes called the American Party, was generally called the Know

Nothing Party, a name which came from the answer each member was expected to make to any inquiry from an outsider, "I know nothing about it."

This party swept Massachusetts in the autumn of 1854. It elected in that year Governor, Lieutenant Governor, all the officers of the State Government, every member of both Houses of the Legislature, except two from the town of Northampton, and every member of Congress. Its candidate for Governor was Henry J. Gardner, a very skilful political organizer. He had a book in which he had the names of men in every town in the Commonwealth whom he attached to his personal fortunes by promises, or flattery, or because in some cases of their sincere belief in the doctrine. He understood better than any other man I ever knew the value of getting the united support of men who were without special influence, even the men who were odious or ridiculous among their own neighbors, but who united might be a very formidable force. He organized with great skill and success the knave-power and the donkey-power of the Commonwealth.

But a good many Anti-Slavery men who thought the party feeling of the Whigs and Democrats was a great obstacle to their cause, joined the movement simply in order that they might get rid of the old parties, and prepare the State as with a subsoil plow for a new one. They had no belief in the proscriptive doctrines, and were willing that men of foreign birth and Catholics should have their just rights, and expected to destroy the Know Nothing Party in its turn when it had destroyed Whiggery and Democracy. Of these was Henry Wilson, who owed his first election to the Senate to the Know Nothing Legislature; and Eli Thayer, who had been the organizer of the Emigrant Aid Society, and the movement for the deliverance of Kansas and Nebraska. Both these gentlemen abandoned the Know Nothing Party the year after its formation. Mr. Thayer was elected as a Republican to Congress in 1856, and reelected in 1858. But he separated from his political associates and espoused the squatter sovereignty doctrines of Stephen A. Douglas. He, I have no doubt, was a sincere Anti-Slavery man. But he liked to do things in peculiar and original ways of his own, and was impatient of slow and old-fashioned methods. So he got estranged from his Republican brethren, was defeated as a candidate for Congress in 1860, took no part in public activities during the time of the war, became somewhat soured, and landed in the Democratic Party. I always had a great liking for him, and deem him entitled to great public gratitude for his services in the rescue of Kansas from what was known as Border Ruffianism.

Neither Charles Sumner nor Charles Allen ever tolerated the Know Nothing movement or made any terms with it. Its proscriptiveness and its secrecy were alike repugnant to their honest, brave and liberty-loving souls. Sumner was advised, as the question of his reelection was coming on in January, 1857, to keep silent about Know Nothingism. He was told that the Slavery question was enough for one man to deal with, and that if he would only hold his peace all the parties would unite in his reelection. He answered the advice with his brave challenge. He went about the Commonwealth, denouncing the intolerant and proscriptive doctrine of the Know Nothings. He told them: "You have no real principle on which you can stand. You are nothing but a party of Gardnerites."

Charles Allen addressed a little company, of which I was one, in the City Hall at Worcester in the autumn of 1854, when Know Nothingism was in the height of its strength. He said:

"Perhaps I am speaking too boldly, but I learned to speak boldly a long time ago. I will speak my sentiments in the face of any organization; or, if it does not show its face, though its secret mines are beneath my feet, and unseen hands ready to apply the match, I will declare those sentiments that a freeman is bound to utter."

The people of Massachusetts elected Gardner Governor in 1854, 1855 and 1856. But in the autumn of 1857 he was beaten under the leadership of General Banks. The party lingered until 1856 when there was an attempt to keep it alive in the Presidential campaign of that year when Millard Filmore was its candidate for the Presidency.

But it was destroyed in the consuming fire kindled by the Civil War, and has not since been heard of by its old name.

The proscriptive and intolerant opposition to Catholicism, especially against men of foreign birth, has shown its head occasionally. It appeared in its most formidable shape in a secret organization known as the A. P. A., of which I shall speak later. It is utterly uncongenial to the spirit of true Americanism, and will never have any considerable permanent strength.

CHAPTER XII

ELECTION TO CONGRESS

In the year 1868 one chapter of my life ended and a very different one began. In the beginning of that year I had no doubt that what remained of my life would be devoted to my profession, and to discharging as well as I could the duties of good citizenship in the community to which I was so strongly attached. But it was ordered otherwise. My life in Worcester came to an end, and I shall if I live to complete my present term in the Senate have spent thirty-eight years in the National service.

This came from no ambition of mine. In May, 1868, I sailed for Europe, broken down in health by hard work. During my absence, some of the leading Republicans of the District issued an appeal recommending me as a candidate for Congress. There were five or six other candidates. They were all of them men of great popularity, with hosts of friends and supporters. Among them was John D. Baldwin, then holding the seat, a veteran in the Anti-Slavery Service, editor of the Worcester *Spy,* one of the most influential papers in New England. It had been the almost unvarying custom of the people of Massachusetts to reelect an old member who had served as faithfully as Mr. Baldwin. Another candidate was Francis W. Bird, one of the founders of the Anti-Slavery Party, and a man who had been a powerful supporter by speech and pen and wise counsel and large influence of the Republican Party since its foundation. He was supported by the powerful influence of Charles Sumner, then at the height of his popularity, and by Adin Thayer, the ablest political organizer in Massachusetts. Another candidate was Amasa Walker, the eminent writer on political economy, whose name has since been rendered still more illustrious by the brilliant public service of his son. Another was Mr. Mayhew, a successful manufacturer, of large wealth, and a deserved favorite in Milford, the second town in the District, where he resided. Another still was Lucius W. Pond, a generous and warm-hearted man, although he afterward fell from his high place. He was a Methodist. That denomination had always been strong and influential in the Worcester District, and its members have always stood stanchly by the men of their own household when candidates for political office. Mr. Pond was also a member of the Masonic Order and of other secret associations. I ought however to say, in justice to the Masonic Fraternity, that I have never been able to see that there was any truth whatever in the charge that the members of that Order deemed it their duty to support each other in politics, or when on juries. Many a client has told me with great alarm that his opponent was a Mason, and that one or more leading Masons were on the jury that were to try the case. I always refused to challenge a juryman on that account, and I never found that the man's being a Mason had the least effect in preventing him from rendering a just verdict. I have many intimate friends both political and personal in that Order, although I never belonged to it and never sympathized with or approved of secret societies in a Republic.

My strength was due to the fact that I had in general the good will of my competitors. So if any one failed to get a majority it was easy to transfer his strength to me. Perhaps also there was a feeling, growing out of the fact that I had had great experience in public speaking at the Bar and in political meetings, that I might be able to take a prominent part in the debates in the House, a faculty which all my competitors lacked, except Mr. Bird. But chiefly I had the advantage of the good will of my associates in my own profession, a body whose influence is always justly very powerful and who were all, with scarcely an exception, my close and strong friends. I had, beside all that, a great many clients in every town in the District who had been in the habit of trusting me with their most intimate and secret concerns, and with whom I had formed the attachment which in those days used to exist between counsel and client.

I had said before I went to Europe that if nominated I would accept the office. I thought it doubtful whether my strength would permit me to continue my professional work without interruption. I had no thought of remaining in Congress, if I were elected, more than one term, or perhaps two. Indeed I did not contemplate the probability of a nomination as a very serious one.

But almost before I got out of sight of land the burden lifted and my health came back. When I got home I was utterly sick of the whole business. But my friends had been committed to my support. They claimed that I could not withdraw honorably after the assurance I had given them before I went away. So, rather to my disgust, I was nominated on the first formal ballot. I had not expected the result. I had gone to take a ride while the Convention was in session. So they were obliged to wait for me. I was found with some difficulty and went in and made a brief speech which I ended by saying: "If I shall fail to satisfy you, the trust you have so freely conferred you can as freely recall. If I shall fail to satisfy myself, I shall at least have the comfort of reflecting that it is by your free choice that this nomination has been conferred. It has not been begged for, or bargained for, or intrigued for, or crawled into. If elected I shall at the close of the term lay down the honors of the office with the same cheerfulness with which I now accept the nomination."

I expected to go back to my home and my profession at the end of one term. My law practice was rapidly increasing. Professional charges in those days were exceedingly moderate as compared with the scale of prices now, and I had inherited the habit of charging low fees from my partner and friend, Emory Washburn. If I had the same class of clients now that I had then, I could at the present scale of charges for professional service easily be earning more than fifty thousand dollars a year, and I could earn it without going to my office in the evening, and also take a good vacation every summer.

My life from that time has been devoted altogether to the public service. I have, what is commonly expected of men who represent Massachusetts in the Senate, delivered a good many literary and historical addresses, and have taken part in political campaigns, and have occasionally eked out a scanty salary by some professional work in the vacations. But I think I may fairly claim that I have done my share of the work of the Senate and of the House to the best of my ability. Senator Edmunds when he left the Senate was kind enough to compliment me by saying that the whole work of the Senate was done by six men, of whom I was one. I do not suppose Mr. Edmunds meant the number six to be taken literally. But he is a gentleman certainly never given to flattery or empty compliment. So I think I might call him as a witness that, in his time, so far as hard work is concerned I did my best. I am not quite so confident that he would testify to the wisdom of my course on all occasions.

I did not, as I have said, expect when I entered to remain in public life more than one term. But I became interested in the bill known as the National Education Bill, and accepted another election with a view to doing what I could to carry that through. At the end of the next term I announced my purpose to withdraw. But there was a very earnest letter to me signed by the principal men in the district, including several gentlemen, any one of whom might very naturally have expected to be my successor, saying it was not for the interest of the people of the district to make a change.

Two years after I made a formal and peremptory refusal to be a candidate again, which was encountered by a like appeal. It was the year of what was called the Tidal Wave which swept the Republicans from power in the House of Representatives. It was very doubtful whether they could carry the Worcester District. The Democrats elected a majority of the Massachusetts delegation in the National House of Representatives. I was elected by a few hundred only, although I was elected by several thousand on former occasions. I could not very well refuse to accept the nomination at a time of great political peril. So I continued once more. At the end of that time I wrote another peremptory refusal, and my successor was nominated and elected.

I have been often charged with a blind and zealous attachment to party. The charge is sometimes made by persons who consider that I desire to do right, but think that my understanding and intellectual faculties are guided and blinded by that emotion. Others are not so charitable. One very self-satisfied critic, Mr. William Lloyd Garrison, sometimes in prose and sometimes,

> A screechin' out prosaic verse
> An' like to bust,

says that I differ from my honorable colleague, Mr. Lodge, in that Mr. Lodge has no conscience, while I have a conscience but never obey it. If any man be disposed to accept these estimates, it is not likely that I can convince him to the contrary by my own certificate. But I will say two things:

1. I have never in my life cast a vote or done an act in legislation that I did not at the time believe to be right, and that I am not now willing to avow and to defend and debate with any champion, of sufficient importance, who desires to attack it at any time and in any presence.

2. Whether I am right or wrong in my opinion as to the duty of acting with and adherence to party, it is the result not of emotion or attachment or excitement, but of as cool, calculating, sober and deliberate reflection as I am able to give to any question of conduct or duty. Many of the things I have done in this world which have been approved by other men, or have tended to give me any place in the respect of my countrymen, have been done in opposition, at the time, to the party to which I belonged. But I have made that opposition without leaving the party. In every single instance, unless the question of the Philippine Islands shall prove an exception, and that is not a settled question yet, the party has come round, in the end, to my way of thinking. I have been able by adhering to the Republican

Party to accomplish, in my humble judgment, ten-fold the good that has been accomplished by men who have ten times more ability and capacity for such service, who have left the party.

When Governor Boutwell, the President of the Anti-Imperialist League, wrote me that he thought I could do more good for that cause by staying in the Republican Party than by leaving it, and when he declared in a public interview in Boston that of course Mr. Hoar would remain in the Republican Party, he was right. If he had taken the same course himself, he would have been a powerful help in saving the country from what has happened. If the gentlemen who acted with him in that way had remained Republicans, and the gentlemen who agreed with him, who have remained Republicans, who abandoned public life, had kept in it, they would have saved the country from what they and I deemed a grievous mistake and calamity. There was but one vote lacking for the defeat of the Spanish Treaty. There was but one vote lacking for the passage of the Teller resolution. If Mr. Speaker Reed, the most powerful Republican in the country, next to President McKinley, had stayed in the House; if Mr. Harrison, as I earnestly desired, had come back to the Senate; if Governor Boutwell and Mr. Adams had uttered their counsel as Republicans, the Republicans would have done with the Philippine Islands what we did with Cuba and Japan. I could cite a hundred illustrations, were they needed, to prove what I say to be true. There was undoubtedly great corruption and mal-administration in the country in the time of President Grant. Selfish men and ambitious men got the ear of that simple and confiding President. They studied Grant, some of them, as the shoemaker measures the foot of his customer. Mr. Sumner and Mr. Schurz and Mr. Trumbull and Mr. Greeley and the New York *Tribune,* and the Springfield *Republican,* and the Chicago *Tribune,* and the St. Louis *Republican,* and scores of other men and other papers left the party. They were, so long as they maintained that attitude, absolutely without political influence from that moment. When the great reforms which were attempted were accomplished, they were not there. The reforms were accomplished. But their names were wanting from the honorable roll of the men who accomplished them. President Grant himself and President Hayes and Judge Hoar and Mr. Cox and General Garfield, and others, if there are other names honorable enough to be mentioned along with these, stayed in the Republican Party. They purified the administration. They accomplished civil service reform. They helped to achieve the independence of American manufacture. They kept the faith. They paid the debt. They resumed specie payment. They maintained a sound currency, amid great temptation and against great odds. To this result our friends who were independent of party contributed no jot or tittle.

Our system differs from that which prevails in England in that it is hard to change the political power from one party to another and hard to restore it when it is once lost. We elect our President for four years. We elect our Senators for six years. Therefore in determining whether it is your duty to forsake a party which is wrong on some single question you are to decide, first, whether that question is important enough to warrant sacrificing every other measure in which you agree with your party, and having every measure espoused by the other which you think bad enacted if it get control. Second, you have not only in such cases to sacrifice every other thing you think desirable to prevent the one thing you think undesirable, but you must decide whether, in regard to that particular matter, the party you are asked to substitute in power for your own will accomplish what you desire if it get power. For example, there are some worthy Republicans who are free-traders. But they agree with the Republican Party in everything else. If you ask them to put a Democratic President and Congress into power in order to get free trade they must consider whether if they get power they will give them free trade. Otherwise they sacrifice everything else for that chance and get no benefit in that respect. The Republican free-trader who voted for Mr. Cleveland in 1892 did not get free trade. He got only what Mr. Cleveland denounced as a measure of infamy. In the third place you have under our Constitutional system to determine whether the chance to accomplish what you want in regard to one measure warrants placing the political power in hands you deem unfit, so that the party, in your judgment right on one thing, but wrong in every other, will have the fate of the country in its hands for a four years' term, and deal with every new and unexpected question as it shall think fit. I was bitterly reproached for supporting Mr. McKinley, and refusing to support Mr. Bryan, when I differed from Mr. McKinley on the great predominant question how we should deal with the people of the Philippine Islands. But the men who criticised me most bitterly were some of them the men who applauded my purpose to do so when it was first declared. One of them, the President of the Anti-Imperialist League, wrote me a letter saying that I could be more useful to that cause by remaining a Republican than in any other way, and declared in a public interview that of course Mr. Hoar would remain a Republican. The Secretary of the same organization, after I had made a speech in which I had declared my purpose to continue to support Mr. McKinley, in spite of his grievous error in this respect, wrote me a letter crowded with the most fulsome adulation, and declared that my position was as lofty as that of Chatham or Burke. I could cite many other instances to the same effect. But what other men think, however respectable they may be, is of course of no importance. Every man must settle for himself the question of his individual duty. I could not find that the chance that Mr. Bryan, who had urged the adoption of the Spanish Treaty and had committed himself to the opinion that it was right to do everything we promised to do in that Treaty, would act wisely or righteously if he were trusted with power, or that he could get his party to support him if he were disposed to do so, warranted my running the risk of the mischief he was pledged to accomplish; still less running the risk of giving the government of this country to his supporters for the next four years. There are many good men in the Democratic Party. But the strength of that organization in 1900, as it is to-day, was in Tammany Hall, in the old Southern leaders committed to a policy of violence and fraud in dealing with ten million of our American citizens at home, aided by a few impracticable dreamers who were even less fitted than the Democratic leaders to be trusted with political power.

The Republican Party, whatever its faults, since it came into power in 1860 has been composed in general of what is best in our national life. States like Massachusetts and Vermont, the men of the rural districts in New York, the survivors and children of the men who put down the Rebellion and abolished slavery, saved the Union, and paid the debt and kept the faith, and achieved the manufacturing independence of the country, and passed the homestead laws, are on that side, and in general they give and will hereafter give direction to its counsels. On the other hand their antagonist has been, is, and for an indefinite time to come will be, controlled by the foreign population and the criminal classes of our great cities, by Tammany Hall, and by the leaders of the solid South.

I entered the House of Representatives of the United States at the spring session which began March 4, 1869, at the beginning of Grant's Administration. It then contained a very interesting and important group of men, the most brilliant and conspicuous of whom was, undoubtedly, Mr. James G. Blaine. The public, friends and foes, judged of him by a few striking and picturesque qualities. There has probably never been a man in our history upon whom so few people looked with indifference. He was born to be loved or hated. Nobody occupied a middle ground as to him. In addition to the striking qualities which caught the public eye, he was a man of profound knowledge of our political history, of a sure literary taste, and of great capacity as an orator. He studied and worked out for himself very abstruse questions, on which he formed his own opinions, usually with great sagacity. How far he was affected in his position by the desire for public favor I will not undertake to say. I think the constitution of his mind was such that matters were apt to strike him in much the same way as they were apt to strike the majority of the people of the North, especially of the Northwest, where he was always exceedingly popular. He maintained very friendly personal relations with some of the more intelligent Southerners, especially with Lamar. One incident in his relations with Butler was intensely amusing. They were never on very friendly terms, though each of them found it wise not to break with the other. When Blaine was a candidate for Speaker, to which office he was chosen in the spring session of 1869, his principal competitor was Henry L. Dawes. Dawes's chances were considered excellent until Butler, who had great influence with the Southern Republican members of the House, declared himself for Blaine. Butler was exceedingly anxious to be Chairman of the Committee on Appropriations. This would have been an offence in the nostrils of a large portion of the Republican Party. Mr. Dawes, learning Butler's proposed defection, was beforehand with him by rising in the caucus and himself nominating Mr. Blaine. This secured Blaine's unanimous nomination. Butler, however, still pressed eagerly his own claim for the Chairmanship of the Appropriations. Blaine was altogether too shrewd to yield to that. The committees were not appointed until the following December. Butler suspected somehow that there was doubt about his getting the coveted prize. He accordingly went to the door of the Speaker's room, which was then opposite the door of the House of Representatives, by the side of the Speaker's chair. He found Blaine's messenger keeping the door, who told him that Mr. Blaine was engaged and could not see anybody. "Very well," said General Butler, "I will wait." Accordingly, he took a chair and seated himself at the door, so that he might intercept Blaine as he came out. Blaine, learning that Butler was there, went out the window, round by the portico, and entered the House by another entrance. Somebody came along and, seeing Butler seated in the corridor, said: "What are you about here, General?" "Waiting for Blaine," was the reply. "Blaine is in the chair in the House," was the answer. "It isn't possible," said Butler. "Yes, he is just announcing the committees." Butler rushed into the House in time to hear Mr. Dawes's name read by the Clerk as the Chairman of Appropriations. He was very angry, and bided his time. They had an altercation over the bill to protect the rights of the freedmen in the South, the story of which I tell in speaking of Grant. But as the end of the Congress approached, Butler endeavored to get up an alliance between the Democrats and what were called the "Revenue Reformers." There was a large number of Northwestern Republicans who were disposed to break away from the party because of its policy of high protection. This included representatives of a good many States that afterward were the most loyal supporters of the tariff policy. Butler showed me one day a call he had prepared, saying: "How do you think something like this would answer?" It was a call for a caucus of all persons who desired a reform in the tariff to meet to nominate a candidate for Speaker. I was never in Butler's confidence, and I suppose he showed me the paper with the expectation that I should tell Blaine. Blaine circumvented the movement by giving assurances to the friends of revenue reform that he would make up a Committee of Ways and Means with a majority of persons of their way of thinking. This ended Butler's movement. Blaine kept his word. Mr. Dawes, a high protectionist, was made Chairman, and Mr. Kelly, also a high protectionist, was second on the Committee of Ways and Means; but a majority were revenue reformers. The committee reported a bill which would have been exceedingly injurious to the protected industries of New England. That bill was pressed and reported to the House from the Committee of the Whole; but the member of the committee who had it in charge, by some strange oversight, forgot to demand the previous question. Mr. Dawes, quick as lightning, took from his desk a bill which he had previously prepared, but which had been voted down by his committee, added to it a clause putting tea and coffee on the free list, and, I believe, containing also one or two other items which were specially popular in some parts of the country, and moved that as an amendment to the committee's bill, and himself demanded the previous question.

The cry of a free breakfast-table was then specially popular. There were enough members who did not dare to vote against putting tea and coffee on the free list to turn the scale. Dawes's amendment was adopted, the bill passed, the New England industries saved, and the tariff reformers beaten. The persons who saw only the quiet and modest bearing with which Mr. Dawes conducted himself in the Senate do not know with how much vigor, quickness of wit, readiness and skill in debate, he conducted himself amid the stormy sessions of the House of Representatives during Grant's first Administration. There has never been, within my experience, a greater power than his on the floor of the House. He had mighty antagonists. There were not only very able Democrats, like Randall and Kerr and Holman, but there were mighty leaders among the Republicans. There was little party discipline. Each of them seemed bent on having his own way and taking care of himself, and ready to trip up or overthrow any of his rivals without mercy or remorse. Among them were Butler and Farnsworth and Garfield and Logan and Schenck and Kelly and Banks and Bingham and Sargent and Blaine and Poland.

I was not in the habit of going often to the White House when Grant was President. When I did, he received me always with great kindness. He always seemed to be very fond of my brother; and I suppose that led him to receive me in a more intimate and cordial fashion than he would otherwise have done. I was first introduced to him in the cloak-room of the House of Representatives the Saturday evening before his inauguration. He came, I think, to see Mr. Boutwell, then a member of the House, afterward his Secretary of the Treasury. He came to Worcester in the summer of that year, and I went with him in a special car to Groton in the afternoon. He was not very talkative, though interested in all he saw. He expressed special delight in the appearance of the boys of the Worcester Military School, who turned out to escort him. One of his sons, a well-grown lad, was upon the train. The general had not seen him for some time, and he sat with one arm around him, as one might with a little girl.

It used to be thought that Grant was a man without much literary capacity. Since the publication of his "Memoirs," this notion has been discarded. I can testify to his great readiness as a writer. I saw him write two messages to Congress, both of a good deal of importance, without pause or correction, and as rapidly as his pen could fly over the paper. The first was the message he sent in on the adoption of the Fifteenth Amendment to the Constitution. I was much interested in a bill in aid of national education. I called on the President when the last State needed had ratified the Fifteenth Amendment, and suggested to him that it might be well to send a special message to Congress congratulating them on the result, and urging the policy of promoting education for the new citizens. I told him of General Washington's interest in a national university, and what he had said about the importance of education in his writings. I said I supposed he had them in his library. He said he believed he had, but he wished I would get the books and bring them to him. I accordingly got the books, carried them up to the White House, showed him the passages, and Grant sat down and wrote in a few minutes, and quite rapidly, the message that was sent to Congress the next day. The other occasion was when he sent in the message at the time of the controversy between the House and the Senate in regard to the policy to be pursued in dealing with the outrages in the South. The Senate had passed a bill giving a discretion to the President to take some firm measures to suppress these disorders, and to protect the colored people and the Republicans of the South, and if in his judgment he thought it necessary, to suspend the writ of *habeas corpus*. This measure, which had a considerable majority in the Senate, was voted down in the House under the influence of Speaker Blaine, Mr. Dawes, General Farnsworth, and other prominent Republicans. During the controversy Mr. Blaine left the chair and engaged in the debate, being provoked by some thrust of Butler's. There was a lively passage at arms, in which Blaine said he was obliged to leave the chair, as his predecessor Mr. Colfax had been compelled to do, "to chastise the insolence of the gentleman from Massachusetts." Butler replied by some charge against Blaine, to which Blaine, as he was walking back to take the gavel again, shouted out: "It's a calumny." My sympathies in the matter, so far as the measure of legislation was concerned, were with Butler, though I had, as is well known, little sympathy with him in general.

The House undertook to adjourn the session, but the Senate refused to do so without action on the bill for the protection of human rights at the South. While things were in this condition, I was summoned one morning into the President's room at the Capitol, where I found President Grant, his Cabinet, several of the leading Senators, including Mr. Conkling, I think Mr. Edmunds, Mr. Howe of Wisconsin, and I believe General Wilson, Judge Shellabarger of Ohio, and one or two other members of the House. All the persons who were there were favorable to the proposed legislation, I believe. President Grant said that he had been asked to send in a message urging Congress to pass a law giving him larger powers for the suppression of violence at the South; but he had sent for us to explain the reason why he was unwilling to do it. He thought that the country would look with great disapprobation upon a request to enlarge the powers of the President, and especially to suspend the writ of *habeas corpus* in time of peace, and that he felt especially unwilling to subject himself to that criticism as he had not come to that office from civil life, but had been a soldier, and it might be supposed he favored military methods of government. Several of the gentlemen present expressed rather guardedly their dissent from this view, but Grant seemed to remain firm. I kept silent, as became a person young in public life, until Mr. Howe and Judge Shellabarger whispered together, and then came to me and said: "Mr. Hoar, you may perhaps, be able to have some influence on him. Won't you say something?" I then made a little speech to the President, in which I said that there was no question of the existence of these disorders and crimes; that they would be likely to be increased, and not diminished, especially as the elections in the Southern States approached. He could not allow them to continue.

He would be compelled, in my judgment, to interpose and go to the verge of his authority, or to leave to their fate these people whom we were bound by every consideration of honor to protect. I asked him if he did not think it would be better, instead of exercising a doubtful authority of his own, acquired without legislative sanction, to obtain the necessary authority from Congress in advance. I thought it much less likely to be imputed to him that he was acting in the manner of a soldier and not of a statesman if he were careful to ask in advance the direction of the lawmaking power, and the people understood he was unwilling, even if he had the authority, to act without the sanction of Congress. This view produced an instant change of mind. Grant took a pen, wrote a brief message with great rapidity, read it aloud to the persons who were assembled, and sent it in that very day without the change of a word. It is a clear and excellent statement. The result was that the Republican opposition to the measure in the House was withdrawn, the two Houses came to an agreement, and adjourned without day soon afterward.

One of the most important acts of President Grant's Administration was his veto of the Inflation Bill, which provided for a considerable increase of the large volume of legal tender paper money, which at that time was not redeemed by the government. This veto is regarded by most persons as the turning of the corner by the American people, and setting the face of the Government toward specie payment and honest money. It was during the hard times that followed the crisis of 1873. It is said that President Grant had made up his mind to sign the bill, and sat down to write out his reasons, but that he found them so unsatisfactory that he changed his mind and sent in his veto message. I had not been disposed to believe this until I was told, a little while ago, by Secretary Boutwell that he had the statement that that was the fact from the lips of Grant himself. If that be true, the President must have changed his mind twice. When the bill was pending in the House of Representatives, my wife's father, a very simple-hearted and excellent merchant of Worcester, who spent seventy years of life in business on the same spot, visited us in Washington. I took him up to see Grant. The General was alone and, contrary to his usual custom, in a very talkative mood. He seemed to like Mr. Miller, who had a huge respect for him, and evidently saw that we were not there for any office-seeking or other personal end. He talked with great freedom about himself and his visit to Worcester. He expressed his wonder that the town had grown and prospered so without any advantage of river or harbor or water power, or the neighborhood of rich mines or rich wheat-fields. He then asked me how the bill for an increased issue of greenbacks was coming on in the House. I told him it seemed likely to pass. He then went on to express very earnestly his objection to the measure and to the whole policy, and his dislike of irredeemable paper. He said that it was an immense injury to all classes of the people, but that it bore heavily upon poor and ignorant men. He said that speculators and bankers and brokers could foresee the changes which came about from the fluctuations of paper money and protect themselves against them, but the workingmen and poor men had no such advantages—that they were the greatest sufferers. He added a suggestion I never heard before, that there was in many parts of the country great loss from the counterfeiting of paper money—a loss which fell almost wholly upon poor and ignorant men. I never in my life heard Grant talk so freely on any occasion. I never in my life, but once, saw him apparently so deeply moved. I said: "Mr. President, you know the story of old Judge Grier and the Pennsylvania jury." "No," said he. "Well," said I, "there was once a jury in Pennsylvania, when Grier was holding court, who brought in a very unjust verdict. The judge said: 'Mr. Clerk, record that verdict and enter under it, "Set aside." I will have you to know, Gentlemen of the Jury, that it takes thirteen men in this court to steal a man's farm.' It takes three powers, Mr. President, under our government to pass a law." Grant laughed and said: "Well, if you send it up to me, make it just as bad as you can." There can be no possible question that he then desired and meant to veto the bill. His desire that it might be as bad as possible was that it might be more easy to defend his action.

I had another exceedingly interesting conversation with the President on my return from New Orleans. In the winter of 1875 I went to New Orleans, as Chairman of a Committee of the House of Representatives, to investigate and to ascertain which of the rival State governments had the true title. Louisiana was in a terrible condition. Sheridan was in command of the United States troops there, and it was only their presence that prevented an armed and bloody revolution. The old rebel element, as it was, had committed crimes against the freedmen and the white Republicans which make one of the foulest and bloodiest chapters in all history. Sheridan had much offended the white people there by his vigorous enforcement of laws, and especially by a letter in which he had spoken of them as banditti. I stopped, during my stay in New Orleans, at the St. Charles Hotel, where Sheridan also was a guest. When he came into the crowded breakfast-room every morning, there were loud hisses and groans from nearly the whole assembled company. The morning papers teemed with abusive articles. The guests would take these papers, underscore some specially savage attack, and tell the waiter to take it to General Sheridan as he sat at table at his breakfast. The General would glance at it with an unruffled face, and bow and smile toward the sender of the article. The whole thing made little impression on him. No violence toward him personally was ventured upon. The night before I started on my return to Washington, General Sheridan called to take leave. I was much amused by the simplicity and *naïveté* with which he discussed the situation. He said, among other things: "What you want to do, Mr. Hoar, when you get back to Washington, is to suspend the what-do-you-call-it." He meant, of course, the *habeas corpus*. He knew there was some very uncomfortable thing which stood in his way of promptly suppressing the crimes in Louisiana, where he said more men had been murdered for their political opinions than were slain in the Mexican War. When I got back to Washington, the President sent for me and Mr. Frye of Maine, a member of the committee, to come to the President's room in the Capitol to report to him the result of our observations. During the conversation, Grant expressed what he had often expressed on other occasions, his great admiration for Sheridan. He said: "I believe General Sheridan has no superior as a general, either living or dead, and perhaps not an equal. People think he is only capable of leading an army in battle, or to do a particular thing he is told to do. But I mean, all the qualities of a commander which enable him to direct over as large a territory as any two nations can cover in war. He has judgment, prudence, foresight, and power to deal with the dispositions needed in a great war. I entertained this opinion of him before he became generally known in the late war." I was so impressed with this generous tribute of one great soldier to another that, as soon as the interview was over, I wrote it down and asked Mr. Frye to join with me in certifying to its correctness. It is now before me, and has the following certificate: "The foregoing is a correct statement of what General Grant said to me and Mr. Frye in a conversation this morning in the President's room. February 15, 1875. George F. Hoar." "I heard the above conversation, and certify to the correctness of the above statement of it. William P. Frye."

I heard General Grant express a like opinion of Sheridan under circumstances perhaps even more impressive. I was a guest at a brilliant dinner-party given by Mr. Robeson, Secretary of the Navy, where Grant, General Sherman, General Sheridan, Commodore Alden, Admiral Porter, Chief Justice Chase, Attorney-General E. R. Hoar, Lyman Trumbull, Mr. Blaine, and some other men of great distinction were present. There were about twenty guests. Mr. James Russell Lowell was of the company. I believe no one of that brilliant circle is now living. Commodore Alden remarked, half in jest, to a gentleman who sat near him, that there was nothing he disliked more than a subordinate who always obeyed orders. "What is that you are saying, Commodore?" said President Grant, across the table. The Commodore repeated what he had said. "There is a good deal of truth in what you say," said General Grant. "One of the virtues of General Sheridan was that he knew when to act without orders. Just before the surrender of Lee, General Sheridan captured some despatches from which he learned that Lee had ordered his supplies to a certain place. I was on the other side of the river, where he could get no communication from me until the next morning. General Sheridan pushed on at once without orders, got to the place fifteen minutes before the rebels, and captured the supplies. After the surrender was concluded, the first thing General Lee asked me for was rations for his men. I issued to them the same provisions which Sheridan had captured. Now if Sheridan, as most men would have done, had waited for orders from me, Lee would have got off." I listened with wonder at the generous modesty which, before that brilliant company, could remove one of the brightest laurels from his own brow and place it on the brow of Sheridan.

I had another memorable conversation with Grant, not so pleasant. It revealed a capacity of intense passion which I do not know that he ever manifested on any other occasion. He had sent into the Senate the nomination of William A. Simmons for the important office of Collector of Boston. This was due to the influence of General Butler. Mr. Sumner, whose controversy with the President is well known, was then the senior Senator from Massachusetts. The nomination had been made, of course, without consulting him, with whom Grant was not on friendly terms, and without consulting any of the members of the House of Representatives except Butler. There was a very earnest opposition to this nomination. I went up to the White House to endeavor to induce President Grant to withdraw it, but he had gone out. I repeated my visit once or twice, but failed to find the President. The third or fourth time that I went up, as I was coming away I saw President Grant on the other side of Pennsylvania Avenue, walking alone on the sidewalk adjoining Lafayette Square. I suppose it was not in accordance with etiquette to join the President when he was walking alone in the street; but I overtook him, and said: "Mr. President, I have been to the White

House several times, and been unable to find you in. The business of the House is very urgent just now, and it is difficult for me to get away again. Perhaps, therefore, you will kindly allow me to say what I have to say here." The President very courteously assented. I walked along with him, turned the corner, and walked along the sidewalk adjoining the east side of Lafayette Square, until we came to the corner opposite the house then occupied by Sumner, which is now part of the Arlington Hotel. I told the President that I thought the Republicans in Massachusetts would be much dissatisfied with the nomination of Simmons, and hoped it might be withdrawn. The President replied that he thought it would be an injustice to the young man to do so, and that the opposition to him seemed to be chiefly because he was a friend of General Butler. I combated the argument as well as I could. The whole conversation was exceedingly quiet and friendly on both sides until we turned the corner by Mr. Sumner's house, when the President, with great emphasis, and shaking his closed fist toward Sumner's house, said: "I shall not withdraw the nomination. That man who lives up there has abused me in a way which I never suffered from any other man living." I did not, of course, press the President further. But I told him I regretted very much the misunderstanding between him and Mr. Sumner, and took my leave. It was evident that in some way the President connected this nomination with the controversy between himself and Sumner.

I have always lamented, in common with all the friends and lovers of both these great men, that they should have so misunderstood each other; yet it was not unnatural. They were both honest, fearless, patriotic, and brave. Yet never were two honest, fearless, patriotic, and brave men more unlike each other. The training, the mental characteristics, the field of service, the capacities, the virtues, the foibles of each tended to make him underestimate and misunderstand the other. The man of war, and the man of peace; the man whose duty it was to win battles and conduct campaigns, and the man who trusted to the prevalence of ideas in a remote future; the man who wielded executive power, and the man who in a fierce contest with executive power had sought to extend the privileges, power, and authority of the Senate; the man who adhered tenaciously to his friends through good and evil report, and the man whose friendships were such that evil report of personal dishonor never dared assail them; the man of little taste for letters, and the man of vast and varied learning; the man of blunt, plain ways, and the man of courtly manners; the man of few words, and the man who ever deemed himself sitting in a lofty pulpit with a mighty sounding board, with a whole widespread people for a congregation—how could they understand each other? Grant cared little for speech-making. It sometimes seemed as if Sumner thought the Rebellion itself was put down by speeches in the Senate, and that the war was an unfortunate and most annoying, though trifling disturbance, as if a fire-engine had passed by. Sumner did injustice to Grant; Grant did injustice to Sumner. The judgment of each was warped and clouded, until each looked with a blood-shotten eye at the conduct of the other. But I believe they know and honor each other now.

CHAPTER XIII

SUMNER AND WILSON

When I took my seat on the 4th of March, 1869, the Commonwealth of Massachusetts had a position of power in both Houses of Congress never held by any other State before or since, unless we except that held for a short time in early days by Virginia. Charles Sumner was beyond all question the foremost figure on the National stage, save Grant alone. He had seen the triumph of the doctrines for which he had contended all his life. He had more than any other man contributed to fetter the hands of Andrew Johnson and drive him from power. Henry Wilson was the most skilful political organizer in the country. Sumner was at the head of the Committee on Foreign Relations, and Wilson of that of Military Affairs. In the House Henry L. Dawes was at the head of the Committee on Appropriations, Benjamin F. Butler of the Committee on Reconstruction, William B. Washburn of the Committee on Claims, Nathaniel P. Banks of the Committee on Foreign Affairs. These Committees with the Committee on the Judiciary of which General Butler was a member, and the Committee on Ways and Means, controlled the policy of the House on all the great questions then interesting the country. Samuel Hooper had the third place on the Committee on Coinage, Weights and Measures. But he was its dominant member and in a later Congress introduced the Bill for Reforming the Currency, a wise and salutary measure. It is known, however, among ignorant people in some parts of the country as "The Crime of '73."

Sumner and Wilson are so well known to the American people that it would be superfluous for me to attempt to describe either elaborately. I have spoken of each at some length elsewhere.

Charles Sumner held a place in the public life of the country which no other man ever shared with him. He held a place in the public life of the world shared by very few indeed. He was an idealist. He subjected every measure to the inexorable test of the moral law. Yet, at the same time, he was a powerful political leader, and in a time when the fate of the Republic was decided accomplished vast practical results. Where duty seemed to him to utter its high commands he could see no obstacle in hostile majorities, and no restraint in the limitations of a written Constitution. It is right, therefore Constitutional, was the logical formula with which he dealt with every question of State. We should be deaf and blind to all the lessons of history, if we were to declare it to be safe that men trusted with Executive or even with Legislative power should act on that principle. Unfortunately, humanity is so constituted that the benevolent despot is likely to work more mischief even than a malevolent despot. His example of absolute disregard of constitutional restraints will be followed by men of very different motives. Yet the influence of one such man pressing and urging his companions forward in a Legislative body like the Senate of the United States, keeping ever before the people the highest ideals, inspired by the love of liberty, and ever speaking and working in the fear of God, is inestimable.

Charles Sumner lacked that quality which enables the practical statesman to adjust the mechanism of complicated statutes. He had no genius for detail. It would not have been safe to trust him with Appropriation Bills, or Bills for raising revenue. But he was competent to deal with questions of the greatest moment to the State. He knew what are its governing forces. He retained his hold on those forces. He directed them. He caused sound principles of action to take effect in the Government of the State in great emergencies. He converted the people to his opinion. He inspired the people with lofty desires. He accomplished wise public ends by wise means. He maintained his hold on power in an important time. He took a prominent part in great debates and was the acknowledged leader of one side of the question. He believed that the conscience of the people was a better guide than individual ambitions. He always did the thing he could best do. He did the thing that most needed to be done, the thing most effective at the time, the thing that no other man did or could do. He left to others to do what hundreds of others could do well enough. He contributed largely to the Government of his country, in the most trying period of our history, its motive and its direction. That is a pretty practical contribution to the voyage which furnishes to the steamship its engine and its compass. His figure will abide in history like that of St. Michael in art, an emblem of celestial purity, of celestial zeal, of celestial courage. It will go down to immortality with its foot upon the dragon of Slavery, and with the sword of the spirit in its hand, but with a tender light in its eye, and a human love in its smile. Guido and Raphael conceived their "inviolable saint,"

> Invulnerable, impenetrably armed:
> Such high advantages his innocence
> Gave him above his foe; not to have sinned,
> Not to have disobeyed. In fight he stood
> Unwearied, unobnoxious to be pained
> By wounds.

The Michael of the painters, as a critic of genius akin to their own has pointed out, rests upon his prostrate foe light as a morning cloud, no muscle strained, with unhacked sword and unruffled wings, his bright tunic and shining armor without a rent or stain. Not so with our human champion. He had to bear the bitterness and agony of a long and doubtful struggle, with common weapons and against terrible odds. He came out of it with soiled garments and with a mortal wound, but without a regret and without a memory of hate.

It was fortunate for Sumner and fortunate for the Commonwealth and the country that he had Henry Wilson for his colleague. Wilson supplied almost everything that Sumner lacked. I cannot undertake to tell the story of his useful life in the space at my command here. If I were to try I should do great injustice to him and to myself.

He was a very impressive and interesting character, of many virtues, of many faults. His faults he would have been the first to acknowledge himself. Indeed, I do not know of any fault he had that he would not have acknowledged and lamented in a talk with his near friend, or that he would have sought to hide from the people.

The motives which controlled his life from the time when he snatched such moments as he could from his day's work on a shoemaker's bench and studied far into the night to fit himself for citizenship, down to the time when he died in the Vice-President's chamber—the second officer in the Government—and if his life and health had been spared, he very likely would have been called to the highest place in the Government—were public and patriotic, not personal. He was not without ambitions for himself. But they were always subordinate in him to the love of liberty and the love of country. He espoused the unpopular side when he started in life, and he stuck to it through all its unpopularity.

He was a skilful, adroit, practised and constant political manager. He knew the value of party organization, and did not disdain the arts and diplomacies of a partisan. He carried them sometimes farther, in my judgment, than a scrupulous sense of honor would warrant, or than was consistent with the noble, frank, lofty behavior which Massachusetts and the American people expect of their statesmen. The most conspicuous instance of this was his joining the Know Nothing Party, in whose intolerance he had no belief.

But it was done as an instrument for destroying the existing political parties, which were an obstacle to freedom, and clearing the field for a new one. This object was successfully accomplished, and in its accomplishment Wilson had a large share. But it was, in my judgment, doing evil that good may come. Wilson freely admitted this before he died, and said—I have no doubt with absolute sincerity —that he would give ten years of his life if he could blot out that one transaction.

He was a very valuable legislator. He was the author of many important measures in the war, during which he was chairman of the Committee on Military Affairs of the Senate, and showed much ability in the way of practical and constructive statesmanship. I do not believe any man in the Senate in his time, not even Sumner, had more influence over his colleagues than he.

There was not a drop of bigotry, intolerance, or personal hatred in him. As you would expect from a man who raised himself from the humblest to the loftiest place in the republic, he was a believer in pure manhood, without respect of persons or conditions.

He was a powerful stump orator. He never made speeches that were quoted as models of eloquence or wisdom. But he knew what the farmer and the mechanic and the workman at his bench were thinking of, and addressed himself always to their best and highest thought. He was a great vote-making speaker. When Mechanics Hall, in Worcester, or the City Hall was filled to hear Henry Wilson in a close campaign, many men who entered the hall undecided or against him, went away to take earnest part on his side.

He had a good many angry political strifes. But he never bore malice or seemed to keep angry over night. General Butler once wrote him a letter pouring out on his head the invective of which he was so conspicuous a master. Wilson brought the letter into the office of a dear friend of mine in Boston when I happened to be there, handed it to us to read, and observed: "That is a cussed mean letter." I do not think he ever spoke of it or scarcely thought of it again.

But his chief gift and faculty is one which I can hardly think of words to describe fitly. The few of his old friends who are left will understand what I mean. But I can hardly make those who did not know him, or live in his time, comprehend it. That was his rare and unequalled gift of gathering and uttering the sentiment of the people. When new and doubtful matters of pith and moment were to be dealt with, and after a long apparent hesitation, and backing and filling, and what people who did not know him thought trembling in the balance, he would at last make up his mind, determine on his action, and strike a blow which had in it not only the vigor of his own arm, but the whole vigor and strength of the public sentiment which he had gathered and which he represented. He was an ubiquitous person. He would travel all over the State, spending the day, perhaps, in visiting forty shops and factories in the neighborhood of Boston; then take a nine or ten o'clock train at night and go up to Springfield, get in there at two or three o'clock in the morning, call up out of bed some active politician and tell him he had come to sleep with him; spend the night in talking over the matter about which he was anxious until six or seven o'clock in the morning (I do not believe he ever slept much, either with anybody or alone), and then, perhaps, up to Northampton or Greenfield to see some person whom he called Tom, Dick, or Harry, but who knew the local feeling there; and after a week or two spent in that way, never giving his own opinion, talking as if he were all things to all men, seeming to hesitate and hesitate and falter and be frightened, so if you had met him and talked with him you would have said, if you did not know him well, that there was no more thought, nor more steadiness of purpose, or backbone in him than in an easterly cloud; but at length, when the time came, and he had got ready, the easterly cloud seemed suddenly to have been charged with an electric fire and a swift and resistless bolt flashed out, and the righteous judgment of Massachusetts came from his lips.

With all his faults, Peace be to the ashes of Henry Wilson. He was a leader and tribune of the people. We do not seem to have such leaders now-a-days. I liked Charles Sumner better. But it was a great thing for Massachusetts, a great thing for human liberty, and a great thing for Charles Sumner himself that he had Henry Wilson as a friend and ally, a disciple and a co-worker.

If Wilson had lived, in my opinion, it is quite likely that he would have been the Republican candidate for the Presidency in 1876, and would have been triumphantly elected. There was a very powerful movement going on all over the country to bring that about. Wilson's hold upon the affection of the people everywhere was very strong indeed.

Wilson became Vice-President of the United States, March 4, 1873. He died two years afterward. I was asked to write the inscription for a tablet placed in the Vice-President's Room in the Capitol by order of the Senate in 1902. It follows here.

IN THIS ROOM
HENRY WILSON
VICE PRESIDENT OF THE UNITED STATES
AND A SENATOR FOR EIGHTEEN YEARS,
DIED NOVEMBER 22 1875.
THE SON OF A FARM LABORER, NEVER AT
SCHOOL MORE THAN TWELVE MONTHS, IN
YOUTH A JOURNEYMAN SHOEMAKER, HE
RAISED HIMSELF TO THE HIGH PLACES OF
FAME, HONOR AND POWER, AND BY UNWEARIED
STUDY MADE HIMSELF AN AUTHORITY IN THE
HISTORY OF HIS COUNTRY AND OF LIBERTY,
AND AN ELOQUENT PUBLIC SPEAKER TO
WHOM SENATE AND PEOPLE EAGERLY
LISTENED. HE DEALT WITH AND CONTROLLED
VAST PUBLIC EXPENDITURE DURING A GREAT
CIVIL WAR, YET LIVED AND DIED POOR, AND
LEFT TO HIS GRATEFUL COUNTRYMEN THE
MEMORY OF AN HONORABLE PUBLIC SERVICE,
AND A GOOD NAME FAR BETTER THAN RICHES.

CHAPTER XIV

PERSONALITIES IN DEBATE

I HAVE been, in general, enabled to avoid angry conflicts in debate or the exchange of rough personalities. My few experiences of that kind came from attacks on Massachusetts, which I could not well avoid resenting. The only two I now think of happened in my first term. In one case, Mr. S. S. Cox of New York, who was one of the principal champions on the Democratic side of the House, a man noted for his wit, undertook to make an attack on the Massachusetts Puritans, and to revive the old slander that they had burned witches. I made some slight correction of what Mr. Cox said but he renewed the attack. I was then comparatively unknown in the House. Mr. Cox treated me with considerable contempt, and pointing to Mr. Dawes, who had charge of the bill then under discussion, but who had not given any reply to Cox's attack, said, with a contemptuous look at me: "Massachusetts does not send her Hector to the field," to which I answered that it was not necessary to send Hector to the field when the attack was led by Thersites. The retort seemed to strike the House favorably, and was printed in the papers throughout the country, and Cox let me and Massachusetts alone thereafter.

I had a like encounter with Daniel W. Voorhees of Indiana, who was a more formidable competitor. Mr. Voorhees made the same charge against the people of Massachusetts of having burned witches at the stake in the old Puritan time. It was in a debate under the five-minute rule. After reiterating the old familiar slander that the State of Massachusetts in her early history had burned witches at the stake, Mr. Voorhees added that in 1854 or 1855 the Know Nothings broke up convents, burned Catholic churches, and would have burned Catholics and Sisters of Charity themselves at the stake within her borders, if they had dared to do so.

I declared both of these charges to be utterly false, and said that no human being was ever burned at the stake in Massachusetts for the crime of witchcraft, and though at a time when the whole civilized world believed in witchcraft on the authority of certain passages in the Old Testament, the courts of Massachusetts did execute some nineteen or twenty persons of both sexes for the alleged crime of witchcraft, it was also true that the people of Massachusetts were the first among men to see the error and wickedness of this course; that although late in the following century, many people were condemned for witchcraft in England and on the Continent, the love of justice and the intelligence of Massachusetts first exposed that error and wickedness.

I explained that a convent was burned in Massachusetts, not in 1854 or 1855 by the Know Nothings, but in 1836, by a mob excited by a rumor that some terrible cruelty had been inflicted upon some young women who had been placed in a convent in Charlestown; that the criminals were arrested, tried and sentenced, and that their crime left no more stain upon the State than any criminal act committed within the limits of any civilized country. In conclusion, I said it did not become the political friends of the men who had burned our soldiers alive at Fort Pillow, or who burned orphan asylums in New York, and hung negroes on lamp posts, to talk of cruelties in a past age.

This retort angered Voorhees beyond endurance, and before I could finish my sentence, he sprang to his feet and cried out in great anger: "Every word the gentleman says is false and he knows it." There was a demand that my words be taken down and that the words of Mr. Voorhees be taken down. That was done. The chairman of the committee, Mr. Ingersoll, brother of the famous Robert G. Ingersoll, declared that the words of Mr. Voorhees were unparliamentary, and ruled that my language was "rather pungent but not unparliamentary." Whereupon the committee arose amid great laughter, and the transaction ended.

CHAPTER XV

THE NATIONAL HOUSE OF REPRESENTATIVES IN 1869

The House, when I entered it, contained many very able men. Some of them remained long enough in public life to fill a large and prominent place in the history of the country. Others retired early. I will mention only a few:

I do not think his countrymen have estimated Nathaniel P. Banks at his true value. When he left office at the ripe age of seventy-five a public service ended surpassed in variety and usefulness by that of few citizens of Massachusetts since the days of John Adams. He bore a great part in a great history. Men who saw him in his later life, a feeble, kindly old man, with only the remains of his stately courtesy, had little conception of the figure of manly strength and dignity which he presented when he presided over the Constitutional Convention in 1853, or took the oath of office as Governor in 1858. He raised himself from a humble place, unaided, under the stimulant of a native and eager desire for excellence. He was always regarded by the working people of Massachusetts as the type of what was best in themselves and as the example and representative of the great opportunity which the Republic holds out to its poorest citizens and their children. He was a natural gentleman, always kindly and true. From this trait and not because of want of fidelity to his own convictions he found as warm friends among his political opponents as among his political associates.

Gen. Banks was Chairman of the Committee on Foreign Relations in 1869. He was then beginning to lose somewhat his oratorical power and the splendid qualities which made him so important a force in the history of Massachusetts and of the country. But still on fit occasions he showed all his old vigor and brilliancy. When the delegation gave a dinner to William B. Washburn on his election as Governor Banks presided. He kept up a running stream of eloquence and wit as he introduced the different speakers and punctuated their remarks with interjections of his own, which I have never known equalled, though I have attended many like occasions. Banks was a man of humble origin. He used to be known as the Waltham Bobbin Boy. He worked in his boyhood and youth in a factory in Waltham. He had very early a passion for reading. When Felton was inaugurated President of Harvard, Banks was Governor. As is the custom, he represented the Commonwealth and inducted the new President into office. There were famous speakers at the Dinner,—Daniel Webster, old Josiah Quincy, Edward Everett, Dr. Walker, Winthrop, and Felton himself. But the Governor's speech was the best of the whole. He described the time of his poverty in his youth when he used to work in a mill five days in a week, and on Saturday walk ten miles to Boston to spend the day in the Athenæum Library and ten miles back at night. He told how he used to peer in through the gate as he passed Harvard College with an infinite longing for the treasures of learning that were inside. That refined and fastidious audience was stirred by an unwonted emotion.

The older public men of Massachusetts did not take very kindly to Banks. He was a man of the people. He was sometimes charged, though unjustly, with being a demagogue. He sometimes erred in his judgment. But he was a man of large and comprehensive vision, of independence, and exerted his vast influence with the people for high ends. He might justly be called, like the negro Toussaint, L'Ouverture,—The Opener. His election as Governor extracted the people from the mire of Know Nothingism. His election as Speaker of the Massachusetts House of Representatives was part of the first victory over the Whig Dynasty which had kept the State, contrary to its best traditions, in alliance with slavery. His election as Speaker of the United States House of Representatives was the first National Republican victory. His taking a little slave girl on a cannon during the War in his march through the Shenandoah Valley was hailed throughout the country as an omen that the War would not end until slavery was abolished. He rendered a special service to the Commonwealth and to the cause of good learning which I think never would have been accomplished without his personal influence. When Agassiz had been in this country but a few years he seriously contemplated going back to Europe. It was understood that he would stay if a sufficient fund could be raised to enable him to prosecute his researches here and to establish a museum where his collections could be cared for and made useful to science. There was a meeting in Boston to see about raising the fund. The Governor was invited to attend. The gentlemen present spoke rather doubtfully of the prospect of success. Governor Banks was asked what he thought the Commonwealth would do. He replied: "The Commonwealth will give a hundred thousand dollars." The Legislature had been of late years economical, not to say niggardly, in such matters. Governor Banks's declaration was received with entire incredulity. One gentleman present said that he was very much discouraged by what His Excellency had said. If he had said some moderate sum there might have been hope that it would be given, but it was utterly hopeless to expect that any such extravagant sum as that would be contributed by the State. The gentleman seemed to be well warranted in what he said. The three colleges, Harvard, Amherst and Williams, had united in an application for one hundred thousand dollars shortly before. It was supported by the eloquence of Edward Everett and the authority of Mark Hopkins and President Hitchcock. Harvard was then so poor that they had not money to spare when they wanted to move the pulpit from the end to the side of the Chapel. But the application was denied. Banks replied in his somewhat sonorous fashion: "You need not trouble yourself, Sir. The Commonwealth will give a hundred thousand dollars." And she did. This was followed by the grant, under Banks's influence, for the endowment of the Boston

Institute of Technology, large grants to the colleges and grants to some of the endowed schools.

General Banks's statue should stand by the State House as one of the foremost benefactors of the great educational institutions of the Commonwealth, and as an example of what a generous ambition can accomplish for the humblest child in the Republic.

Governor Boutwell, who is still living, became a member of President Grant's Cabinet in March, 1869, and remained in the House only a day or two of the spring session which lasted about ten days. He was succeeded in the following December by George M. Brooks, who had been my friend from early boyhood. He would in my judgment have had an eminent political career if he had remained in public life, but for his great modesty. He never seemed to value highly anything he accomplished himself. But his sympathy and praise were always called out by anything done by a friend. I think Brooks took much more pleasure in anything well done or well said by one of his colleagues than in anything of his own. He was a man of an exceedingly sweet, gracious and affectionate nature, loving as a child, yet as men of such natures often are, thoroughly manly. He was incapable of any meanness or conscious wrong-doing. He had a very pleasant and ready wit. The people of Middlesex County, especially of Concord, were very fond of him, and would have kept him in public life as long as he desired. But his health was not good in Washington. The climate of the place and the bad air of the House were unfavorable. He did not fancy very much the strife and noise of that turbulent assembly. So he gladly accepted an appointment to the office of Judge of Probate of Middlesex County which was absolutely suited to him. He administered that important office to the entire satisfaction of the people until his death. I think George Brooks's smile would be enough to console any widow in an ordinary affliction.

William Barrett Washburn, afterward Governor and Senator, was Chairman of the Committee on Claims.

He is one of the best recent examples of a character whose external manifestations change somewhat with changing manners and fashions, but the substance of whose quality abides and I believe will abide through many succeeding generations. He was a New England Puritan. He brought to the service of the people a purity of heart, a perfect integrity, an austerity of virtue which not so much rendered him superior to all temptation as made it impossible to conceive that any of the objects of personal desire which lead public men astray could ever to him even be a temptation.

There were few stronger or clearer intellects in the public service. His mind moved rapidly by a very simple and direct path to a sound and correct result in the most difficult and complicated cases. The Chairmanship of the Committee on Claims was then with two or three exceptions the most important position in the House. He spoke very seldom and then to the point, stating very perfectly the judgment of a clear-headed and sound business man. But his opinion carried great weight. He was universally respected. Every man felt safe in following his recommendation in any matter which he had carefully investigated.

Congress was beset by claims to the amount of hundreds and hundreds of millions, where fraud seemed sometimes to exhaust its resources, where, in the conflict of testimony, it was almost impossible to determine the fact, and where the facts when determined often presented the most novel and difficult questions of public law and public policy. Mr. Washburn's dealing with these cases was the very sublimity of common sense. He very soon acquired the confidence of the House so completely that his judgment became its law in matters within the jurisdiction of his committee. I became acquainted with him, an acquaintance which soon ripened into cordial friendship, when I entered the House in the spring of 1869. I think I may fairly claim that it was the result of what I said and did that he was agreed upon by the opponents of General Butler as their candidate for Governor, and was Butler's successful antagonist.

Beneath his plain courtesy was a firmness which Cato never surpassed. Upon a question of morality, or freedom or righteousness there was never a drop of compromise in his blood. He could not be otherwise than the constant foe of slavery, and the constant friend of everything which went to emancipate and elevate the slave. It was his good fortune to record his vote in favor of all the three great amendments to the constitution, and to be the supporter, friend and trusted counsellor of Abraham Lincoln.

After his election to fill Sumner's unexpired term I had a letter from Adin Thayer in which he said: "Washburn hates Butler with an Evangelical hatred which you know is more intense than a Liberal Christian can attain to."

James Buffington was a shrewd and amusing character. He understood the temper of the House very well and had great influence in accomplishing anything he undertook. He prided himself on the fact that he never missed answering to his name at roll call during his whole term of service. He understood very well the art of pleasing his constituents. He made it a rule, he told me, to send at least one document under his own frank every year to every voter in his District. On one occasion in a hotly contested election he had four votes more in a town on Cape Cod than any other candidate. He was curious and inquired what it meant. The Chairman of the Selectmen told him that there were four men who lived in an out-of-the-way place, who never came to town meetings and nobody seemed to know much about them. They were a father and his three sons, living together on the same farm. But at that election they appeared at town meeting. All four voted for Buffington and for no other candidate and disappeared at once. The Selectman asked him why he voted for Buffington. "If he knew him?" "No!" said the old fellow. "He knows me. He sends me and each of my sons a document every winter."

Buffington was very anxious about the matter of patronage and of getting offices for all his constituents. A great many men applied for his support; frequently there were many applications for the same office. He did not like to refuse them. So he made it a rule to give all of them a letter of recommendation to the Departments. But he had an understanding with the appointing clerks that if he wrote his name Buffington with the g he desired that man should be appointed, but if he wrote it Buffinton without the g he did not wish to be taken seriously.

Beyond all question the leader of the Massachusetts delegation, and of the House, was Henry L. Dawes. He had had a successful career at the bar and in public life before his election to Congress. In Congress he made his way to the front very rapidly. No member of the House of Representatives from Massachusetts and few from any part of the Union had an influence which could be at all compared with his. He became in succession Chairman of the two foremost Committees, that of Appropriations and that of Ways and Means. He was a prominent candidate for the office of Speaker when Mr. Blaine was elected and was defeated, as I have said elsewhere, only by the adroit management of Butler.

Mr. Dawes represented the Berkshire District in the House for eighteen years when he declined further service there. He was then elected to the Senate where he remained eighteen years longer, when he declined further service there. During the last part of his last term he was troubled with a growing deafness which I suppose had much to do with his declining to enter upon the contest for another re-election. He was regarded by the manufacturers of Massachusetts as their faithful and powerful representative. He had several contests for his seat in the Senate when his opponents thought they were sure of success; but they found themselves left in the minority when the vote came to be taken. They never fully comprehended what defeated them. They would get the support of men who were active in caucuses and nominating conventions and supposed with excellent reason that they were safe. But there was in every factory village in Massachusetts some man of influence and ability and wealth, frequently a large employer of labor, who had been in the habit of depending on Mr. Dawes for the security of his most important interests, so far as they could be affected by legislation. They knew him and they knew that he knew them, and their power when they chose to exert it could not be resisted.

Persons who saw Mr. Dawes in his later years only, when he sat quietly in his seat in the Senate, taking little part save in a few special subjects, could not realize what a power he had been when he was the leading and strongest champion in that great body which contained Blaine and Bingham and Butler and Schenck and Farnsworth and Allison and Eugene Hale and Garfield.

When Mr. Dawes left the Senate in 1893, his associates gave a banquet in his honor, at which I made the following remarks. They were, I believe, approved by the entire company. I record them here as my deliberate judgment:

"If there be any admirer of other forms of government who think unfavorably of our republican fashion of selecting our rulers, I would invite him to examine the list of men whom Massachusetts for a hundred years has chosen as her Senators of the first class. I do not claim for her any superiority over other Commonwealths in this respect—but certainly she has given you of her best. She has sent men who were worthy to be the peers of the men who have represented her sister States, and if that be true, they surely have been worthy to be peers in any Senate that was ever gathered upon earth. The line begins with Tristram Dalton, save Washington the stateliest gentleman of his time, rich in every mental accomplishment, whose presence graced and ennobled every assembly that he entered. Next to him comes George Cabot, the wise statesman and accomplished merchant, beloved friend of Hamilton, trusted counsellor of Washington, whose name and lineage are represented at this table to-night, who shared with his successor, Benjamin Goodhue, the honor of being the first authority in finance in their generation, save Hamilton alone.

"Then comes John Quincy Adams, who left the Senate, after years of illustrious public service, in 1808, but to begin another public service of forty years, still more illustrious. He served his country in every department of public occupation. He was Minister to five great Powers in succession. He was present as Secretary when the treaty of peace was signed in 1783. He negotiated and signed the Treaty of Ghent, the Commercial Treaty of 1815, the French Treaty of 1822, the Prussian Treaty, and the treaty which acquired Florida from Spain. He was Senator, Representative, Foreign Minister, Secretary of State, and President. He breasted the stormy waves of the House of Representatives at the age of eighty, and when he died in the Capitol, he left no purer or loftier fame behind him.

"Next came James Lloyd, the modest gentleman, the eloquent orator and the accomplished man of business. Then came Gore and Ashmun and Mellen and Mills, each great among the great lawyers of a great generation. Next in the procession comes the majestic presence of Daniel Webster, whose matchless logic and splendid eloquence gave to the Constitution of the country an authority in the reason and in the hearts of his countrymen equal to anything in judicial decision and equal to that of any victory of arms. With his reply to Hayne, it has been said that every Union cannon in the late war was shotted. His power in debate was only equalled by his wisdom in council. It was said of him by one whose fame as a great public teacher equals his own: 'His weight was like the falling of a planet, his discretion the return of its due and perfect curve.'

"Then comes Rufus Choate, next to Webster himself the foremost forensic orator of modern times, against whose imperial eloquence no human understanding, either on the Bench or in the jury box, seemed to be proof. Following them is he who still lives in his honored age, with his intellectual powers unshattered, the foremost citizen of his native Commonwealth, the accomplished and eloquent Winthrop. Next comes Rantoul, who died when his foot had scarcely crossed the threshold of the Senate Chamber, whose great hope was equal to the greatest of memories. Next is the figure of the apostle of liberty, Charles Sumner, the echo of whose voice still seems to linger in the arches of the Capitol. To those of us who remember him, he seems, as Disraeli said of Richard Cobden, 'still sitting, still debating, still legislating' in the Senate Chamber.

"No two of these men were alike in the quality they brought to the public service. Their mental portraiture is as different and as individual as the faces painted by Titian or Van Dyke or Holbein. But each brought to the service of the State what she most needed in each generation. The constructive statesman, the framer of the Constitution and statutes, the financier, the debater, the lawyer, the man of business, the diplomatist, the reformer, the orator, are all there, and all are there at their best.

"It is enough, and not too much, to say of my colleague that, as he lays down his office, the State that has been proud of them is proud of him. The State that has been satisfied with them is satisfied with him. In all this illustrious line, there is none other who has more faithfully and more successfully discharged every duty of Senatorial service, and who has more constantly represented the interests and character of the dear old Commonwealth, who has maintained a higher or firmer place in her confidence and respect than he whom we greet and with whom we part to-night. Mr. Dawes was elected to the Massachusetts House of Representatives in 1847. Every year since, with one exception, he has held some honorable public station from the gift of his native State. Everywhere, at the Bar, in the State Legislature, in the Representative Chamber, in the Senate Chamber, he has been a leader. Some great department of public service has depended upon him for a successful administration. He has always been appointed to some special service or duty or difficulty which he has discharged to the entire satisfaction of his constituents and his political associates. His work has been as remarkable for its variety as for its dignity and importance, or the length of time for which it has continued. He has proved himself fit for every conspicuous position in our Republican army except that of trumpeter. When the duty was done, he has not sought for personal credit or popular applause. His qualities have not been those for which the people manifested their regard by shouting or clapping of hands, or stamping of feet in public meetings; he has had no following of ambitious politicians whom he has sought to repay for their political services at the public expense.

"But he has had a place second to that of no other man in the solid and enduring esteem of the people of the Commonwealth. He has been content to do a service, and has left the other men who sought for it the credit of doing it. His official action has tended to make or unmake great industries. Great fortunes have depended upon it. He has affected values of millions upon millions, and yet he retires from office with unstained hands, without fortune, and without a spot upon his integrity. He has no children pensioned at the public charge. He will leave behind him no wealth gained directly or indirectly from his public opportunities. He will go back to a humble and simple dwelling not exceeding in costliness that of many a Massachusetts mechanic or farmer. But honor, good fame, the affection of his fellow citizens, the friendship of his fellow Senators will enter its portals with him, and there they will dwell with him until he leaves it for his last home."

Mr. Dawes was a very powerful and logical reasoner. He was a very successful advocate when at the Bar and he was always a strong antagonist in debate and very effective as a campaign speaker. He stuck closely to his subject. He had a gift of sarcasm with which he could make an adversary feel exceedingly uncomfortable, although he rarely indulged in it. He almost never attempted eloquence, except so far as it is found in his grave and effective statement of his case. One sentence of his which I myself heard deserves to be remembered among the best things in American eloquence. Speaking to thirty or forty people at a club in Boston of the power and greatness of the Republic, he said: "If we cannot say of our country, as Mr. Webster said of England, 'that her morning drum-beat circles the earth with an unbroken strain of her martial airs,' we can at least say that before the sun sets upon Alaska he has risen upon Maine."

In my first Congress the leadership was shared between my colleague, Mr. Dawes, and Robert C. Schenck of Ohio.

General Schenck was an old Whig. He had served with distinction in the time of Webster and Clay and Calhoun and Corwin. He had the gift of vigorous, simple Saxon English. He was a very powerful debater, a man of wisdom and of industry. He was Chairman of the Committee on Ways and Means, and carried through to success, against odds and difficulties, an important tariff bill. At one time he found the measure, which he had introduced, overloaded and destroyed by amendments. He abandoned it in disgust, declaring that it had been "nibbled to death by pismires." But he afterward introduced the measure in another form, and came off successful and triumphant in the end.

He was afterward sent abroad by General Grant to succeed Mr. Motley. He got into trouble there by giving a letter of recommendation which was unwisely used to promote an enterprise known as the Emma Mine. He gave the recommendation, I have no doubt, in entire good faith. The stock of that mine went down. The investors lost their money, and great complaint was made that he had used his official position to promote a fraudulent scheme. He was compelled to withdraw from the Mission. He was not recalled, but came home on leave of absence, and resigned here. So he was not obliged to take formal leave. But the stock of the mine afterward became exceedingly valuable, and the public regretted the unjust judgment they had formed about General Schenck. I had and have a great regard for him. There was not a dishonest hair on the old fellow's head. His health failed soon after, so he had no opportunity to render further service, which would undoubtedly have caused that unpleasant affair to be forgotten.

Judge Luke P. Poland of Vermont was another very interesting character. He was well known throughout the country. He had a tall and erect and very dignified figure, and a fine head covered with a beautiful growth of gray hair. He was dressed in the old-fashioned style that Mr. Webster used, with blue coat, brass buttons and a buff-colored vest. His coat and buttons were well known all over the country. One day when William Lloyd Garrison was inveighing against some conduct of the Southern whites, and said: "They say the South is quiet now. Order reigns in Warsaw. But where is Poland?" An irreverent newspaper man said: "He is up in Vermont polishing brass buttons."

The Judge was a very able lawyer, and a man of very great industry. He and Judge Hoar went over together the revision of the United States statutes of 1874, completing a labor which had been neglected by Caleb Cushing. Judge Poland had a good deal of fun in him, and had a stock of anecdotes which he liked to tell to any listener. It was said, I do not know how truly, that he could bear any amount of whiskey without in the slightest degree affecting his intellect. There was a story that two well-known Senators laid a plot to get the Judge tipsy. They invited him to a room at Willards, and privately instructed the waiter, when they ordered whiskey to put twice as much of the liquid into Poland's glass as into the others. The order was repeated several times. The heads of the two hosts had begun to swim, but Poland was not moved. At last they saw him take the waiter aside and heard him tell him in a loud whisper: "The next time, make mine a little stronger, if you please." They concluded on the whole that Vermont brain would hold its own with Michigan and Illinois.

One of the most amusing scenes I ever witnessed was a call of the House in the old days, when there was no quorum. The doors were shut. The Speaker sent officers for the absentees. They were brought to the bar of the House one after another. Judge Poland happened to be one of the absentees. My colleague, Mr. Dawes, was in the chair. Poland was brought to the bar. Mr. Dawes addressed him with solemnity: "Mr. Poland, of Vermont, you have been absent from the session of the House without its leave. What excuse have you to offer?" The Judge paused a moment and then replied in a tone of great gravity and emotion: "I went with my wife to call on my minister, and I stayed a little too long." The House accepted the excuse, and I suppose the religious people of the Judge's district would have maintained him in office for a thousand years by virtue of that answer, if they had had their way. A man who had been so long exposed to the wickedness and temptations of Washington, and had committed only the sin of staying a little too long when he called on his minister might safely be trusted anywhere.

Judge Peters, of Maine, did not speak very frequently and did not attract much public attention. But he had a strong influence with the members of the House. He was on the Judiciary Committee. He made brief, pithy speeches which generally convinced the House. He declined to continue in the National service, where the people of Maine would have been willing to keep him until his dying day. He afterward became Chief Justice of Maine, and sustained the high character which the Bench of that State has had from the beginning.

There is one anecdote of him, which does not come within the sphere of my recollections, but which I think perhaps my readers will prefer to anything that does. A few years ago a young man who kept a grocery store was tried before Judge Peters for larceny. He was a very respectable young tradesman. The Salvation Army had engaged quarters next to his store, where they disturbed him and his customers a good deal by playing on the drum and other similar religious services. But that was not all. They used to come out on the sidewalk and beat a large drum and sing and kneel in prayer just before his door, much to the disturbance of his customers and the aggravation of the young grocer. One day he purloined and hid the large drum. He was detected and indicted for larceny. The Attorney-General, for the Government, maintained that everything that went to constitute the crime of larceny existed there. He had taken secretly another man's property from his possession, for purposes of his own. Whether he meant to destroy it or to hide it or to convert it to his own use made no difference in the offence against the owner or against the law. On the other hand the defendant's counsel argued that it was a mere matter of mischief; that there was no felonious intent, and no purpose to deprive the owner permanently of the property. The Chief Justice charged very strongly for the Commonwealth. The jury very reluctantly brought in a verdict of guilty. The poor fellow was sorely distressed. He was convicted as a thief. His life seemed to be blighted and ruined past hope. The Chief Justice said: "Mr. Clerk, you may record the verdict. I may as well sentence him now. I shall fine him a dollar, without costs. I once stole a drum myself."

John A. Logan was a member of the House when I entered it, and I served with him in the Senate also. He was a man of remarkable power, and remarkable influence, both with the Senate and with the people. It is, I believe, agreed by all authorities that we had no abler officer in the Civil War than he, except those who were educated at West Point. He was always a great favorite with the veteran soldiers. He was rough in speech, and cared little for refinements in manner. He was said to be an uneducated man. But I believe he was a man of a good many accomplishments; that he spoke some foreign languages well, and had a pretty good knowledge of our political history. He was exceedingly imperious and domineering, impatient of contradiction in any matter which he had in charge. So he was rather an uncomfortable man to get along with. He was especially sensitive of any ridicule or jesting at his expense. He was supposed, I know not how truly, to be exceedingly impatient and ready for war on any man who crossed his path. But his behavior when he was ordered to supersede General Thomas, just before the battle at Nashville and Franklin, is a noble instance of magnanimity.

When Sherman started for the sea, Hood, with a large rebel army, was in his rear. Gen. Thomas was ordered to attack him. But he delayed and delayed till the authorities at Washington grew impatient and ordered Logan to supersede Thomas. Everybody knows the intensity of the passion for military glory. General Logan could have carried out his orders, taken advantage of Thomas's dispositions, and won himself one of the most brilliant victories of the war, which would have had a double lustre from the seeming lukewarmness of his predecessor; but when he arrived at the place of operations and learned Thomas's dispositions and the reason for his delay, he became satisfied that the great Fabius was right and wise. His generous nature disdained to profit by the mistake at headquarters and to get glory for himself at the expense of a brave soldier. So he postponed the execution of his orders, and left Thomas in his command. The result was the battle of Nashville and the annihilation of Hood. Where in military story can there be found a brighter page than that? That one act of magnanimous self-denial gave to American history two of its brightest names,—the name of Thomas and the name of Logan.

Another very able member of the House was Thomas A. Jenks of Rhode Island. He never seemed to care much for that field of service, but preferred to enjoy the practice of his profession, in which he was largely employed, and was earning a large income. But he is entitled to honorable memory as the originator and father of the reform of the civil service in this country. He made a very able speech in its favor in 1867 or 1868, which was the beginning of a movement which has been successful, for which I think the public gratitude should be shared between him and Dorman B. Eaton.

Elihu B. Washburn, of Illinois, was appointed Secretary of State by General Grant, whose constant friend and supporter he had been through his whole military career. Washburn was brave, vigorous and far-sighted, a man of great influence in his State and in the House. He was prominently spoken of for the Presidency. But with Grant and Logan as his competitors from his own State, there was not much chance for him. He was afterward Minister to France, and gained great distinction and credit by remaining in Paris throughout the siege, and giving shelter and support to persons who were in danger from the fury of the mob. He earned the gratitude alike of the Germans and the French ecclesiastics.

He was known as the watch dog of the Treasury, when he was in the House. Few questionable claims against the Government could escape his vigilance, or prevail over his formidable opposition. But, one day, a private bill championed by his brother, Cadwallader, passed the House while Elihu kept entirely silent. Somebody called out to the Speaker: "The watch dog don't bark when one of the family goes by."

When I entered the House, William B. Allison, of Iowa, had already acquired great influence there. He manifested there the qualities that have since given him so much distinction in the Senate. He was understood to favor what was called Revenue Reform, and moderation in the exercise of all doubtful national powers.

But his chief distinction has been gained by a service of thirty years in the Senate. He was out of public life two years, and then was elected to the Senate, where he has been kept by the State of Iowa, maintaining the confidence of his State and of his associates in public life. During all that time he has done what no other man in the country, in my judgment, could have done so well. He has been a member of the great Committee on Appropriations for thirty years, most of the time Chairman, and for twenty-six years a member of the Committee on Finance. He has controlled, more than any other man, indeed more than any other ten men, the vast and constantly increasing public expenditure, amounting now to more than 1,000 millions annually. It has been an economical, honest and wise expenditure. He has been compelled in the discharge of his duties to understand the complications and mechanism of public administration and public expenditure. That is a knowledge in which nobody else in the Senate, except Senator Hale of Maine, and Senator Cockrell of Missouri, can compare with him. He has by his wise and moderate counsel drawn the fire from many a wild and dangerous scheme which menaced the public peace and safety.

He almost never takes part in the debates, unless it becomes necessary to explain or defend some measure of which he has charge. It is said that he is very careful not to offend anybody, and that he is unwilling to take responsibilities or to commit himself. There is undoubtedly some truth in that criticism. Indeed if it were otherwise, he would find it very hard to maintain the personal influence necessary to success in the duties to which he is immediately devoted. But he never avoids voting. His name, since he has been Senator, has been first or second alphabetically on the roll of the Senate. He is found in the Senate Chamber unless engaged in his committee-room on work which requires him to be there during the sessions,—and he always votes when his name is called.

I have never seen any indication that he is interested in anything, or has any special knowledge or accomplishment, except what is necessary to the line of his duty. I do not know that he has any interest in history or literature or science or music. What he does in his time of recreation—if he ever has any time for recreation—I cannot tell. He never seems to take any active interest in any of the questions which determine the action of the party or the destiny of the State, except those that relate to its finances. I use the word finances in the largest sense, including means for raising revenue and maintaining a sound currency, as well as public expenditures. He is like a naval engineer, regulating the head of steam but seldom showing himself on deck. I think he has had a good deal of influence in some perilous times in deciding whether the ship should keep safely on, or should run upon a rock and go to the bottom.

There is a good story told that after Thaddeus Stevens died, a friend of Mr. Blaine's was walking with him one day through the Rotunda of the Capitol toward the House of Representatives. Mr. Blaine said: "The death of Stevens is an emancipation for the Republican Party. He kept the party under his heel." His friend replied: "Whom have you got for leaders left?" Blaine said: "There are three young men coming forward. There is a young man who will be heard from yet." He pointed to Allison, who happened to be just approaching. "James A. Garfield is another." There was a little pause, and his friend said:

"Well, who is the third?" Blaine gazed straight up into the dome, and said: "I don't see the third."

I give my estimate of James A. Garfield later in this book.

I think I ought not to leave out of an account of the very able and remarkable Massachusetts delegation in the Congress of 1869 the name of George S. Boutwell, although he remained in the House only a few days after I entered it and is still living. He had been a very faithful, useful and prominent member of the House from the time he entered it in March, 1863, at the middle of the War.

It was the desire of his associates in the House that he should be a Member of General Grant's Cabinet. When General Grant's Cabinet was announced the name of Governor Boutwell did not appear, and my brother, Judge Hoar, was nominated for Attorney-General. He had a high opinion of Mr. Boutwell and had been very earnest, so far as he could properly do so, in advocating his original nomination to Congress. In the evening after the Cabinet had been announced Mr. William B. Washburn, afterward Governor, called upon me at my room. Mr. Washburn and I were not then intimate, although we afterward became close friends. He said that he had been requested by the delegation to tell me that they had earnestly hoped that Mr. Boutwell might have a place in the Cabinet, and that, although they had great regard for Judge Hoar, they hoped that some arrangement might still be made which would bring about the selection of Mr. Boutwell. I told Mr. Washburn that I was sure that the appointment of Judge Hoar would be a surprise to him, as it was to me, and that I thought it quite doubtful whether he would wish to leave his place on the Bench for a seat in the Cabinet, but that I could not speak for him or judge for him. I telegraphed at once to Judge Hoar not to commit himself in any way until he reached Washington and could see me. I met him at the depot, told him of the communication of the Massachusetts delegation and that, especially considering President Johnson's quarrel with Congress, it seemed quite important that General Grant, who had no experience whatever in political life, should have some person among his counsellors who had the full confidence of the leaders in Congress. The Judge strongly appreciated that view. When he called upon President Grant his first conversation consisted in urging upon him very strongly the selection of Governor Boutwell. He supposed then that it would be quite unlikely that the President would take two men from the same State and supposed that selection would require his own refusal of the offer of the office of Attorney-General. President Grant said that he would think it over and not decide the question that day. The next morning he sent for the Judge and said: "Judge, I think I would like to have you take the oath of office." He handed the Judge his commission. The Judge looked at it and saw that it was not signed. He said: "I think perhaps it would be better if you were to sign it." Grant laughed and complied with the suggestion. Judge Hoar's first official duty was to give an opinion upon the question whether Mr. Stewart, who had been nominated for Secretary of the Treasury, could under the law undertake the office. Mr. Stewart proposed to make some conveyances of his business in trust, by which he should part with his legal title to it while he held the office of Secretary of the Treasury and come back to it again after his term ended. But the Attorney-General advised the President that that was impracticable, and the result was the withdrawal of Mr. Stewart's name and the appointment of Mr. Boutwell a day or two afterward.

I have had some serious differences with Mr. Boutwell since he left the Democratic Party after his term of service as Governor. They have, I believe, never been differences of political principle. My differences of opinion with him have been mainly upon the question what individuals were fit to be trusted with political office and power, and with the leadership in political parties, and upon the question whether certain men and influences were to be tolerated, or whether the public safety required unsparing warfare upon them. So, while we have agreed in general as to policies, we have always had an entirely different set of friends and companions.

Mr. Boutwell has borne an honorable part in our history. His titles to a place in the grateful memory of his countrymen are not likely to be overlooked.

One of them deserves special mention. I am but repeating what I said many years ago. As a leading member of the House of Representatives, and as Secretary of the Treasury under President Grant's Administration, he had, of course, a large influence upon our financial history. He saw very early the importance of devoting every resource of the country to the reduction of the National debt. It was not with him, as I understand it, a question whether a little saving could be made in the way of taxes by postponing the payment until the rate of interest should be less or the National resources greater. He saw that it was important that the people should not get accustomed, as the English people are, to consider a National debt as something that was to continue always. He saw that it was important to the character of the people, as to an individual, that they should be impatient and restless under the obligation of debt, and should consider it alike the Nation's first duty and its greatest pride and luxury to get rid of the burden. This has always been the temper of the State of Massachusetts, of her towns, and, in general, of her citizens.

Accordingly he insisted that the debt should be reduced so rapidly that the people would take pride in having paid it, and would be relieved from the temptation of listening to the specious and seductive arguments of persons contriving dishonest methods of getting rid of it by issuing fiat money, or any device of direct or indirect repudiation. Many persons can remember in what dangerous forms this temptation came, and how many men, who otherwise deserve to be held in high esteem, yielded to it wholly or partly. Mr. Boutwell's powerful influence was a very important factor in attaining the result in which we all now take so much satisfaction, and keeping the American people in the path of duty and honor.

William A. Wheeler, of New York, entered the House in 1869. I soon became very well acquainted with him, an acquaintance which ripened into a very intimate friendship. He was a very serious, simple-hearted and wise man. There was no man in his time who had more influence in the House. His ancestors dwelt in my native town of Concord in the early generations, and in Lincoln, which had been part of Concord. One of the family emigrated to Vermont. Wheeler's father went from Vermont to Malone, New York, where he was born, and where he was left by his father an orphan in very early youth. The widow and children were without any property whatever, but got along somehow. Wheeler got an education, spending two or three years in college, and became the foremost man in his part of New York. The people of his district were in character and way of thinking very much like our best Massachusetts constituencies. Wheeler had little respect for the devious and self-seeking politics which are supposed to have been needed for success in that State. He very much disliked Roscoe Conkling, and all his ways. Conkling once said to him: "Wheeler, if you will join us and act with us, there is nothing in the gift of the State of New York to which you may not reasonably aspire." To which Wheeler replied: "Mr. Conkling, there is nothing in the gift of the State of New York which will compensate me for the forfeiture of my own self respect."

Mr. Wheeler was one of the sub-committee, of whom Mr. Frye and myself were the other two Republican members, to inquire into the condition of the legality of the Kellogg State Government of Louisiana. He suggested what is known as the Wheeler compromise, the acceptance of which by both sides was due to his influence and capacity for conciliation. The compromise consisted in an agreement to allow the Republican State officers to remain in office during the remainder of their terms, without turbulent or factious opposition, to submit quietly to their authority on the one hand, and that the two Houses of the Legislature, on the other hand, should seat the Democratic contestants whom our sub-committee found entitled to their seats. This compromise in reality gave effect to the opinion of the committee, as if they had been a tribunal of arbitration. Of course they had no authority to enforce their opinion against the objection of either party.

As soon as the nomination of President Hayes was declared in the Convention of 1876, I spent a very busy hour in going about among the delegates whom I knew, especially those from the Southern States, to urge upon them the name of Mr. Wheeler as a suitable person for Vice-President. I have no doubt I secured for him a great many votes, and that those votes secured him his election. Mr. James Russell Lowell was a Massachusetts delegate. He was a little unwilling to vote for a person of whom he had no more knowledge. I said to him: "Mr. Lowell, Mr. Wheeler is a very sensible man. He knows the 'Biglow Papers' by heart." Lowell gave no promise in reply. But I happened to overhear him, as he sat behind me, saying to James Freeman Clarke, I think it was: "I understand that Mr. Wheeler is 'a very sensible man.'"

Wheeler was one of the best parliamentarians and one of the best presiding officers I ever knew. He had no children. It is pathetic to remember the affection which existed between him and his wife. Their long living together had brought about a curious resemblance. She looked like him, talked like him, thought like him, and if she had been dressed in his clothes, or he had been in hers, either might have passed for the other. When she died Wheeler seemed to lose all interest in this world, shut himself off from all ordinary activities, and died a year or two after, I suppose with a broken heart.

CHAPTER XVI

POLITICAL CONDITIONS IN 1869

WHEN the Republican Party came into power in 1869 under its great and simple-hearted President, it found itself confronted with very serious duties. They were enough to fill ordinary men in ordinary times with dismay. The President was without political experience. He had never held civil office. He had voted but twice in his life. He had voted the Whig ticket once and the Democratic ticket once. So he could not justly be charged with being an offensive partisan. He had no experience in business except in a humble way and in that he had been unfortunate. Congress and the President could only act under the restraint of a written Constitution. Everything done by either must pass the ordeal of the Supreme Court, a majority of whose members then had no sympathy with a liberal interpretation of the National powers. The Chief Justice had been a great Republican leader. But he had quarrelled with Lincoln, and was an eager aspirant for the Democratic nomination for the Presidency.

Of the eight years after the inauguration of Lincoln more than four had been years of actual war and more than five passed before formal declaration of peace. During all this time nothing could be considered but the preservation of the Union. From the end of the War to the accession of President Grant, Congress and the President had been engaged in a struggle with each other for power. President Johnson had been impeached and put on trial before the Senate. So there could be no important legislation from the summer of 1866 until March, 1869, that did not command the assent of two thirds of both Houses.

Yet the feeling everywhere among Republicans in Washington and throughout the North was of exultant and confident courage. The strength of the Nation had been tried and not found wanting. It had overthrown a mighty rebellion. The burden of slavery, which had hung like a millstone about the neck of the Republic, had been thrown off. Congress had been triumphant in its contest with the President. The loyal people of the country looked to Grant with an almost superstitious hope. They were prepared to expect almost any miracle from the great genius who had subdued the rebellion, and conducted without failure military operations on a scale of which the world up to that time had had no experience. So the dominant party addressed itself without fear to the great work before it.

They had to determine on what conditions the States that had been in rebellion should come back to their place under the Constitution.

They were to determine on what terms the men who had taken part in the rebellion should be fully restored to citizenship.

They were to determine the civil and political condition of more than five million people just set free from slavery.

They were to secure fair elections in fifteen States, where for many years neither free elections nor free speech had been tolerated.

If they could, they were to reconcile the North and the South, estranged by a strife so bitter that even before the War the life of no Northern man who dared to utter Northern opinions was safe in half the States of the country, and which had been intensified by four years of bloody war —bellum plus quam civile—which had left nearly every household in the country mourning for its dead.

They were to confront the greatest temptation that ever besets men of Anglo-Saxon race, a race ever restless and ever hungry for empire. Hungry eyes were already bent on San Domingo and Cuba. Good men were rendered uneasy by the tales of Spanish oppression in Cuba. Men who were looking for the union of the two oceans by a canal across the Isthmus, or who hoped that we should extend our dominion in this continent southward, looked upon the island belonging to the Negro Republics of Hayti and San

Domingo as a desirable addition to our military and naval strength.

They were to provide for the payment of an enormous debt.

They were to accomplish the resumption of specie payment.

They were to consider and determine anew the question of currency. What should be the standard of value and a legal tender for the payment of debts?

They were to get rid of the vast burden of war taxes which pressed heavily upon all branches of business.

They were to decide whether the duties on imports which had been laid to meet the heavy cost of war should be kept in peace and whether to follow the counsel of Hamilton and his associates in the first Administration of Washington, or the counsel of the free traders and the English school of political economists, in determining whether American industry should be protected.

The people felt that they had suffered a grievous wrong from England, and that unless there were reparation, which England had so far steadily refused either to make or consider, the honor of the country required that we should exact it by war.

The emigrants from foreign lands who had come to our shores in vast numbers, and were coming in rapidly increasing numbers, were made uneasy by the doctrine of perpetual allegiance on which all Europe insisted. They claimed that they were entitled to protection like native-born American citizens everywhere on the face of the earth.

The number of civil officers appointed by the Executive had largely increased. This put an undue and most dangerous power into the hands of the party controlling the Government. There was a strong feeling that this should be checked.

Besides; during the controversy with Andrew Johnson the members of the two Houses of Congress had come to think that they were entitled to control all appointments of civil officers in their own States and Districts, and they were ready with scarce an exception to stand by each other in this demand. They had passed, over the veto of President Johnson, an act of disputed and quite doubtful constitutionality, seriously crippling the Executive power of removal from office, without which the President's constitutional duty to see that the laws are faithfully executed cannot be performed. So each Senator and Representative was followed like a Highland Chieftain "with his tail on," by a band of retainers devoted to his political fortunes, dependent upon him for their own, but supported at the public charge.

This not only threatened the freedom of election, but itself brought a corrupting influence into the Administration of the Government.

But there was a still greater danger than all these in the corruption which then, as always, followed a great war. Unprincipled and greedy men sought to get contracts and jobs from the Government by the aid of influential politicians. This aid they paid for sometimes, though I think rarely, in money, and in contributions to political campaigns, and in the various kinds of assistance necessary to maintain in power the men to whom they were so indebted. This corruption not only affected all branches of the Civil Service, especially the War and the Navy and the Treasury, but poisoned legislation itself.

They had to deal with claims amounting to hundreds of millions of dollars, some wholly fraudulent, some grossly exaggerated and some entirely just. Some of these belonged to persons who had contracts with the Government for constructing and supplying a powerful Navy, or for supplies to the Army. There were demands still larger in amount from the inhabitants of the territory which had been the theatre of the War. This class of claims was wholly new in the history of our own country. There were few precedents for dealing with them in the experience of other countries, and the Law of Nations and the law of war furnished imperfect guides.

Men wounded or disabled in the Military or Naval Service, and their widows and orphans, were to be provided for by a liberal pension system.

These were a part only of the questions that must be studied and understood, under the gravest personal responsibility by every member of either House of Congress. Under the Administration of Grant and those that succeeded, of course, there was a constant struggle on the part of the party in power to keep in power and on the part of its opponent to get power. So that it was necessary that a Representative or Senator who would do his duty, or who had the ordinary ambition, or desired that the counsel best for the country should prevail, should master these subjects and take a large part in discussing and advocating the policy of his party.

During the thirty-two years from the 4th of March, 1869, to the 4th of March, 1901, the Democratic Party held the Executive power of the country for eight years. For nearly four years more Andrew Johnson had a bitter quarrel with the Republican leaders in both Houses of Congress. For six years the Democrats controlled the Senate. For sixteen years they controlled the House of Representatives. There is left on the Statute Book no trace of any Democratic legislation during this whole period except the repeal of the laws intended to secure honest elections. The two Administrations of President Cleveland are remembered by the business men and the laboring men of the country only as terrible nightmares. Whatever has been accomplished in this period, which seems to me the most brilliant period in legislative history of any country in the world, has been accomplished by the Republican Party over Democratic opposition. The failure to secure honest National elections and the political and civil rights of the colored people is the failure of the Republican Party and the success of its Democratic antagonist. With that exception, to all the problems which confronted the country in 1869 the Republican Party has given a simple, wise, final and most successful solution. It has done it not only without help, but over the constant opposition of its Democratic antagonist.

Every State that went into the Rebellion has been restored to its place in the Union.

There has been complete and universal amnesty. No man has been punished for his share in the Rebellion.

In spite of dishonest and subtle counsel, and in spite of great temptation, we have dealt with the public debt on the simple and honest principle that the only thing to do with a debt is to pay it. The National credit is the best in the world, and the National debt has ceased to be an object either of anxiety or consideration.

Specie payments have been resumed. Every dollar issued by the Government, or by national banks under government authority, passes current like gold. Indeed the ease with which it can be transported and the certainty of its redemption makes the paper money of the United States better than gold.

The United States has joined the commercial nations of the first rank in making gold the world's standard of value. In doing this we have never departed from the theoretical principle of bimetallism as announced by Hamilton and Washington and Webster and all our statesmen without exception down to 1869. The contest was an exceedingly close one. The arguments in support of the free coinage of silver were specious and dangerous. Undoubtedly for a time, and more than once, they converted a majority of the American people. The battle for honest money would have been lost but for the wisdom of the Republican statesmen who planted the party not only upon the doctrine of theoretical bimetallism, but also upon the doctrine that the question of the standard of value must be settled by the concurrence of the commercial nations of the world and that if there were to be one metal as a standard, gold, the more valuable metal, was the fittest for the purpose. That was the doctrine of Alexander Hamilton. To have avowed any other principle would have reinforced our opponents with the powerful authority of Hamilton and all his disciples down to the year 1873.

The war taxes have been abolished. The weight of the burden which has been in that way lifted from the shoulders of the people may perhaps be understood from the statement of a single fact. The Worcester District, which I represented, paid in the direct form of taxes to the National Treasury the enormous sum of $3,662,727 for the year ending June 30, 1866. For the year ending June 30, 1871, the taxes so paid amounted in all to $225,000, and for the year ending June 30, 1872, they amounted to about $100,000.

The policy of protection to American industry, which, like the question of honest elections, has been always in contest between the Republican Party and its Democratic antagonist has, unless during the two Administrations of President Cleveland, been successfully maintained. As a consequence of that policy our manufacturing independence has been achieved. The United States has become the foremost manufacturing nation in the world. We are penetrating foreign markets, and have built up a domestic commerce, the like of which has never been seen before, and whose extent surpasses the power of human imagination to conceive and almost of mathematics to calculate.

The temptation to extend our territory by unlawful exercise of power over Cuba and San Domingo was resisted by the American people. Cuba has been liberated and has taken her place among the free nations of the world.

For the great offence committed against us by Great Britain in the hour of our peril we have exacted apology and reparation. There were not wanting counsellors enough to urge the American people that we should nurse this grievance and lie in wait until the hour for our revenge should come. But the magnanimous American people preferred peace and reconciliation to revenge. I ought to except this from the list of achievements due to the Republican Party alone. In the matter of the British Treaty, the Democratic leaders contributed their full share to its successful accomplishment. Mr. Justice Nelson of the United States Supreme Court was a distinguished member of the Commission that made the Treaty.

Under General Grant's Administration treaties were negotiated with nearly all the great powers of the world by which they renounced the old doctrine of perpetual allegiance, and the American citizen of foreign birth is clothed with all the rights and privileges of a native-born citizen wherever on the face of the earth he may go.

The vast number of National offices has ceased to be a menace to the safety of the Republic and has ceased to be a source of strength to the Administration in power, or to become the price or reward of political activity. The offices of trust and profit now exist to serve the people and not to bribe them.

The conflict between the Senate and the Executive which arose in the time of Andrew Johnson, when Congress undertook to hamper and restrict the President's Constitutional power of removal from office, without which his Constitutional duty of seeing that the laws are faithfully executed cannot be performed, has been settled by a return to the ancient principle established in Washington's first Administration.

The vast claims upon the Treasury growing out of the war have been dealt with upon wise and simple principles which have commanded general assent and in the main have resulted in doing full justice both to the Government and to the claimant.

A disputed title to the Executive power which threatened to bring on another civil war, and which would not have been settled without bloodshed in any other country, has been peacefully and quietly disposed of by the simple mechanism devised for the occasion and by the enactment of a rule which will protect the country against a like danger in the future.

With all these matters I have had something to do.

As to some of them my part has been a very humble one. As to others I have had a part of considerable prominence. As to all I have had full and intimate knowledge at the time and have been in the intimate counsel of the men who were responsible for the result.

Beside all these things there has been during a large part of my public service, especially the part immediately following the Civil War, a battle to maintain the purity of elections and the purity of administration and government expenditure against corruption. The attempt to get possession of the forces of the Government for corrupt purposes assumed its most dangerous form and had its most unscrupulous and dangerous leader in Massachusetts. It was my fortune to have a good deal to do with maintaining the ancient honor of the Commonwealth and defending and vindicating the purity of her political organization.

Upon all these matters I formed my opinions carefully in the beginning. I have adhered to those opinions, and acted on them throughout. I formed them in many cases when they were shared by a few persons only. But they have made their way, and prevail. They are the opinions upon which the majority of the American people have acted, and the reasons which have controlled that action, seem to me now, in looking backward, to have been good reasons. I have no regret, and no desire to blot out anything I have said or done, or to change any vote I have given.

The duties of a Representative and Senator demand a large correspondence. I have had always the aid of intelligent and competent secretaries. Disposing of the day's mail, even with such aid, is not infrequently a hard day's work, especially for a man past three score and ten.

Political campaigns in Massachusetts with its small territory and compact population are easy as compared with most of the other States. But I have been expected every second year to make many political speeches, commonly from thirty to forty. Mr. Blaine, and Mr. Frye, and Mr. Reed, and a great many others who could be named, were called on for a much larger number. A man at all prominent in public affairs is also expected to give utterance to the voice of the people on all great occasions of joy or sorrow, at high festivals, or at colleges and schools, on great National anniversaries, when great men die and great historical events are celebrated. So it was a life of hard work upon which I entered when I took my seat in the House of Representatives on the 4th of March, 1869. The thirty-four years that have followed have been for me years of incessant labor.

CHAPTER XVII

RECONSTRUCTION

THE reconstruction policy of the Republican Party has been bitterly denounced. Some men who supported it are in the habit now of calling it a failure. It never commanded in its fullest extent the cordial support of the whole party. But it was very simple. So far as it applied to the Southern whites who had been in rebellion it consisted only of complete amnesty and full restoration to political rights. No man was ever punished for taking part in the rebellion after he laid down his arms. There is no other instance of such magnanimity in history. The War left behind it little bitterness in the hearts of the conquerors. All they demanded of the conquered was submission in good faith to the law of the land and the will of the people as it might be constitutionally declared.

Their policy toward the colored people was simply the application to them of the principles applied to the whites, as set forth in the Declaration of Independence and in the Constitution of nearly every State in the Union. There was to be no distinction in political rights by reason of color or race. The States were left to regulate such qualifications as residence, character, intelligence, education and property as they saw fit, only subject to the condition that they were to apply to all alike.

It was the purpose of the dominant party to leave the control of the election of national officers, as it had been left from the beginning, in the hands of the local or State authorities. The power was claimed, indeed it is clearly given by the Constitution, as was asserted in the debates in the Convention that framed it, to conduct those elections under National authority, if it should be found by experience to be necessary. But in fact there was at no time any attempt to go further with National election laws than to provide for punishment of fraudulent or violent interference with elections or for a sufficient provision to ascertain that they were properly conducted, or to protect them against violence or fraud.

Beside this it was the desire of many Republican leaders, especially of Mr. Sumner and General Grant, that there should be a provision at the National charge for the education of all the citizens in the Southern States, black and white, so far as the States were unable or unwilling to afford it, such as had been provided for in the State of the North for all their citizens. It was never contemplated by them to give the right to vote to a large number of illiterate citizens, without ample provision for their education at the public charge. General Grant accompanied his official announcement to Congress of the adoption of the Fifteenth Amendment with an earnest recommendation of such a provision. Earnest efforts were made to accomplish this result by liberal grants from the National treasury. Many liberal and patriotic Southern Democrats supported it. But it was defeated by the timidity, or mistaken notions of economy, of Northern statesmen. In my opinion this defeat accounts for the failure of the policy of reconstruction so far as it has failed. I do not believe that self-government with universal suffrage could be maintained long in any Northern State, or in any country in the world. without ample provision for public education.

It has been claimed with great sincerity and not without plausible reason that a great hardship and wrong was inflicted by the victorious North on their fellow citizens when the political power in their States was given over to their former slaves. This consideration had great force in the minds of many influential Republicans in the North. Governor Andrew of Massachusetts, Governor Morton of Indiana, afterward Senator, men whose influence was probably unsurpassed by any other two men in the country, save Grant and Sumner alone, were of that way of thinking. They thought that our true policy was to let the men who had led their States into the Rebellion take the responsibility of restoring them to their old relations.

It is not unlikely that the strength of the Republican Party would have been seriously impaired, perhaps overthrown, by the division of sentiment on this subject. But the white Democrats in the South were blind to their own interest. President Johnson permitted them in several States to take into their hands again the power of government. They proceeded to pass laws which if carried out would have had the effect of reducing the negro once more to a condition of practical slavery. Men were to be sold for the crime of being out of work. Their old masters were to have the preference in the purchase. So the whole Republican Party of the North came to be united in the belief that there could be no security for the liberty of the freedman without the ballot.

It is said that this reconstruction policy has been a failure. Undoubtedly it has not gained all that was hoped for it by its advocates. But looking back now I do not believe that any other policy would have done as well as that has done, although a large part of what was designed by the Republican leaders of the period of reconstruction never was accomplished.

A complete system of education at the National charge was an essential element of the reconstruction policy. It was earnestly advocated by Sumner and by Grant and by Edmunds and by Evarts. But there were other Republicans of great influence who resisted it from the beginning. Among these was Senator Eugene Hale of Maine, a very accomplished Senator, an able debater and a man of large influence with his colleagues. His public life has been one of great distinction and usefulness. While an earnest partisan he has given an example of independence of action on several notable occasions. But he always seemed to be possessed by what seems to prevail among the Republicans of Maine to a great extent, dislike for what is called sentimental politics. Mr. Hale always seemed to think that the chief function of Congress was to provide for an honest, economical, wise and at the same time liberal public expenditure, to keep in the old paths and leave other matters alone. He dislikes new doctrines and new policies. He is specially adverse to anything like legal restraint. He once in my hearing used a very felicitous phrase, full of wisdom, "Government by good nature." John Sherman, who had originally been an earnest advocate of a liberal National expenditure for education, joined the ranks of its opponents, putting his opposition largely on the ground that he was unwilling to trust the Southern States with the expenditure of large sums of money. He feared that the money would not be fairly expended as between the two races, and that it would be made a large corruption fund for political purposes.

So this most essential part of the reconstruction policy of Sumner and Grant never took effect. Mr. Sumner deemed this matter vital to success. He told me about a week before his death that when the resolution declaring the provision for public education at the National charge an essential part of the reconstruction policy, was defeated in the Senate by a tie vote, he was so overcome by his feelings that he burst into tears and left the Senate Chamber.

Another part of the Republican plan for reconstruction was never accomplished. That was the securing of a fair vote and a fair ascertainment of the result in National elections by National power. Some partial and imperfect attempts were made to put in force laws intended to accomplish this result. They never went farther than enactments designed to maintain order at the polls, to secure the voter from actual violence, and to provide for such scrutiny as to make it clear that the vote was duly counted and properly returned, with a right to appeal to the Courts of the United States in case of a contest, the decision of the Court to be subject to the final authority of the House of Representatives. These laws, although they had the support of eminent and zealous Democrats and although they were as much needed and had as much application to the Northern cities as to the Southern States, were the object of bitter denunciation from the beginning. Good men in the North listened with incredulity to the narrative of well established facts of cruelty and murder and fraud. These stories were indignantly denied at the time, although they are not only confessed, but vauntingly and triumphantly affirmed now. The whole country seems to be made uneasy when the old practice to which it had been accustomed everywhere of having offences tried by a jury taken by lot from the people of the neighborhood, and the result of election ascertained by officers selected from the bystanders at the polls, is departed from. Besides, no strictness of laws which provide only for the proceedings at the elections will secure their freedom if it be possible to intimidate the voters, especially men like the colored voters at the South, from attending the elections, by threats, outrages and actual violence at their homes. Against these the election laws could not guard. Congress attempted some laws to secure the Southern Republicans against such crimes under the authority conferred by the Fourteenth Amendment to the Constitution. But the Supreme Court held that these laws were unconstitutional, it not appearing that the States had by any affirmative action denied protection against such offences to any class of their citizens by reason of race, color, or previous condition. It was idle to expect Southern jurors, or State officers to enforce the law against such crimes in the condition of sentiment existing there.

Further, the people of the North would not maintain the Republican Party in power forever on this one issue alone. They were interested in other things. They could not be expected, year after year, election after election, and perhaps generation after generation, to hold together by reason of this one question, differing on other things. So whenever the Democratic Party should come into power it was apparent that all the vigor would be taken out of the election laws. If there be not power to repeal them the House of Representatives can always refuse to make the appropriation for enforcing them. So it became clear to my mind, and to the minds of many other Republicans, that it was better to leave this matter to the returning and growing sense of justice of the people of the South than to have laws on this subject passed in one Administration, only to be repealed in another. A policy to be effective must be permanent. I accordingly announced in the Senate after the defeat of the Elections Bill in 1894 that in my judgment it would not be wise to renew the attempt to control National election by National authority until both parties in the country should agree upon that subject.

We should have had little difficulty in dealing with the Negro or the Indian, or the Oriental, if the American people had applied to them, as the Golden Rule requires, the principles they expect to apply and to have applied to themselves. We have never understood that in some essential matters human nature is the same in men of all colors and races. Our Fathers of the time of the Revolution understood this matter better than we do. The difficult problems in our national politics at this hour will nearly all of them be solved if the people will adhere to rules of conduct imposed as restraints in the early constitutions. The sublimity of the principle of self-government does not consist wholly or chiefly in the idea that self is the person who governs, but quite as much in the doctrine that self is the person who is governed. How our race troubles would disappear if the dominant Saxon would but obey, in his treatment of the weaker races, the authority of the fundamental laws on which his own institutions rest! The problem of to-day is not how to convert the heathen from heathenism, it is how to convert the Christian from heathenism; not to teach the physician to heal the patient, but to heal himself. The Indian problem is not chiefly how to teach the Indian to be less savage in his treatment of the Saxon, but the Saxon to be less savage in his treatment of the Indian. The Chinese problem is not how to keep Chinese laborers out of California, but how to keep Chinese policies out of Congress. The negro question will be settled when the education of the white man is complete.

We make every allowance for ourselves. We expect mankind to make every allowance for us. We expect to be forgiven for our own wrong-doing. We easily forgive our own white fellow citizens for the unutterable and terrible cruelties they have committed on men of other races. But if a people just coming out of slavery or barbarism commit a hundredth part of the same offence our righteous indignation knows no bounds. We have no recognition for their eager desire for civilization or for liberty, no generous appreciation of their improvement and promise. And the thousand things in them that give promise of good in the future are disregarded if there be any trace left in them of the old barbarism.

Has Reconstruction been a failure? Let us see about that. We must remember that the relations of the black and white races to each other, which have existed almost from the foundation of the world, cannot be changed in a single generation. It is but thirty-three years since General Grant and the two Houses of Congress, in political accord with him and with each other, took possession of the Government. That possession has been interrupted more than once. It is but forty years since slavery was abolished. It is less than thirty years since the last of the three great Amendments to the Constitution took effect. What has happened in that time? Slavery has been abolished. That is not a failure. The negro owns his right to his own labor. He cannot be separated from his wife or children. He is not prevented by law from learning to read the Bible. These things are not failures. He can own land. He has schools and colleges. The young colored man is received as an equal into nearly every Northern college and university. He has frequently taken the highest university honors. I suppose he does not know, from the behavior of his companions, that they think of the difference between the color of his skin and theirs. His right to vote is secure in thirty-four of the forty-five States of the Union. So far, there has been no failure. When the Civil War broke out, there were fifteen slave States and sixteen free States. In Maryland, Delaware, and West Virginia the negro seems to have his place now like other citizens. The same thing probably is true in St. Louis, and likely to be true before long throughout Missouri. There are thirty States out of forty-five, and there will before long probably be thirty-five out of fifty in which the old race feeling, growing out of slavery has never got a hold. The old race-hatred of the negro is getting into a corner. So far reconstruction has not been a failure.

Two things are not yet accomplished. There are eleven States in which the negro is not yet secure in his political rights; and there are as many, and perhaps two or three more, in which if he be suspected of a crime of the first magnitude, he is likely to undergo a cruel death, without a trial. That would have been quite as likely, indeed a good deal more likely to have happened, if the reconstruction measures had never been enacted.

It is a bad thing that any man who has the Constitutional right to vote should fail to have his vote received and counted. But I think it is a fair question whether the existence of this condition throughout so large a country, with the prospect that slowly and gradually as the negro improves he will get his rights, be not better than the alternative which must have been his reduction to slavery again, or what is nearly as bad, a race of peons in this country. That is the question into the answer of which so much prejudice enters that it is hardly worth while to reason about it. My opinion is that as the colored man gets land, becomes chaste, frugal, temperate, industrious, veracious, that he will gradually acquire respect, and will attain political equality. Let us not be in a hurry. Evils, if they be evils, which have existed from the foundation of the world, are not to be cured in the lifetime of a single man. The men of the day of reconstruction were controlled by the irresistible logic of events; by a power higher than their own. I could see no alternative then, and I see no alternative now, better than that which was adopted.

CHAPTER XVIII

COMMITTEE SERVICE IN THE HOUSE

THE career of a Member of either House of Congress is determined, except in rare cases, by his assignment to Committees. In the House that is wholly dependent on the favor of the Speaker. In the Senate those assignments are made by Committees of the two parties, chosen for the purpose, who first agree on the representation to be assigned to each. After the Senator has been assigned to a Committee he remains there unless he himself desire a change, and if the Members older in the service retire he succeeds in the end to the Chairmanship of the Committee. There has been no instance of a departure from this rule, except when there is a change in the political control of the body, and no instance of deposing a Member from a Committee without his consent, except the single and well-known case of Mr. Sumner.

I was always on friendly terms with Mr. Blaine during my entire service of eight years in the House of Representatives. But I owed nothing to any favor of his in the matter of Committee assignments. When I entered the service I was put on the Committee of Education and Labor and on the Committee of Revision of the Laws, both obscure and unimportant. In my second term I served a little while on the Committee on Elections. I was also placed on the Committee of Railroads and Canals. I was made Chairman of a special Committee to visit Louisiana and inquire into the legality of what was called the Kellogg Government and report whether Governor Kellogg or his Democratic rival should be recognized as the lawful Governor of Louisiana. I was afterward placed on the Judiciary Committee, a position of great honor, which I liked very much.

With the exception of the last none of these appointments had any attraction for me. They were all out of the line of my previous experience in life and the service they required of me was disagreeable. I was placed on the Committee on the Judiciary by Mr. Speaker Kerr, a Democrat. Mr. Blaine at the time very earnestly pressed Mr. Martin I. Townsend of New York for the place. I do not conceive that I had any right to complain of Mr. Blaine in this matter. I never made any request of him for any appointment within his gift and he was beset behind and before by the demands of men he was unable to gratify, to many of whom he conceived himself under great obligation. It should be stated too that in Mr. Blaine's time the Members from Massachusetts older in the service than myself had very important places indeed. So it was hardly just to increase the number of important Committee appointments from our State.

But it happened to me by great good fortune that I had an opportunity, of which I was very glad, to accomplish something by reason of my place on each Committee on which I served, which I could not have accomplished without it.

An amusing piece of good fortune happened to me at the beginning of my service. I was placed, as I said, on the Committee on the Revision of the Laws. My law practice had been in the interior of the Commonwealth. So I had little knowledge of United States jurisprudence. I determined in order to fit myself for my new duties to make a careful study of the statutes and law administered in the United States Courts. I took with me to Washington a complete set of the Reports of the Supreme Court of the United States and purchased Abbott's Digest of those decisions, then just published. The first evening after I got settled I spent in reading the opinions of the Supreme Court. I took the Digest beginning with the letter A, reading the abstracts, and then reading the cases referred to. I got as far as Adm and read the cases relating to admiralty practice. The next morning the Speaker announced his Committees and the House adjourned. After the adjournment, Judge Poland, Chairman of the Committee on the Revision of the Laws, called the Committee together and laid before them a letter he had just received from Mr. Justice Miller of the Supreme Court, asking for a change in the law in regard to monitions for summoning defendants in Admiralty. The change had been made necessary by some recent decisions of the Court. The others members of the Committee looked at each other in dismay. None of them was familiar with the question, or knew at all what it was all about. I then stated to them the difficulty, the necessity for a remedy, and the recent decisions, giving them the names of the cases and the volumes where they were found. They were all quite astonished to find a man from the country, of whom probably none of them had ever heard before, having the law of Admiralty at his tongue's end. If the question had related to anything in the Digest under Adr, or anything thereafter, I should have been found probably more ignorant than they were. But Judge Poland took me into high favor, and I found his friendship exceedingly agreeable and valuable. I do not remember that the Committee on the Revision of the Laws had another meeting while I belonged to it.

I was also, as I have said, put on the Committee of Education and Labor. The Bureau of Education had been lately established and the Commissioner appointed. But the office was exceedingly unpopular, not only with the old Democrats and the Strict Constructionists, who insisted on leaving such things to the States, but with a large class of Republicans. A very zealous attack was made on the Bureau, led by Mr. Farnsworth of Illinois, and by Cadwallader C. Washburn, a very able and influential Republican from Wisconsin. The Committee on Appropriations, of which my colleague, Mr. Dawes, was Chairman, reported a provision for abolishing this Bureau. Mr. Dawes, himself, however, dissented. The Republicans on the Committee of Education and Labor took up the cudgels for the Bureau. We beat the Committee of Appropriations. The result of the strife was that the Bureau was put on a firmer footing with a more liberal provision, and it has since been, under General Eaton and Dr. Harris, the accomplished and devoted Commissioners, of very great and valuable service to the country.

That led me to give special study to the matter of National education. I introduced a bill for establishing an educational system by National authority in States which failed to do it themselves. Later, I introduced and carried through the House a measure for distributing the proceeds of the public land and sums received from patents and some other special funds, among all the States in aid of the common schools. This bill passed the House, but was lost in the Senate mainly because Senator Morrill of Vermont, a most excellent and influential statesman, insisted that the money should go to the agricultural colleges, in which he took great interest, and not to common schools. Later when I became a member of the Senate I succeeded in getting a like measure twice through the Senate. But it failed in the House. So the two Houses never agreed upon it. But the movement and discussion aroused public attention throughout the country and were of great value.

While I was on that Committee, I think during my second term, there was referred to it a bill to rebuild William and Mary College in Virginia. The principal building of that College had been destroyed by fire. The Union and Rebel forces had fought for possession of it. It had been held by the Union soldiers and a court martial was sitting there when it was attacked by the other side and the Union men driven out, and the insurgents held the building for a few hours. They abandoned it very soon. But before the Union soldiers had got back in force some stragglers set fire to the building. It was totally destroyed.

William and Mary was the oldest college in the country, except Harvard. It numbered among its children many famous statesmen, including Jefferson, Marshall, Peyton Randolph, and Monroe. Washington was its Chancellor for twelve years. Its graduates loved it ardently. I came to the conclusion that it would tend very much to restore the old affectionate feeling between the States to rebuild this College without inquiring too strictly into the merits of the case, as tested by any strict principle of law. I accordingly reported and advocated a bill for appropriating sixty or seventy thousand dollars to rebuild the College. Afterward, when on the Committee of Claims in the Senate, I advocated extending the same principle to all colleges, schools and other institutions of education and charity destroyed by the operations of the War without regard to the question who was in fault. This policy was, after a good deal of opposition and resistance, successfully carried out.

But the William and Mary College Bill was reported at the time when the passions excited by the War were still burning in the breasts of many Republican statesmen. The measure was received with derision. I was hardly allowed to go on with my speech in order, and the ordinary courtesy of a brief extension of time to finish it was refused amid great clamor. But I got the Bill through the House the next winter. I had a powerful ally in Mr. Perce of Mississippi, a Northern soldier, who had settled in that State after the War. It was not considered in the Senate. The measure was renewed again later in the House. But it was bitterly attacked by Mr. Reed of Maine, afterward Speaker, and defeated. Afterward I succeeded in getting it through the Senate when the Democrats had possession of the House, during the Administration of President Harrison, and it became a law.

I have been assured by many Southern men that that measure, and the report and speech in which I advocated it, had a very strong and wide influence in restoring good feeling toward the Union in the minds of the people of Virginia. Several of the graduates of William and Mary who afterward became Republicans have assured me of this with great emphasis. I was much pleased to get the following letter from Governor Henry A. Wise, the eminent Virginia statesman, who was, with two or three exceptions, the most powerful and influential advocate of secession in the South.

RICHMOND VA
Feby 13th 1872.

Hon Mr Hoar
   of Massts.
Honored Sir.

I write for no reason but one of pure feeling of respect—not even for a reply. I am a visitor of W^m & Mary College—truly of the most venerable of the "Mothers of Thought"—and have read your excellent appeal to the H. Reps: in her behalf. It was worthy of that Grand old Comth, Massts, the elder sister of this once glorious Comth, which hailed her heartily in the Night of Revolution against Tyranny. It was worthy of sweet memories—worthy of Letters—it was pious and patriotic. Let me just add a sentence more, to say that if Rebellion and Sectional Hate are to be eradicated—and I hope they are—*that is the way to do it.* Your speech & the passage of such bills, catholic in every sense of love & charity, will do more to heal our Country's wounds than all the caustic of reconstruction which can be applied.

With unaffected gratitude for your Speech, I pray you will not pause upon it, but keep the bill to its passage through both Houses of Congress. I know you would if you could see the destitution of instruction, and the poverty which cant pay for it, on the Consecrated peninsula of Jas Town, York Town, and Williamsburg. Ah! tear down every parapet of War—cruel War, wanton war call it if you will—but for the Past, for Piety's sake, for Learning and Moral's sake let Old W^m & Mary stand a Beacon Light for the guide of the Future.

   Very sincerely
      Yrs
   Henry A. Wise.

Governor Wise had a very conspicuous career in the United States House of Representatives. He was a very zealous supporter of the Southern doctrine before the War. He was regarded as a good deal of a fire eater. He was Governor of Virginia when John Brown was executed. But in spite of the horror and indignation that the people of the South felt for John Brown's raid he did full justice to the heroic quality of the man. He declared him "the gamest man" he ever saw.

I served in my second term on the Committee on Elections under the Chairmanship of George W. McCrary. Election cases in the House up to that time were, as they always were in the English House of Commons and as they have been too often in the Senate, determined entirely by party feeling. Whenever there was a plausible reason for making a contest the dominant party in the House almost always awarded the seat to the man of its own side. There is a well-authenticated story of Thaddeus Stevens, that going into the room of the Committee of Elections, of which he was a member, he found a hearing going on. He asked one of his Republican colleagues what was the point in the case. "There is not much point to it" was the answer. "They are both damned scoundrels." "Well," said Stevens, "which is the Republican damned scoundrel? I want to go for the Republican damned scoundrel."

We had a good many contests. But the Committee determined to settle all the questions before it as they would if they were judges in a court of justice. The powerful influence of Mr. McCrary, the Chairman, aided largely to bring about that result. The Democratic minority soon discovered that we were sincere and in earnest. They met us in a like spirit. I believe the Committee on Elections during that Congress reported on every case with absolute impartiality, and the House followed their lead. I formed a very pleasant friendship on that Committee with Judge William M. Merrick, a Maryland Democrat, who had made himself very much disliked by the Republican authorities during the War because of his supposed sympathy with Rebellion. I do not think he sympathized with the Rebellion. But he construed the Constitution very strictly and was opposed to many measures of the Administration. He was nominated by President Cleveland to be Judge of the Supreme Court of the District of Columbia. The Judiciary Committee of the Senate reported against him, putting their objection on the ground of the conduct imputed to him during the War, and also of his age. He was then sixty-seven years old. I dissented from the Committee, of which I was a member, and I exerted myself with all my might to secure his confirmation, and was successful. He made a most admirable Judge, and my action was abundantly vindicated by the result.

I have taken special satisfaction in two reports which I made for that Committee. I have a right to say that I dealt with the subjects with the same freedom from bias or prejudice with which it would have been my duty to give to the question if I had been sitting on the Bench of the Supreme Court of the United States.

The case of Cessna *vs.* Myers was perhaps the most interesting and important of those in which I made a report for that Committee. John Cessna had served the State of Pennsylvania for several terms. He was a very popular and eminent Republican member. According to the returns, Myers, his adversary, had a majority of 14. Cessna showed beyond question, and his antagonist admitted, that more than 14 illegal votes were cast for Myers. On the other hand Myers claimed that there were many illegal votes cast for Cessna, the evidence of which, so far as appeared, came to his knowledge first when introduced in the case. When the evidence was taken Cessna claimed to have evidence that 328 illegal votes were cast for Myers, and that ten legal votes, cast or offered for him, were rejected. On the other hand the sitting member claimed that there were 341 votes illegally thrown for the contestant, and of those Cessna admitted that 81 had proved to be illegal. So the Committee were obliged to examine by itself the evidence in regard to the right to vote of each of several hundred persons.

The case turned finally on some very interesting questions of the law of domicile. It appeared that a considerable number of persons who were entitled to vote, if they were residents of the district where they voted, were workmen employed in the construction of a railroad. They had come from outside the district for that purpose alone, and had no purpose of remaining in the district after the railroad should be completed, and meant then to get work wherever they could find it, there or elsewhere. There were also a number of votes cast by students who had gone to college for the purpose of getting an education, having no design to remain there after their studies terminated. Still another class of voters whose right was in dispute, were the paupers abiding in the public almshouse, and maintained in common by a considerable number of townships and parishes. These paupers voted in the district where the almshouse was situated, although it was not the district of their domicile or residence when they were removed to it.

The Committee held in the case of the laborer,—in spite of the very earnest contention to the contrary, that if the laborer elected in good faith when he came into the district to make it his legal residence, it became his legal residence, even if he intended to leave it and get another after his job was done.

We applied a like doctrine to the case of the students, holding that a student of a college, being personally present in any district, had the right if he so desired, to take up his abode there, and make it by his election his legal residence for a fixed and limited time.

The question of the paupers we left undecided, as it turned out that whichever way it were decided, Mr. Cessna had not overcome his opponent's legal majority.

We also decided an Arkansas case where the title to his seat of a well known Republican member of Congress was at stake, in favor of the Democratic contestant.

I was somewhat gratified in the midst of a storm of vituperation which I had encountered for some political action of mine, in which I was charged by almost the entire Democratic press of the country with being a bitter partisan to find two Democratic gentlemen who had owed their seats to the impartiality of the Committee on Elections, coming very zealously to the rescue.

I served also from 1873 to 1875 on the Committee on Railroads and Canals. I have no recollection of doing anything on that Committee, except aiding in reporting a bill for the regulation by National authority of railroads engaged in interstate commerce, in defence of which I made an elaborate speech. But I was able to secure the passage of one very interesting and important measure. James B. Eads, the famous engineer, architect of the great St. Louis bridge, had a plan for opening to commerce the mouth of the Mississippi River by a system of jetties. He had submitted his plan to the Board of Engineers appointed by the War Department. But he could get no encouragement, and of the twenty members of that Board, only one, General Barnard, the President, looked with any approval upon his scheme. The Board thought that a very long and costly canal was the only method of securing a water-way which would enable ocean steamers to reach New Orleans, and the product of the Mississippi Valley to be carried to Europe that way. Captain Eads appeared before the Committee on Railroads and Canals and urged his scheme in a speech of great interest and ability. The Committee adjourned for a week. They were to take up the question at the next meeting. The vote was unanimous against Mr. Eads's Bill. When the Committee came out of their room he was waiting outside the door to learn his fate. I saw the look of disappointment and despair on his face when he was told of the vote. I asked him to come with me into another room, which he did. I told him that I was satisfied from what I had heard that his plan was a good one, although I had voted against it with the rest of the Committee. It seemed to me that it would be presumptuous in me, having no special knowledge in such matters, to go against the practically unanimous report of the United States Board of Engineers. But I said: "Captain Eads, can you not frame a bill, which will provide that you shall not have any money from the Treasury for your work until you have accomplished something. If you deepen the channel of the river a foot that will have done some good. Suppose you provide that when you have deepened the river a certain number of feet you shall have so much of your pay, when it is deepened further so much more, and so on until the work is done." Captain Eads eagerly caught at the plan. He said that he was willing to do it, and that he was perfectly willing that his getting his pay should depend upon the certificate of the engineers of his having accomplished the result. He agreed to have a bill drawn on that principle. He brought it to me afterward. I went over it very carefully, inserting some additional securities for the Government. I then took it to the next meeting of the Committee, moved a reconsideration of the vote of the previous week. That was carried by a bare majority of one vote. I then moved the new bill as a substitute for the old one. It was adopted. The bill passed the House and Senate under which the Eads jetties were constructed and vessels drawing over twenty-eight feet of water passed freely up and down to and from New Orleans. The depth before that time, I think, had been twelve feet. Captain Eads afterward sent me a beautifully bound copy of the history of the Eads's jetties with an inscription certifying to the facts I have stated, in his own handwriting. I told this story afterward at a meeting of the business men of Boston. Mr. Corthell who happened to be present made a speech after I got through. He is himself a very eminent water engineer. He said that he was associated with Captain Eads at the time and had often heard Captain Eads tell the story.

Captain Eads afterward had a scheme which always seemed to me very feasible for a ship-railway across the Isthmus of Tehuantepec. His project was to construct a railway with a sufficient number of tracks, and to raise ships of the largest size on the principle applied in locks of ordinary canals. He had a contrivance made of stout beams which would hold and support a loaded vessel to which it was adjusted. The beams were to operate something like the keys of a piano, and the whole operation was something like that by which hatters measure and record the shape of a man's head. This plan received the hearty commendation of some very eminent engineers, including Major Reed of England, the highest authority on such subjects, the constructor of the dry docks at Malta. The scheme had a good many supporters in Congress. I think it would have been adopted but for Captain Eads's premature death.

Rather a singular coincidence took place when I was interesting myself in this matter which possibly may be not too trivial to record. One Thanksgiving morning I received by express a beautiful copy of Wordsworth, which I had bought in Boston the day before. Just as I was opening it the morning mail was brought in. I opened the book at random and turned to Wordsworth's poem, "The Highland Broach." My eye caught the following lines:

> Lo! Ships from seas by nature barred,
> Mount along ways by man prepared;
> Along far stretching vales, whose streams
> Seek other seas, their canvas gleams,
> And busy towns grow up on coasts
> Thronged yesterday by airy ghosts.

I turned my eye from these verses to the mail in which was a copy of a New York illustrated journal containing an account of the Eads ship-railway.

The inscription in Eads's "History of the Jetties," above referred to, is as follows:

To Hon. George F. Hoar, who, as a member of the House Committee which matured the Jetty Act, prepared the *first report* in its favor, this book is presented; with the assurance that his unfaltering support of the enterprise through all its struggles, entitled him to a prominent place among the statesmen to whom the producers in the Valley of the Mississippi are most largely indebted.

JAS B. EADS

Washington, D. C.,
   February
      1881

I had the pleasure of receiving a telegram from New Orleans shortly after the completion of the jetties saying that a loaded steamer, drawing between twenty-seven and twenty-eight feet of water, had safely passed through them to New Orleans.

The Commission appointed by the Government insisted upon having the jetties constructed at the south pass of the

Mississippi River. This Captain Eads strenuously resisted and urged the superiority of the southwest pass for the purpose. The House when it passed the jetty bill adopted Mr. Eads's plan. But the Senate insisted on taking the opinion of the Commission, much to his distress. The Senate was firm, and the House was obliged to yield. I think everybody now agrees that Eads was right, and that the scheme would have been perfectly successful, and would have continued to perform all that was desired of it, if his counsel had been taken. As it is, the jetties have been of great value and well worth their cost. But it will probably be necessary some time to construct a similar work in the southwest pass.

During my first term in the House on the Committee on Education and Labor I had the important duty of investigating the conduct of the Freedman's Bureau and other charges made against General Oliver O. Howard. I wrote nearly the whole of the report, all of it containing the arguments of the Committee, and the summing up of the evidence. A few passages are by the Chairman, Mr. Arnell. The Freedman's Bureau was established to aid the colored people who had been suddenly emancipated by President Lincoln's Proclamation, to attain a condition where they could get their living in comfort, and their children could be educated. General Howard, a very eminent officer in the Civil War, afterward at the head of the Army, was a man singularly fitted for this duty. He was profoundly religious, absolutely incorruptible, a man of very kind heart, not afraid to break out new paths, apt to succeed in all his undertakings, a lover of Liberty and thoroughly devoted to his work. The resources at his command were the unclaimed pay of the negro soldiers and some other sums specially granted from the Treasury. But the work was one entirely different from anything which had been accomplished by government agency in this country before. He purchased tracts of land, which were divided into building lots, which were sold to the colored people. Money was advanced to them to build houses, the Freedman's Bureau taking a mortgage as security. The Bureau endowed Howard University, of which General Howard was made President. A large Congregational Church was built in Washington with moneys advanced by the Bureau, the religious society giving its bonds at seven per cent. for which the structure was ample security. General Howard had incurred the bitter animosity not only of the enemies of the negro race, who disliked the whole object for which the Bureau was founded, but of other persons whom he had offended. I believe in no instance was there any loss to the Government, or to the fund in his charge. He was able to establish in comfortable homes, and to educate and to provide work for many thousand freedmen who had flocked to Washington during the disturbed period immediately following emancipation. After a thorough investigation, where the prosecution was conducted by Fernando Wood, a very distinguished and able Representative from New York, formerly Mayor of the City, General Howard was completely exonerated by the report of the majority of the Committee. The report was accepted by the House.

In 1873 I visited Louisiana, as Chairman of a special committee raised for the purpose of inquiring into the conditions there, and ascertaining which of two rival State governments was the lawful one. The investigation disclosed a terrible story of murder, brutality and crime. I made the report, signed also by Mr. Wheeler, afterward Vice-President, and Mr. Frye, now Senator and President pro tempore of the Senate. It told the dreadful story of these things with absolute truth and fidelity. It is not worth while to revive these memories now. But at the same time I endeavored to do full justice to the better qualities of the Southern people and to explain how it happened that men otherwise so honorable and brave and humane could be led by the passions of a political warfare and race prejudice to commit such offences. Mr. Lamar, of Mississippi, one of the most brilliant and able statesmen of his time, sought an interview with me after the report went in and thanked me for what I had said of the Southern people, and told me that "I was the first Northern man who seemed to be capable of doing them justice." What he thought will be found also stated by him.

In a speech made before a Democratic meeting in the spring of 1875, Mr. Lamar said ("Life of Lamar," p. 221):

"Well, the character of that last Committee—especially of its Chairman, Mr. George F. Hoar—was such as to lead to no expectation that there would be any indulgence shown to the people of the South, or any very harsh criticisms of his own party. By inheritance, by training, by political association, he was intensely anti-Southern. His manners toward Southern men, so bitter are his feelings, are often cold and reserved; and nothing but his instinct and refinement as a gentleman, which he is in every respect, saved him from sometimes being supercilious; acute in intellect, cultured, trained to the highest expansion of his powers, quick in his resentments and combative in temperament, we certainly expected no quarter from his hands. But beneath all this there were genuine truth and manhood in Hoar that lifted him above the sordid feeling of malignant passion. He went, then, to that country, and he made a report; and, while there is much in it that saddened my heart, while there is much which I say is unwise and unjust in his observations, there are some things, fellow citizens, which you people of the North should hark to bear in mind, while you are coming to your conclusions with reference to the relations which you intend to sustain to the prostrate people of my section. Here, fellow citizens, is what Mr. Hoar says in reference to the South: 'We do not overlook the causes which tended to excite deep feeling and discontent in the white population of Louisiana. (I must read these extracts to you because a people's interest, a people's destiny, hang largely upon the action of the people of New Hampshire and other Northern States.) There has been great maladministration; public funds have been wasted (that means public funds have been embezzled, appropriated by these governments that are sucking the blood, the life blood, from a people already impoverished by four years of calamitous war); public lands have been wasted, public credit impaired.' Now, fellow citizens, that is the testimony of one of the most uncompromising Republicans in this country."

Mr. Lamar would not have used, I am sure, the word "bitter" after we came to know each other better. Perhaps I may be forgiven if I insert here a letter from Mr. Lamar's nephew, just elected a member of Congress from the State of Florida. I know I must attribute the eulogy which it contains to his kindness of heart, and desire to meet more than half way my own cordial feeling toward the portion of my countrymen to whom he belongs. I do not take them literally. But I confess I like to leave on record, if I may, some evidence which will contradict the charge so constantly made by critics near home, that I am a man of intense partisan and personal bitterness.

TALLAHASSEE, FLA.,
Mch 10th, 1903

SENATOR GEORGE F. HOAR,
    Washington, D. C.
Dear Sir:

I would like very much to have a copy of your address lately made before the Union League of Chicago. I see notices of the speech in the newspapers.

Also your address made before the New England Society some three years ago, if you have a copy.

Your picture, sent to me at my request, hangs in my room. It is the face and form of a great American statesman. One whom our people have learned to admire and love.

Our people venerate your years, still in vigorous life and in full possession of great faculties of mind and heart. We look to you and other great Northern men to keep us in our sectional and racial questions. In one way these questions mean so little to the sections of the country not immediately interested in them, but they mean so much to the Southern people who have to deal with them as live, every day matters.

I left the Attorney-General's office in this State on February 28th, ult., after fourteen years service and two years yet to run. On March 4th, inst., I became Congressman from the new Third Congressional district.

I go to Washington as a Democrat, but with full knowledge that my party does not contain all the right or all the wrong in it. And I hope that in the vexing questions of the future, that by a temperate course of thought and action, that my influence may be worth something, however, small, to my people beyond even a party view.

But after all I feel that great and representative men of other sections can assist the Southern people in these questions quite as much, if not more, than we can assist ourselves.

I hope to meet you next winter. The biography of my Uncle Justice Lamar shows how much he esteemed you and your regard for him. I am with much respect,

Very truly yours,
(Signed) W. B. LAMAR.

I was also placed by Mr. Blaine on the Committee to investigate the Union Pacific Railroad and the Credit Mobilier. I shall give an account of this matter in a separate chapter.

There was great public excitement on the subject. After the report on the Union Pacific Railroad, and within about a week of the end of the Congress, the House adopted a resolution to make a like investigation of the affairs of the Central Pacific Railroad. It was absolutely impossible to accomplish such an inquiry within the few remaining days of the session. But if we failed to attempt it the political newspapers and what are called Independent newspapers, always much less fair to public men than political opponents, would have charged us with failing to make the investigation from a desire to screen the offenders. The charge would have been greedily believed in the excited condition of the public mind, which our explanation would never reach. So I advised the Committee to call Mr. Huntington, the President of the Central Pacific Railroad, and ask him to produce the accounts and records of his Company. To this it was anticipated that he would reply that these records were in California and that he could not get them before Congress and the authority of the Committee would expire. Mr. Huntington was accordingly summoned. He brought with him Mr. William M. Evarts, as counsel, and testified as was expected. He then, however, asked leave of the Committee to make a statement in regard to the relation of his road to the National Government. This was granted. He then went on to say what a great public benefactor his company had been. It had connected the two oceans by a great railroad across the continent, saving millions upon millions to the commerce of the country. But beside that he said it had saved to the Government more than all the moneys the Government had advanced toward its construction, by preventing Indian wars. One winter especially his railroad corporation had fed a hostile Indian tribe when the Government supplies had failed to reach them, saving them from the danger of starvation and saving the Government from a bloody and costly Indian war. I said, Mr. Huntington—Was not that ultra vires for a railroad corporation? He answered: "No, Sir! no, Sir! we never gave them anything as strong at that." He evidently thought he was being charged with supplying the Indians with liquor, and that ultra vires meant extra strength.

The only other important committee work that I now recall during my service in the House related to the investigation of the conduct of Mr. Speaker Blaine. He was charged with having received stock in a railroad at a price much less than its then value with the expectation of paying for it by aiding the passage of legislation in which the road was interested, by political service as a Member of the House of Representatives, and especially by his great influence as Speaker. It was further claimed that in letters addressed by him to a man named Mulligan he had demanded conveyances of such stock in compensation for a ruling he had before made by which a measure in conflict with the interest of the road was defeated. These charges were referred to the Committee of the Judiciary. The House was then Democratic and the majority of the Committee was made up of Mr. Blaine's political opponents. The investigation was conducted in a spirit of bitter hostility to him. The evidence was taken by a sub-committee of which I was not a member. But as disputed questions of procedure and as to the admission of evidence were constantly coming up which were referred always to the full committee, which was considered in session all the time for that purpose,— the members were every day, sometimes several times a day, summoned from their seats in the House to the meeting of the Committee. I was familiar with the whole case as it went in. It was expected that there would be a hostile report, and it was understood that I should be charged with the duty of making a minority report.

I studied that evidence as thoroughly and faithfully as I could. I have gone over the matter very carefully since. I was then satisfied, and am satisfied now, that the charges against Mr. Blaine of any corruption or wrong-doing were totally unsustained. They would never have found credit for a moment except in minds deeply excited by the bitter political passion which at that time raged to a degree wholly unknown in our political strife to-day. All Mr. Blaine did was to say when he applied for the purchase of the stock to the men who were then trying to dispose of it that "he should not be a dead-head." He meant by that only that he was able to be of advantage to any undertaking in which he should be interested, an assurance which his known ability and energy and large acquaintance with business men thoroughly warranted him in making. There was no action of Congress expected, or legislation in which the railroad was likely to have an interest. All that it expected to get from Congress had been obtained already.

The other charge that he demanded a favor in this purchase as compensation for a ruling he had made as Speaker was, in my judgment, equally unfounded and trivial. He simply alluded to the fact that he had made a ruling which had saved the road from hostile legislation. Every lawyer has doubtless many times had jurymen remind him of the fact that they had been on juries that gave verdicts in his favor. Every Member of Congress likes to meet a pensioner for whom he has secured a pension. Neither has any thought of wrong in reviving such a memory. The ruling Mr. Blaine had made was simply stating a clear rule of the House about which there could be no doubt whatever. At the same time, I said at the time, what I deem it my duty to repeat now, I think Mr. Blaine erred, when he thought it proper to embark in such a speculative investment. Members of legislative bodies, especially great political leaders of large influence, ought to be careful to keep a thousand miles off from relations which may give rise to even a suspicion of wrong. Their influence and character are the property of their country, and especially valuable to their political associates. The great doctrines of which they are the influential advocates must not be imperiled by any smell of fire on their garments. But an error of judgment, or of good taste, on their part, is very far from being corruption. Henry Clay was a gambler. Other eminent statesmen both in this country and in Europe have made no secret of even worse vices than that. They are undoubtedly to be disapproved, in some cases severely condemned. But the people always have made and always will make a distinction between such offences and the final unpardonable guilt of corruption in office.

James G. Blaine was a man of many faults and many infirmities. But his life is a part of the history of his country. It will be better for his reputation that the chapter of that history which relates to him shall be written by a historian with a full and clear sense of those faults and infirmities, concealing nothing, and extenuating nothing. But also let him set nought down in malice. Mr. Blaine was a brilliant and able man, lovable, patriotic, far-seeing, kind. He acted in a great way under great responsibilities. He was wise and prudent when wisdom and prudence were demanded. If he had attained to the supreme object of his ambition and reached the goal of the Presidency, if his life had been spared to complete his term, it would have been a most honorable period, in my opinion, in the history of the country. No man has lived in this country since Daniel Webster died, save McKinley alone, who had so large a number of devoted friends and admirers in all parts of the country.

CHAPTER XIX

SALMON P. CHASE

AMONG the very interesting characters with whom I have formed an acquaintance in Washington was Chief Justice Salmon P. Chase. I saw him but a few times. But on those occasions he spoke to me with a freedom with which famous public men seldom speak, even to intimate friends. I incline to think it was his habit to speak freely to comparative strangers. But of that I know nothing.

When I first went to Washington, in the spring of 1869, I was invited by Commissary-General Eaton, whose daughter was the wife of my cousin, to attend a meeting of a club at his house. The club was composed of scientific men who met at each other's houses. The reading of a paper by the host was followed by a supper. The host was permitted to invite such guests as he saw fit, not members of the club. Chief Justice Chase was one of the guests. I was introduced to him there for the first time, except that I went, when I was quite a young man, long before the war, to hear him speak and, with a great many other persons, went up and shook hands with him after the speech was over.

The Chief Justice left General Eaton's house when I did, and asked me if I were going his way. So we walked together about a mile. He talked all the way about the next nomination for the Presidency; about the prospects of the various candidates, and the probability of the success of the Democratic Party if they had a candidate who would be satisfactory to the Republicans who were disaffected with the present policies. It was evident that this great man had this subject, to use a cant phrase, "on the brain." This was before the Chief Justice had his paralytic shock. He was in the full vigor of health, a model of manly strength and manly beauty, giving every evidence that his great intellectual power was undiminished.

Not long afterward a friend of mine went to Ohio with his wife. In those days it was necessary for persons going from Washington to the Northwest to cross Baltimore in a carriage—the Washington station and the Ohio station being in different parts of the city. A friend of my friend went to Baltimore to see his wife, who was going to Ohio, across the city and then to return to Washington. He knew Chief Justice Chase. He introduced him to my friend on the cars, and they rode across Baltimore in one carriage, the two gentlemen, the Chief Justice, and the wife. The Chief Justice talked to him whom he had just met for the first time during the whole ride of half an hour on the same engrossing subject, as he had to me before.

I think there can be no doubt that Chief Justice Chase, like many other great men, was consumed by an eager and passionate ambition for the Presidency. That has been true of other great statesmen as well as of many small statesmen. It has been specially true of great orators. The American people are fond of eloquent speech. They make their admiration known to the speaker in a way that is quite likely to turn his head. In Plato's day the bee lighted on the lips of the orator, and the sweet honey of Hymettus mingled with the discourse as it came forth. To-day the bee lights in his ear and fills his fancy with delightful dreams of a hive by the Potomac, thatched with flowers and redolent with the incense of flattery.

I do not doubt that if Salmon P. Chase had been elected President of the United States he would have administered that lofty office honorably and to the advantage of the country. But I think that this ambition clouded his judgment, and inclined him, perhaps unconsciously, to take an attitude as a Judge on some of the political questions on which parties were divided after President Grant came in, which would be acceptable to the Democrats, and would make it possible for him to accept their nomination. But all this is merest speculation. If he had maintained his mental and physical vigor it is quite likely that he would have been nominated when Greeley was nominated. If he had been, it is not unlikely, in my opinion, that he would have been elected. I thought at the time that if Mr. Adams had been nominated in 1872, he might have been chosen. The discontent with Grant was far-reaching, for the reasons I have stated elsewhere. But the nomination of Greeley was ludicrous and preposterous. Almost every attack on the first Administration of President Grant was answered by the political speakers on his side by a quotation from Greeley or the New York *Tribune*. A candidate seeking an election by reason of the mistakes his antagonist has made in accordance with his own advice, does not stand much chance of winning. The Southern people, even the white Democrats, always had a kindly feeling for Grant. They did not resent what he had done as a soldier, as they resented what Greeley had said as a politician. They knew too, in spite of their strong differences with Grant, the innate honesty, justice and courage of the man.

Chase would have been a far stronger candidate than Greeley. However any political antagonist might dislike him, every antagonist must respect him, and nobody could laugh at him.

The question of the constitutional power of Congress to make Treasury notes legal tender for all debts, whether incurred before or after they were issued, came up for the decision of the Court when Chase was Chief Justice. It was a question which profoundly interested and excited the public. The Democratic Party, which more lately favored the payment of all debts, public and private, in irredeemable paper money, had assailed the Republican Administration during the war for providing, under an alleged necessity that the Treasury notes, called greenbacks, should be legal tender for the discharge of all debts. The constitutionality of that law had been affirmed by the courts of fifteen States. It had been denied by one court only, that of Kentucky, the eminent Chancellor dissenting. There was scarcely a Republican lawyer or a Republican judge in the country who doubted the constitutional power of Congress to impose such a quality upon the paper currency if, in the opinion of Congress, the public safety should require it.

The question came before the Supreme Court of the United States in the case of Hepburn *v.* Griswold, and was decided by that Court in December, 1869.

The Court were all agreed that Congress has power under the Constitution to do not only what the Constitution expressly authorizes, but to adopt any means appropriate, and plainly adapted to carry into effect any such express power. So the two questions arose: First, Was the power to issue legal tender notes an appropriate, and plainly adapted means to any end which the National Government has a right to accomplish? Second, Who are to judge of the question whether the means be so appropriate, or plainly adapted?

There were then seven Justices of the Supreme Court. Chief Justice Chase, with the three Democratic Justices held the Legal Tender Law unconstitutional, and declared that a law making anything but gold or silver legal tender for debts was neither appropriate nor plainly adapted to carrying on war, or any other end for which the National Government was created.

He had, when Secretary of the Treasury during the War of the Rebellion, originally advised the issuing of these legal tender notes. He had visited the Capitol. He had called members of the two Houses of Congress from their seats and, by his great urgency, overcome their reluctance to vote for the Legal Tender Law. My late colleague, Mr. Dawes, has more than once told me, and others in my hearing, that he was exceedingly reluctant to resort to that measure, and that he was induced to support it by Mr. Chase's earnest declaration that it was impossible that the War should go on without it, that he was at the last extremity of his resources. A Government note had been formally protested in the city of New York. I have heard a like statement from many public men, survivors of that time. It is not too much to say, that without Mr. Chase's urgent and emphatic affirmation that the war must stop and the Treasury be bankrupt and the soldiers without their pay, unless this measure were adopted, it never could have passed Congress.

Notwithstanding this, Mr. Chase puts his opinion in the Legal Tender Cases on the ground that this was not a necessary, or plainly adapted means to the execution of the unquestionable power of carrying on a great war in which the life of the Republic was in issue.

The question whether this necessity existed was a question of fact. Now questions of fact cannot be determined by the courts. If the fact be one on which depends the propriety of legislation it must be determined by the lawmaking power. Of course, where facts are of such universal or general knowledge that the court can know them judicially, without proof, like the fact of the time of the rising of the sun, or the laws of mechanics, or the customs prevailing in great branches of business, the court may take judicial notice of them. But how could Mr. Chase, as a judge, judicially declare as a fact that the issue of legal tender notes was not necessary for carrying on the war, when he had, as Secretary of the Treasury, having better means of knowledge than any other man, so earnestly and emphatically declared such necessity? How could he, as a judge of one court, determine as of an unquestionable fact of universal knowledge that the issue of a legal tender note was not necessary for maintaining the Government in that terrible war, when fourteen State tribunals, and a minority of his own court, had declared the fact to be the other way?

This decision gave rise to an attack upon the Administration of President Grant and especially upon Judge Hoar, then Attorney-General, which, although it has no foundation whatever in fact, is occasionally revived in later years, that the Court was packed by appointing two new Judges to reverse the decision. The decision in Hepburn *v.* Griswold was announced in the Supreme Court February 7, 1870. The court met at twelve o'clock. The decision was read by the Chief Justice after several opinions had been read by other judges, so that the afternoon must have advanced considerably before it was promulgated. It had not been made known to the public in advance by the press, and President Grant and Attorney-General Hoar both affirmed that they had no knowledge of the decision and had no expectation of what it would be before it was announced. I myself had a conversation with Attorney-General Hoar in the afternoon of that day. He had just heard the decision from the Chief Justice with great astonishment and surprise.

Four judges concurred in the decision. There were two vacancies in the court—one occasioned by the withdrawal of Mr. Justice Grier, and one by the Act of Congress of the previous Session providing for an additional judge. At twelve o'clock in the morning of that day, before the decision in Hepburn v. Griswold was made known, President Grant had sent to the Senate, and the Senate had received the communication nominating Messr. Strong and Bradley to these vacancies. They were regarded as the ablest lawyers in the circuits where they dwelt. By common consent of the entire profession they are among the ablest judges who ever sat on the Supreme Bench. In my opinion Mr. Justice Bradley has had no superior, save Marshall alone, on that court, in every quality of a great judge. I doubt if he has had, on the whole, an equal, save Marshall alone. They have both joined in opinions since their appointment in very important political questions, in which the policy of the party to which they belonged was not sustained. An offer to them of these vacancies in their circuits was the most natural and proper thing that could have been done. There was no Republican lawyer in the country, of any considerable prominence, so far as I know, who questioned the constitutionality of the Legal Tender Act, of distinction enough to make him thought of anywhere for a place on the Supreme Bench. So far as I now remember, there is but one instance of an appointment by the President of the United States to the Supreme Court of a man not belonging to his own political party. That is the case of Mr. Justice Jackson, who was appointed by President Harrison on my own earnest recommendation. There has never been made in any quarter, so far as I know, a statement or pretence that there existed any evidence that President Grant made these appointments, or that any member of his Cabinet advised it because of its possible effect on the Legal Tender Law. Yet this foolish and dirty charge has found extensive credit. I read it once in the London *Times*. It was, however, in a communication written by a degenerate and recreant American who was engaged in reviling his own country. It was also referred to by Mr. Bryce in his book on the United States. I sent him a copy of a pamphlet I prepared on the subject, and received from him a letter expressing his satisfaction that the story was without foundation. It is the fashion still, in some quarters, to speak, in spite of the decisions of the Supreme Court and the numerous State courts, to which I have referred, as if it were too clear for argument that Congress had no right to make the Government notes a legal tender. The gentlemen who talk in that way, however, are almost universally men of letters, or men without any legal training or any considerable legal capacity. They are of that class of political philosophers who are never trusted by their countrymen to deal with authority with any practical question either legislative, administrative, or judicial.

While saying this, I wish to affirm my own belief that, while it may be in some great emergencies like that of our late Civil War essential to the maintenance of the Government that this power which I believe Congress has, without a shadow of a reasonable question, should be exercised, yet I should hold it a great calamity if it were exercised except on such an occasion. It is a dangerous power, like the power of suspending the writ of *Habeas corpus,* or the power of declaring war, or the power of reckless and extravagant public expenditure, never to be exercised if it can possibly be helped. I think the American people have, in general, settled down on this as the reasonable view, in spite of the clamor of the advocates of fiat money on the one side, and the extreme strict constructionists on the other.

CHAPTER XX

ADIN THAYER

THE political history of Massachusetts from 1850 until 1888 cannot be written or understood without a knowledge of the remarkable career of Adin Thayer. When I was first nominated for Congress, he was my earnest opponent. That was due, so far as I know, to no dislike to me, but only to his strong friendship for Mr. Bird. After my election, he became my stanch friend. Our friendship continued without interruption to his death. The name of Adin Thayer is dear to my memory and to my heart.

I have often said that there were four men who honored me with their friendship, whose counsel I liked to get under any difficult public responsibility, and that when these four men approved or agreed with anything I myself said or did, I did not care what the rest of mankind thought. It would have been better to say that, although I did care very much what the rest of mankind thought, I knew that when these men were on my side, the wisdom and conscience of Massachusetts would be there also.

One of them was John G. Whittier. He added to the great genius which made him a famous poet the quality of being one of the wisest and most discreet political advisers and leaders who ever dwelt in the Commonwealth.

Another was my own brother, Judge Hoar, of whom I will not now undertake to speak. He was the last friend of mine who always performed the act of friendship to which Adin Thayer was never unequal, that of telling me my faults and mistakes with much more thoroughness and plainness of speech than he ever used in praising any of my virtues.

The third was Samuel May, who died in an honored old age at Leicester, his sunset hour cheered by the memories of noble service and the consciousness of having borne his full share in the greatest achievement of human history accomplished by mere political instrumentalities—the freedom of the slave.

The fourth was Adin Thayer, a man quite as remarkable in his way as either of the others in his. Each of them gave high and brave counsel in great emergencies. Each of them had a great part in the overthrow of the political forces that were on the side of slavery, and in the triumphant overthrow of the combination which would, if successful, have corrupted Massachusetts and made of her the worst instead of the best example on earth of republican self-government.

There is hardly room here for more than a sketch of Adin Thayer. He was a very striking, original and picturesque figure in the history of the Commonwealth. He was a strong, brave, wise, unselfish man. His life, so far as he took part in political affairs, was devoted to objects wholly public, never personal. He was the greatest organizer of righteousness in his generation. We must go back to Sam Adams to find any one who deserves to be compared with him in this respect. I cannot now undertake to tell the story of his important services to the Commonwealth at some very critical periods, or to narrate the history of all the political events in which he bore so conspicuous a share. The time to do this has not come. It can be done only when the correspondence, the inner personal life of men who were the leaders of Massachusetts during the stormy period through which she has lately passed, shall be given to the world.

Worcester County, from the day of Rufus Putnam until to-day, has in every generation contributed eminent persons to the service of the Commonwealth. But the service of none of them has been in the same field as his. Indeed, as I have just said, we must go back to the days of the Revolution to find a conspicuous character who united so completely absolute disinterestedness of character, inflexible integrity, passionate love for Massachusetts, devotion to the loftiest ideals, and was at the same time a most skilful and efficient organizer of political forces.

Adin Thayer was born in the town of Mendon, in the County of Worcester, December 5, 1828. His birthplace was near Chestnut Hill, in the territory which was incorporated into the town of Blackstone in 1845. He was the son of Caleb Thayer and Hannah, the daughter of Peter Gaskill of Mendon. His ancestors, so far as known, in all the line of descent, were New England farmers. No better race ever existed for the development of the highest intellectual and moral quality. They wrung a difficult livelihood from the soil and forest. They were educated by the responsibilities of self-government. They were accustomed to meditate and discuss with each other the profoundest questions of theology and of the State. Their local traditions had made them familiar with a stimulant and heroic history, in which every family had borne its share. In these Puritan communities life was a perpetual gymnasium. At the time of Mr. Thayer's birth, the strictness of the Puritan manners had softened somewhat. A milder theology was slowly making its way, but the race which settled in New England still remained without a tincture of any foreign element.

The town was one of the oldest in Worcester County. In every generation it had contained men of large influence in the Commonwealth, who had kept alive the interest of the people in public affairs. Jonathan Russell, who, with Adams, Bayard, Clay and Gallatin, negotiated the treaty of Ghent, and who met rather an ignominious defeat afterward in an attempt to measure lances with John Quincy Adams; the Hastings family, three of whom were eminent lawyers, two of them having represented the district in Congress; were of a generation that passed from the stage at about the time of Judge Thayer's birth.

The people were fond of discussing public questions, not only in town meeting, but in neighborhood gatherings and debating societies. The Judge used often to tell of the eager interest with which in his boyhood he listened to these encounters. There were two men, one of whom survived until Judge Thayer came to manhood, the other of whom died recently in an honored old age, who were less known abroad than those I have named, but who exerted a powerful influence upon the community and upon the character of the observant and impressible boy. One of them was Dan Hill, the other the Reverend Adin Ballou.

Dan Hill was one of the most remarkable men Worcester County ever contained. He was not bred to the bar, and was without the advantage of what is called a liberal education. But he had a wonderful aptness for understanding legal principles and the weight and effect of evidence. His neighbors when in trouble instinctively sought him as a shield. He was an unerring counsellor in the conduct of complicated affairs. His aid was extensively sought in the preparation of causes, in settling estates, and as guardian and trustee. He was concerned in hundreds of cases. It would be hard to name one in which he had anything to do that did not terminate to the advantage of the party who employed him. He had none of the arts of the pettifogger. He cared little for his own personal advantage. He had a native and lofty scorn for dishonesty and meanness. He was never better pleased than when, without prospect of gain for himself, he was employing his talents in the protection of poor and honest men against fraud and oppression. He had a large public spirit. He was early an anti-slavery man, and one of the founders of the Free Soil Party. He was specially at home in the Mendon and Blackstone town meetings, in the meetings of the school district, in the caucus, in the temperance and anti-slavery meetings and other neighborhood gatherings where the people discussed matters which concerned the public welfare. In all these he gave sensible counsel in common affairs and high counsel in high affairs.

The influence of Adin Ballou, of whom Judge Thayer delighted to speak in his later years, may be traced in the strong sympathy the Judge always showed for aspirations, although exhibited in most crude and grotesque fashion, for the reconstruction of society according to the laws of a newer and more spiritual life. Mr. Ballou, a man of clear intellect, stainless life, sweet and amiable temper, undertook with about thirty companions and disciples to form a community which should have the Beatitudes for constitution, charter and by-laws. This community was established at Hopedale, now a separate town, then part of Milford, formerly part of Mendon. Some of the most important members of this body withdrew from it, doubting its ability to maintain itself financially, and it was abandoned. But if its sweet and gracious influence on the social life in its neighborhood be any measure of its success, it was highly successful.

Hopedale became famous afterward as the dwelling-place of George Draper, one of the most eminent manufacturers and sagacious and public-spirited citizens—founder of the Home Market Club—the reputation and honor of whose name has been still more extended by his sons, the eldest of whom is the admirable soldier, Representative to Congress and Minister to Italy, General William F. Draper.

Judge Thayer was named for Adin Ballou, although he afterward dropped the middle name. Mr. Ballou gives his estimate of his namesake in the following letter:

HOPEDALE, MASS., Aug. 20, 1888.

HON. GEORGE F. HOAR,—
 My Dear Sir,—
Your lines of 11th inst. were duly received. I am very glad to learn that a Biography of Hon. Adin Thayer is in process of preparation, and that the work is in such competent hands. I reckoned him among my highly esteemed personal friends, and was painfully shocked by the news of his lamentable death. I knew his grandfather before him, his father and mother, and the whole family connexion more or less intimately. They were often attendant on my public ministrations, and I have been with them, during my long life, on many occasions of interest, joy and sorrow. They have all been persons of strong common sense, downright honesty and solid worth. Judge Thayer descended from a sturdy, intelligent and respectable yeoman stock. And he has honored his heredity by his own intellectual and

moral excellence. Although my personal intimacy with him has never been close enough to enable me to describe the footsteps of his upward career with graphical exactness, or to enrich my memory with interesting anecdotes, I can bear witness in a general way to his good characteristics, especially in his youth while he was nearest under my observation, and to some extent those of his mature years. He was an industrious, affectionate, and dutiful son from childhood to maturity. He evinced early intelligence, rationality and moral principle of a superior type, availing himself by close application of every opportunity for acquiring useful knowledge, and did so, as the sequel proved, successfully. He was always an independent, acute and logical thinker on a wide range of subjects, as well outside of his professional life as inside. But his constitution practically confined his ambition and pursuits to the state of the world's affairs as manageable for the time being, rather than to expending his energies for the realization of theories greatly in advance of current public opinion. In this respect he differed from his friend who writes this graphic contribution; whom nevertheless he always respected. But he was by no means a fossil conservative lagging in the rear of progress. He marched just as far forward in the column as he was sure it could command the ground. Thus he espoused the anti-slavery movement in politics in its germinal stage, and became one of the most sagacious and efficient organizers of the Republican Party in his native State. Of this, however, others are better qualified to treat than this friend. The same is true of his pecuniary and financial achievements; also of his legal, judicial and official attainments. Let abler pens in those departments eulogise him. Whatever this writer saw of him in the judicial chair or legal forum was unexceptionably creditable to him.

On the great themes of theology his conceptions and beliefs accorded mainly with those of the writer. They were sublimely liberal and regenerative, excluding all notions of the divine attributes and government in the least degree derogatory to the character of God as the Supreme, All-Perfect Father of the Universe.

Hoping that his numerous personal friends in the various relations of life will do greater justice and honor to his memory than this pen can, the foregoing is respectfully tendered.

Very respectfully yours,
Adin Ballou.

But it is not necessary to seek an explanation of Judge Thayer's interest in life beyond the native tendencies which came to him by lawful inheritance. More than one person of his name and blood in former generations were noted for their public spirit and exercised a large influence in the affairs of the town. Traditions of two brothers, Captain Caleb Thayer and 'Squire Elisha Thayer, are still fresh. Captain Caleb Thayer was the great-grandfather of Adin Thayer, Esquire. Elijah was grandfather of Hon. Eli Thayer, member of Congress from the Worcester district, and founder of the Emigrant Aid Society, which had so illustrious a share in saving Kansas from slavery. Eli Thayer tells me Elijah governed Mendon. He always carried in town meeting what he wanted to carry, and killed what he wanted to kill.

Caleb Thayer, the father of the Judge, was an early anti-slavery man, and one of the founders of the Free Soil Party. He was a man of vigorous sense and great public spirit. He had large interests in Mendon and Blackstone. He represented Mendon in the Legislature and helped elect Charles Sumner to the Senate in 1851. He was generally sociable and cheerful, but subject to occasional periods of depression of spirits, when he liked to remain in solitude until the time of gloom passed by.

Adin Thayer's education was chiefly in the district schools of his neighborhood. Hosea Biglow may be taken as the type of the ordinary Yankee country boy of that day. Adin had the advantage, better, if you can have but one, than any university, of being brought up in the country. He was a member of that absolute democracy, the old-fashioned New England country town, where character and worth were the only titles to respect in the community, where the son of a President or the son of a Senator or of a Governor stood on an absolute and entire social equality with the son of the washerwoman. If the son of a President or Governor gave himself any airs on that account, he had applied to him a very vigorous and effective remedy well known to our Saxon ancestors.

Adin Thayer came to manhood when the hosts of slavery and freedom were marshalling for the great contest for the territory between the Mississippi and the Pacific.

He was soaked in Scripture, especially in the Old Testament, a soaking which has somewhat the same effect on the moral and mental fibre that seven years in a tanner's vat used to have upon sole leather. How often I have known Adin, on some great political occasion or crisis, to crush some sophistry or compromise, or attempt to get things on a lower plane, by indignantly flashing out with some old text, such as, "Righteousness exalteth a nation," or "Sin is a reproach to any people," or answer, as he did once, to a gentleman who wanted him to sacrifice some moral principle for the sake of harmony in the Republican Party, "My friend, we will be first pure, and then peaceable."

Adin Thayer was a member of the School Committee of Worcester for some years. He was Senator from Worcester, I think, for two years, in 1871 and 1872. He was appointed Collector of Infernal Revenue for the eighth district by President Lincoln on August 26, 1862, and gave way to a successor appointed by President Johnson, September 14, 1866. He was reappointed by President Grant, June 22, 1872, and held the office until January, 1877, when the eighth and tenth districts were consolidated. He was appointed Judge of Probate by Governor Rice in the fall of 1877, and held that office until his death. He was Chairman of the State Committee in 1878. He gave to the public three or four essays or speeches printed in newspapers, and some of them in pamphlet form. They were, under one title or another, treatises on the moral duties of citizenship and appeals to the youth of the State to take their full and patriotic share in its administration.

But his function in life was that of an organizer. He was an ambitious man. But he never suffered his ambitions to stand in the way of what he thought was the good of the Commonwealth or of the party. Many and many a time, as there are plenty of persons who can testify, it had been the expectation that he would be the choice of his party for Senator or for Representative of the district in Congress, or some important municipal office, but when the time came, Mr. Thayer was the first to suggest that victory and harmony or the public advantage would be best attained by some other candidate, to whose service he gave a zeal and efficiency which he never would have given in his own behalf. He believed in party in politics, in organization, in work in the ward and in the school district. But he believed in those things because they were, in his judgment, essential to the accomplishment of the highest results in the country and in the Commonwealth. He was absolutely incorruptible, either by money or by office. He was a man of clean hands and a pure heart. His methods were open as the daylight. He conducted the great campaign against General Butler, when he was Chairman of the State committee. He came to Boston and found the knees of Boston trembling, people shaking in their shoes and their teeth chattering. He went into the committee room, put things to rights, organized a campaign never approached for thoroughness and efficiency in this Commonwealth, and during the whole time there sat at the table next his own a beautiful and refined young lady hearing and knowing everything that went on from the beginning of the campaign until the end. He had no political secrets. He never, to use a common phrase, "laid his ear to the ground." He never listened for the stamping of feet or the clapping of hands or the shouting or excitement or acclaim of the multitude. His ear was to the sky. He used to speak with infinite scorn of settling questions of righteousness by a show of hands. He had a perfect faith in the American people and the people of Massachusetts, but it was a faith in the American people and the people of Massachusetts, governed by reason and not by passion, acting under constitutional restraints, listening ever for the voice of duty, a people acting not on the first impulse, but on sober second thought. He was often in the minority, and once or twice in his life a bolter. He was never afraid of being in the minority. But he never was contented until he had changed or helped to change that minority into a majority. He was a politician almost from his cradle to his grave. He believed that the highest human occupation was to take a share in the leadership and direction of a self-governing people. He was a very tolerant, friendly and considerate man, in dealing with men who differed from himself. He would pardon sinners. He would pardon politicians with whose efforts there was, as he thought, even a mingling of ambition and self-seeking. But he had nothing but hatred and contempt for men who received all the benefits of the Republic, but shrank from any labor or sacrifice in its behalf. To his mind the one base creature in the Commonwealth was the man who said he was no politician. He thoroughly believed in Ralph Waldo Emerson's saying, which he borrowed from his brother Charles: "That is the one base thing in the universe, to receive benefits and render none." He had a clear business sense. He was the best adviser I knew of in Worcester, with but one possible exception, for clients who were in financial difficulties. He was a man of absolute integrity, of absolute veracity, and of a tender and boundless compassion. One of the most touching scenes I ever beheld was, when at his funeral, among the men of high station and of honor, there came forward a little group of Negroes and fugitive slaves who had been attracted to Worcester by its reputation as the home of freedom. They passed by the coffin with bowed heads and moistened eyes, every one of them probably knowing him as the friend and benefactor who had made life possible for them in this strange and unaccustomed community. He did not get carried off his feet by any sentimentalities.

He was the best of company. You could not talk with him or tackle him without a bright and entertaining answer. He was no great respecter of persons in such an encounter. I remember meeting him one day, when he said he had just been spending Sunday in Canton. "Indeed!" said I, "my great-grandfather used to live there, and is buried there." "Well, sir," he answered, "it may be a very respectable town for all that." A master of English fiction, who has won fame abroad, and who dwelt for some little time in this country, has given a most vivid and accurate description of Judge Thayer, his speech and his style and eloquence and sense in a novel lately published. One of the persons of the novel asks an English friend to the club, which he calls the State Club. He goes to the Club, and this is what happens:

"The State Club held its meeting in the parlor of the well-known Warrener House. There were some fifty members present, who received the Mayor with cheers, as he entered with his two friends. A good deal of smoke was made, and a good many speeches.

"Sir Hugh found interest in listening to some of the speakers, and in looking at some of the members. Montaigne pointed out all of the notables. One of the speakers[*] was a short man, with a corpulent body and a large open face; but he was a born orator of a certain type. Rounded and polished, mellow and musical, his sentences rolled from his mouth in liquid cadence and perfect balance. Sir Hugh put him down as his ideal after-dinner speaker. He made his points clearly, neatly, and with occasional vigor that was always surprising.

"'He reminds me of the Younger Pitt. Who is he?' asked Sir Hugh, with a touch of enthusiasm that was in striking contrast with his habitual and aristocratic insouciance.

"'Oh, that,' said Montaigne, with a smile, 'is Mr. William Shortley, commonly called Billy Shortlegs. He is very popular, well up in classics, and stands a good chance of being Governor some day. Shall I introduce you?'

"'Thank you, presently. Whom are they calling for now?' inquired Sir Hugh, as a chorus of voices cried out

[*] John D. Long.

'Amos Blackstone! Amos Blackstone! Amos, Amos, Amos!'

"Montaigne himself was chanting 'Blackstone! Blackstone!' with great gusto. When that gentleman rose, a perfect storm of cheers went up, during which Montaigne said: 'Now you will hear something, Sir Hugh. I shall want to know what you think of him.'

"Sir Hugh put up his eye-glass, not that his sight was defective but the occasion was important. Mr. Amos Blackstone had arrived at the dignified age of three score years. In some respects he curiously resembled the previous speaker, though considerably his senior. He stood perhaps five feet five inches in his boots. With the exception of his legs, he was a heavily built man, with a large head, an ample brow, a hairless face, very red, with large cheeks, and an under jaw like a lion. His eyes were small, but wonderfully bright and intelligent. He looked so portentously solemn, that when you learnt that he was perfectly well in mind, body and estate, the inclination to laugh was irresistible. This remarkable man began to speak in a husky, asthmatical voice, that gradually came out of the clouds and grew clear. His subject was, 'The Abstention of our Young Men from Politics: Causes and Cure.' He was evidently a master of his subject, and spoke without notes. He was absolutely without any pretence to oratory; and yet for thirty minutes he played upon his audience as it were a pipe, and plucked out the heart of its mystery. He was by turn, serious, merry, doleful, witty, pathetic, humorous, ironical and gravely philosophic. When he was gay in speech, his face was funereal, and during the utterances of his grave reflections, his face was lighted up with a winning smile. There were moments when one might have heard a pin drop; when one could not have heard his name, if shouted, for laughter; when one's eyes gathered a sudden mist.

"Sir Hugh did not once remove his eye-glass; he would have put up half a dozen glasses had he had them.

"'Well,' enquired Montaigne, as the after-cheering subsided. 'A grave, melancholy intellect, with a sprightly temperament; a wonderful man. Who is he?' asked Sir Hugh, dropping his glass.

"'His name, as you know, is Amos Blackstone; he lives some miles away; but he is a household name.'

"'Is he in business?'

"'Yes, a lawyer; a patent lawyer. Have you ever heard of an institution called the Political Boss?'

"'Oh, yes. At home we use him to a degree, as a sort of political Black Bogey, to scare naughty children who like to play at Radicalism.'

"'Well, Amos Blackstone is a specimen of the Political Boss.'

"'Indeed? You surprise me,' gasped Sir Hugh. 'Don't mistake me; they are not all like him. He is a lion among jackals; the best political organizer in the State. But he is getting crowded out by younger men. We soon turn our war-horses out to pasture, in this country,' explained Montaigne."

No man among his contemporaries in Massachusetts had a larger number of devoted friends than Adin Thayer. Many people who were not counted among his acquaintances were attached to him by sympathy of political opinions and by gratitude for his important service to the Commonwealth. He did a thousand things for the benefit of the city, for the benefit of the State. Many bad men found that somehow their ambitions were nipped in the bud by a process they could hardly understand, and many good men were called into the public service in obedience to a summons from a hand the influence of which they never discovered. But there were four things he largely helped to do which were important and conspicuous in our history; I will not say things that he did, but they were things which would not have been done, in my judgment, if the power and influence of Adin Thayer had been subtracted; things accomplished with difficulty and with doubt. He stood by Charles Sumner when that great and dangerous attempt was made to banish him from public life in the year 1862. It was a time when Charles Sumner, as he told me himself, could not visit the college where he was graduated and be sure of a respectful reception, when a very important Republican paper, the most important and influential Republican paper in Massachusetts, declared that Charles Sumner could not address a popular audience in New York with personal safety; when, under the lead of the United States District Attorney, one of the most successful managers of a political meeting who ever existed in Massachusetts, an attempt was made to defeat a resolution of confidence in him, in the Republican State Convention (when the whole of the House of Representatives, or of the Caucus, or of the Convention, was on one side and Richard H. Dana was on the other, it was about an even chance which came out ahead), Thayer stood by Mr. Sumner in that memorable State Convention, and helped save his great career to the country and to liberty.

He was a devoted supporter of John A. Andrew. Andrew had been Governor the traditional three years, and there were men eager to supplant him. When Adin heard of a formidable meeting called for that purpose, he exclaimed—I remember very well the indignation with which he said it—"They shall not lay their hands on the Lord's Anointed." He sent a message to the meeting that he would fight their candidate in every school district in Massachusetts. The scheme was abandoned.

He was largely responsible for the defeat of the scheme for substituting biennial for annual elections, and biennial sessions of the Legislature for yearly sessions in Massachusetts, although it did not receive its deathblow at the hands of the people until after his death.

But his chief service, after all, was in keeping the government of Massachusetts clean and incorruptible, at the time of the great raid which was made upon the Republican Party in the years between 1871 and 1883. And yet, in all these services and contests he never appealed to a base passion or to a low ambition in any man. He summoned the nobility in men, and it answered to his call. He loved with the whole intensity of his nature, his country, his Commonwealth, and the city which was his home. He loved the great cause of human freedom and equality with the passionate devotion which a lover feels for his mistress. He was the most disinterested man I ever knew in public life. He was not devoid of ambition. He believed that the holding of public office was the best method of accomplishing public results. But, as I have already said, when the time came, he always subordinated his own desire to what he deemed the welfare of the public.

He had, I think, one favorite poem. He was fond of all good literature, especially the Bible, and was never without its resources to illustrate or make emphatic what he had to say. But there was one poem which was written to describe his and my intimate friend, George L. Stearns, which I think was his favorite above all the literature with which he was acquainted. I have often heard him quote its verses. They set forth the character and quality and life of Adin Thayer himself. If Thayer had died before Stearns, I believe Whittier would have written the same thing about him. They are familiar to my readers, I am sure, but I will close this brief and imperfect tribute by citing them once more:

>   He has done the work of a true man,—
>   Crown him, honor him, love him.
>   Weep over him, tears of women,
>   Stoop, manliest brows, above him!

>   . . . . . .

>   For the warmest of hearts is frozen,
>   The freest of hands is still;
>   And the gap in our picked and chosen
>   The long years may not fill.

>   No duty could overtask him,
>   No need his will outrun;
>   Or ever our lips could ask him,
>   His hands the work had done.

>   He forgot his own soul for others,
>   Himself to his neighbor lending;
>   He found the Lord in his suffering brothers,
>   And not in the clouds descending.

>   . . . . . .

Ah, well!—The world is discreet;
  There are plenty to pause and wait;
But here was a man who set his feet
  Sometimes in advance of fate,—

Plucked off the old bark when the inner
  Was slow to renew it,
And put to the Lord's work the sinner
  When saints failed to do it.

Never rode to the wrong's redressing
  A worthier paladin.
Shall we not hear the blessing,
  "Good and faithful, enter in!"

CHAPTER XXI

POLITICAL CORRUPTION

JOHN JAY said that the greatest achievements of diplomacy were often little noted by history and that their authors got, in general, little credit. He compared it to the work of levelling uneven ground of which the face of the earth will show no trace when it is done. The same thing is true of successful battles with political corruption in high places, the most formidable peril to any Government and, if it be not encountered and overcome, fatal to a Republic. A nation will survive a corrupt minister or monarch, but a corrupt people must surely and speedily perish. We have had sporadic examples of corruption in high office at several periods in our history. The first sixteen years after the inauguration of the Constitution, including the Administrations of Washington, John Adams, and the first four years of Jefferson, were by no means free from it. But it never got so dangerous a hold upon the forces of the Government, or upon a great political party, as in the Administration of General Grant.

General Grant was an honest and wise man. History has assigned him a place among our great Presidents. He showed almost unerring judgment in military matters. He rarely, I suppose, if ever, made a mistake in his estimate of the military quality of a subordinate, or in a subordinate's title to confidence. But he was very easily imposed upon by self-seeking and ambitious men in civil life. Such men studied his humors and imposed upon him, if not by flattery, yet by the pretence of personal devotion. He had been himself bitterly and most unjustly assailed by partisan and sectional hostility. When any person to whom he had once given his confidence was detected in any low or corrupt action Grant was very unwilling to believe or even to listen to the charge. He seemed to set his teeth and to say to himself: "They attack this man as they attack me. They attack him because he is my friend. I will stand by him." So it happened that attempts to secure pure and unselfish administration got little help from him, and that designing and crafty men whose political aims were wholly personal and selfish got his ear and largely influenced his appointments to office.

Hamilton Fish, the Secretary of State, always retained his influence with President Grant. He was a wise, able and thoroughly honest man. But as was fit, and indeed necessary, he kept himself to the great interests which belonged to his Department, and took little share, so far as the public knew, in other questions.

General Cox, of Ohio, was an able, brave and upright man. He resigned from President Grant's Cabinet, alleging as his reason that he was not supported in his fight with corruption. Judge Hoar strenuously insisted that the Judges of the newly created Circuit Courts of the United States should be made up of the best lawyers, without Senatorial dictation. President Grant acted in accordance with his advice. The constitution of the Circuit Courts gave great satisfaction to the public. But leading and influential Senators, whose advice had been rejected, and who were compelled by the high character of the persons nominated to submit, and did not venture upon a controversy with the President, were intensely angry with the Attorney-General The result was that when he was nominated by the President for the office of Associate Justice of the Supreme Court of the United States, he was rejected by the Senate. A few Senators avowed as a pretext for their action that there was no Judge on that Bench from the South, and that the new appointee ought to reside in the Southern Circuit. But these gentlemen all voted for the confirmation of Mr. Justice Bradley, a most admirable appointment, to whom the same objection applied. Judge Hoar never doubted that the service of a clean, able, upright Circuit Court, appointed without political influence, and entirely acceptable to the public, was well worth the sacrifice. Indeed the expression of public regard which came to him abundantly in his lifetime, and which was manifested in the proceedings of the Bar of Massachusetts, and the Massachusetts Historical Society, and in the press of the country after his death, was more valued by those to whom his memory is dear, than a thousand offices.

When I entered Congress in 1869 the corridors of the Capitol and the Committee rooms were crowded with lobbyists. The custom of the two Houses permitted their members to introduce strangers on the floor. It would not be profitable to revive all the scandals of that time. In general the men elected to the Senate and the House were honest and incorruptible. There were some exceptions. Adroit and self-seeking men were often able in the multitude of claims which must necessarily be disposed of by a rapid examination, to impose on Committees of the two Houses.

As one of the managers of the Belknap trial, I alluded to some of the more prominent and undisputed examples of corruption, in the following words:

"I said a little while ago that the Constitution had no safeguards to throw away. You will judge whether the public events of to-day admonish us to look well to all our securities to prevent or power to punish the great guilt of corruption in office. We must not confound idle clamor with public opinion, or accept the accusations of scandal and malice instead of proof. But we shall make a worse mistake if, because of the multitude of false and groundless charges against men in high office, we fail to redress substantial grievances or to deal with cases of actual guilt. The worst evil resulting from the indiscriminate attack of an unscrupulous press upon men in public station is not that innocence suffers, but that crime escapes. Let scandal and malice be encountered by pure and stainless lives. Let corruption and bribery meet their lawful punishment.

"My own public life has been a very brief and insignificant one, extending little beyond the duration of a single term of Senatorial office; but in that brief period I have seen five judges of a high court of the United States driven from office by threats of impeachment for corruption or maladministration. I have heard the taunt, from friendliest lips, that when the United States presented herself in the East to take part with the civilized world in generous competition in the arts of life, the only product of her institutions in which she surpassed all others beyond question was her corruption. I have seen in the State in the Union foremost in power and wealth four judges of her courts impeached for corruption, and the political administration of her chief city become a disgrace and a by-word throughout the world. I have seen the chairman of the Committee on Military Affairs in the House, now a distinguished member of this court, rise in his place and demand the expulsion of four of his associates for making sale of their official privilege of selecting the youths to be educated at our great military school. When the greatest railroad of the world, binding together the continent and uniting the two great seas which wash our shores, was finished, I have seen our national triumph and exultation turned to bitterness and shame by the unanimous reports of three committees of Congress—two of the House and one here—that every step of that mighty enterprise had been taken in fraud. I have heard in highest places the shameless doctrine avowed by men grown old in public office that the true way by which power should be gained in the Republic is to bribe the people with the offices created for their service, and the true end for which it should be used when gained is the promotion of selfish ambition and the gratification of personal revenge. I have heard that suspicion haunts the footsteps of the trusted companions of the President.

"These things have passed into history. The Hallam or the Tacitus or the Sismondi or the Macaulay who writes the annals of our time will record them with his inexorable pen. And now when a high Cabinet officer, the Constitutional adviser of the Executive, flees from office before charges of corruption, shall the historian add that the Senate treated the demand of the people for its judgment of condemnation as a farce, and laid down its high functions before the sophistries and jeers of the criminal lawyer? Shall he speculate about the petty political calculations as to the effect on one party or the other which induced his judges to connive at the escape of the great public criminal? Or, on the other hand, shall he close the chapter by narrating how these things were detected, reformed and punished by Constitutional processes which the wisdom of our fathers devised for us, and the virtue and purity of the people found their vindication in the justice of the Senate?"

This passage was quoted very extensively by the Democratic speakers all over the country, and was circulated as a campaign document. I was reproached by some of my Republican associates for furnishing ammunition for the enemy. But I was satisfied, and I am now, that in saying what I did I rendered a great service to the Republican Party. What was said helped to arouse public attention, and the masses of the people—always pure and incorruptible—set themselves earnestly and successfully to reform the abuses.

It never occurred to me that these abuses furnished any reason for placing the powers of the Government in the hands of the Southern Democracy, or their ally, Tammany Hall. If the men who saved the Union were not to be trusted to keep it pure; if the men who abolished slavery could not carry on a Government in freedom and in honor, certainly it was not likely that the men of Tammany Hall, or the men who had so lately attempted to overthrow the Government, would do it any better.

I happened to be at lunch with General Garfield just after the Belknap trial. He spoke of my argument, and expressed his strong sympathy and approval. I told him that I had been looking into the history of the first sixteen years of the Government, which included the Administrations of Washington and John Adams and the first term of Jefferson, and that in my opinion there was not only more corruption in proportion then than there had been under Grant, but there had been more in amount, notwithstanding the difference in population. I stated to him a good many instances. He urged me to make a speech in which I should say publicly what I had said to him. I acted on his advice, and in the course of a speech, in reply to Mr. Lamar, of Mississippi, I spoke as follows:

"The Republican Party, as I have said, has controlled the Government for sixteen years, a term equal to that which covers the whole Administration of Washington, the whole Administration of John Adams, and the first term of Jefferson. It has been one of those periods in which all experience teaches us to expect an unusual manifestation of public corruption, of public disorder, and of evils and errors of administration. A great war; the time which follows a great war; great public debts; currency and values inflated; the exertion of new and extraordinary powers for the safety of the State; the sudden call of millions of slaves to a share in the Government—any one of these things would be expected to create great disturbance, and give rise to great temptations and great corruptions. Our term of office has seen them all combined. And yet I do not scruple to affirm that not only has there been less dishonesty and maladministration in the sixteen years of Republican rule proportionally to the numbers and wealth of the people than in the first sixteen years after the inauguration of Washington, but there has been less absolutely of those things.

"Now, Mr. Speaker, I do not wish to be misunderstood. I do not wish to be misrepresented in this matter. Let no man assert that I refer to the evils of those days as either excuse or palliation for the evils of ours. That generation was a frugal and honest generation in the main, and they would have visited with the swiftest condemnation and punishment, every breach of public trust, whether through dishonesty or usurpation. But they did not send to England for Benedict Arnold. They did not restore the Tories to power. They did not go down on their knees to George III. and ask him to take them back into favor. They believed that if the Constitution could not be administered honestly by a majority of the friends of the Constitution, it could not be administered honestly by a majority of its enemies; that if liberty were not safe and pure in the hands of those who loved her, then liberty was a failure upon the earth, and they did not think of intrusting her to the hands of those who hated her. So in this generation, had they lived to-day, they would have done simply what a distinguished president of the convention in my own State, whom the gentleman quotes, recommended; they would have taken the Government from the hands of the lovers of liberty who are dishonest and put it into the hands of men who entertain the same sentiments but who are honest. It never would have occurred to them that because among one hundred thousand men there are found some few who will not keep the eighth commandment, 'Thou shalt not steal,' which is a mandate for all the public service, they should put in power men who have no regard for the sixth, 'Thou shalt not kill.' "

There were several conspicuous instances of corruption with which I had personally to deal.

1. One was the Credit Mobilier.

Two Committees were appointed to investigate the affairs of the Union Pacific Railroad Company, and the Credit Mobilier of America. One Committee investigated the conduct of some members of the two Houses of Congress against whom charges had been made. Of that Committee Judge Poland of Vermont was the Chairman. The other Committee investigated the history of the Union Pacific Railroad Company to report whether its charter had been forfeited. Of that Committee Jeremiah M. Wilson of Indiana, a very able lawyer and accomplished gentleman, was Chairman. The next member to him on the Committee was Judge Shellabarger of Ohio. Owing to reasons, stated later, it fell to me as the next in rank to conduct the greater part of the examination, and to make the report.

2. Another was the impeachment and trial of General William W. Belknap, Secretary of War, for receiving a bribe for the appointment of a Post Trader.

3. A third example of the prevalent laxity of morals that occurred was the case of the Sanborn contracts. I was a

member of the House when they were investigated, but took no special part in the proceedings.

4. A fourth example was the claim of Senators and Representatives which had been asserted in Andrew Johnson's Administration, and to which General Grant had partly yielded, to dictate the appointment of executive officers. In that way a vast army of public servants, amounting to more than one hundred thousand in number, who were appointed and removed at the pleasure of the Executive, became first the instrument of keeping the dominant party in power, and afterward became not so much the instruments and servants of party as the political followers of ambitious men to whom they owed their office, and on whose pleasure they depended for maintaining them. I made, in a speech at West Newton in 1876, an earnest attack on this system, and afterward in the Senate had a good deal to do with framing the Civil Service Law, as it was called, which put an end to it.

5. Perhaps the most dangerous attack upon the purity of the Government was the attempt of General Butler to get possession of the political power in Massachusetts, and ultimately that of the country. What I was able to do to resist and baffle that attempt is the most considerable part of the public service of my life, if it has been of any public service.

I shall speak of each of these a little more fully.

The responsibility for three of these, I regret to say, rested upon Massachusetts men, members of the Republican Party. The Union Pacific Railroad Company and the Credit Mobilier were made up largely of prominent Massachusetts men for whom General Butler acted as counsel. When Mr. Ames was on trial before the House of Representatives General Butler, then a member of the House, appeared as a member and took part and made the extraordinary statement to the House that he was there as counsel for Mr. Ames.

Sanborn, who made the contracts, was a Massachusetts man. His profits were used largely in affecting elections in Massachusetts. The Treasury officials who were in fault, whether through carelessness or corruption, were Massachusetts men, and the arch contriver of the scheme was a Massachusetts man.

Yet the lesson which these things have taught me is that the American statesman who believes that the doctrines of his party are sound should never abandon his principles or quit political life because of its corruption. Let him never for any political advantage support or tolerate a corrupt man, or vote for a corrupt candidate. If a man whose principles are good will yield to an evil motive, it is not likely that the man whose principles are bad will resist it. The American people are upright and honest. They will vindicate and stand by any man in the contest for honesty and uprightness, be he Democrat or Republican, so long as they believe that the ends for which he is striving are for the public good. They will not sustain a man whose counsel they think bad, however honest he may be in his own conduct, or however much he may desire to secure honesty in the conduct of others. No man ever yet accomplished much good by abandoning his party while he continued to hold its principles. Many men have accomplished a great deal of good by striving to purify it.

Every account of political history from the inside will exhibit abundant evidence of wickedness, wrongdoing, and petty personal motives, of low ambitions, of bargains and sales, of timidity, of treachery. The reverse of the most costly tapestry looks mean and cheap. It is said that no man is a hero to his valet. The reason is not that the hero is mean or base, but that the valet cannot see anything that is great and noble, but only what is mean and base. The history of no people is heroical to its Mugwumps. But, thank God, what is petty and personal is also temporary and perishable. The voice of all history, especially the voice of the history of our Republic, speaks to us the lesson which our great philosopher taught and so implicitly believed,

> Saying, What is excellent,
> As God lives, is permanent.

CHAPTER XXII

CREDIT MOBILIER

DURING the election of 1872 many rumors appeared in the press of the country that there had been great corruption in the management of the affairs of the Union Pacific Railroad. It was charged that members of the House and Senate, some of whom were named, had been bribed by gifts of stock in the Credit Mobilier to secure their influence in legislation affecting the Union Pacific Railroad.

The Credit Mobilier Co. had been formed to take the contract for building the Union Pacific Railroad. The stockholders of the two companies were identical. Each stockholder of the Credit Mobilier owned a number of shares of the Union Pacific Railroad proportionate to his holding in the former company.

The Union Pacific Railroad Company and Central Pacific Railroad Company received liberal land grants from the Government of the United States, that they might each build a part of a line which should connect the Atlantic States with the Pacific Ocean. In addition to the land grants, each road was to receive a loan of Government bonds, payable in thirty years, of $27,000,000, for which the Government was to pay interest, which interest was not required to be repaid by the roads. The roads were also authorized to give a mortgage on their properties for a like amount, of $27,000,000 each, which mortgage was to be prior to the Government's lien for its loan. The charter of the Union Pacific Railroad was granted by the Government of the United States. That of the Central Pacific was from the State of California. The Government undertook to remove all Indian titles from the public land granted to the Union Pacific Railroad for a space of 200 feet in width on each side of its entire route, and conferred the right to appropriate by eminent domain necessary private land for depots, turnouts, etc., and public lands to the amount of ten alternate sections per mile, within the limits of twenty miles on each side of the road. It was required by the charter of the Union Pacific Railroad that its stock should be paid in full in cash, and that the interests of the Government should be specially protected by the appointment by the President of five Government Directors. The Government bonds were to be handed over on the certificate of an officer appointed by the President, as the road advanced to completion. It was required that a Government Director should be a member of every Committee, standing or select.

The managers of the Union Pacific Railroad acquired the franchise of a Pennsylvania Company, known as the Credit Mobilier, divided its stock among themselves in proportion to their ownership in the Union Pacific Railroad, mortgaged the road to the extent permitted by the act of Congress, being a little more than $27,000,000, and mortgaged their land grants for a further sum of $10,000,000. Then they made a contract with the Credit Mobilier Company to construct the road at a price which would exhaust all the resources of the road, including the proceeds of the bonds of all kinds, and divided the proceeds among themselves as dividends on the stock of the Credit Mobilier. This left the Union Pacific Railroad to begin business mortgaged to its full value, without any resources for its operation, and utterly stripped of the ample endowment which the bounty of the Government had provided for it.

Congress supposed when this munificent grant of land and loan of credit was made it would create a great public highway across the continent for the use of the Government and the people, in war and peace, which should be a strong, solvent corporation, ready for every emergency, and as secure for the public use as New York Harbor, or as the Pacific Ocean.

The devisers of this scheme soon got to quarrelling among themselves. One faction was made up largely of Boston capitalists, and the other of men belonging in New York, New Jersey and Connecticut. The former wanted to have the headquarters of the corporation in Boston, with a Boston man for President; and the latter desired to have its management in New York. A suit in equity was brought, and the Boston men, headed by Oakes Ames, a member of Congress, and his brother Oliver, both eminent and highly respected business men of Massachusetts, were enjoined from voting at a stockholders' meeting held in New York, for the election of officers. The injunction was issued by Judge Barnard, who was afterward impeached, and removed from office. On the day of the stockholders' meeting General Butler, counsel for the Ames faction, found Judge Barnard at lunch, and got him so to modify the injunction as to permit that the votes might be cast, the result of the election not to be declared until the further order of the Court. The other faction who had rested with fancied security under their injunction were taken by surprise.

The Ames ticket had a majority. Thereupon one of the other faction wrote a letter to Elihu B. Washburne, at Washington. He was an influential member of the House of Representatives, known as the "Watch Dog of the Treasury." The letter was put in the post-office. It exposed the whole transaction. He then informed his opponents what he had done. They knew very well that if Washburne moved an investigation by the House of Representatives, which was likely, the game was up. No further bonds would come from the United States Treasury. Judicial proceedings would in all likelihood be taken at once to annul the charter, or restrain further action under it. They instantly came to terms. The two factions agreed on a Board of Directors. The letter to Washburne was withdrawn from the mail. Oakes Ames received a quantity of the stock of the Credit Mobilier, which he was to distribute among influential members of Congress at par, "putting it," according to his testimony given before a Committee afterward, "where it would do the most good." A list of members of the two Houses was agreed upon, to whom the stock should be offered. It was expected that they would pay for it at par. But there had been already a large dividend assigned to it, which with the dividend expected to be paid shortly, would amount to much more than the nominal par value of the stock. So the purchase of one of the shares was like purchasing for $1,000 a bank account which already amounted to, or shortly would amount to, more than double that sum.

A list of the men who were to be induced to take this stock was made out with wonderful and prophetic sagacity. It contained some of the ablest and most influential men in the two Houses of Congress, representing different parts of the country. It included men as conspicuous for integrity as for ability. Each of them occupied already a great place in the respect of his countrymen, and nearly every one of them attained a much greater place afterward. This is the list of the members of Congress to whom stock was to be conveyed:

List of Members of Congress to Whom Stock Was to be Sold Agreed Upon in New York, Entered in Oakes Ames's Memorandum Book, and Taken by Him to Washington.

James G. Blaine of Maine.
Senator James W. Patterson of New Hampshire.
Senator Henry Wilson of Massachusetts.
Schuyler Colfax of Indiana.
Thomas D. Eliot of Massachusetts.
Henry L. Dawes of Massachusetts.
George S. Boutwell of Massachusetts.
James A. Garfield of Ohio.
Glenni W. Schofield of Pennsylvania.
William D. Kelley of Pennsylvania.
Joseph F. Fowler of Tennessee.
John A. Bingham of Ohio.
Senator James A. Bayard of Delaware.
William B. Allison of Iowa.
James F. Wilson of Iowa.
Roscoe Conkling of New York.
James Brooks of New York.
John A. Logan of Illinois.

When Mr. Ames got to Washington he added the names of several Senators to his list, some of whom took the stock.

It will be seen by an examination that men of great ability and influence were very skilfully selected. Two of them afterward became Vice-Presidents of the United States. One of them became President of the United States. Another became Secretary of the Treasury. Two others became Speakers of the House. Five others were very prominent candidates for the Presidency. Another was Chairman of the Judiciary Committee of the House. Another became Chairman of the Committee on Appropriations. Another became Chairman of the Committee on Appropriations and subsequently of Ways and Means. Nine of these gentlemen, then members of the House, were afterward elected to the Senate.

Mr. Blaine, Mr. Eliot, Mr. Bayard, Mr. Conkling and Mr. Boutwell refused absolutely to have anything to do with the transaction. All the others were fully acquitted on investigation, by the judgment of the House, of any corrupt purpose or any desire to make money or get private advantage by reason of their official influence, or of any expectation that they would be likely to be called upon to take or refuse any action by reason of their relation to these corporations. It was thought that they had been careless in that they had not been put on their guard by the fact that so large a dividend was to be paid on the stock. In all cases the amounts received were very small, in general not amounting to more than $1,000. In two or three instances the people thought there was want of candor or frankness in telling the full transaction to the public, when the newspaper charges first made their appearance.

Henry Wilson never had any of the stock. But some of his friends made a present of a small sum of money to Mrs. Wilson, and the persons having the matter in charge invested a portion of it in Credit Mobilier stock. As soon as Wilson heard of it, he directed that the stock be reconveyed to the person from whom it had been received, and gave his wife a small sum of money to make up the difference of what turned out to be the value of the stock and the value of the investment which had been made in its place. There was no lack of the most scrupulous integrity in the transaction. Wilson met at a great public meeting Gen. Hawley, who was one of the speakers. Hawley told Wilson on the platform just before his speech that he understood that his name had been mentioned in the papers as the owner of Credit Mobilier stock. Wilson answered that he never had any of it. Thereupon Hawley in his speech alluded to that matter and said he was authorized by Mr. Wilson to say that he never owned any of the stock. Mr. Wilson did not get up and say, No, I never owned any. But my wife once had a present of a little money which was invested in it, and as soon as I heard of it, I immediately had it returned to the person from whom it came, and I made up the loss to my wife myself. Such, however, was the public excitement that his omission to do that was held in some quarters as culpable want of frankness.

All the persons who received any of the stock and told the story frankly at the investigation were acquitted of any wrongdoing whatever, and never in the least suffered in esteem in consequence.

But Schuyler Colfax and Senator Patterson of New Hampshire were found by the Committee, and believed by the people to have been disingenuous in their account of the transaction. The Senate Committee of investigation reported a resolution for the expulsion of Senator Patterson. The case was a very hard one indeed for him. The Senate adjourned, and his term expired without any action on the resolution, or any opportunity to defend himself.

Schuyler Colfax was also held to have given an untruthful story of the transaction. But the public attention was turned from that by the discovery, in the investigation of his accounts which the Committee made, that he had received large sums of money from a person for whom he had obtained a lucrative Government contract. But his term of office as Vice-President expired before any action could be taken, and he died soon after.

Mr. Ames, whose character as a shrewd and skilful investor and manager of property stood deservedly high, recommended to his friends the stock of the Credit Mobilier as a safe investment, and one in his judgment very sure to prove profitable.

It has been often asked how the managers of the Credit Mobilier could be guilty of bribing men when nobody was guilty of being bribed. But the answer is easy. The managers of the Credit Mobilier knew that they had violated the law, and that an investigation would ruin their whole concern. The men who received the stock were in ignorance of this fact. It was as if the managers of a railroad whose route under State laws is to be determined by a city council, or a board of selectmen or some other public body, should induce the members of such board to take stock in their enterprise, intending afterward to petition the body to which the subscribers belonged to adopt a route very near land owned by them, which would much increase its value, the receivers of the stock being ignorant of their scheme. The person who should do that would be justly chargeable with bribery, while the persons who received the stock would be held totally innocent. That was the judgment of the House of Representatives which acquitted the members who had received the stock, but held Ames, who had conducted the transaction, censurable. A large number of the members voted for his expulsion. Ames was a successful business man. He was regarded by his neighbors as a man of integrity. He was generous and public spirited. But he and his associates in the Union Pacific Railroad seemed, in this matter, to be utterly destitute of any sense of public duty or comprehension of the great purposes of Congress. They seemed to treat it as a purely private transaction, out of which they might get all the money they could, without any obligation to carry out the act according to its spirit, or even according to its letter, if they could only do so without being detected. They seemed to have thought that they were the sole owners of the Union Pacific Railroad and of the Credit Mobilier corporation, and that the transaction between the two concerned themselves only and not the public. They treated it as if they were transferring money from one pocket to another.

When Congress met in December, Mr. Blaine, the Speaker, who had been one of the persons implicated by public rumor, although in fact he had refused absolutely to have anything to do with the transaction, left the Chair, and, calling Mr. Cox of New York to his place, introduced a resolution providing for an investigation of the affairs of the Union Pacific Railroad.

Two Committees were appointed. One, of which Judge Poland was Chairman, undertook to deal with the charges against the members of the House of Representatives. The other, of which Jeremiah M. Wilson of Indiana was Chairman, was directed to inquire into the entire management of the affairs of the Union Pacific Railroad and the Credit Mobilier. I was a member of this last Committee. A Committee was appointed also in the Senate, with direction to inquire into the charges so far as they affected Senators. The whole country was profoundly excited by the affair.

I stood third on the Committee on which I was a member. It was thought best that Mr. Wilson, the Chairman, who was a very able and distinguished lawyer, should go to Boston where the books of the Companies were kept, and make a searching examination of their books and accounts. Mr. Shellabarger of Ohio, the second member on the Committee, one of the ablest lawyers in the House, was in poor health. He consented to serve only on the condition that he should not be compelled to do any duty requiring any considerable labor. So I had to a large degree the charge of the investigation in Washington, where the witnesses were examined, and in the end the duty of preparing the report.

We did not deal in our report with the alleged misconduct of the individual members of the House, but solely with the two corporations. The report sets forth the transaction at length, and contains the following summary of the Committee's conclusions:

The purpose of the whole act was expressly declared to be "to promote the public interest and welfare by the construction of said railroad and telegraph line, and keeping the same in working order, and to secure the Government at all times, but particularly in time of war, the use and benefit of the same for postal, military, and other purposes.''

Your committee cannot doubt that it was the purpose of Congress in all this to provide for something more than a mere gift of so much land, and a loan of so many bonds on the one side, and the construction and equipment of so many miles of railroad and telegraph on the other.

The United States was not a mere creditor, loaning a sum of money upon a mortgage. The railroad corporation was not a mere contractor, bound to furnish a specified structure and nothing more. The law created a body politic and corporate, bound, as a trustee, so to manage this great public franchise and endowment that not only the security for the great debts due the United States should not be impaired, but so that there should be ample resources to perform its great public duties in time of commercial disaster and in time of war.

This act was not passed to further the personal interests of the corporators, nor for the advancement of commercial interests, nor for the convenience of the general public, alone; but in addition to these the interests, present and future, of the Government, as such, were to be subserved. A great highway was to be created, the use of which for postal, military, and other purposes was to be secured to the Government "at all times," but particularly in time of war. Your committee deem it important to call especial attention to this declared object of this act, to accomplish which object the munificent grant of lands and loan of the Government credit was made. To make such a highway, and to have it ready at "all times," and "particularly in time of war," to meet the demands that might be made upon it; to be able to withstand the loss of business and other casualties incident to war and still to perform for the Government such reasonable service as might under such circumstances be demanded, required a strong, solvent corporation; and when Congress expressed the object and granted the corporate powers to carry that object into execution, and aided the enterprise with subsidies of lands and bonds, the corporators in whom these powers were vested and under whose control these subsidies were placed, were, in the opinion of your committee, under the highest moral, to say nothing of legal or equitable obligations, to use the utmost degree of good faith toward the Government in the exercise of the powers and disposition of the subsidies.

Congress relied for the performance of these great trusts by the corporators upon their sense of public duty; upon the fact that they were to deal with and protect a large capital of their own which they were to pay in money; upon the presence of five directors appointed by the President especially to represent the public interests, who were to own no stock; one of whom should be a member of every Committee, standing or special; upon the commissioners to be appointed by the President, who should examine and report upon the work as it progressed; in certain cases upon the certificate of the chief engineer, to be made upon his professional honor; and lastly, upon the reserved power to add to, alter, amend, or repeal the act.

Your committee find themselves constrained to report that the moneys borrowed by the corporation, under a power given them, only to meet the necessities of the construction and endowment of the road, have been distributed in dividends among the corporators; that the stock was issued, not to men who paid for it at par in money, but who paid for it at not more than thirty cents on the dollar in road making; that of the Government directors some of them have neglected their duties and others have been interested in the transactions by which the provisions of the organic law have been evaded; that at least one of the commissioners appointed by the President has been directly bribed to betray his trust by the gift of $25,000; that the chief engineer of the road was largely interested in the contracts for its construction; and that there has been an attempt to prevent the exercise of the reserved power in Congress by inducing influential members of Congress to become interested in the profits of the transaction. So that of the safeguards above enumerated none seems to have been left but the sense of public duty of the corporators.

The Judge Poland Committee investigated the conduct of the members who were suspected and acquitted all but two. The House accepted their decision. They recommended the expulsion of Mr. Ames and of James Brooks, one of the Democratic members. There were some special circumstances in the case of Brooks, which it is not necessary to recite. Brooks died before a vote on his case was taken. The House by a majority amended the resolution reported by the Committee in the case of Mr. Ames, and recommended a vote of censure, which was passed. Ames felt the disgrace very keenly, and did not live very long afterward.

These disclosures did much to bring about the uneasy condition of the public mind which led to the Republican defeat in the election of members of the House of Representatives in the fall of 1874, and brought Tilden so near to an election in 1876.

But it may fairly, I think, be said for the majority of the Republican Party in both houses of Congress, and the majority of the Republican Party in the country, that they did their very best to deal firmly and directly with any fraud or wrongdoing that came to light, even if their own political associates were the guilty parties. The political atmosphere has been purified as compared with the condition of those days. The lobbyist is not seen in the Committee Room or the Corridor of the Capitol, as was the case when I entered Congress in 1869. I ought perhaps to say that I think the acquittal of Belknap on the ground that the Senate has no jurisdiction to render judgment against a civil officer on process of impeachment after he has left office, was influenced by political feeling. I do not think most of the Republican Senators who voted that way would have so voted if the culprit had been a Democrat. But there were many able lawyers who thought the opinion of these Senators right.

CHAPTER XXIII

THE SANBORN CONTRACTS

THE forty-second Congress, at its second session, repealed all laws which provided for the payment of moieties, or commissions, to informers, so far as related to internal revenue taxes. But a provision was inserted by the Conference Committee, which attracted no attention, providing that the Secretary of the Treasury might employ not more than three persons to assist the proper officers of the Government in discovering and collecting any money belonging to the United States whenever the same might be for the interest of the United States. The Secretary was to determine the conditions of the contract, and to pay no compensation except out of money recovered. No person was to be employed who did not file a written statement, under oath, stating the character of the claim under which the money was withheld or due, and the name of the person alleged to withhold the same.

Under this law John D. Sanborn of Massachusetts, an active supporter of General Butler, applied for a contract which he obtained on the 15th of July, 1872, for the collection of taxes illegally withheld by thirty-nine distillers, rectifiers and purchasers of whiskey. He was then himself an employee of the Government as Special Agent for the Treasury Department. Secretary Boutwell being then absent or otherwise unable to attend to his duties, this contract was signed by Assistant Secretary William A. Richardson. Sanborn had already been employed to work up certain whiskey cases for which he had been paid $3,000 by the Government, and these cases were included in the foregoing contract.

On the 25th of October, 1872, Sanborn made application to have added to his contract the names of 760 persons, alleged to have withheld taxes imposed on legacies, successions and incomes. An additional contract for that purpose was signed by the Assistant Secretary Richardson. On the 19th of March, 1873, Sanborn applied to have the names of more than 2,000 other like persons added to his contract, which Mr. Richardson permitted. On the 1st day of July, 1873, Sanborn again asked to amend his contract, and Assistant Secretary Richardson signed the contract by which the names of 592 railroad companies were included. That was substantially a complete list of the railroad companies of the country. Some of them had been examined by Government officials before the day of the contract, and the claims had been brought to light and found due. Sanborn had no knowledge of any delinquency, except as to about 150 of them. When he so represented to the officers of the Treasury Department he was told that it did not make any difference, and to put them all in. Thereupon he took oath that they were all delinquent, and had them added to the contract.

The form of this contract was taken, in part, from one prepared by Secretary Boutwell, which he had carefully considered with Mr. Kelsey, a subordinate in the Treasury, in June, 1872. That prepared by Mr. Boutwell, if adhered to, would have amply protected the Government. But it was departed from in essential particulars. Under Secretary Boutwell's contract only a small number of claims was included. Sanborn collected, in the course of a year or two, $427,000, on which sum he received 50 per cent.

The unanimous report of the Committee of the House who investigated the matter was written by Charles Foster of Ohio, afterward Governor, and Secretary of the Treasury. The Committee comprised the following gentlemen: Henry L. Dawes of Massachusetts; W. D. Kelly of Pennsylvania; Horatio C. Burchard of Illinois; Ellis H. Roberts of New York; John A. Kasson of Iowa; Henry Waldron of Michigan; Lionel A. Sheldon of Louisiana; Charles Foster of Ohio; James B. Beck of Kentucky; William E. Niblack of Indiana; Fernando Wood of New York.

The Committee found that a large percentage of the $427,000 was not a proper subject for contract under the law, and that it would have been collected by the Internal Revenue Bureau in the ordinary discharge of its duty. The law provided that the person with whom it was made should assist the Treasury officials in discovering and collecting, so that the collections were to be made by the Treasury. But the contract in fact signed authorized Sanborn to make the collections, and required the Treasury officials to assist him.

The Committee further called attention to the fact that the law provided that no person should be employed who should not have fully set forth in a written statement under oath the character of the claim out of which he proposed to recover or assist in recovering the moneys for the United States, the laws by the violation of which the same had been withheld, and the name of the person, firm or corporation having withheld such moneys. This provision was disregarded utterly.

The Committee found that the Commissioner of Internal Revenue was not consulted in the matter, nor was any official of his Bureau, nor was he advised as to the making of the contracts or of the character of the claims, although the proper officials of the Government, referred to in the statute, could only have been the officials of the Internal Revenue Bureau. It was shown that the Commissioner of Internal Revenue wrote a letter protesting against the manner of these collections to the Secretary of the Treasury, which was never answered. The Committee found that the Commissioner was studiously ignored by the Secretary of the Treasury and the officials in his office.

The wicked and fraudulent character of the transactions is shown in the report.

When the Committee made their report the matter was debated in the House of Representatives by Governor Foster and other gentlemen who had taken part in the investigation. All these Sanborn transactions were with the Assistant Secretary in Mr. Boutwell's absence, until later Mr. Richardson became Secretary of the Treasury. The Committee unanimously agreed to report a resolution that the House had no confidence in the Secretary of the Treasury, Mr. Richardson, and demanded his removal. President Grant was notified of this conclusion. He sent for the members of the Committee and personally urged them to withhold the resolution, and offered that the Secretary should resign, and that he should be provided for in some other department of the public service. To this the Committee agreed. It was never thought that the Secretary himself profited corruptly by the transaction, but only that he had suffered himself to be hoodwinked. It was unfortunate that nearly all the persons who were connected with this transaction were from New England, most of them from Massachusetts, and several of them from Lowell.

CHAPTER XXIV

BENJAMIN F. BUTLER

No person can adequately comprehend the political history of Massachusetts for the thirty-five years beginning with 1850 without a knowledge of the character, career and behavior of Benjamin F. Butler. It is of course disagreeable and in most cases it would seem unmanly to speak harshly of a political antagonist who is dead. In the presence of the great reconciler, Death, ordinary human contentions and angers should be hushed. But if there be such a thing in the universe as a moral law, if the distinction between right and wrong be other than fancy or a dream, the difference between General Butler and the men who contended with him belongs not to this life alone. It relates to matters more permanent than human life. It enters into the fate of republics, and will endure after the fashion of this world passeth away.

I cannot tell the story of my life at a most important period without putting on record my estimate of him, and the nature of his influence over the youth of the Commonwealth. Besides, it is to be remembered that he took special pains to write and to leave behind him a book in which he gave his own account of the great controversies in which he engaged, and bitterly attacked some of the men who thwarted his ambitions. This book he sent to public libraries, including that of the British Museum, where he had good reason to expect it would be permanently preserved.

I shall say nothing of him which I did not say in public speeches or published letters while he was living and in the fulness of his strength, activity and power. History deals with Benedict Arnold, with Aaron Burr, with the evil counsellors of Charles I. and Charles II., with Robespierre, with Barère and with Catiline, upon their merits, and draws from their lives examples, or warnings, without considering the fact that they are dead. This especially is a duty to be performed fearlessly, though with due caution, when it is proposed in some quarters to erect monuments or statues to such men for the admiration of the youth of future generations.

Benjamin F. Butler was born November 5, 1818. He was graduated at Waterville College, now Colby University, in the year 1838. He began the practice of law in Lowell. Compared with other men of equal ability and distinction, he was never a very successful advocate. Quiet and modest men who had the confidence of the courts and juries used to win verdicts from him in fairly even cases. He was fertile in resources. He liked audacious surprises. He was seldom content to try a simple case in a simple way. So that while he succeeded in some desperate cases, he threw away a good many which with wise management he might have gained.

Butler's practice in the beginning was chiefly in the defence of criminals, or in civil cases where persons of that class were parties. There was very likely to be a dramatic scene in court when he was for the defence. His method of defence was frequently almost as objectionable as the crime he was defending. He attacked the character of honest witnesses, and of respectable persons, victims of his guilty clients, who were seeking the remedy of the law. He had many ingenious fashions of confusing or browbeating witnesses, and sometimes of misleading juries. He once asked a medical expert who undertook to testify about human anatomy, in a case of physical injury, this question: "State the origin and insertion of all the muscles of the forearm and hand from the elbow to the tips of the fingers"; and another, "Give a list of the names and the positions of all the bones in the body." This was something like asking a man who claimed to know the English language to give off hand all the words of the English language beginning with a. But it confused a worthy and respectable country doctor, and misled the jury. The best citizen of a country village, or his wife or daughter, who had to testify against a thief or burglar who had broken into a house had to encounter his ruffianly treatment on the witness stand. So Butler became a terror, not to evil-doers but to the opponents of evil-doers throughout the county of Middlesex. Few lawyers liked to encounter his rough speech and his ugly personalities.

He was a Democrat in politics and became quite popular with the poorer class of foreign immigrants who gathered in manufacturing towns and cities like Lowell. He had at first little success in politics for the reason that his party was a small minority in Massachusetts. He was elected to the House of Representatives for the Legislature of 1853. During that session there was a memorable struggle on the part of the Whigs to repeal so much of the act providing for an election of delegates to a Constitutional convention as required the election to be by secret ballot. There was also, as an incident to this struggle, an angry contest in the joint convention of the two Houses held for the purpose of electing some officers required by the Constitution to be chosen by joint ballot. The dispute related to the extent of the authority of the President of the Senate, as presiding officer, to control the joint assembly. Butler was conspicuous in that scene of turbulence and disorder. On the occasion of some ruling by the Whig Speaker, Mr. George Bliss, a worthy and respectable old gentleman, Butler called out in a loud voice: "I should like to knife that old cuss." That utterance was quoted not only all over the Union, but in foreign countries, in England, and on the continent, and in the West Indies, as a proof of the degradation and licentiousness of popular governments. It is a singular fact that a like question as to the authority of the presiding officer of a joint convention of two legislative bodies came up in Congress when the electoral vote was counted, at the time of the election of General Grant in 1868. Butler repeated on a larger stage his disorderly conduct, until Schuyler Colfax, Speaker of the House—although Mr. Wade, President of the Senate, was then presiding over the joint convention—resumed the chair of the House, in order, as Mr. Blaine described it afterward, "to chastise the insolence of the member from Massachusetts."

He was chosen in 1860, when the Democratic Party was divided between the supporters of Douglas and the supporters of Breckenridge, a delegate to the National Convention at Charleston, South Carolina, by the Douglas Democrats of Massachusetts, under instructions to vote for Douglas. Instead, he voted thirty-seven times for Jefferson Davis. There has been but one other instance, I believe, in the history of Massachusetts of such a betrayal of trust. That other related not to candidates but to principles.

Under our political arrangements the presidential elector is but a scribe. He exercises no discretion, but only records the will of the people who elect him. The real selection of the president is made by the nominating conventions. The nominee of the party having a majority becomes the president. A breach of trust by a delegate to a nominating convention is an act of dishonor of the same class with that to which no presidential elector in the United States has yet stooped—a breach of trust by an elector.

General Butler's career upon the national stage began with the episode at Charleston. From that time until his death he was a very conspicuous figure in the eyes of the whole country. There are two or three public services for which he deserves credit. They ought not to be omitted in any fair sketch of his life and character.

First. When, in the earlier days of the Rebellion, there was a doubt whether the Democratic Party would rally to the support of the country, he promptly offered his services. His example was of great importance in determining the question whether the war of sections was also to be a war of parties. He had a large clientage, especially among that class of Irish Americans who were apt in Massachusetts to vote with the Democratic Party. His conduct so far was in honorable contrast with that of some of his influential political associates, and that of some of the old Whigs who never got over their chagrin at the success of the Republican Party.

Second. When the question what would be the treatment of the negroes by the commanders of the Union army was doubtful, and when many persons wished to conciliate the old slaveholders in the border states by disclaiming any purpose of meddling with the institution of slavery, General Butler made a bright and important contribution to the discussion by declaring the negro "contraband of war." I do not know whether this phrase was original with him or no. It has been claimed that he borrowed it. But he undoubtedly made it famous. This tended somewhat to obliterate the effect of the shock caused to the lovers of liberty by his offer to the Governor of Maryland on the day his regiment landed at Annapolis, of his own services and those of the forces under his command, to put down any slave insurrection, in case the negro people should attempt to assert their heaven-born rights.

Governor Andrew wrote to General Butler censuring his offer of the use of the Massachusetts troops, as the first operation of the war, to improve the security of rebels that they might prosecute with more energy their attacks upon the Federal government. The Governor adds: "I can perceive no reason of military policy why a force summoned to the defence of the Federal Government, at this moment of all others, should be offered or diverted from its immediate duty to help rebels, who stand with arms in their hands, in obstructing its progress toward the city of Washington." General Butler answered that "if the contest were to be prosecuted by letting loose the slaves, some instrument other than myself must be found to carry it on." He had been, with a large part of his party, an advocate and supporter of the Fugitive Slave Law, in the days before the war.

Third. He governed the rebel city of New Orleans with great vigor. He understood how to deal with a turbulent and ugly populace. He was not imposed upon by shams or pretences, and treated the old Southern Democracy with little respect. It is probable that his vigorous remedy saved the city from yellow fever.

Fourth. Another thing should be added to his credit, not of moral quality, but of that quality which accounts largely and naturally for his influence with the people. He had a gift of clear, racy and simple speech. He could convey his thought to the apprehension of common men without any loss in the process. His style was of the same class with that of William Cobbett and Horace Greeley, without ornament, not very copious, but simple, clear and vigorous. When these things have been said, nothing remains to be said in his favor.

He had a ready, though rough and coarse wit, suited to the tastes of illiterate audiences and to that class of men who are always delighted when anything is said in disparagement of anybody. I recall two or three examples. He was rather fond of appropriating the bright sayings of others, whether jesting or serious, and claiming credit for them. But he also had a capacity of his own for such things.

I heard him argue a case involving the constitutionality of the bill to annex Charlestown to Boston, before the Supreme Court of Massachusetts. He was interrupted by the Mayor, who was on the other side, a fussy and self-important little person. Butler made the point that the meetings at which the citizens had voted for annexation had not been legal, the notice being not sufficient. The Mayor, who had irritated Butler by previous interruptions, jumped up and said that it was the practice in Charlestown to hold public meetings on a notice not longer than the one in question. He added: "We only gave a week's notice for our election of Mayor." Butler looked at him a moment, and said: "I should think they got up their Mayor on short notice."

His thrust at S. S. Cox in the House of Representatives attracted the attention of the country. It was in a five-minute debate. Cox had attacked Butler savagely. Butler replied, taking up nearly the whole five minutes with arguing the question before the House, taking no notice of Cox till just he was about to finish. He then said: "There is no need for me to answer the gentleman from New York. Every negro minstrel just now is singing the answer, and the hand organs are playing the tune, 'Shoo Fly, don't bodder me.'"

In the Constitutional Convention of Massachusetts twenty-seven different schemes for a system of representation were pressed. Somebody moved to refer them all to a committee to consist of the persons who had proposed the schemes. "As well refer twenty-seven babies to their twenty-seven mothers to decide which is the prettiest," exclaimed Butler.

His military career was, with the exception I have stated, disgraceful to himself and unfortunate to the country. From the beginning of Butler's recruiting for the war, wherever he was in command came rumors of jobs, frauds, trading with rebels through the lines, and the putting of unfit persons in responsible positions. The scandal became so great that Governor Andrew—than whom there was never a truer, nobler, braver or more upright man in the executive chair of any State in this country—was compelled to put on public record his indignant denunciation. He said in a letter to Charles Sumner and Henry Wilson, Senators in Congress, December 21, 1861:

"I am compelled to declare with great reluctance and regret, that the course of proceeding under Major-General Butler in this Commonwealth seems to have been designed and adapted simply to afford means to persons of bad character to make money unscrupulously, and to encourage men whose unfitness had excluded them from any appointment by me to the volunteer militia service, to hope for such appointment over Massachusetts troops from other authority than that of the Executive himself."*

The first considerable military operation of which he took charge was a movement upon the rebel forces at Big Bethel. It was rash, unskilful, blundering and lacking both in perseverance and courage. His troops were repulsed with great and needless slaughter.

It is a doubtful and debated question whether General Butler was personally to blame for this terrible and disgraceful repulse. If it were only his misfortune, it is a sample of the misfortunes which attended him throughout

* Schouler's "Massachusetts in the War," Vol. I., p. 276.

the war. It would not have happened to a great or even a fairly good general officer. The best that can be said for him is that if he were without personal blame, that it is the chief incident of a campaign which he went through without credit.

But the worst example of timidity and inefficiency in American military history, not excepting Hull's surrender, was the attempt and repulse at Fort Fisher. I do not mean when I say timidity, personal cowardice. But I mean the fear of the ordinary risks which accompany every bold and successful operation in war. This timidity is not infrequently, as it was in this case, characteristic of men who thrust themselves into places for which they are not fit.

It was highly important to capture Wilmington, of which Fort Fisher was the key. It was the last remaining gateway for the admission of necessary supplies and ammunitions of war to the rebellious States from the outer world. It was a military position of great importance, a chief centre of the rebellion, and a great object in our military operations. General Butler entered upon this undertaking with every advantage. He had special detailed instructions from Grant, the greatest living military commander; and he had under him and to cooperate with him Admiral Porter who, with one possible exception, was the ablest naval commander in our service.

Wilmington was stripped of troops. The fort was garrisoned by four companies of infantry and one light battery. With all the reinforcements which the enemy could muster but a thousand and seventy-seven men were in the fort. The greatest armada ever in American waters was under Butler's command—fifty vessels, thirty-three for attack, and seventeen in reserve, including four iron-clads. The iron-clads opened fire upon the fort, throwing one hundred and fifteen shells a minute.

"Fort Fisher replied at once with all its guns. But those on the northeast face were silenced almost as soon as the monitors opened their terrific fire, and by the time the last of the large vessels had anchored and got their batteries into play, only one or two of the enemy's guns were able to reply. The shower of shells had driven the gunners to the bomb-proofs. In one hour and fifteen minutes after the first gun was fired, not a shot came from the fort. Two magazines had been blown up, and the fort set on fire in several places. Such a torrent of missiles was falling and bursting that it was impossible for anything human to stand."*

In this condition of things General Butler arrived upon the scene. Not a soldier had been hurt on the Union side.

"General Curtis was now within fifty yards of the fort, and sent word to General Ames that he could take the work, whereupon Ames, not knowing Butler's determination, gave orders for an assault. Curtis at once moved forward, but by the time he reached his position, night had come on, and the fleet had nearly ceased its fire. . . . At this juncture Butler's orders to reembark arrived, and no assault was made. Curtis and the officers with him, declared that the fort could have been carried; that at the moment they were recalled, they virtually had possession, having actually approached so close that a rebel flag had been snatched from the parapet and a horse brought away from the inside stockade.

"That night Butler informed the Admiral that he and Weitzel were of the opinion that the place could not be carried by assault. . . . I shall therefore sail, he said, for Hampton Roads as soon as the transport fleet can be got in order."†

"Porter replied that he could fire much faster than he had been doing, and would keep the enemy from showing himself until our men were within twenty yards of the fort, and he begged that Butler would leave some brave fellows like those who had snatched the flag from the parapet and taken the horse from the fort."

Butler was unchangeable. He got all his troops aboard, except Curtis's brigade, and started back. In doing this

*Badeau's "Military History of General Grant," Vol. 3, p. 314.
† Ibid., p. 317.

Butler made a fearful mistake. "My instructions to the officer who went in command of the expedition," says Gen. Grant, "were explicit in the statement that to effect a landing would be of itself a great victory, and if one should be effected, the foothold must not be relinquished; on the contrary, a regular siege of the fort must be commenced and, to guard against interference by reason of storms, supplies of provisions must be laid in as soon as they could be got on shore. But Butler seems to have lost sight of this part of his instructions, and was back at Fort Monroe on the 28th." *

The Admiral, however, was of a different mind from Butler and replied to him: "I have ordered the largest vessels to proceed off Beaufort, and fill up with ammunition, to be ready for another attack, in case it is decided to proceed with this matter by making other arrangements. We have not commenced firing rapidly yet, and could keep any rebels inside from showing their heads, until an assaulting column was within twenty yards of the works. I wish some more young gallant fellows had followed the officer who took the flag from the parapet, and the brave fellow who brought the horse from the fort. I think they would have found it an easier conquest than is supposed."†

On the 27th Butler arrived at Fort Monroe, and on the 28th had an interview with Grant, after which the General-in-Chief telegraphed to the President:

"The Wilmington expedition has proven a gross and culpable failure. Many of the troops are back here. Delays and free talk of the object of the expedition enabled the enemy to move troops to Wilmington to defeat it. After the expedition started from Fort Monroe, three days of fine weather were squandered, during which the enemy was without a force to protect himself. Who is to blame, will, I hope, be known."‡

* Grant's "Memoirs," Vol. II., p. 394.
† Ibid., Badeau, p. 318.
‡ Ibid., p. 318.

Grant's statement, just quoted, was made when he had heard Butler's side of the story alone. What he thought when he had heard the whole story will appear a little later.

Admiral Porter said, in his official dispatch: "My dispatch of yesterday will give you an account of the operations, but will scarcely give you an idea of my disappointment at the conduct of the army authorities in not attempting to take possession of the fort. . . . Had the army made a show of surrounding it, it would have been ours; but nothing of the kind was done. The men landed, reconnoitred, and, hearing that the enemy were massing troops somewhere, the orders were given to reembark. . . . There never was a fort that invited soldiers to walk in and take possession more plainly than Fort Fisher. . . . It can be taken at any moment in one hour's time if the right man is sent with the troops."

On the 30th of December Grant sent this message to Porter:

"Please hold on wherever you are for a few days, and I will endeavor to be back again, with an increased force, *and without the former commander.*"

Grant at once took measures for renewing the attack and for changing the commander. On the 31st of December the Secretary of the Navy telegraphs to Porter: "Lieutenant-General Grant will send immediately a competent force, *properly commanded,* to cooperate in the capture of the defences of Federal Point."

So in every instance in which the head of the military or naval department of this country issued an order to cooperate in this expedition he found it necessary to assure the officer to whom he gave his orders that the expedition would be properly commanded. The Secretary adds in his dispatch to Admiral Porter: "The Department is perfectly satisfied with your efforts thus far." On the next day Porter writes to General Grant: "I have just received yours of December 30th. I shall be all ready; and thank God we are not to leave here with so easy a victory at hand. Thank you for so promptly trying to rectify the blunder so lately committed. I knew you would do it." He adds, speaking of the late expedition: "We lost one man killed. You may judge what a simple business it was."

On the 2d of January Grant directs that Terry, who is to command this new expedition, be sent to City Point to see him. "I cannot go myself," he adds to the Secretary of War, "so long as Butler would be left in command."

January 4th, the next day but one, Grant asks for the removal of Butler. He says: "I am constrained to request the removal of Major-General Butler from the command of the department of Virginia and North Carolina. I do this with reluctance, but the good of the service requires it. In my absence General Butler necessarily commands, and there is a lack of confidence felt in his military ability, making him an unsafe commander for a large army. His administration of the affairs of his department is also objectionable."

Stanton had just left the capital on a visit to Sherman, at Savannah, and this letter at first received no answer; but Grant was very much in earnest, and on the sixth he telegraphed direct to the President: "I wrote a letter to the Secretary of War, which was mailed yesterday, asking to have General Butler removed from command. Learning that the Secretary left Washington yesterday, I telegraph you asking that prompt action be taken in this matter."

That was practically the end of Butler's military service. He never received another command.

There is no country in the world, other than ours, where an officer guilty of such conduct, whether it came from incapacity or cowardice, would not have been promptly cashiered and probably shot. This would have been true, as in the case of Admiral Keppel, if his fault had been merely a failure to attack. But Butler's fault was an express disobedience of orders. The order which he disobeyed was unknown to the subordinate on whose advice he claimed to have relied. General Grant expressly ordered him that in case of failure to attack the fort by assault, he should remain and entrench his troops on the peninsula, and cooperate with the fleet for the reduction of the place. When

Grant learned the circumstances he declared that, in leaving after he had landed, Butler had violated his express orders.

It is a source of just pride that a New England commander, and one of Massachusetts descent, General Terry, was successful in the new attempt. Grant's instructions to him said: "I have served with Admiral Porter, and know that you can rely on his judgment and his nerve to undertake what he proposes. . . . The first object to be attained is to get a firm position on the spit of land on which Fort Fisher is built, from which you can operate against the fort. You want to look to the practicability of receiving your supplies, and to defending yourself against superior forces sent against you by any of the avenues left open to the enemy. If such a position can be obtained, the siege of Fort Fisher will not be abandoned until its reduction can be accomplished, or another plan of campaign is ordered from these headquarters."

The fort which had enabled 397 vessels to pass the blockade was taken by a great New England Captain, and largely by New England troops. Butler made one contribution, and only one, to that victory. That contribution was his absence. It was a curious coincidence which would have brought a blush of shame upon any forehead but his, that when he was testifying before an investigating committee of Congress, who were inquiring into the cause of his great and shameful failure to take the fort, and just after he had testified that Fort Fisher was impregnable and that it was impossible for any Union force to take it, a dispatch was received in the Committee Room announcing its fall.

General Grant says in his "Memoirs":

"I had no idea of General Butler accompanying the expedition until the evening before it got off from Bermuda Hundred, and then did not dream but that General Weitzel had received all the instructions, and would be in command. I rather formed the idea that General Butler was actuated by a desire to witness the effect of the explosion of the powder-boat. The expedition was detained several days at

Hampton Roads, waiting the loading of the powder-boat. The importance of getting the Wilmington expedition off without any delay, with or without the powder-boat, had been urged upon General Butler. The powder-boat was exploded on the morning of the 24th, before the return of General Butler from Beaufort; but it would seem, from the notice taken of it in the Southern newspapers, that the enemy were never enlightened as to the object of the explosion until they were informed by the Northern press." *

"General Butler, in direct violation of the instructions given, ordered the reembarkation of the troops and the return of the expedition." †

"I advised Admiral Porter to hold on, and that I would send a force and make another attempt to take the place. This time I selected Major-General A. H. Terry to command the expedition." "At my request Major-General B. F. Butler was relieved." ‡

I will not undertake to give a detailed account of the blundering strategy of what General Grant aptly called the "Bottling up at Bermuda Hundred" which enabled a powerful Union army to be held in check by a small Confederate force, leaving free the bulk of their army for hostile operations against the Union forces.

So the contribution of General Butler's military genius to the success of the United States in the war consisted of a scheme to blow up a powder-boat in the capture of Fort Fisher, somewhat after the Chinese fashion of warfare, which General Grant said hardly had the effect to excite the curiosity of the occupants of the fort which it had been intended to demolish; and of his scheme of engineering at Dutch Gap and Bermuda Hundred.

General Grant got tired of him at last and ordered him to report at Lowell. So ended the military career of incompetence, boasting and failure.

Massachusetts soldiers from those of the humblest origin to those who came from the most cultivated circles have

*" Personal Memoirs, U. S. Grant," p. 604 appendix.
† Ibid., p. 605.
‡ Ibid., p. 607.

always had the reputation of gentlemen. I know of but one conspicuous exception in her entire military history. During the trial of Andrew Johnson, Butler, who was one of the managers, employed spies to visit, in his absence, the room of William M. Evarts, counsel for the President, and to search his waste basket in the hope of spying upon his correspondence. Of this he shamelessly afterward boasted. Later he employed dishonest persons to get from the wires the private telegraphic dispatches of Henry L. Pierce, then his colleague in the House of Representatives, sent to the Hon. W. W. Rice at Worcester.

But this is not all. Wherever Butler is found in military command there were constant rumors of the same story which Governor Andrew told in the beginning. It is like the ointment of the hand which bewrayeth itself. Jobs, fraudulent contracts, trading through the lines, relatives enriched by public plunder, corrupt understanding with the enemy. These stories pursued him to New Orleans and from New Orleans back to Lowell. Is there another Union General, at least was there ever another Massachusetts General to whose integrity such suspicion attached? He scarcely undertook to discuss the matter himself. After the war a New Orleans bank, on which Butler had made a requisition for eighty thousand dollars in gold, employed the late Edwards Pierpont to bring an action against General Butler on the ground that the money had never been paid over to the Government, but that he had kept it himself. Butler saw the counsel for the plaintiffs and said he had received the money in an official capacity and had paid it over to the United States. Mr. Pierpont answered: "If you will show that, it will constitute a good defence." In the course of the conversation Pierpont said: "Your neighbors in Lowell will not think very well of it when they see you riding in your carriage through the streets, and know it was paid for out of money you have taken unlawfully from this bank." Before the time came for the trial Butler surrendered and paid over the money. After the matter was settled he said to Mr. Pierpont: "Well, you beat me. But I want to tell you that you made one mistake. You said the people of Lowell would not think very highly of me when they saw me riding through the streets in my carriage and knew it was paid for by the money of this bank. The people would think I was a fool for not having taken twice as much.''

General Butler was appointed treasurer of the National Soldiers' Home. He mingled the money of that institution with his own, got the use of it, got interest upon it, for which he never accounted. An attempt was made to investigate his accounts and he refused on the ground that he could not do it without showing his private account books, which he was not compelled to do.

He had a powerful political influence which made him an object of terror to timid and ambitious men. So, much to the shame of our public authorities, the investigation was not pressed. He was allowed to pay over only such sum as he himself admitted to be due.

General Butler's chief title to distinction in political life was a scheme which Massachusetts has pronounced a scheme of dishonesty and infamy in every method by which her sentiment can be made known. This scheme was to pay off the national debt and all other debts public and private, including all widows' and soldiers' pensions, in irredeemable paper money. He proposed to issue a series of government bonds bearing interest, payable like the principal, in greenbacks, and providing that the greenbacks should never be redeemed, but that the holder might at any time, on demand, get from the Treasury the equivalent in bonds. This scheme had been announced by General Butler for several years before the Presidential election of 1876. In that year General Butler, who had been defeated for reelection to Congress from the Essex district in 1874, was a candidate for the Republican nomination in the Middlesex district, which included his home in Lowell. There was much opposition to him. But the party feeling was very strong and no other person of large enough reputation or of conspicuous ability could be found to take the Republican nomination. General Butler was accordingly nominated with the distinct promise on his part that he would surrender his plans in regard to finance out of deference to the known wishes of his constituents, and would act with the Republican Party upon financial questions. To this pledge he owed, if not his nomination and election, certainly his great majority in the convention and at the polls. This pledge, as in the case of the trust which had been committed to him by the Douglas Democrats before the war, he most unblushingly and shamelessly violated. He renewed and advocated his fiat money scheme. The result was that at the next convention of the Republican Party in his district the following resolution was passed, without a dissenting vote:

"*Resolved,* That we warn the people of the Commonwealth, whose votes General Butler is now soliciting by promises to serve them faithfully, that his professions when seeking office have been found in our experience to be easily made and as easily repudiated when the time for redeeming them came.

"That they are neither gold nor good paper, but are a kind of fiat currency, having no intrinsic character, being cheap, delusive, irredeemable and worthless."

This convention represented a large and overwhelming majority of the people of the Middlesex district. It was made up as such conventions in Massachusetts always are made up, of men of high standing and character and of great personal worth. Can there be found in the history of Massachusetts such a record of shameless dishonor and such a terrible indictment and conviction?

A like judgment was expressed a little later by Mr. Edward Avery, a Democrat of high standing, who declared that the Democratic Party had found his promises and pledges could not be trusted.

He was once elected Governor. It so chanced that the Republican Party had been disappointed by the defeat in their State Convention of Mr. Crapo, a gentleman of the highest standing, who had rendered conspicuous service to his country in the National House of Representatives, and who was doubtless the choice of a majority of his party.

His successful competitor was a man of much personal worth and highly esteemed. But it was thought that his nomination had been compassed by skilful political management by which the will of the people had been baffled and defeated, and many Republicans declined to vote. There was a certain curiosity, as many men expressed it, to see what Butler would do and to test his professions of reform, with a feeling that he would be quite harmless with a Republican Legislature and Council. So the experiment was tried. The people of the Commonwealth had no desire to try it a second time. The matter of General Butler's title to public respect, if the rest of his record could be erased as by a wet sponge, might be determined by the experience of a single year. There was never such an exhibition as that made by him in the executive chair of Massachusetts. He proceeded to attack, to promote his own ambitions, the fair name and fame of the Commonwealth itself. One of his speeches was so gross in its nature that the principal Democratic paper of Boston refused to print it, declaring it unfit for publication.

General Butler declared in one of his public speeches when a candidate for Governor, thereby insulting the Commonwealth, especially the citizen-soldiery of Massachusetts, that the soldiers of Massachusetts "needed but a word from him to clean out the State House."

But he had his eye on a still higher prize. He hoped to compass the Democratic nomination for the Presidency. That nomination depended on his conciliating the old Democratic, rebel element at the South, then powerful in National Democratic councils. He made an attack upon the administration of the State Almshouse at Tewksbury, in which he declared that "the selling and tanning of human skins was an established industry in Massachusetts." He charged the Commonwealth with desecrating the graves and selling the bodies of deceased inmates of her public institutions for money. General Butler's charges were refuted to the public satisfaction by the simple certificate of Mrs. Clara Leonard, a member of the State Board of Lunacy and Charities, who knew all about the matter, and in whose high integrity and capacity to decide the question everybody had implicit confidence.

There was an investigation, and Butler signally failed to sustain himself. One incident at the hearing revealed perfectly his character and that of his affected sympathy for downtrodden humanity. Some human remains were brought into the presence of the committee, which it was alleged had come from the almshouse. Butler was in an angry mood at something that had occurred and called out peremptorily: "Give me the skin that came off the nigger."

I will not undertake myself to impute the motive which inspired this attack upon his own State. Whether it were anger inspired by the knowledge of the estimate in which the majority of her people held him; whether it were a gross nature with blunted sensibilities; whether these expressions were uttered in haste or anger, I will not say. The Honorable William P. Frye, an able and justly distinguished Representative and Senator from Maine, with an intimate knowledge of General Butler, which came from a long association in the public service, charged General Butler in a public speech in Massachusetts, in the autumn of 1883, in my hearing, what he repeated at many places elsewhere in the Commonwealth—that Butler had made this foul charge against Massachusetts in order that he might win the favor of the slave-holding and rebel Democratic elements of the South by catering to their prejudices against her. If that be true, this charge of General Butler's is the most disgraceful single utterance that ever came from American lips. If it be not true, what must be the nature of which the gentle, charitable and kindly Senator Frye could believe it true after an intimate knowledge so many years?

General Butler was disappointed in his expectation of Democratic support in the country at large. He had thereafter no rest in politics for the sole of his foot. The remainder of his life was spent in speculation and manufacturing enterprises.

I repeat what I said of General Butler in his lifetime, when he was at the height of his power, with a full knowledge of his vindictive character, that the success of his attempt to use and consolidate the political forces of Massachusetts would have been the corruption of her youth, the destruction of everything valuable in her character, and the establishment at the mouth of the Charles River of another New York with its frauds, Tweed rings and scandals.

General Butler made an earnest effort to get the Republican nomination for Governor in 1871. He had built up what was called a Butler party, in which he had had the aid of the National Administration, and of all persons whom he could either seduce by hope of reward or terrify by fear of his vengeance. It was not a question in considering candidacy for office with him whether the man had rendered honest service in civil or in military life, whether he was a man of honor or of good or bad character, but only whether he was a Butler man. He conducted his own campaign for Governor in 1871 and again in 1873. In the former he summoned his adherents to the State Convention, issuing a circular in which he advised them to bring three days' rations in the expectation of a long and angry struggle.

I was invited by the State Central Committee to preside at the Convention of 1871. It was quite likely that the Convention might break up in disorder and the result would be two factions, each claiming to be the regular Republican organization. I told the gentleman of the State Central Committee, who communicated to me their desire, that I would do it on condition that there should be provided one hundred skilled and trustworthy police officers who would obey my orders, and, if it became necessary, would remove from the hall General Butler or any other person who should defy the authority of the Convention. This the committee promised to do. This promise was in substance kept. The gentleman who made it as the organ of the State Central Committee had himself been for many years a sheriff of the County of Worcester, and had been a General in the Civil War, and was a man of large capacity for handling disorderly assemblies. He came to me afterward and said that in a hall like Mechanics Hall a well-disciplined force of not more than fifty men would be better for the purpose of keeping order than a more numerous one, and he had taken the liberty of departing from our agreement to that extent. To this I assented.

When I went to the Hall that morning in taking leave of my wife I told her that the chances were that I should come home the most disgraced man in Massachusetts. If General Butler succeeded in breaking up the Convention in disorder the blame would be laid upon the presiding officer.

But we got through safely. General Butler had calculated that his opponents, who were divided among several candidates, could not agree upon any one. But such an agreement was effected upon William B. Washburn. His plan then, I supposed, was to find some excuse for breaking up the Convention under circumstances which would enable him to claim to President Grant that he represented the regular Republican organization and that his opponents were the bolters. My duty on the other hand was so to conduct the Convention that there should be no pretext on his part for such a course. The Convention was in continuous session from 11 o'clock in the forenoon until half-past one next morning. There were several contests in which Butler conducted the case on his own side. But his opponents held together and nominated William B. Washburn. With the exception of the National Convention of 1880, at which I also presided, this was the most difficult duty in the way of presiding over a deliberative assembly which ever fell upon any person in this country so far as I know.

In the year 1873 General Butler made another attempt to get the Republican nomination for Governor. A meeting was called at Hamilton Hall, in Boston, of a few persons opposed to his candidacy, which resulted in an address to the people recommending the reelection of Mr. Washburn. I signed the address of which I wrote a few sentences. Judge Hoar made a bright and characteristic speech in which he said that "the people of Massachusetts would not yield the office of Governor to a Tichborne claimant, whether with or without a bond." This name, "the Claimant," stuck to Butler for the rest of his life.

In 1871 my opposition to General Butler and support of Governor Washburn was well known. I announced my preference for the latter in a letter to the Springfield *Republican*. This did not occasion any personal quarrel with Butler, although our relations were never cordial. But in 1873 he was very angry with the persons who signed the address in favor of the renomination of Governor Washburn. He wrote a letter to the people of Massachusetts in which he angrily attacked many persons in the Republican party whom he believed to be his opponents. Among them he bitterly attacked me. He sent a copy of this letter in the form of a broadside to every newspaper in Massachusetts, I believe, and had it folded into every copy of the paper. I instantly replied, setting forth as well as I could the character and quality of General Butler and the nature of his influence upon the youth of the Commonwealth. The letter contained the following sentences:

"When General Butler proposed to pay off our national debt in irredeemable paper, General Grant silenced him with the ringing sentence in his inaugural, 'Let it be understood that no repudiator of one farthing of our public debt will be trusted in public place,' because he knew that he was trying to tempt this people to escape from a burden by a mean and base act.

"He has quarrelled with Grant and Wilson, and Colfax and Blaine, and Andrew, and Sumner, and the Washburnes, and Bingham, and Schenck, and Dawes, because he is quarrelsome. They have been compelled, each in his own way, to chastise and punish him because he deserved to be whipped.

"Among the unprincipled adventurers who gained favor in the corrupt times of the Stuarts, and whose evil counsels brought Charles the First to his doom, the most notorious was Buckingham. Gaining favor by lending himself as the subservient tool in accomplishing every evil purpose: restless, ambitious, unscrupulous, selfish, revengeful, thrusting himself into military employments for which he was unfit and from which he was compelled to retire in disgrace; getting a 'competent private fortune' by dishonest practices, which he lavished in overcoming the virtue of timid and venal men, his name is the shame of England. Nugent says of him: 'His shrewdness in judging of men was employed only to enable him to found his influence upon their weaknesses and vices; so that, when opposed to men of capacity, or thwarted by what remained of public virtue in the country, he found himself in conflict with weapons of which he knew not the use; and his counsels were dangerous, and his administration unprosperous. His only wisdom was the craft with which he managed weak or bad men, and his only virtue the courage with which he overawed timid ones.' Such counsellors, fatal to a monarch, are full of peril to a republic. Such men can only prosper in times of public corruption.

"General Butler has done, unless he has egregiously imposed upon us, two things well. He out-blackguarded a New York mob in 1864, and with a United States army at his back, he kept down a rebel city in 1862. Massachusetts is not likely soon to stand in need of either of these processes. But he never has accomplished anything else of much importance when his point could not be carried by sheer blustering. The history of all his other attempts may be comprised in three words—*Swagger, quarrel, failure.*

"Other men have aspired before now to the office of Governor of Massachusetts. It is an honorable ambition. They were content to leave their claims to be set forth by others, and were glad to waive them if by so doing they could promote the harmony of the party. This man seeks nothing but his own selfish ends, utterly regardless of the wishes, the welfare, or the harmony of the great party to which he professes to belong. The people of Massachusetts have sometimes elected to this high office men who in some particulars are not deserving of respect. But the people respected them, and chose them because they deemed them worthy, and the persons so chosen endeavored to deserve the public confidence. This man, if he is chosen at all, is to be chosen without having the respect of the men to whom he looks for support. It would be hard to find a leading supporter of General Butler who will say that he deems him honest, truthful, disinterested, or incapable of using power to gratify both his ambition and his revenge. The men whom General Butler will beat are the men whom he persuades to support him."

The morning after his defeat in the State Convention each of the principal morning papers in Boston headed its account of the Convention with the words "Swagger, Quarrel, Failure."

General Butler made no further reply by letter. But he came to Worcester, where I dwelt, and addressed an enormous meeting in Mechanics Hall. I suppose many more people than those that got in were obliged to go away because the Hall would not hold them. The General devoted his speech largely to a powerful and bitter attack upon me. I replied at a meeting at the same place a few days after. My speech ended with the following sentences. After describing the heroism of the youth of Worcester in the battle with slavery and the battle with Rebellion, I added:

"And now, after the war, another enemy, unarmed, but bringing even greater danger, menaces the Republic. The battle with corruption is the duty of the hour. The blow which rebellion aimed at the Nation's life you could ward off. The wounds it inflicted are already in the process of cure. But this poison, this rotting from the core, when the virtue of our public servants is corrupted, is far more dangerous to the Republic. There is already danger that the operations of the Tweeds and Goulds in New York may be repeated on more gigantic scale at the National capital. The mighty railroads to whom our public domain has been so lavishly granted, in some cases I doubt not, wisely, afford infinite opportunity for plunder and corruption. All these are at the cost of the labor of the country. The increased tax falls in the end on the consumer. With the waste of our public land are diminished the resources of the laborer. Following bad precedents Congress has itself been induced to set the pernicious example of which you have heard so much discussion. (This referred to the measure known as the Salary Grab.) The author of the measure tells you that he knew what he was doing, and if you didn't like it you could vote against him. Are you quite ready to declare to the country that in this great contest with extravagance and corruption, wherever the Republicans of the rest of the country may array themselves, the Republicans of Massachusetts fight under the banner of General Butler?

"You are doubtless familiar with Victor Hugo's description of the marine monster said to be found in the vicinity of the Channel islands, and known as the Devil Fish. It is apparently formed of an almost transparent jelly, colorless, almost indistinguishable from the water which surrounds it, armed with long slender limbs, numerous as the feet of the centipede, and strong in their grasp as bands of iron. The bather in those waters habitually provides himself with a long keen blade, which, when he finds himself encountered by one of these monsters, he elevates above his head in his extended right hand. As the creature approaches, the bather feels himself slowly enveloped in the powerful limbs which twine about him, holding him in their iron grasp. Suddenly a head appears, and drawing itself nearer the animal seeks to fasten its mouth upon the lips of the victim and deprive him of life. At this moment the bather strikes with his knife into the head of the monster. Instantly the limbs relax their hold, the hideous creature slowly disappears, and the bather is left unharmed and safe. Our Republic finds itself to-day assailed by a monster as dangerous and as hideous as that of the Channel islands; insensible, unpalpable, soft, horrible but strong—strong as bands of iron. The limbs of this monster of Corruption have seized upon our noble Republic, but at last there is a head coming in sight, and I think the Republicans of Massachusetts are able to bear the knife and strike the blow which will destroy its horrible life so that it shall fall powerless forever!"

That closed the discussion so far as we were concerned for that campaign.

In 1876 Judge Hoar, who had been, very much against his will, elected to Congress from the Middlesex District declined a renomination. General Butler, who had been defeated at the polls in the Essex District two years before, was thereupon nominated, having pledged himself to the Republicans that he would abandon his fiat money doctrines in obedience to the declared will of the people; a pledge which as stated above he shamefully violated. There was no expectation of defeating him. But some few Republicans who were unwilling to support him desired a candidate on whom to unite, and they applied to Judge Hoar. He said he had no desire to go to Congress. But he thought there ought to be a Republican candidate against Butler and that he had no right to ask another man to take a position from which he flinched himself, and accordingly he was nominated. But Butler was elected by a large majority.

That however was substantially the end of his relation with the Republican Party. After the Inauguration of President Hayes he tried to have the public officers in his District who had refused to support him removed. On President Hayes's refusal he left the Republican Party and became, a year or two after, the Democratic nominee for Governor for two or three years and, as has been seen, was elected in 1883. I of course supported the Republican candidate and made, I suppose, thirty or forty speeches in each of those years. He had said in explaining and defending his fiat money scheme that the word "fiat" means "let there be." God said "fiat lux," "let there be light," and there was light. He argued that fiat money was excellent from the very fact that it cost nothing and had no intrinsic value. So if a bill were lost or destroyed a new one could be supplied without cost. He also said that it would stay in the country and would not be sunk in the morasses of Asia, especially in China and India, where silver and gold were absorbed and never heard of in civilized nations afterward. I quoted these sentences with the following comment: "That, Fellow-citizens, is precisely the difference between Omnipotence and Humbug, between the Almighty and General Butler. God said let there be light and there was light. General Butler says let there be money and there is—rags. This is the first time in our history that the

American workingman has been gravely asked to take for his wages money it costs nothing to make, that it is no loss to lose, that it is no gain to get, and that even a Chinaman won't touch." Butler was very angry and answered, rather irrelevantly, as it seemed to me, by saying that I did not go to the War, to which I replied as follows:

"I see that the Greenback candidate for Governor has seen fit to taunt some persons, including myself, who have ventured to exercise the privilege of free speech in this campaign, that they did not go to the war; while he boasts that he not only went to the war but hung a rebel. Those persons who did not go to the war may, perhaps, possess at least this advantage, that they can form an impartial opinion of the merits of those who did. It is the pride and the honor of this noble Commonwealth of ours, that of the hundred thousand brave soldiers and sailors she sent to the war, there was but one notorious braggart; there was but one capable of parading up and down the Commonwealth, vaunting that he had hung a man; exhibiting himself as the Jack Ketch of the rebellion. I bow reverently to the brave, modest, patriotic soldier, who, without thought of personal gain, gave youth, health, limb, life to save the country which he loved. I am willing to abide by his opinion, and to yield to him every place of honor and of office. But to you, General Butler, whose military career is made up of the blunder and slaughter of Big Bethel; of the powder explosion at Fort Fisher; of the engineering at Dutch Gap; of the "bottling-up" at Bermuda Hundred; of the trading with the rebels through the lines in North Carolina; of the scandals of New Orleans; to you, who were ordered by General Grant to go home in disgrace; to you whose best service had been, if you, too, had stayed at home, I have no such tribute to offer. When Benedict Arnold taunts Jefferson that he did not go into battle in the Revolution, when Aaron Burr taunts John Adams with want of patriotism, then it will be time for you to boast yourself over the men who performed the duties of civil life during the Rebellion."

We have had turbulent and exciting times in our State and National politics before and since that day. But I think there has been nothing in Massachusetts, and so far as I am aware there has seldom been anything in the country anywhere like the years from 1869 until 1877, when General Butler's power was at its height. You could hardly take up a morning paper without dreading that you should read of the removal from some position of honor of some brave honest soldier who had deserved well of his country, and the substitution of some disreputable person in his place. All the dishonesty of the time seemed to be combined and rallied to his support. Three of his trusted lieutenants in different parts of the Commonwealth were convicted of crime and sent to the State Prison. Another was detected in crime punishable by imprisonment in the State Prison, but escaped prosecution by a compromise. Still another was compelled to flee the country for a series of forgeries, finding refuge in a South American State with which we had no treaty of extradition. Still another was indicted for frauds which wrecked a National bank, and escaped conviction by a technicality. Still another was compelled to flee from the Commonwealth by the detection of some notorious frauds. And now more recently, in 1898, another has been arrested, a fugitive from justice, and brought back to Massachusetts, having wrecked two banks and embezzled their funds.

In the autumn of 1883 General Butler was a candidate for reelection. He was so confident that he had prepared his grounds for a magnificent illumination. But he was signally defeated. I took a leading part in the campaign. I give the following extract from my speech at Worcester:

"But we are thinking to-night of the matter of electing a Governor. Character is more important than opinion; good name to the State, as to the citizen, is better than riches. I suppose it is true of each one of you as of myself that among his chief comforts and pleasures in life is his pride in being a Massachusetts citizen. The honor and good fame of our beloved State is far above any question of party. I think I do you no more than justice when I declare that you lament as much as I do the personal character of the contest which is upon us. It has never been the habit of Republicans to deal in personalities. The Republican press and the Republican platform in Massachusetts has been singularly free from these things. What Democratic candidate can be named other than the present Governor to whom the Republicans have not delighted to pay the respect due to honorable and respected opponents. Have Gaston or Thompson or either Adams or Hancock or any of their candidates for Congress, anything to complain of in this respect? If we deal differently with General Butler, it is because the difference is in him. We have selected our own candidate on a very simple principle. In determining on whom we would confer the title, His Excellency, we have sought a man who represented in his own person our standard of excellence. We sought a man whom the fathers and mothers of the Commonwealth would be willing to hold up to their children for imitation. We sought a man, tried and proved in important public trusts, faithful, sincere, upright, downright, who would continue and maintain the honored line of Massachusetts Governors. We have found such a man in George D. Robinson. I will sum up what I have to say of Mr. Robinson by saying that he is in every respect the reverse of his antagonist. We are told that we must not discuss the record of the candidate of our antagonists before his election last year. That was all condoned. I do not concede for myself that truth is necessarily determined by majorities. I have a high respect for the people, but they do not change men's characters by their votes. But, be it so, let bygones be bygones. Let us concede that the career of our present governor as citizen and soldier and statesman furnishes a lofty example of every virtue under heaven. Let us admit that it was love of liberty that advocated the Fugitive Slave Law in the old Democratic days; that it was fidelity that was sent to Charleston, to vote for Douglas, and voted fifty-seven times for Jefferson Davis; that it was patriotism of which Governor Andrew said in 1861: 'I am compelled to declare with great reluctance and regret that the whole course of proceedings under Major General Butler in this Commonwealth seems to have been designed and adopted to afford means to persons of bad character to make money unscrupulously;' that it was good generalship that caused the blunder and slaughter of Big Bethel; that it was skilful engineering that made the canal at Dutch Gap a laughing-stock to the civilized world; that it was a great strategist that was bottled up at Bermuda Hundred; that it was courage that retreated from the uncaptured Fort Fisher; that it was purity that caused the scandals of New Orleans, and integrity that traded through the lines in North Carolina; that it was a great soldier that was ordered by General Grant to report at Lowell; that it was zeal for the public service that defended the Sanborn Contracts; that it was modesty that has gone so often up and down the State blowing his own trumpet; that it was honesty that mingled the funds of the Soldiers' Home with its own; that it was good faith that sought to juggle the public creditor out of his debt; that it was care for the poor and the working men that sought to give our laborers rags for wages and our soldiers waste paper for pensions; that it was a faithful representative that promised the men of the Middlesex District that if he might go once more to fight the Rebel brigadiers he would faithfully represent their opinions on finance and then proposed that marvellous scheme of fiat money, which he represented it would be no loss to lose and no gain to get, and that even a Chinaman would not touch, so that the same constituency demanded his resignation and 'resolved, that we warn the people of the Commonwealth, whose votes General Butler is now soliciting by promises to serve them faithfully, that his professions when seeking office have been found in our experience to be easily made and as easily repudiated when the time for redeeming them came; that they are neither gold nor good paper, but a kind of fiat currency, having no intrinsic value, cheap, delusive, irredeemable and worthless;' that it was an honest Democrat, of whom Mr. Avery, President of this year's Democratic Convention, declared that his promises and pledges could not be trusted; that it was consistency which has belonged to every party in turn. We will put the issue of this election upon the record of the year's administration. He has shown an utter want of understanding of the true theory of the Constitution. This is illustrated in his removal of Warden Earle. He told his friends at the prison that he made the removal because Earle would not obey his orders. He had no more right to give an order to Earle than to you or me. The Governor and Council have the right to prescribe rules for the government of the prison—not the Governor. The Board of Prison Commissioners have the right to give directions to the Warden, but not the Governor. His telling Earle to obey his orders on pain of dismissal was as flagrant a violation of law and of the fundamental principles of the Constitution, as it was an injustice to as brave an officer, as honest a man as ever tied a sash around his waist. He traduced the Commonwealth in his vile Tewksbury speech. I believe every charge he made broke down on his own evidence or was thoroughly refuted. But if the thing were decent to do, it might be done decently. Those of you who have delighted to listen to the classic eloquence of Everett, to the lofty speech of Sumner, to the noble appeals of Andrew, aye, to the sincere and manly utterances of Robinson, take that speech and read it. He insulted womanhood in the person of a defenceless girl. He insulted purity by a speech so gross that the principal Democratic paper in Boston declares it unfit for circulation, and demands that it be suppressed. He insulted every colored man in the State, when, in an unguarded moment, speaking from his very soul, he called out: 'Give me the skin that came off the nigger.' He insulted the citizen soldier of Massachusetts when he declared that they needed but a word from him to clean out the State House. He insulted the common school system of Massachusetts when he said that if his witness were a person of immoral character, the school system was responsible. He insulted the whole Commonwealth in trying to cast upon her the foul imputation that she was inhuman and indifferent to her poor and unfortunate, and intimated that the tanning of human skins was a recognized Massachusetts industry. Another insult is the menace of fraud that comes from Boston. The law requires the appointment of election officers, to be chosen equally from the two great parties, and every mayor of Boston, Republican and Democrat alike, Pierce, Gaston and Green, have fairly and honorably discharged their duty. It is one of the most important trusts that can be imposed upon a public official, to guard the purity of the vote of their fellow citizens. The Republican Committee this year submitted its lists and the names upon them were changed, and other men substituted, Butler men, Democrats and criminals, all charged to the Republican account. Our neighbor, Judge Nelson, a few years ago, tried at the bar of his court a man whom Governor Butler defended. He was convicted, sentenced and went to jail. He is now out of prison, and has been substituted for a Republican, probably by the influence of his former counsel, to count the ballots of the citizens of Boston. You have heard of such proceedings in other States, but never in Massachusetts. Unless the people of this Commonwealth rise in their might and crush out this attempted fraud, they will have at the mouth of the Charles River another New York, with its frauds, Tweed rings and scandals.''

He answered that by an attack on the memory of my father who had died more than twenty-five years before. Thereupon the controversy, so far as it had anything personal in it, ended.

It happened that the year when General Butler was Governor I was elected President of the Harvard Alumni Association. It was the custom of the College to invite the Governor to the dinner of the Alumni on Commencement day as the guest of the University and to confer upon him the degree of Doctor of Laws. It would have been my duty to preside at the dinner and to walk with him at the head of the procession, to have him seated by my side at the table, and to extend to him the courtesies of the University. I hardly knew what I ought to do. I must either walk with him and sit by his side in silence or with a formal and constrained courtesy which would in itself be almost an affront, or on the other hand, I must take his hand, salute him with cordiality as becomes a host on a great occasion in dealing with a distinguished guest, and converse with him as I should have conversed with other persons occupying his high place. It did not seem to me that I ought to do either, especially in the case of a man whose offence had not been merely against me, but who had made a gross and unfounded attack upon the memory of my father, and of whose personal and public character I entertained the opinion I had so often publicly expressed. Accordingly I declined to accept the office of President. My place was filled by Joseph H. Choate, who discharged the duty, of course, very much better than I could have done it.

Mr. James F. Rhodes in his able and most impartial history of the United States, speaking of the events of the summer of 1864 and the disintegrating and discouraging condition of the Army of the Potomac, says:

"Circumstances seemed to indicate the bitterness of disappointment at the failure of the high hopes and expectations which filled the soul of Grant when he crossed the Rapidan. It was commonly believed in the Army that his misfortune had driven him again to drink, and on this account and others Butler with crafty method acquired a hold on him which prevented him from acting for the best interests of the service. It is not a grateful task to relate the story of Butler using Grant as a tool to accomplish his own ends. The picture of such a relation between the two is repulsive, but it may be fraught with instruction as men of the type of Butler are never absent from our political life." *

"Butler had some hold on the Commander of the Armies of the United States and in the interview of July 9th showed his hand."†

I do not suppose that the secret of the hold which General Butler had upon General Grant will ever be disclosed. But-

* Rhodes, " History," Vol. 4, p. 493.
† Rhodes, Ibid., Vol. 4, p. 495.

ler boasted in the lobby of the House of Representatives that Grant would not dare to refuse any request of his because he had in his possession affidavits by which he could prove that Grant had been drunk on seven different occasions. This statement was repeated to Grant by a member of the House who told me of the conversation. Grant replied without manifesting any indignation, or belief or disbelief in the story: "I have refused his requests several times." In the case of almost any other person than President Grant such an answer would have been a confession of the charge. But it ought not to be so taken in his case. Unless he desired to take into his full confidence the person who was speaking to him he was in the habit of receiving most important communications with entire silence or with some simple sentence which indicated his purpose to drop the subject. My own belief is that at some time during the War, or before the War in times of discouragement Grant may have been in the habit of drinking freely and may at some time have done so to excess. During the whole time of his Presidency I had a good opportunity to observe him in personal intercourse. I was familiar with many men who were constantly in his company at all hours of the day and often far into the night. They assured me that there was no foundation for any imputation that he was in the habit of drinking to excess then. If at any time he had formed such a habit he had put it under his feet. For that I think he is entitled to greater honor than if he had never yielded to temptation. My explanation of Butler's influence over Grant is to some extent conjecture. But I believe Grant thought him a powerful political leader and that he was entitled to respect as representing the opinions of large numbers of men. Beside that Butler had a great influence over some ambitious men who were his confederates and over some timid men who were afraid of him. Their influence with Grant was on Butler's side. Then Grant was apt, as I have said in another place, to sympathize with men who were bitterly attacked, especially men who were charged with dishonesty or corruption, because such charges were made against him. So without undertaking to explain Butler's influence with Grant, I content myself with stating it and with lamenting it. He led Grant to make some very bad appointments in Massachusetts which were totally repugnant to the feeling of her people. But for those appointments, in my opinion, the strong objection felt by her people to giving any President of the United States a third term would not have prevented her supporting him for renomination in 1880, a support which would have insured his success.

After President Hayes came into power General Butler tested the President's willingness to permit him to control the patronage of Massachusetts. He demanded the appointment of a man recommended by him to the office of Postmaster at Methuen. The term had expired. President Hayes carefully examined the matter in person, got a list of the principal patrons of the office, and compared it with the petitions. He determined to reappoint the incumbent, who was an excellent officer, and a Republican who had refused to vote for General Butler. The man whom General Butler recommended had lost a leg in the War. He had an artificial limb so well made that many people, even those who worked in the same shop with him, did not know that he had lost his leg. Butler went before the Senate Committee on Post Offices to get them to reject President Hayes's nominee, taking his own candidate with him. He had the man leave off his artificial leg and come on crutches to get greater sympathy. He made an earnest and angry speech before the Committee attacking President Hayes. But he made no impression, and the old Postmaster was confirmed and reappointed. Thereupon Butler left the Republican party, first declaring himself an Independent and attempting in that capacity to get elected as Governor of the State. Failing in that he avowed himself a Democrat, and was, as has been already said, elected by the Democrats in the fall of 1882. This transaction terminated his relation to the Republican Party, and his defeat for Governor terminated his political life with the exception that he was the Greenback candidate for the Presidency in 1884. But he received little support.

CHAPTER XXV

BELKNAP IMPEACHMENT

MARCH 3, 1876, a message was sent to the Senate from the House of Representatives, impeaching General Belknap, the Secretary of War. He was charged with having received corruptly a large sum of money, payable in quarterly instalments, for the appointment of a Post Trader, an officer appointed by the Secretary of War. This was a very lucrative position, the profits of which depended very largely upon the Secretary. I was chosen one of the Managers of the Impeachment by the House. There was no serious question of the guilt of the Secretary. But he resigned, and his resignation was accepted, after the discovery of his misconduct, before the proceedings of impeachment were inaugurated. The whole struggle was over the question of the Constitutional right of the Senate to convict a public officer on impeachment proceedings instituted after he had left office. Upon that question I made a careful and elaborate argument. A majority of the Senate (37 to 25) were for sustaining the proceedings. But the Senators who thought the Senate had no jurisdiction to enter a judgment of guilty when the proceedings were commenced after the person left office, deemed themselves constrained to vote Not Guilty as the only mode of giving that opinion effect.

So General Belknap was acquitted for the want of the two-thirds vote for his conviction. Every Democrat voted for conviction except Mr. Eaton of Connecticut. The following Republicans voted for conviction: Booth, Cameron of Pennsylvania, Dawes, Edmunds, Hitchcock, Mitchell, Morrill, Oglesby, Robertson, Sargent, Sherman, and Wadleigh.

It is difficult to believe that the Senators who voted for acquittal were not, perhaps unconsciously, influenced by the desire to shield a political associate from punishment. The power to impeach public officers after leaving office had been exercised in England from time immemorial. It is well settled that when in the Constitution or legislation of the United States a term of the English law is used, that the meaning customarily given to the term in English jurisprudence is to be ascribed to it here.

The history of this clause as found in the proceedings of the Convention that framed the Constitution, makes very clear the understanding of that body. They first inserted the words: "The Senate of the United States shall have power to try all impeachments, but no person shall be convicted without the concurrence of two-thirds of the members present, which in case of impeachment shall not extend further than to removal from office and disqualification to hold and enjoy any office of trust and profit under the United States." The framers of the Constitution regarded the power of impeachment as absolutely essential to the working of the Government.

That clearly gave the two Houses of Congress the common law powers of impeachment, as exercised by Parliament. At a later time there was added: "The Vice-President and all civil officers of the United States shall be removed from office on impeachment and conviction." That was added as a limitation on the tenure of office. It seems incredible that they should have intended, without debate or division, to wholly change and so greatly limit and narrow the clause previously adopted.

It is obvious that impeachment and removal from office will be in many cases an insignificant and unimportant part of the remedy as compared with perpetual disqualification from holding office. It seems incredible that it could ever have been intended that this judgment of perpetual disqualification to hold office could only be rendered when the defendant is willing, and can be avoided by his voluntary resignation.

The framers of the Constitution were very skilful Constitutional mechanics. I am satisfied that the opinion of the majority of the Senate will prevail hereafter, unless the case where the question shall come up be, like that of Belknap, strongly affected by party feeling.

President Monroe said: "The right of impeachment and of trial by the Legislature is the mainspring of the great machine of government. It is the pivot on which it turns. If preserved in full vigor, and exercised with perfect integrity, every branch will perform its duty."

I received a good many letters expressing approval of my argument. Perhaps, without inordinate vanity, I may be permitted to preserve those which follow. The approval of my honored and beloved instructor, Judge Thomas, gave me special satisfaction.

I am led to publish these letters partly because I think the opinion of the writers on the question is worth preserving for future reference, but chiefly, I believe, from what I hope will be deemed a pardonable vanity. Mr. Sumner, in editing the thirteen volumes of his speeches, has given in regard to all of them, letters from friends and correspondents, expressing their approval. I do not suppose it would ever have occurred to Daniel Webster to publish similar certificates as to any speech or act of his.

FROM GEORGE S. BOUTWELL, GOVERNOR; SECRETARY OF THE U. S. TREASURY; U. S. SENATOR, ETC., TO JUDGE E. R. HOAR.

UNITED STATES SENATE,
WASHINGTON, May 8th, 1876.

My dear Judge,

It was the opinion of all who heard your brother's argument in the Belknap case that it was the best of the arguments yet given and that it will rank with the best at any time delivered in the Senate.

I do not write this because I was in any degree surprised, but it cannot be otherwise than agreeable to you to know that there is a concurrence in the view I have expressed.

Very truly,
GEO. S. BOUTWELL.

To The Honble
E. R. Hoar,
Concord, Mass.

From Judge Benjamin F. Thomas of the Supreme Court of Massachusetts.

No. 9 Pemberton Sq
Boston May 25th '76.

My Dear Sir

I am greatly obliged to you for sending me a copy of your admirable argument on the question of jurisdiction in the impeachment cause

The argument is sensible and exhaustive, the style clear, forcible and attractive and the whole tone temper and spirit becoming a jurist and statesman

Very truly yours
Benj F. Thomas.

Hon Geo F. Hoar

From William M. Evarts, Secretary of State; United States Senator, etc.

New York, May 22, 1876.

My dear Mr. Hoar,

I am much obliged to you for sending me your speech, as manager, on the question of jurisdiction. I had seen it applauded in the newspapers and am happy to add mine to the general suffrage. It seems to me a very complete and able presentation both of law and reasons of State on your side.

My own opinions are strongly adverse to the jurisdiction, and I should greatly lament its maintenance by the Senate. In ordinary times I should not suppose it possible, and I do not think it probable, now.

I hope the defendant's counsel presented the argument as satisfactorily from their side as you have done for yours. But I have little hope that it is so.

Yours very truly,
(Signed) Wm M. Evarts.

The Hon'ble
Geo F. Hoar.

From Judge Dwight Foster of the Supreme Court of Massachusetts.

Boston, 20 May, '76.

My Dear Sir:

I have read with satisfaction and admiration your exhaustive and conclusive argument in the Belknap impeachment case. It would have convinced me, if I had not been of your opinion already. In thought I doubted a little at first. My mind was soon satisfied that the narrow construction which left the accused to decide whether to abide his trial or by resignation to defeat the jurisdiction of the court could not possibly be correct.

Congratulating you on your success.

I am
Yours sincerely

Honble Geo F. Hoar   Dwight Foster

From Charles Devens, Jr., Attorney-General, etc.

Worcester
May 18, '76

My Dear Hoar

I have just read with the greatest interest and satisfaction your speech on the jurisdiction in the impeachment case. It seems to me most able profound and convincing and I congratulate you immensely on the effort which is spoken of by all who have read it as most vigorous and successful. It could not have been better done.

Yours most truly
Chas Devens Jr

From Charles Allen, Judge of the Supreme Court of Massachusetts.

Boston May 18 1876

Dear Mr. Hoar

Thanks for your argument in the Belknap case. Massachusetts is very proud of what you have done in this case; and I, among the rest.

Yours very truly

Hon. G. F. Hoar.   Charles Allen.

CHAPTER XXVI
ELECTORAL COMMISSION

WHEN the Presidential election of 1876 was over both sides claimed the victory. When the certificates of the result in the different States reached the President of the Senate, in accordance with the requirement of the Constitution and the law, it turned out that there was one majority for Hayes and Wheeler, upon the face of the returns, if the returns from the State of Oregon were construed in accordance with the Republican claim.

The Governor of Oregon gave a transcript of the record and declared his opinion that it showed one of the lawful electors to have voted for Mr. Tilden. That would have given one majority for Tilden. The Republicans claimed that upon the record the election showed that all the Republican candidates for elector had been chosen in Oregon, and that they had all voted for Hayes and Wheeler.

The Democrats declared that the boards authorized to ascertain and return the result of the election for Presidential electors in South Carolina, Florida and Louisiana had corruptly and unlawfully rejected votes that ought to be counted for them, and counted votes for the Republicans that ought not to be so counted; and had in that way changed the result which, if it had been correctly ascertained and reported, would have shown a Democratic majority in those three States.

The country was deeply excited. Threats of civil war were heard in many quarters. When I went to Washington for the session of December, 1876, while I did not believe there would be a civil war, and supposed there would be some method of escape devised, I confess I saw no such method. I now believe that but for the bitter experience of a few years before, with its terrible lesson, there would have been a resort to arms. It would have been a worse civil war than that of the Rebellion, because the country would have been divided not by sections, but by parties.

But, as I have related elsewhere, a majority in Congress agreed to submit the question to a Commission composed of five Senators, five Representatives, and five Judges of the Supreme Court, who, proceeding in accordance with an ingenious and skilfully devised mechanism, were to determine the case.

I believe that as time goes on, the great self-restraint of the American people in dealing with the momentous peril of 1877, and the constructive ability which created the simple but perfect mechanism of the Electoral Commission, will receive, as they deserve, the admiration of mankind. There was at the time, as would be expected, some anger and disappointment at the result. Occasionally some bigot who can find nothing but evil in the history and life of his country, generally some recluse who has little knowledge of affairs, charges the Commission with having wickedly deprived the majority of the people of the fruits of an honest and lawful victory. But, in general, wherever I go I find that intelligent men of both parties are satisfied with the righteousness of the decision, and admit that a different judgment would have wrought the destruction of the Republic.

When the decision of the Electoral Commission was accepted every Democratic vote in the two Houses was against it, and every Republican vote, save two, given in its favor. Of these two, one shortly afterward left the Republican party and became a bitter and angry Democrat. The other, a most admirable and excellent college president, told me that he thought the Commission were technically right. But he thought it better for the effect on the country that the Democratic contention should be sustained. As if in a question of Constitutional proceeding, or rather a question of Constitutional power, a determination could be technically right, and wrong upon the merits. If Congress, technically, that is according to the mandate of the Constitution, had no power to decide the result of the elections in the

States, but that power was committed to State tribunals, how was it possible that any member of either House of Congress, who had sworn to support the Constitution, could usurp that power without being forsworn? Beside, it must be conceded by everybody to be utterly impossible that the power of investigating disputed questions, as to the choice of presidential electors by the States, should be exercised by Congress. There is no time for such an investigation by Congress. It could only be done where a few precincts or votes were in dispute, in places near the seat of Government. It would have been impossible to do it in time for the inauguration of the new President before the day of railroads and telegraphs for any State in the country. It would be impossible now to do it in parts of the country distant from the seat of Government. The choice of electors takes place in November. The result must be ascertained; the electors must meet; their votes must be given; they must be certified to Congress; the count must be made and result declared in Congress before the 4th of March, a period of less than four months. If there should be a contest made in each of the forty-five States, an investigation might be demanded for every election precinct in the country.

It seems to me clear that the power to judge of elections, returns, and qualifications of presidential electors is not given by the Constitution to the two Houses of Congress, or either of them. The power which it was deemed necessary carefully to express in regard to their own members, it could hardly have been intended to bestow by implication from the right to be present when the certificates are opened, or even from the right to count the votes. It is a power which it is utterly impracticable for Congress to exercise between the time when the certificates are brought officially to its knowledge, and the time when it must be determined who has been chosen President. Indeed, the distinguished counsel who closed the case for the Tilden electors[*] conceded this difficulty, to which his only answer was the suggestion that such an inquiry, like the right to

[*] Mr. Charles O'Connor.

the writ of *quo warranto,* must be limited by discretion; in other words, that the two Houses may go as far into the inquiry, who were duly chosen electors in any State, as they in their discretion think fit, or as time will permit.

The statement of this position seems to be its refutation. We are now discussing a question of jurisdiction. In whom is the power to determine who have been appointed electors —in Congress or in the State? It was gravely answered that it is in Congress when the State to be investigated is near the seat of Government, or the inquiry to a few election precincts only, but it is to be left to the State in other cases; that Congress may exert a power of inquiry into an election in Delaware which is impossible as to California, or may inquire into one election district in New York, but cannot into twenty or a hundred. This claim would never have arisen in any man's mind before the days of railroads and telegraphs. Such investigations, possible only to the most limited extent now, would have been wholly impossible as to most of the States when the Constitution was adopted.

It is asked, is there no remedy if the officers to whom the States intrust the power of ascertaining and declaring the result of the election act fraudulently or make mistakes? The answer is that the Constitution of the United States gives no jurisdiction to Congress, when the certificates are opened and the votes are to be counted, to correct such mistakes or frauds. A like question may be put as to every public authority in which a final power of decision is lodged. The danger of mistake or fraud is surely quite as great if the final power be lodged in Congress, and the framers of the Constitution acted in nothing more wisely than in removing from Congress all power over the election of President.

There was never yet a political party in this country, or in England, which decided ordinary election cases, except in the clearest case, on other than party considerations. In England and Canada it has been found necessary to commit to the courts the consideration of election cases. It is seldom that either House of Congress has resisted partisan temptation in election cases, when one seat only was the prize of the contest. Is it likely that public virtue would withstand the temptation of the Presidency?

The simple doctrine on which the Commission proceeded was that the right to determine absolutely and finally who are the duly chosen presidential electors is committed by the Constitution to the States. The judgment of the tribunal established by the State for that purpose is conclusive on all the world. Congress is only to count the votes of the officials found by the State to have the right to cast them.

It is said that in the Oregon case the Commission departed from this principle, which they had acted upon in the case of South Carolina, Florida and Louisiana. But there is not the slightest truth in that suggestion. In all of those three cases the laws of the State had established a tribunal with absolute right to determine all questions arising out of the election. The tribunal had the right to reject votes, or count votes, according as they found the votes to be lawful or unlawful. They had the right to reject returns from election precincts where they found there could have been no lawful or orderly election by reason of violence, or where they found the returns untrustworthy by reason of fraud. This power they exercised, and from it there was no appeal.

On the other hand the laws of Oregon did not provide for a board of State canvassers, but provided that the Secretary of State should canvass the votes in the presence of the Governor, and prepare duplicate lists thereof, which lists should be signed by the Governor and Secretary. These lists, certified by the Secretary, were before the Electoral Commission, and disclosed the choice of Republican electors. The Governor, however, undertook to declare his opinion of the result. That opinion was that a Democrat was chosen who had received less than a majority of the votes, or to use the phrase of the Governor, "received the highest number of votes cast for persons eligible," because his Republican competitor was not eligible; and he, therefore, certified that the Democrat had the largest number of votes cast for persons eligible. That Democratic elector proceeded then to hold a meeting, at which he was the only person present, and as the two Republicans whom everybody admitted were lawfully chosen, did not meet with him, he proceeded to fill two vacancies himself.

The Secretary of State made the canvass required by law, recorded it and filed it in his office. He made that canvass in the presence of the Governor. He could not change it. He could not tamper with it. He had completed his official duty when he had completed it. So that the Governor's certificate as to the effect of the election was of no more official character than a like certificate of the Governor-General of India would have been.

There was no claim or pretence in any quarter that the Republicans did not have a lawful majority of the votes cast for electors in Oregon. The only claim was that one of the electors was postmaster, and that he did not lawfully resign before he was chosen elector. He was postmaster at the time of the election, but resigned a few days after. He was also chosen after he had resigned to fill the vacancy in the Electoral College, if his ineligibility created a vacancy, in regular form according to the laws of Oregon. There was no question or pretence in any quarter that the will of the people of Oregon was not given due effect by the judgment of the Electoral Commission.

I do not believe that there are any considerable number of intelligent persons in the country, now that the excitement of the time has gone by, who doubt that the will of the people of South Carolina and Florida and Louisiana was carried into effect by the judgment of the Commission; and that their judgment baffled an unscrupulous conspiracy to deprive the majorities in those States of their lawful rights in the election because those majorities were made up largely of negroes.

CHAPTER XXVII

FOUR NATIONAL CONVENTIONS

1876

IT has been my fortune to be a delegate from Massachusetts in four National Conventions for the nomination of President and Vice-President—those of 1876, 1880, 1884 and 1888. In the first I was a delegate from the Worcester district, which I then represented in Congress. In the other three I was at the head of the delegation at large. I presided over that of 1880.

The history of these conventions is of great interest. It shows the rudeness of the mechanism by which the Chief Executive of this country is selected, and what apparently slight and trivial matters frequently determine the choice. As is well known, the framers of the Constitution, after considering very seriously the question of entrusting the power of choosing the President to the Senate, determined to commit that function to electoral colleges, chosen in the several States in such manner as their legislatures should determine, all the electors to give their votes on the same day. It is generally stated that the President and Vice-President cannot be from the same State. That is not true. The Constitutional provision is that electors in their respective States shall vote by ballot for President and Vice-President, one of whom, at least, shall not be an inhabitant of the same State with themselves.

It was intended that the choice of the President should not be a direct act of the people. It was to be committed to the discretion of men selected for patriotism, wisdom and sobriety, and removed as far as might be from all the excitements of popular passion.

The Constitution further provides that no Senator or Representative, or person holding an office of trust or profit under the United States, shall be appointed an elector. It was undoubtedly the chief object of this last provision to prevent the perpetuation of power in the same hands, or under the same influences, by removing the choice of President wholly from the control of persons wielding National authority. In a considerable measure this purpose has been defeated. The elector, in practice, is a mere agent or scribe. He records and executes the will of the nominating convention of the party to which he belongs, in which the real power of selection is in fact lodged. In these conventions members of Congress, and holders of National office, take frequently an active and influential share. It is remarkable, however, how often the nominating conventions have discarded the candidates who were favored by the holders of executive office or the two Houses of Congress. And where such candidates have been nominated by the convention of either party, they have often been defeated at the polls. General Harrison, in 1840, was nominated instead of Webster or Clay, who were the leaders of the Whig Party, and doubtless the favorites at Washington. In 1844, when Mr. Clay received the Whig nomination, he was defeated by Mr. Polk, who had, I suppose, hardly been heard of as a candidate in political circles at the Capital. In 1848 the popular feeling again compelled the nomination of a candidate, General Taylor, over the favorite leaders at the Capital. In 1852 Fillmore and Webster were both rejected by the Whigs for General Scott, and General Pierce was summoned from private life for the Democratic nomination. In 1860 Seward was rejected for Lincoln. And in 1876 Hayes, whose National service had consisted of but one term in the House of Representatives, was chosen as the result of a contest in which Blaine, Conkling, Morton and Bristow, distinguished National statesmen, were the defeated competitors. So, in 1880, Garfield, who had not been much thought of in official circles, was selected as the result of a mighty struggle in which Grant and Blaine were the principal champions, and in which Edmunds and Sherman, who had long been prominent in the Senate, were also candidates.

Republican National Conventions since the War of the Rebellion have been embarrassed by another influence, which I hope will disappear. In many of the Southern States the Democratic Party consists almost entirely of whites who have possessed themselves of the forces of government by criminal processes, which have been a reproach not only to this country, but to civilization itself. The Republicans, however numerous, and although having a majority of lawful voters in most of these States, have been excluded from political power. They have however, of course, had their full proportionate representation in the National Conventions of the Republican Party. Their delegates have too often been persons who had no hope for political advancement in their own States, and without the ambition to commend themselves to public favor by honorable public service, of which that hope is the parent. They have been, therefore, frequently either National office-holders who may reasonably be supposed to be under the influence of the existing Administration, or likely to be governed by a hope of receiving a National office as a reward for their action in the convention; or persons who can be influenced in their actions by money. This Southern contingent has been in several of our National Conventions an uncertain and an untrustworthy force.

The Republican nominating convention of 1876 was held at Cincinnati on June 14. The delegates from Massachusetts were:

At Large.—E. R. Hoar, Richard H. Dana, Jr., Paul A. Chadbourne, John M. Forbes.

From Districts.—William T. Davis, Robert T. Davis, John E. Sandford, Edward L. Pierce, Henry D. Hyde, J. Felt Osgood, Alpheus Hardy, C. R. McLean, James M. Shute, James F. Dwinal, George B. Loring, Henry Carter, William A. Russell, C. H. Waters, James Freeman Clarke, James Russell Lowell, A. J. Bartholomew, George F. Hoar, James F. Moore, William Whiting, Edward Learned, S. R. Phillips.

The struggle for the nomination equalled in bitterness and in importance many of the contests between different political parties that had preceded it. While the great majority of the Republicans retained confidence in the personal integrity and patriotism of President Grant, it had become painfully manifest that he was often an easy victim to the influence of unscrupulous and designing men. Grant never lost his hold upon the hearts of the Northern people. Wherever there was a contest in any State for political supremacy the least worthy faction frequently got his ear and his confidence. He never wavered in his attachment to the doctrines of his party—protection, sound principles of finance and currency, honesty in elections. But the old political leaders, whom the people most trusted, were more and more strangers to his presence, and ambitious and designing men, adventurers who had gone South to make fortunes by holding office, men interested in jobs and contracts, thronged the ante-chambers of the White House. The political scandals, always likely to follow a great war, seemed to be increasing rather than diminishing during his second term of office.

I never thought that the proper way to put an end to this state of things was to abandon what I deem sound political principles, or to abandon the party that was formed to establish them. I should as soon have thought of turning Tory because of like complaints in the Revolutionary War, or of asking George III. to take us into favor again because of like scandals which existed during the Administrations of Washington and John Adams. But I thought, in common with many others, that a party of sound principles could be made and should be made a party of pure politics.

The two divisions in the Republican Party, which I have indicated, marshalled their forces for the struggle in the convention of 1876. The friends of Mr. Blaine were generally those Republicans who had been dissatisfied with the conduct of the Administration. They embraced, also, the larger number of the enthusiastic young Republicans, who were attracted by Blaine's brilliant qualities, as were those who had come in contact with him by the marvellous personal charm of his delightful and gracious manners. Roscoe Conkling was regarded as the leader of the other party. The House of Representatives, by an almost unanimous vote, had adopted the resolution declaring that it was contrary to sound principle to elect a President for a third term. So General Grant himself was not a candidate.

But as the time for the convention drew near, there had been an investigation in the House of Representatives into the affairs of the Little Rock and Fort Smith Railroad, which had resulted in some uncomfortable revelations with reference to Mr. Blaine. He was charged with having acquired stocks in railroads which were to be affected by National legislation, either without consideration or for a consideration far below their true value, and of having eagerly sought to acquire other similar stocks, the real consideration which he paid, or expected to pay, being the use of his official influence in behalf of these corporations. This investigation, ordered by the Democratic House of Representatives, was conducted by a majority of the committee charged with it, in a spirit of bitter hostility. The investigation was still in progress when the Republican Convention met. The facts, which were distorted and discolored in public report, impressed many excellent persons unfavorably to Mr. Blaine, and a few with a belief of his guilt. They were used dexterously by his political opponents and by his rivals in his own party, and by some conspicuous persons who had, or thought they had, personal grievances against him, to excite the public mind. On the other hand, as is natural in such cases, the great body of Mr. Blaine's friends clung all the closer to him from a belief that he was the object of unjust and malignant slander.

I did not think it, under the circumstances, wise to nominate Mr. Blaine, either in 1876 or later. I believed then, and now believe, that he would have been an admirable President of the United States. But I did not think it wise to put at the head of a movement for reform and for purity of administration, a man whose supporters must defend him against such charges, and who must admit that he had most unwisely of his own accord put himself into a position where such charges were not only possible, but plausible. But I was exceedingly anxious that a candidate should be found who would be not only agreeable to Mr. Blaine and his supporters, but whom, if possible, they should have a large influence in selecting.

Such a candidate, it was hoped, might be found in Mr. Bristow. He was a great favorite in his own State. He was a man of spotless integrity and great ability. He had been a Union soldier. He was from Kentucky, and his selection as a candidate would remove the charge of sectionalism from the Republican Party, and tend to give it strength with the white people of the South. He had made an admirable Attorney-General, and an admirable Secretary of the Treasury. He had been appointed to the Cabinet by Grant. He had not been long enough in public service to have encountered the enmities which almost always attach themselves to men long in office, and he represented no clique or faction. He was a man of clean hands and of pure heart. For a good while it seemed as if the rival aspirations of Blaine and Bristow might exist without ill-feeling, so that when the time came, the supporters of either might easily give their support to the other, or agree without difficulty in the support of some third person. I gave a banquet at Wormley's in the spring of 1876, which I hoped might have some tendency toward this desired harmony. There were about forty guests. Mr. Blaine sat on my right hand as the guest of honor, and Mr. Bristow on the left. They talked together, as I sat between them, during the whole evening in the most friendly and delightful way, telling humorous anecdotes relating to their own campaigns, as pleasantly as if they had been describing the canvass of some third person whom they were both supporting. I do not believe there was at that time in the heart of either a tinge of anger against the other.

But as the contest went on, Mr. Blaine seems to have become possessed with a belief that the bitter public attacks upon him were instigated by Bristow. Some of the Kentucky papers had been specially bitter. The Republican Convention opened in Cincinnati, Wednesday, June 14.

The Sunday morning before Mr. Blaine fell in a swoon on the steps of the church at the corner of G and Tenth Streets in Washington. He was carried to his house on Fifteenth Street. Bristow was in his office in the Treasury Department when a friend called upon him, and gave him the news of Blaine's attack, and said: "Would it not be well for you to go round and express your interest?" Bristow took his hat, and the two friends went together to Mr. Blaine's house.

An occurrence took place there which satisfied them both that the feeling against Bristow on the part of Mr. Blaine and his near friends was exceedingly strong and implacable. The story was immediately telegraphed in cipher to Mr. Bristow's principal manager at Cincinnati, from whom I had it a day or two before committing it to paper. The facts were communicated by him in confidence to members of the Kentucky delegation.

On the first six ballots the total number of votes cast was 754. Three hundred and seventy-eight were necessary for a choice. Mr. Blaine received votes varying from 285 on the first ballot to 308 on the sixth. On all these ballots, but two, Bristow had the second largest number, ranging from 111 to 126. On the first and second ballot he was led by Morton, who had 124 and 120 votes, and was closely followed by Conkling, whose highest vote was 99. At the end of the sixth ballot it had become manifest that the opponents of Blaine, if they expected to succeed, must unite on a candidate. A portion of the Pennsylvania delegation had already voted for Blaine, who was a native of that State. Others had been held in restraint from voting for him with difficulty, by the influence of Don Cameron, chairman of the delegation and a strong adherent of Grant. The New York Conkling men and the majority of the Pennsylvania delegation, led by Cameron, determined to cast their votes for Hayes, of Ohio, to prevent the nomination of Blaine. In doing that they were to unite with their most earnest antagonists and give their support to a candidate who probably sympathized with them less than any other on the list. It was manifest to the Kentucky delegation that they must make their choice between Blaine and Hayes, and that their choice would decide the nomination. They had a hurried consultation and determined to vote unanimously for Hayes. The going over of Kentucky to Hayes was followed by the other States that had opposed Blaine. Hayes had on the final ballot 384 votes, Blaine 351, and there were 21 cast for Bristow, which had been cast by States standing earlier in alphabetical order on the roll, who had cast their votes before the stampede began. If Kentucky had cast her 24 votes for Blaine, he would have been nominated. I was told by the close friend of Bristow, of whom I have spoken, and I have no doubt he is right, that the Kentucky Republicans had felt very kindly toward Blaine, and their action was determined by the knowledge of the transaction I have just related. They thought that if this bitterness and anger and dislike of Mr. Bristow existed in the mind of Mr. Blaine, it was hardly worth while for Bristow's friends and supporters to clothe him with the Presidential office. If Bristow had not visited Blaine's house that Sunday morning, Blaine would, in my opinion, have been the Republican candidate for the Presidency.

What would have been the result if Mr. Blaine had been nominated in 1876, it is now idle to speculate. I am satisfied, in looking back, that I myself underrated his strength as a candidate. But it seems likely that he would have had the votes of all the States which President Hayes received, and would have been stronger than Hayes in New York.

Mr. Hayes came to the Presidency under circumstances of great difficulty and embarrassment. He was in my judgment one of the wisest, sincerest and most honest and patriotic men who ever held the office.

But President Hayes's Administration was embarrassed by the disputes about his title. The House of Representatives was against him in the first Congress of his term, and in the second Congress the Senate and House were in the hands of his political opponents. He also throughout the whole term had to encounter the hardly disguised hostility of nearly all the great leaders of his own party in both Houses of Congress. Conkling never spoke of him in public or private without a sneer. I suppose he did not visit the White House or any Department during President Hayes's term. Mr. Blaine was much disappointed by President Hayes's refusal to give Mr. Frye a place in the Cabinet, which he desired as a means of composing some incipient jealousies in Maine. Hamlin, who was a very influential Senator, was much disgusted by the President's inclination to reform the civil service. This feeling was largely shared by Simon Cameron, of Pennsylvania, an able and patriotic man, who ruled the Republican Party in that State with a despotic hand, and had as little respect for the doctrines of the civil service reformers as you might expect from one of his Highland ancestors who ruled over the Clan Cameron in the days of the Scotch Stuarts. Cameron had also a personal grievance, although I do not think that made any difference in his feeling. He had been proposed by the Pennsylvania delegation for the appointment to the English Mission. But the proposition had not been received with favor by President Hayes. Under these difficulties, it is greatly to his honor that so much of public good was accomplished in his time, and that he handed over the Government to a Republican successor.

CHAPTER XXVIII

FOUR NATIONAL CONVENTIONS

1880

As the time approached for the Republican Convention of 1880, it had become clear that it would witness a mighty struggle. Conkling, Don Cameron, who had succeeded to his father's power in Pennsylvania, and Logan, of Illinois, the most distinguished volunteer soldier of the war, and a great favorite with his old comrades, were the most conspicuous leaders of the party who desired to restore the old Grant regime. They were seconded by Howe, formerly Senator from Wisconsin and later Postmaster-General under President Arthur, Creswell, of Maryland, Postmaster-General in President Grant's first term, Governor Boutwell, of Massachusetts, who had a very distinguished public career as Governor, member of the House of Representatives, Secretary of the Treasury, and Senator. They selected as their candidate their old chieftain, General Grant. He was strong not only in the powerful support of these great political leaders, but in the solid confidence of the business men of the country, in the attachment of the great Methodist denomination to which he belonged, in the love of the old soldiers, in the memory of his great public service, both in war and peace, and the general respect of the whole American people. Against this was the unwritten, but well-understood, rule of action by which the people had been governed since the time of Washington, that no person should be elected to the office of President for more than two terms. Against him, also, was the feeling that his judgment, which had been sound and unerring in the selection of fit men for good military service, was very much at fault in choosing men in whom he should confide in civil affairs. There was a further feeling that the influence of unworthy politicians, which had been powerful with him during his second term, would be more powerful if he should go back to the Presidency with their aid.

Mr. Blaine's old popularity had been increased in the four years since his former defeat. Many people believed that he had been not only unjustly but cruelly treated, and were eager to record their verdict of acquittal from the malignant charges which had been made against him since 1876. There was a third class, of whom I was one, who felt that it would be unwise to nominate either General Grant or Mr. Blaine. While they had a great respect for the character of Grant, they dreaded the influences which would be sure to surround him, if he should come to the Presidency again. While they had the kindliest feeling for Mr. Blaine and shared the public indignation at the character of the attacks of which he had been the victim, they did not like to have a candidate who would be so handicapped. Mr. Blaine's own imprudence had unquestionably given an opportunity and a plausibility to these slanders. They thought, also, that the nomination of either Grant or Blaine would create a feeling of anger and disappointment in the supporters of the defeated candidate, which would seriously endanger the election. They looked about, therefore, for a person who might not be obnoxious to either the Blaine men or the Grant men, and found such a person in Mr. Edmunds of Vermont. He was a man of ability and long public service. He was not a person calculated to inspire much popular enthusiasm, but answered very well as a standard-bearer, although his supporters were ready to transfer their support to another candidate, other than Blaine or Grant, on whom a majority of the Convention should be brought to unite. Mr. Sherman had also a considerable body of supporters who respected him for his eminent talents and long and valuable services.

General Grant had a peculiarly strong hold on the Republicans of Massachusetts. They shared with all patriotic men throughout the country a profound gratitude for his illustrious military services. They had been impressed by a feeling of great respect for his personal qualities. The modesty which led him to refuse to enter Richmond in triumph at the close of the war; the simplicity of his behavior; the magnanimity which led him to claim so little praise for himself and give so much of the credit to which he was entitled to Sheridan and Sherman, and others of his military associates; his incorruptible personal honesty; his soundness and firmness in dealing with all questions affecting the public credit, the integrity of the currency, and the rights of citizenship, had endeared him to the people of a Commonwealth which ever valued such traits in her public men. The Methodist denomination, always large in Massachusetts and powerful in her Republican councils, was proud that this statesman and warrior was of its fold. As the time for the convention approached, four ex-Governors, men of great personal influence, leaders in the Republican Party, yet of highly different character, who represented very different shades of Republican opinion—Boutwell, Bullock, Claflin and Rice—declared themselves in favor of nominating him again. Nothing could have prevented his carrying Massachusetts as by a great wave, but the fact that he had been, in his second term, subject to a most unworthy influence in the matter of appointments to public office. The whole National executive patronage in Massachusetts seemed given up to advancing the personal fortunes of General Butler. Brave soldiers, honored Republicans, were turned out of post-offices and customhouses, and other high Federal offices, to be replaced by incompetent and dishonorable adventurers, odious in the neighborhoods from which they came, to please this ambitious and unscrupulous man. This excited a deep indignation which culminated when William A. Simmons was made Collector of Boston. No personal respect for General Grant could induce the Massachusetts Republicans to run the risk of having again a President who was subjected to personal influences like these. But for the appointment of Simmons as the principal Federal officer in Massachusetts, I think she would have supported Grant for a third term. The Edmunds movement would never have been made, and his nomination at Chicago would have been certain.

The State Convention passed resolutions in favor of Mr. Edmunds, and elected as Delegates-at-Large, George F. Hoar, Worcester; Charles R. Codman, Boston; John E. Sanford, Taunton; and Julius H. Seelye, Amherst.

The District Delegates were: Charles W. Clifford, New Bedford; Azariah Eldridge, Yarmouth; William C. Lovering, Taunton; F. A. Hobart, Braintree; Phineas Pierce, Boston; Choate Burnham, Boston; Eustice C. Fitz, Chelsea; J. Otis Weatherbee, Boston; Henry Cabot Lodge, Nahant; Daniel Russell, Melrose; Dudley Porter, Haverhill; N. A. Horton, Salem; George S. Boutwell, Groton; George A. Marden, Lowell; R. M. Morse, Jr., Boston; George W. Johnson, Milford; W. S. B. Hopkins, Worcester; William Knowlton, Upton; Alpheus Harding, Athol; Timothy Merrick, Holyoke; Wellington Smith, Lee; M. B. Whitney, Westfield.

Of these, three were in favor of Grant, namely, Boutwell, Eldridge, Marden; two were in favor of Sherman, and one for Washburn.

The others voted for Mr. Edmunds in the beginning, meaning to defeat both Grant and Blaine if they could, and were ready to agree on any man of respectable character and capacity by whom that defeat could be accomplished.

George F. Edmunds had a high reputation in the country as an able lawyer, and a faithful and independent Senator. He had unquestionably rendered great public service in the Senate. If elected, I believe he would have administered the Presidency on the principles which a large majority of the people of Massachusetts held. He was an excellent debater He was very fond of criticising and objecting to what was proposed by other men. He seemed never so happy as when in opposition to the majority of his associates. But he possessed what persons of that temper commonly lack, great capacity for constructive statesmanship. Any measure of which he was the author would be likely to accomplish its purpose, and to stand fire.

David Davis, who was President pro tempore of the Senate, used to say he could always compel Edmunds to vote in the negative on any question by putting the question in the old New England fashion, "Contrary-minded will say no," for Edmunds was always contrary-minded. I once told him, borrowing a saying of an Englishman, that if George Edmunds were the only man in the world, George would object to everything Edmunds proposed.

The morning after the Massachusetts Convention of 1880, when the convention passed resolutions, proposing Edmunds as a candidate for the Presidency, and placing me first on the delegation at large, Edmunds came to me and said, I have no doubt with absolute sincerity: "I have seen the proceedings of your convention yesterday. If I know myself, I have no desire to be President of the United States. I do not think I am fit for it, and if I were, I should much prefer my present service as Senator. I would say so in a public letter, but I suppose the chances of my nomination are so slight that it might seem ridiculous to decline." I said: "But, Edmunds, just think of the fun you would have vetoing bills." He smiled, and his countenance beamed all over with satisfaction at the idea, and he replied, with great feeling: "Well, that would be good fun."

So while, as I have said, the Massachusetts delegates, most of them, supported Mr. Edmunds as a person likely to hold some votes until the opposition to Grant might be concentrated on some other candidate to be agreed on as the proceedings of the convention went on, and while I think he would have made an excellent President if he had been chosen, his candidacy was never a very strong one.

This convention was menaced by a very serious peril. A plan was devised which, if it had been successful, would, in my judgment, have caused a rupture in the convention and the defeat of the Republican Party in the election. The Chairman of the Republican National Committee was Don Cameron of Pennsylvania, then and for some years afterward a Senator of the United States from that State. He was an ardent supporter of President Grant and had been Secretary of War in his Cabinet, as his father had been in the Cabinet of President Lincoln. Like his father before him, he had ruled the Republican Party of Pennsylvania with a strong hand. He was not given to much speaking. He was an admirable executive officer, self-reliant, powerful, courageous and enterprising, with little respect for the discontent of subordinates. He was supported by a majority of the delegates from Pennsylvania, although Blaine, who was a native of that State, had a large following there. The New York delegation was headed by Roscoe Conkling, who had great influence over Grant when he was President, and expected to retain that influence if he became President again. The Maryland delegation was headed by J. A. J. Creswell, who had been Postmaster-General more than five years in Grant's two Administrations. On the Massachusetts delegation, as I have said, was Governor Boutwell, Grant's Secretary of the Treasury during nearly the whole of his first term, and on that from Illinois John A. Logan. These men had a large following over the whole country. There were three hundred and eight persons in the convention who could be counted on to support Grant from beginning to end, and about a dozen more were exceedingly disposed to his candidacy. The State Conventions of the three largest and most powerful States, New York, Pennsylvania and Illinois, and possibly one or two others, that I do not now remember, had instructed their delegates to vote as a unit for the candidate who should be agreed upon by the majority. Grant had a majority in each of these States. But there was a minority of 18 in Illinois, 26 in Pennsylvania, and 19 in New York, who were for other candidates than Grant. If their votes had been counted for him it would have given Grant on the first ballot 367 votes, 13 less than the number necessary for a choice. As his votes went up on one of the ballots to 313, it is pretty certain that counting these 63 votes for Grant would have insured his nomination. But there were several contests involving the title of their seats of 16 delegates from the State of Louisiana, 18 from Illinois, and three others. In regard to these cases the delegates voted in accordance with their preference for candidates. This was beside several other contests where the vote was not determined by that consideration. Now if the vote of Illinois, Pennsylvania and New York had each been cast as a unit, in accordance with the preference of the majority of the delegation in each case, these 37 votes would have been added to Grant's column and subtracted from the forces of his various antagonists; and the 63 votes of the minority of the delegations in these three States would also have been added to the Grant column, which would have given him a total vote of more than 400, enough to secure his nomination. So the result of the convention was to be determined by the adoption or rejection of what was called the unit rule.

Don Cameron, the Chairman of the National Committee, left the Senate for Chicago about ten days, I think, before the day fixed for the meeting of the convention. It was whispered about before his departure that a scheme had been resolved upon by him and the other Grant leaders, which would compel the adoption of the unit rule, whatever might be the desire of the convention itself. It was his duty, according to established custom, to call the convention to order and to receive nominations for temporary presiding officer. He was pledged, upon those nominations, as it was understood, to hold that the unit rule must be applied. In that way the sitting members from the disputed States and districts would be permitted to vote, and the votes of the three States would be cast without dissent for the Grant candidate. When the temporary President took his place he would rule in the same way on the question of the choice of a permanent President, and the permanent President would rule in the same way on the conflicting votes, for the appointment of committees, for determining the seats of delegates, and finally the nomination of the candidates for President and Vice-President. If the minority claimed the right to vote and took an appeal from his decision, he was to hold that on the vote on that appeal the same unit rule was to apply. If a second point of order were raised, he would hold, of course, that a second point of order could not be raised while the first was pending.

So the way seemed clear to exclude the contesting delegates, to cast the votes of the three great States solid for Grant, and compel his nomination.

But the majority of the National Committee, of which Cameron was Chairman, was opposed to Grant. They met, I think, the day before the meeting of the convention to make the preliminary arrangements. Mr. Cameron, the Chairman, was asked whether it was his purpose to carry out the scheme I have indicated. He refused to answer. A motion was then made that the Chairman, after calling the convention to order, be instructed to receive the vote of the individual delegates without regard to the instruction of the majority of their delegation. Cameron refused to receive motions on that question, saying that it was a matter beyond the jurisdiction of the committee. A large part of the entire day was spent in various attempts to induce Cameron either to give a pledge or permit a resolution to be entertained by the committee, instructing him as to his action. He was supported by Mr. Gorham, of California, who I believe was not a member of the committee, but was present either as Secretary or as *Amicus Curiæ*. He was an experienced parliamentarian, and for a long time had been Secretary of the Senate of the United States. The discussion for the majority was conducted largely by Mr. Chandler, of New Hampshire, afterward Secretary of the Navy, and later Senator. After spending a large part of the day in that discussion, some time in the afternoon an intimation was made, informally, and in a rather veiled fashion, that, unless they had more satisfactory pledges from Mr. Cameron, he would be removed from the office of Chairman, and a person who would carry out the wishes of the committee be substituted. The committee then adjourned until the next morning. Meantime the Grant managers applied to Colonel Strong, of Illinois, who had been already appointed Sergeant-at-Arms by the committee, and who was a supporter of Grant, to ascertain whether, if the committee were to remove Cameron and appoint another chairman, he would recognize him as a person entitled to call the convention to order and preside until a temporary

Chairman was chosen, and would execute his lawful orders, or whether he would treat them as without effect and would execute the orders of Cameron. He desired time for consideration, which was conceded. He consulted Senator Philetus Sawyer of Wisconsin, who was himself in favor of General Grant, but who desired above all things the success of the Republican Party, and was not ready for any unlawful or revolutionary action. Mr. Sawyer was a business man of plain manners, and though of large experience in public life, was not much versed in parliamentary law. He called into consultation ex-Senator Timothy O. Howe, of Wisconsin, formerly Senator from that State, and afterward Postmaster-General under Arthur. He was a very able and clear-headed lawyer, and had a high reputation for integrity. He advised Mr. Strong that the committee might lawfully depose their Chairman and appoint another, and that it would be his duty, as Sergeant-at-Arms, to recognize the new Chairman and obey his lawful orders. Strong was under great obligations to Sawyer, who had aided him very largely in business matters, and had a high respect for his judgment. He gave his response to the Grant leaders in accordance with the advice of Mr. Howe, in which Senator Sawyer concurred. They had intended to make General Creswell the President of the convention. But finding it impossible to carry their plans into effect, in order to prevent the severe measure of deposing the Chairman of the committee, they consented that the assurances demanded should be given. There was then a negotiation between the leaders on the side of Grant and of Blaine for an agreement upon a presiding officer. It was well known that I was not in favor of the nomination of either. Senator Hamlin, formerly Vice-President and then a Senator, proposed my name to Mr. Conkling as a person likely to be impartial between the two principal candidates. Mr. Conkling replied that such a suggestion was an insult. Hamlin said: "I guess I can stand the insult." But on consultation of the Grant men and the Blaine men it was agreed that I should be selected, which was done accordingly. I was nominated orally from the floor when Mr. Cameron called the convention to order, and chosen temporary President by acclamation and unanimously. As proceedings went on it was thought best not to have any division or question as to a permanent Chairman and it was at the proper time ordered, also without objection, that I should act as permanent President.

But the Grant leaders were still confident. They felt sure that none of their original votes, numbering three hundred and more, would desert them, and that it would be impossible for the rest of the convention, divided among so many candidates, to agree, and that they would in the end get a majority.

I was myself exceedingly anxious on this subject. I also felt that if the followers of Grant could get any pretext for getting an advantage by any claim, however doubtful, that they would avail themselves of it, even at the risk of breaking up the convention in disorder, rather than be baffled in their object. So the time to me was one of great and distressing responsibility. The forces of Grant were led on the floor of the convention by Roscoe Conkling, who nominated him in a speech of great power and eloquence. The forces of Blaine were led, as they had been in 1876, very skilfully by Senators Hale and Frye. Garfield was the leader of the supporters of Mr. Sherman. One of the greatest oratoric triumphs I ever witnessed was obtained by Garfield. There had been a storm of applause, lasting, I think, twenty-five minutes, at the close of Conkling's nominating speech. It was said there were fifteen thousand persons in the galleries, which came down very near the level of the floor. The scene was of indescribable sublimity. The fate of the country, certainly the fate of a great political party, was at stake, and, more than that, the selection of the ruler of a nation of fifty millions of people —a question which in other countries could not have been determined, under like circumstances, without bloodshed or civil war. I do not think I shall be charged with exaggeration when I speak of it in this way. I can only compare it in its grandeur and impressiveness to the mighty torrent of Niagara. Perhaps I cannot give a satisfactory reason for so distinguishing it from other like assemblies that have gathered in this country. But I have since seen a great number of persons from all parts of the country who were present as members or spectators, and they all speak of it in the same way. A vast portion of the persons present in the hall sympathized deeply with the supporters of Grant. Conkling's speech, as he stood almost in the centre of that great assembly on a platform just above the heads of the convention, was a masterpiece of splendid oratory. He began:

> And when asked what State he hails from,
> Our sole reply shall be,
> He comes from Appomattox,
> And its famous apple-tree.

It was pretty difficult for Garfield to follow this speech in the tempest of applause which came after it. There was nothing stimulant or romantic in the plain wisdom of John Sherman. It was like reading a passage from "Poor Richard's Almanac" after one of the lofty chapters of the Psalms of David. Garfield began, quietly:

"I have witnessed the extraordinary scene of this convention with deep solicitude. Nothing touches my heart more quickly than a tribute of honor to a great and noble character. But as I sat in my seat and witnessed this demonstration, this assemblage seemed to me a human ocean in a tempest. I have seen the sea lashed into fury and tossed into spray, and its grandeur moves the soul of the dullest man; but I remember that it is not the billows, but the calm level of the sea from which all heights and depths are measured. When the storm has passed and the hour of calm settles on the ocean, when the sunlight bathes its peaceful surface, then the astronomer and surveyor take the level from which they measure all terrestrial heights and depths.

"Gentlemen of the Convention, your present temper may not mark the healthful pulse of our people. When your enthusiasm has passed, when the emotions of the hour have subsided, we shall find below this storm and passion that calm level of public opinion from which the thoughts of a mighty people are to be measured, and by which their final action will be determined.

"Not here, in this brilliant circle where fifteen thousand men and women are gathered, is the destiny of the Republic to be decreed for the next four years—not here, where I see the enthusiastic faces of seven hundred and fifty-six delegates, waiting to cast their lot into the urn and determine the choice of the Republic; but by four millions of Republican firesides, where the thoughtful voters, with wives and children about them, with the calm thoughts inspired by love of home and country, with the history of the past, the hopes of the future, and reverence for the great men who have adorned and blessed our nation in days gone by, burning in their hearts—*there* God prepares the verdict which will determine the wisdom of our work to-night. Not in Chicago, in the heat of June, but at the ballot-boxes of the Republic, in the quiet of November, after the silence of deliberate judgment, will this question be settled."

Conkling, while exciting the admiration of all men for his dexterity and ability, lost ground at every step. He made a foolish attempt to compel the passage of a resolution depriving of their rights to vote delegates who refused to pledge themselves to support the choice of the convention whoever it might be. His speech nominating Grant contained a sneer at Blaine. So, while he held his forces together to the last, he made it almost impossible for any man who differed from him in the beginning to come to him at the end. On the contrary everything that Garfield said was marked by good nature and good sense. I said on the first day of the convention that in my opinion if the delegates could be shut up by themselves and not permitted to leave the room until they agreed, the man on whom they would agree would be General Garfield. This desire became more and more apparent as the convention went on. At last, on the thirty-sixth ballot, and the sixth day of the convention, the delegates who had previously voted for other candidates than Grant, began to wheel into line for Garfield. Garfield had one vote from the State of Pennsylvania in previous ballots. But on the thirty-fourth ballot Wisconsin, the last State to vote in alphabetical order, had given him her sixteen votes, and on the thirty-sixth ballot she was joined by the delegates who had voted for other candidates than Grant. Grant held together his forces till the last, receiving three hundred and thirteen votes on the thirty-fifth ballot, and three hundred and six on the thirty-sixth. It was a sublime moment, which it was hoped would determine the destiny of the Republic for many years, a hope which was cruelly disappointed by Garfield's untimely death. It was, as might be well believed, a moment of sublime satisfaction to me. Garfield had been my friend for many years. I had sat close to him in the House of Representatives for three terms of Congressional service. He had been my guest at my house in Worcester; and I had been his colleague on the Electoral Commission in 1876. He had been educated at a Massachusetts college. He was of old Middlesex County stock. We were in thorough accord in our love for New England, our firm faith in her hereditary principles, and our pride in her noble history.

Garfield has been charged, in accepting the nomination for the Presidency, with having been untrue to the interests of John Sherman, who was the candidate of Ohio, and whom Garfield had supported faithfully through every ballot. The charge is absolutely unjust. Mr. Sherman's nomination was seen by everybody to have been absolutely impossible long before the final result. I was in constant consultation with leaders of the different delegations who were trying to unite their forces. There never was any considerable number of those persons who thought the nomination of Mr. Sherman practicable, notwithstanding the high personal respect in which they held him. At the close of the thirty-fourth ballot, when Garfield received seventeen votes, he rose, and the following incident took place:

Mr. Garfield, of Ohio: "Mr. President ————"

The President: "For what purpose does the gentleman rise?"

Mr. Garfield: "I rise to a question of order."

The President: "The gentleman from Ohio rises to a question of order."

Mr. Garfield: "I challenge the correctness of the announcement. The announcement contains votes for me. No man has a right, without the consent of the person voted for, to announce that person's name, and vote for him, in this convention. Such consent I have not given."

The President: "The gentleman from Ohio is not stating a question of order. He will resume his seat. No person having received a majority of the votes cast, another ballot will be taken. The Clerk will call the roll."

This verbatim report is absolutely correct, except that where there is a period at the end of Mr. Garfield's last sentence there should be a dash, indicating that the sentence was not finished. I recollect the incident perfectly. I interrupted him in the middle of his sentence. I was terribly afraid that he would say something that would make his nomination impossible, or his acceptance impossible, if it were made. I do not believe it ever happened before that anybody who attempted to decline the Presidency of the United States was to be prevented by a point of order, or that such a thing will ever happen again.

During the thirtieth ballot a vote was cast by a delegate from the Territory of Wyoming for General Philip H. Sheridan. General Sheridan, who was upon the platform as a spectator, came forward instantly, and said: "I am very much obliged to the delegate from Wyoming for mentioning my name in this convention, but there is no way in which I could accept a nomination from this convention, if it were possible, unless I should be permitted to turn it over to my best friend." The President said: "The Chair presumed the unanimous consent of the convention to permit the illustrious soldier who has spoken to interrupt its order for that purpose. But it will be a privilege accorded to no other person whatever." The General's prompt suppression of this attempt to make him a candidate was done in a direct and blunt soldierly fashion. I did not think it best to apply to him the strictness of parliamentary law; and in that I was sure of the approval of the convention. But the precedent of permitting such a body to be addressed under any circumstances by a person not a member would be a dangerous one, if repeated. Perhaps I may with propriety add one thing of personal nature. It has been sometimes charged that the delegates from Massachusetts were without great influence in shaping the result of this convention. They moved, and carried, against a formidable opposition, the civil service plank, which embodied the doctrine of civil service reform as among the doctrines of the Republican Party. Of whatever value may be attributed to the humble services of the President of the Convention, they are entitled to the credit. They had, I think, more to do than any other delegation with effecting the union upon Garfield. Of course the wishes of Mr. Blaine had very great influence indeed. I think he preferred Garfield to any other person except Robert Lincoln, of Illinois, of whom he spoke to me as a person from whom it would be impossible to keep the votes of the colored delegates from the South, and who would be, by reason of the respect felt for his father's memory, highly acceptable through the country. But Mr. Lincoln, under the circumstances, could not have got the support of his own State, and without it it seemed unwise to attempt a union upon him.

But to continue with what is personal to myself and the delegation from Massachusetts. When I got back to the Capitol, as I went into the cloak-room of the Senate to leave my hat, Don Cameron sat there surrounded by a group of interested listeners. He was relating to them the story of the great contest. As I approached the group he looked up and said:

"There comes Massachusetts. There were twenty-three men from Massachusetts who went there to keep six hundred men from doing what they wanted to. And, by God, they did it."

A few Sundays after his inauguration, during the spring session of the Senate, President Garfield invited Mrs. Hoar and myself to dinner at the White House. President Hopkins, his old friend and teacher, and Mrs. Hopkins were there. There were no other guests, except Judge Nott and his wife, President Hopkins's daughter, President Garfield's mother, and, I think, Mr. Archibald Hopkins, President Hopkins's son. President Garfield asked me to remain after President Hopkins had taken his leave. I had a long and interesting conversation with him about his plans and purposes, and especially the difficulties which were then showing themselves in regard to the great New York appointments. Before I went upstairs, he gave his arm to my wife and walked with her about the East room. He said to her: "I hope I may live to repay your husband for all he has done for me." Perhaps I am indulging in an unpardonable vanity in relating this testimony of two of the most interested parties and most competent observers as to the value of the work of the Massachusetts delegation in that convention.

I hope that somewhere before I die I may put on record my estimate of James A. Garfield, when I can say some things which ought to be said, and for which there is not room in this book and was not room in the eulogy delivered just after his death. It is the fashion, even among his friends, to speak of him as a person timid if not time-serving, and as easily swayed and moulded by a strong will. I have heard men who knew him very well say that when he led the House on the Republican side, and had led his party into a position which excited sharp conflict, they never could be sure that he would not get wrong at the last moment, or have some private understanding with the Democrats and leave his own side in the lurch. This was attributed to moral timidity. I feel very sure that this is a great mistake. Garfield's hesitation, want of certainty in his convictions, liability to change his position suddenly, were in my opinion the result of intellectual hesitation and of a habit of going down to the roots of his subject before he made up his mind. He had a great deference for other men's opinions. When, after he had expressed his opinion, some strong and positive man came to him with a confident utterance of a different opinion, unless Garfield had gone to the bottom of the subject himself, he was very likely to defer, to hesitate, to think himself mistaken. But when he had had time and had thought the thing out and made up his mind, nobody and no consideration of personal interest or advantage would stir him an inch. I suppose his courage and genius as a soldier have never been questioned. He performed some very important military exploits. He gave a thorough investigation into the military conditions of Tennessee and Kentucky, and his letter to the Department of War accomplished a great deal toward putting things in a better way. He was a thorough lover of his country. He hesitated long as to the doctrine of protection, and undoubtedly made some inconsistent utterances before he took the ground which he held at last. But he studied the financial question, especially the great subjects of currency and the standard of value, to the very bottom. He stood like a rock when Ohio and the whole West seemed going against him, and when the statesmanship even of John Sherman was of the willow and not of the oak. When his District Convention met and passed resolutions in favor of paying interest on the Government bonds with paper, Garfield declared that he would not take the nomination on such a platform. The good fight he made in Ohio turned the scale in that great struggle. I do not believe he would have been a tool or servant in the Presidency. He would have mastered for himself the great subjects to be dealt with in our foreign policy, as well as in domestic administration and legislation. His will would, in my opinion, if he had been spared to us, have been the dominant will in our Government for eight fortunate and happy years. Next to the assassination of Lincoln, his death was the greatest national misfortune ever caused to this country by the loss of a single life.

I have not the slightest respect for the suggestion that General Garfield in the least violated his honor or good faith in consenting to accept the nomination after he had been elected as a delegate in the interest of Mr. Sherman.

FOUR NATIONAL CONVENTIONS

The office of the President is not personal. There can be no such thing as a personal claim upon it, or a personal obligation in regard to it. President Garfield got no advantage whatever from the fact that he had favored Mr. Sherman. Mr. Sherman's nomination was an impossibility from the beginning. That the majority of the convention united upon Garfield was due to the fact that he had no enemies or antagonists in the convention or among the people and, to some degree undoubtedly, also to the admiration felt by his fellow-delegates for the tact, sense and good nature which he showed in its discussions—qualities which were in marked contrast with those of his very able and powerful antagonist, Mr. Conkling.

Beside, when the voting for Garfield in the Convention began, a dispatch was received from Mr. Sherman urging his friends to unite in Garfield's support. That was before Garfield had taken any action, except an earnest attempt to decline the nomination which, as I have already stated, was suppressed by a peremptory exercise of the authority of the chair.

I have given more than once my estimate of James A. Garfield, although not as fully as I should like. Shortly after his death I delivered a eulogy before the people of Worcester at the request of the City Government. I was asked by John Sherman, who more than anybody else had the matter in charge, to deliver the eulogy before the two Houses of Congress. But Mr. Sherman had spoken without due authority. The Committee of the two Houses determined to invite Mr. Blaine, then Secretary of State. That arrangement was required by every consideration of propriety, and was in all respects the best possible. Mr. Blaine's address on Garfield is one of the treasures of our literature. It would have been a great public misfortune if that noble oration had been lost to the world.

I knew Garfield very intimately. For six of the eight years I served in the House with him my seat was so near his that we could converse with each other in whispers. By a singular chapter of accidents our families had been closely associated in several generations, although neither of us knew it until long after our friendship began.

The land of Captain John Sherman and the land of Captain John Prescott, both my ancestors on the mother's side, adjoined the land of Edward Garfield, the ancestor of the President, in Watertown. His land lay on both sides of what is now the line between Waltham and Watertown. Captain Benjamin Garfield, who may be properly called the founder of Waltham, was the leader of an earnest and protracted controversy in Watertown in which my great-great-grandfather, Joseph Sherman, was leader on the other side.

Lieutenant Thomas Garfield, another of the President's ancestors in the direct line, built a house in that part of Watertown, afterward Weston, which later still was incorporated with parts of Concord and Lexington as the town of Lincoln. He and his son Thomas were among the first incorporators, of whom my great-grandfather, John Hoar, was also one. Thomas Garfield built a house now standing at the end of a grass-grown lane about forty rods from the high road leading from Lincoln to Waltham and about two miles south from the centre of Lincoln. It is a secluded spot of great beauty. The house, a square, unpainted, two-story house with a great chimney in the middle, stands surrounded by old elms and apple trees, in a tract of fertile meadow, with the Lincoln hill in the distance. This estate passed from Lieutenant Thomas Garfield to his son Thomas, Jr., from him to his daughter Rebecca, wife of David Fiske, from her to her son Elijah Fiske, and from him to his children. One of these children married my cousin. I attended the wedding in my boyhood in the old Garfield house.

Abram Garfield, son of the second Thomas, the President's great-uncle, from whom his middle name came to him, was a soldier at Concord Bridge on the 19th of April, 1775, in the Lincoln Company of which my grandfather, Samuel Hoar, was Lieutenant and my two great-grandfathers served as privates. The depositions of Abram Garfield and John Hoar as to the facts of the Concord fight were taken with others by the patriots and sent to England for their vindication. This Abram Garfield died in the summer of 1775, a few months after the battle at Concord. His grave, with that of his father and grandfather, the President's direct ancestors, is close to the graves of my own ancestors in the Lincoln burial-ground.

The President's great-grandfather settled in Westminster. His land was close by the land of my wife's great-grandfather, and not far from the spot where her father was born. His house is still standing in Westminster. My grandfather's uncle, Daniel Hoar, was one of the founders of that town and owned land not far off.

So our friendship came by lawful inheritance. I discovered myself many of these facts relating to his ancestry which had been previously unknown to him. I have from him a letter written the day before he was assassinated in which he promises after visiting Williams College and the White Mountains to meet me at Concord and to spend the night with my brother there and visit the dwelling and burial places of his ancestors in Lincoln and then to come to Worcester as my guest.

James A. Garfield was a man of indefatigable industry and vast information. He seemed constantly possessed by an intelligent curiosity in regard to all subjects. He had a tenacious memory. Its stores were always ready at hand for his use on all occasions. There has been no man in public life in my time, except Charles Sumner, who was always so glad to render any service in his power to literature and science. He was a great friend of the Congressional Library, and helped largely to increase its appropriations. I got his powerful aid in procuring the purchase of the Margry papers, at the instance of Parkman, the historian.

During Garfield's service in the House he was the leader of its best thought. Everything he did and said manifested the serious, reverent love of excellence. He was ever grave, earnest, addressing himself only to the reason and conscience of his auditors. You will search his speeches in vain for an appeal to a base motive or an evil passion. He was remarkably independent in forming his judgments and inflexible in adhering to them on all great and essential questions. His friend and Commander, General Thomas, whose stubborn courage saved the day in the battle for the possession of Tennessee, was well called The Rock of Chickamauga. In the greater battle in 1876 for the Nation's honor Garfield well deserves to be called The Rock of Ohio. There has been hardly any single service to this country in recent times greater than that rendered by him when he stood against the fiat money movement in Ohio.

CHAPTER XXIX

FOUR NATIONAL CONVENTIONS

1884

It happened to me again to be put at the head of the Massachusetts delegation in the convention of 1884. The leading candidates were Mr. Blaine and President Arthur. Mr. Arthur had, in many respects, made a very satisfactory President. He was a man of pleasant manners and skilled in the subtle ways of New York politicians. He had been one of the chief representatives of a faction in the Republican Party, and he never seemed able to shake off the influences which had surrounded him before his election. At a dinner shortly after he was chosen Vice-President, he made an apparently approving allusion to what he called the use of soap, which was understood to mean the use of money for corrupt purposes. He made a fatal mistake, as it always seemed to me, in permitting the resignation of President Garfield's Cabinet and filling their places with men who, like himself, belonged to the Grant faction. If he had said that he would not allow the act of an assassin to make a change in the forces that were to control the Administration so far as could be helped and that he would carry into effect the purposes of his predecessor, wherever he could in conscience do so, he would have maintained himself in the public esteem. But that was not his only mistake. Inconsiderately he lent himself to the popular prejudice against the policy of river and harbor improvements, and, in vetoing a bill passed by large majorities in both Houses of Congress, he sent in a message in which he said in substance that the more corrupt the measure the more votes it was likely to get in Congress. When in the next winter he was asked to specify the objectionable items in the bill he had vetoed, which appropriated about $18,000,000, he was able to point out less than five per cent. of all the appropriations which he could say he thought were for purposes not required by the interests of international or interstate commerce. And his claim was thoroughly refuted even in regard to the items which he specified. He also made some very bad appointments, which deeply offended the best Republican sentiment in many of the States. It is a little singular that the appointment of the Collector of the Port of Boston should have cost two Presidents of the United States a renomination. Yet so it is. The old feeling in Massachusetts that it was not, on the whole, desirable to nominate Mr. Blaine existed in great strength. The business men liked Arthur. They thought their interests were safe with him. But the honest Republican sentiment of Massachusetts was deeply outraged by the appointment to the office of Collector of Boston, of Mr. Roland Worthington, against the protest of her Senators and Representatives in Congress. He had been known only as an unscrupulous supporter of General Butler, and as the editor of a scurrilous newspaper which bitterly attacked the opponents of that person even where they were honest and trusted Republicans. To give this place to Mr. Worthington the President refused to reappoint Mr. Beard, who had made an admirable Collector, and who was supported by a large majority of the best men of Boston. It was believed that this appointment had been made in exchange for assurances of General Butler's support in the approaching election. Worthington made a poor Collector, and, at the State election after his appointment, voted for Butler against the candidate of the Republican Party. But for the indignation caused by this appointment, I think the delegation from Massachusetts, with three exceptions, would have supported Mr. Arthur for reelection. There would have been no movement for Mr. Edmunds, and but for that movement Mr. Arthur would have received the Republican nomination. Upon the final ballot the vote of Massachusetts was seven for Arthur, three for Blaine and eighteen for Edmunds.

A somewhat interesting incident occurred which shows the depth of a feeling, which I think was largely a prejudice, which is still manifesting itself as a disturbing element in American politics. There was a great desire on the part of those who were opposed to both Arthur and Blaine, to find a candidate upon whom they could unite, of such popularity and national distinction as to make it impossible for the managers for these candidates to hold their forces together. We thought that General Sherman was the person that we wanted. It was known that he had written a letter to Mr. Blaine declining to have his name used, and that a telegram had been received from him by a delegate during the session of the convention to the same effect. But it was thought that if he were once nominated he would find it impossible to decline, and that his previous refusal would be an element of strength and not of weakness in the country. After the adjournment, which was at 11:45 A. M., on Friday, June 6, the day before the balloting, I made an arrangement to meet Mr. George William Curtis, the Chairman of the New York delegation, and one or two other gentlemen of the same way of thinking, from one or two other States, and we agreed that when the convention came in again we would cast the votes of our delegates who agreed with us for General Sherman. I had been authorized by a large majority of the Massachusetts delegation to have this interview, and I knew that I represented their opinions, although they had not, all of them, spoken to me about General Sherman. When I got back to the next meeting of the convention, I made known to them what I had done. I was told by several of them that they would stand by me, but that it would cause great dissatisfaction when they got home.

"What is the matter?" I said. "Our people do not want a Father Confessor in the White House," was the answer. Although General Sherman was a Protestant, it is well known that his wife was a Catholic. Soon after, Mr. Curtis came over to my seat and said: "Mr. Hoar, I cannot carry out our agreement." "What is the matter?" said I. "There is an insurrection in the New York delegation," was his reply. "They do not want a Father Confessor in the White House." So we agreed we should have to give it up. When I came back to Washington, I called at John Sherman's house and talked over the convention with him. I told him the story I have just related. He said he was not surprised, and that he believed the unwillingness to have the religious faith of his wife made matter of public discussion had a good deal to do with his brother's refusal to permit himself to be a candidate.

While the convention of 1884 did not nominate the candidate favored by the Republicans of Massachusetts, the action of the State, in my opinion, was decisive in defeating the nomination of President Arthur. But for that there would have been no movement for Edmunds, and his support would have gone to the President. Mr. Blaine, who was nominated, was defeated at the election. The event proved him a much stronger candidate than I had supposed, and his subsequent career in the Department of State, I believe, satisfied a majority of his countrymen that he would have made an able and discreet President. I suppose it would hardly be denied now by persons acquainted with the details of the management of the Democratic campaign, at any rate I have heard the fact admitted by several very distinguished Democrats, members of the Senate of the United States, that the plurality of the vote of New York was really cast for Mr. Blaine, and that he was unjustly deprived of election by the fraud at Long Island City by which votes cast for the Butler Electoral Ticket were counted for Cleveland. I suppose also that but for the utterances of a foolish clergyman named Burchard, Mr. Blaine's majority in that State would have been so large that these frauds would have been ineffectual.

CHAPTER XXX

FOUR NATIONAL CONVENTIONS

1888

IN 1888 there was a very strong, almost irresistible feeling among Republicans in the country that Blaine should be put in nomination again, although he had peremptorily and publicly refused to be a candidate. He was travelling abroad during that year. His mental vigor was unabated, as was shown by his answer to Cleveland's free trade message, which was cabled across the ocean and reached the people almost as soon as the message. But the disease of which he afterward died was then upon him, as was known to some few of his intimate friends. Besides that, he had had an attack at Milan, which deprived him for a good while of the use of his limbs on one side. In 1892 I was in the care, at Milan, of a man who I suppose was the most eminent physician in the north of Italy, Dr. Fornoni, who gave me an account of Mr. Blaine's illness in the very apartments where I was ill, and which Blaine had occupied before me. But when the convention came together they were so eager to nominate Blaine that he was obliged to send another cable, I think, from Paris, insisting that his wishes should be respected. There was a great diversity of opinion as to candidates, but little of the eager antagonism that had characterized the preceding conventions. The Republican Party had been sobered a good deal by four years of adversity. The delegates from Massachusetts were:

At Large.—George F. Hoar, Worcester; Henry S. Hyde, West Springfield; Frederick L. Burden, North Attleboro; Alanson W. Beard, Boston.

District.—Frank S. Stevens, Swansea; Jonathan Bourne, New Bedford; William H. Bent, Taunton; Eben L. Ripley,

Hingham; Arthur W. Tufts, Boston; Edward P. Wilbur, Boston; Jesse M. Gove, Boston; Charles J. Noyes, Boston; Edward D. Hayden, Woburn; Elmer H. Capen, Somerville; William B. Littlefield, Lynn; Samuel W. McCall, Winchester; William Cogswell, Salem; William E. Blunt, Haverhill; Joseph L. Sargent, Dracut; George S. Merrill, Lawrence; J. Henry Gould, Medford; David Farquhar, Newton; William A. Gile, Worcester; George L. Gibbs, Northbridge; John W. Wheeler, Orange; John G. Mackintosh, Holyoke; Emerson Gaylord, Chicopee; and William M. Prince, Pittsfield.

I was very desirous that the vote of Massachusetts should be given to John Sherman. He was, except Mr. Blaine, unquestionably the most distinguished living Republican statesman. He had been an able champion of the opinions which the Republicans of Massachusetts held, and of the policies under which her special industries had been fostered. To nominate him would be to go back to the early habit of placing the greatest and wisest statesmen of the country in its highest offices. But I could not get the majority of the Massachusetts delegation to come to my way of thinking. General Coggswell, a very able and accomplished member of the House of Representatives, and Mr. Edward D. Hayden, also a member of the House—a service which he left greatly to the regret of his own constituents and the people of the State—seemed to have very strong objections indeed to Mr. Sherman. The delegation very kindly offered before the first ballot, and again just before the fourth or fifth ballot, to present my name as the candidate of Massachusetts. It would have been a very great honor to have received such a vote from Massachusetts. I was told also by gentlemen from other States, who spoke to me about it, that I should have had a considerable vote from other parts of the country. I had quite a number of very intimate friends in the convention from States outside of Massachusetts. I thought then, and think now, though that is a matter of conjecture, that I should have got about seventy votes. But I thought my nomination out of the question. I thought also that it would be utterly inexpedient, if it could be accomplished. And I thought also that the office of a Senator from Massachusetts would be more agreeable to me, and better adapted to my capacity than that of the President of the United States. Still the temptation to get the high compliment and honor of such a vote was very strong indeed. But there were thirteen of our delegation of twenty-eight, who were willing to vote with me for Mr. Sherman. If I had consented to the subtraction of their votes from his column on the first ballot, it would have made a serious diminution of his strength.

If I had consented to the same thing on a later ballot it would have put him in the position of having his forces diminishing and falling away. I thought I ought not, for a mere empty honor to myself, to permit such an injury to be inflicted upon him, although I confess I did not then think his nomination likely. But while the Massachusetts delegation does not seem to me to have exerted a very decisive influence upon the result of that convention, it came very near it. After several ineffectual ballotings, in which the votes of the different States were divided among several candidates, the convention took a recess at twelve o'clock to four o'clock of the same day. Immediately a meeting was called by a number of gentlemen representing different delegations in a room in the building where the convention was held, for consultation, and to see if they could agree upon a candidate. The Massachusetts delegation had authorized me to cast their vote as a unit for any candidate whom I should think best, whom sixteen of the delegates —being one more than a majority—approved. I had ascertained their opinion. While as I said there were but thirteen at most who would support Sherman, considerably more than sixteen were willing to support either Harrison or Allison, and perhaps one or two others, who had been prominently mentioned, including, I think, Mr. Depew, although of that I am not certain. We met as I said. The New York delegation had authorized its vote to be cast unanimously for any person on whom the four delegates at large, Platt, Miller, Depew and Hiscock, representing different shades of opinion in the Republican Party of that

State, should agree. Three of these gentlemen, Platt, Miller and Hiscock, were present at the meeting. Mr. Quay, Chairman of the Pennsylvania delegation, was also authorized to cast the vote of the entire delegation as he should think fit. Mr. Spooner of Wisconsin, Chairman of the Wisconsin delegation, was present with a like authority. Mr. Farwell, Chairman of the Illinois delegation, was present with a like authority from his State. Mr. Clarkson, Chairman of the Iowa delegation, was present with authority to vote for Mr. Allison from the beginning. De Young, of California, thought he could speak for his people, though I believe without claiming authority from them. Filley, of Missouri, was also present. There were several other gentlemen of influence, though not all of them delegates, and not all of them entitled to speak for their States, but feeling able to assure the company that their States would accede to whatever agreement might be made there. The names of several candidates were discussed. I made a very earnest speech in favor of Mr. Allison, setting forth what I thought were the qualities that would make him a popular candidate, and would make him an able and wise President.

Finally, all agreed that their States should vote for Mr. Allison when the convention came in in the afternoon. Depew, as I have said, was absent. But his three colleagues said there could be no doubt that he would agree to their action, and there would be no difficulty about New York. We thought it best as a matter of precaution, to meet again a half-hour before the coming in of the convention, to make sure the thing was to go through all right. I suppose that everybody in that room when he left it felt as certain as of any event in the future that Mr. Allison would be nominated in the convention.

But when we met at the time fixed, the three delegates at large from New York said they were sorry they could not carry out their engagement. Mr. Depew, who had been supported as a candidate by his State in the earlier ballots, had made a speech withdrawing his name. But when the action of the meeting was reported to him, he said he had been compelled to withdraw by the opposition of the Agrarian element, which was hostile to railroads. He was then President of the New York Central and Hudson River Railroad Company. He said that this opposition to him came largely from Iowa, and from the Northwest, where was found the chief support of Allison; that while he had withdrawn his own name, he would not so far submit to such an unreasonable and socialistic sentiment as to give his consent that it should dictate a candidate for the Republican Party. The three other delegates at large were therefore compelled to refuse their support to the arrangement which had been conditionally agreed upon, and the thing fell through. If it had gone on, New York, Illinois, Wisconsin, Pennsylvania, Massachusetts, Iowa, California, and perhaps Missouri, would have cast their votes unanimously for Allison, and his nomination would have been sure. I think no other person ever came so near the Presidency of the United States, and missed it.

The result was the nomination of Mr. Harrison. It was a nomination quite agreeable to me. I had sat near him in the Senate for six years, my seat only separated from his by that of John Sherman, who, for a large part of the time, had been President pro tempore. So Sherman's seat was not then occupied and Harrison and I were next neighbors. I had become very intimate with him, and had learned to respect him highly as a very able, upright and wise man, although he developed, as President, an ability which I think his most intimate friends had not known before. Our relations then, and afterward, were exceedingly cordial. He was a wise, pure, upright and able President, and an eloquent orator, capable of uttering great truths in a great way, and able to bring them home to the understanding and conviction of his countrymen. He lacked what gave Mr. Blaine so great a charm, the quality of an agreeable and gracious manner. He had little tact in dealing with individuals. If a man travelled three thousand miles across the continent to say something to President Harrison, he would find himself broken in upon two minutes after the conversation began with a lecture in which the views in opposition to his were vigorously, and, sometimes roughly, set forth. He did this even when he was of the same way of thinking and meant to grant the gentleman's request. Blaine would refuse a request in a way that would seem like doing a favor. Harrison would grant a request in a way which seemed as if he were denying it. An eminent Western Senator said to me once what, of course, was a great exaggeration, that if Harrison were to address an audience of ten thousand men, he would capture them all. But if each one of them were presented to him in private, he would make him his enemy.

However, in spite of all this the country was safe with him. While his hand was on the helm she would keep the course of safety, of honor, of glory, of prosperity, of republican liberty. There would be no fear for the future of the country if we were sure to have in the great office of President a succession of Benjamin Harrisons.

This fault of his is a fault apt to beset good and honest men, especially when they are under the burden of great anxieties and cares. Such men at such times are intent upon the object to be accomplished. They are not thinking of personal considerations, of making friends or allies, or of the impression they are making for themselves upon mankind. But they need to learn a lesson. It is a lesson which many of them learn very late in life, that many a good cause has been jeopardized or lost by this infirmity of men who are leaders on the righteous side. There is written on the walls of one of the great English schools a legend which I suppose has been there for seven hundred years: "Manners Makyth Man." It is a curious fact, however, that this legend illustrates a portrait of a pig.

But while public men ought to be made to see how great a thing this is, the people ought to learn how little a thing it is—how insignificant are these foibles, irritable temper, habits of personal discourtesy, impatience, even vanity and self-confidence, compared with the great things that concern the character, the welfare, and the glory of the State. I beg to assure my readers that I make these observations partly as a critic and partly as a penitent.

I wrote to Benjamin Harrison after the Presidential campaign of 1896, urging him to consent to come to the Senate from Indiana, citing the example of Presidents Adams and Johnson, both of whom came back to public life after they had been President, although Mr. Johnson did not live to render any service in the Senate.

In my letter I expressed my sense of the great value of what he had done in the campaign. In reply I got the following letter. Nobody who reads it will doubt that the man who wrote it had a kind and affectionate heart.

November 10, 1896.
674 North Delaware Street,
Indianapolis, Ind.

My dear Senator:

It is very kind of you to take note of my work in the campaign, and I value very highly what you say of it—though your friendship has perhaps, in some degree, spoiled your judgment. I am thoroughly tired of the cares and excitements incident to public life in our country. To you I may say that the people of this state seem to be more strongly attached to me than ever. I never appear before an audience that I am not deeply moved by the demonstrations of the affectionate interest of my home people.

Possibly they would send me to the Senate this winter if I should intimate a willingness to take the place, but I do not feel that I can, and have said so.

If I could believe that any exigency in public affairs called for me, then my personal wishes would be subservient—but it is not so. My own belief is that as a free citizen I can do more towards giving a right direction to public affairs than I could as a Senator.

. . . .

My wife joins me in the desire to be kindly remembered to Mrs. Hoar.

Most sincerely your friend,
Benjamin Harrison.

Hon. George F. Hoar,
    Worcester, Mass.

I had a great many interesting experiences of Harrison's roughness of manner and honesty and kindness of heart, which it would not be right to relate here. But I may mention two or three.

When the term of General Corse, the Democratic Postmaster at Boston, expired, Mr. Dawes and I earnestly recommended that he should be reappointed. He was, with one or two exceptions, the most eminent living veteran of the Civil War. He was the hero of one of its noted exploits. "Hold the Fort" had made him famous in song and story. The business men of Boston, without distinction of party, were satisfied with him, and recommended that he be continued in the service. There was an association of the principal trades, nineteen in number, in which each trade had three representatives, making fifty-seven in all. Of these fifty-four were Republicans, and three were Democrats. Fifty-four, though not the same fifty-four, recommended the continuance of General Corse in the service. He was recommended by the Republican members from Boston in the Massachusetts Senate, and by most of those in the House, and by several of the Republican members of Congress, whose districts contained a part of the territory served by the office.

President Harrison almost angrily refused to reappoint Corse. He said that while his Marshals were being murdered in Florida, and the execution of the law resisted, he would appoint no man to public office who either sympathized with such things, or belonged to a party that did not oppose and resist them. I said to him: "Mr. President, how do you reconcile this with your declaration that no man would be removed from public office for political reasons?" The President was quite angry, and showed his anger in his reply. I said: "Good morning, Mr. President," and took my leave, also quite angry. But in a moment or two I went back, and said: "Mr. President, if you think there is a man in this country who has a higher regard for you, or a more sincere desire for your success than I have, I will never come here again." Mr. Harrison said, very pleasantly:

"I know that very well, Mr. Hoar." And the difference ended as quickly as it began.

President Harrison sent for me in a few days, and said he had made up his mind not to appoint Corse, but would appoint any Republican I would nominate. I gave a list of six names, of which that of Mayor Thomas H. Hart stood at the head. Next to him was that of Col. Horace Rockwell. Next to him was Wm. A. Russell. I selected Mr. Russell on account of his eminent business capacity, and also because I knew that both the President and Postmaster-General had great regard for him. I told him at the same time that I did not believe Mr. Russell would accept the office. Next to him was Samuel W. McCall, and the fifth name was that of John W. Candler. Next came Congressman Frank W. Rockwell. A messenger was sent to Boston that afternoon. He got there before daylight the next morning, and found Mr. Russell was absent on a long journey to the South. It was not thought the chances of his acceptance made it worth while to keep the office open. So it was offered to Mr. Hart, who accepted it.

Pretty soon afterward there came a vacancy in the United States Circuit Court for the First Judicial Circuit by the resignation of Judge Lowell. I desired to have Judge Putnam, of Maine, succeed him. He, too, was a Democrat. I did not know exactly what to do about it, after my experience in the post-office matter. So I saw Judge Gray of the Supreme Court, who had a high regard for Putnam, and asked him if he would be willing to recommend him to the President. Judge Gray said he would do it if the President applied to him for advice. But he was not willing to offer such advice unasked. He agreed, however, that I might say that Judge Lowell was about to resign, and that when the matter came up, if the President desired to know Judge Gray's opinion, he would be very happy to give it. The resignation took effect in the vacation of Congress. The President invited Judge Gray to come to see him, and determined to accept his advice. When I got to Washington in December, President Harrison sent for me and said:

"Mr. Hoar, I have pretty much made up my mind to appoint Judge Putnam to the Circuit Court, if you approve." I said: "Mr. President, I heartily approve. But I shall look with some curiosity to see how you answer the excellent argument you made against the appointment of a Democrat to office when General Corse's term expired," to which Harrison burst out into hearty laughter; and both incidents closed.

When the bill for rebuilding the William and Mary College building, which had been destroyed during the war, was passed, President Tyler and several other gentlemen interested in the College, were very anxious lest the President should refuse to sign it. They came to Washington to ask me to go with them to see him. This I did. I told him the history of the College, giving a list of the famous men who were graduated from there. I spoke of the great affection that had inspired the people of Virginia for centuries, and reminded him that his own ancestor, General Washington's friend, General Benjamin Harrison of the Revolution, had been a child of the College, and I pointed out what a measure of reconcilement it would be. The President listened with a rather disgusted look, until I got through, and just as I rose to take my leave, said: "Mr. Hoar, have you got any reasons except sentimental ones?" I said I had no others, except those I had stated. The gentlemen went out very down-hearted, and said when they got out that of course he would veto the bill. I said: "I think I know the man pretty well, and I think there is more than an even chance that he will sign it," and he did.

Just before his term of office ended, he was in the President's Room, at the Capitol, to dispose of bills when there was not time to take them to the White House before the hour of twelve o'clock, on the 4th of March. Many measures had been passed within an hour of the time of adjournment, among them a bill for the relief of the widow of Jefferson Davis. She had written a Memoir of her husband, on the sale of which it was understood she depended for her livelihood in her advancing years. But the publishers had neglected a technicality which, if the decision of one Circuit

Judge were good law, made the copyright void. So she was at the mercy of her publishers, and it was feared that they meant to take advantage of the defect. She applied through General Gordon, then a member of the Senate, to Congress for relief. A bill passed the two Houses, which I had drawn, providing that where the copies required by law to be deposited in the Library of Congress, had not been so deposited within the time required by law, the author of the book might deposit them at a later time, and the copyright should not be rendered void. This was made a general law. Just before twelve o'clock, when the Senators were in their seats ready for the inauguration of President Harrison's successor, which was to take place in about ten minutes, General Gordon came to me in great distress, saying: "The Attorney-General says the President means to refuse to sign that bill and that he can do nothing with him. Can you help us?" I had devised the plan, and had got it through the Senate. I went into the President's Room with General Gordon and said to the President that I wanted to speak to him about that bill, and began my story when he broke in upon me, very uncivilly, and said: "We cannot pass laws to take care of hard individual cases." I said: "No, Mr. President, we cannot pass laws to take care of individual cases, but where a general law is just and proper, it is no objection to it that it also affords relief in a case of individual injustice." The President made some remark to the effect that the people of the North would not like that we should go out of our way to help the widow of Jefferson Davis. I had not told my story, nor stated my reasons. I said quite angrily: "Well, Mr. President, if you will not hear me, I will stop now." I made my bow and withdrew from the circle. The President called after me: "Mr. Hoar, I will hear you." Whereupon I told my story. But there was no sign of relenting upon his grim countenance. I went back to my seat with General Gordon, who had accompanied me. He tore off a piece of an order of exercises for the Inauguration, and handed it to a page, telling him to give it to a friend of Mrs. Davis, who was outside. He had written on it: "He won't sign the bill." Just after the page had departed, the Attorney-General came up and told us that the President had signed the bill. General Gordon called back the page. I asked him to give me the torn fragment of the order of exercises, on which he had written the message, which I have kept as a memorial of the transaction, and of him. Perhaps I may be pardoned for adding that General Gordon came to me just afterward with great emotion, and said: "Hoar, save my allegiance to the Democratic Party, I want you to know that you own me."

These stories may seem trifling. But such trifles sometimes give an idea of the character of men like Harrison more than their greater actions.

Benjamin Harrison many times thought rashly and spoke hastily. But he acted always, so far as I knew, under the impulse of a warm, kind and brave heart, and of a great and wise intellect.

Some of my Southern brethren have spoken of me with undeserved kindness in recent years, and they like to say that my heart has softened within the last few years, and that I have become more tolerant and less harsh and bigoted than I was of old. Some Northern papers have taken the same view. What I did to secure the rebuilding of the William and Mary building, and to establish the policy of restoring at National cost all the property of institutions of education, charity and religion destroyed at the South, both of which were in the beginning opposed by the almost unanimous sentiment of my party associates, was done in the first and second terms of my service in the House of Representatives, now thirty-five years ago. A Boston newspaper published a series of articles denouncing me as a bitter partisan and a bigoted and intolerant hater of the people of the South, some years ago. That very week I received a letter from Mrs. Jefferson Davis thanking me for what I had done to save her from privation in her old age; a telegram from the authorities of William and Mary College, thanking me for my service in accomplishing the rebuilding of the College; and a personal call from Judge Howell E. Jackson, of Tennessee, a Southern Democrat and Confederate, thanking me for what I had done toward procuring his appointment as Associate Justice of the Supreme Court of the United States. These things all happened in the same year, I believe, certainly in a very short time after I had done what I could to induce the reappointment of General Corse and the selection of Judge Putnam.

I freely admit that I have believed with all my heart and soul in the principles of the Republican Party. But I think there can be found few members of that party who have been less controlled in their public actions by violent partisanship than I have.

CHAPTER XXXI

SATURDAY CLUB

IN 1877, about the time of my election to the Senate, I was chosen a member of the famous Saturday Club. I always attended the meetings when I could be in Boston until after the death of my brother, when every man who was a member when I was chosen was dead, except Mr. Norton and Judge Gray and the younger Agassiz and Mr. Howells, and all of them had ceased to be constant attendants.

They used to meet at the Parker House in Boston once a month. Each member was at liberty to bring a guest.

I suppose there was never a merely social club with so many famous men in it or another where the conversation was more delightful since that to which Johnson and Burke and Goldsmith and Garrick and Reynolds belonged. There was plenty of sparkling wit and repartee and plenty of serious talk from philosophers and men of letters and science. Agassiz and Jeffries Wyman would sometimes debate Darwin's doctrine of evolution, which Darwin had confided to Asa Gray, another member, long before he made it known to the public. Holmes and Lowell contributed their wit, and Judge Hoar, whom Lowell declared the most brilliant man in conversation he had ever known, his shrewd Yankee sense and his marvellous store of anecdote. Some of the greatest members, notably Emerson and Longfellow and Whittier, were in general quite silent. But it was worth going a thousand miles if but to see one of them, or to hear the tones of his voice.

In the beginning I suspected Dr. Holmes of getting himself ready for the talk at the dinner as for a lecture. But I soon found that was utterly unjust. He was always as good if a new subject were brought up, which he could not have expected and which was wholly out of the range of his experience. His stream was abundant and sparkling and clear, whenever you might tap the cask. "Take another glass of wine, Judge," he said to one of the members who was starting near midnight to drive twenty miles in the cold rain of autumn, "Take another glass of wine; it will shorten the distance and double the prospect."

Dr. Holmes and I were born on the same day of the year, although I was seventeen years behind him. I sent to the delightful Autocrat the following note which reached him on the morning of his eightieth birthday.

WORCESTER, Aug. 28th, 89.

My dear Dr. Holmes: Let me add my salutation to those of so many of your countrymen, and so many who are not your countrymen, save in the republic of letters, on your birthday. You may well be amused to think how many political reputations have risen and set during your long and sunny reign. I was led to think of this by the fact that my own birthday also comes Aug. 29th. But alas!

> Consules sunt quotannis et novi proconsules,
> Solus aut Rex aut Poeta non quotannis nascitur.

Of Governors and Senators we have an annual crop. But Autocrats and Poets come but once in eighty years.

The asteroids must not envy the Georgium Sidus his orbit of fourscore years, but rather rejoice in his beneficent and cheerful light, and in the certainty that it will keep on shining so long as there is a star in the sky.

I am
Faithfully yours
GEO. F. HOAR

I got the following pleasant reply:

BEVERLY FARMS, MASS., August 30, 1889.

My dear Mr. Hoar,

Your note of felicitation upon my having reached that "length of days" which Wisdom, if I remember correctly, holds in her right hand, was the first I received and is the first I answer. Briefly, of course, but with heartfelt sincerity, for I hardly thought that you whose hand is on the wheel that governs the course of the Nation, would find time to remember so small an event as my birthday.

You cannot doubt that it was a great pleasure to me to read your name at the bottom of a page containing so much that it was kind in you to write and most agreeable for me to read.

Please accept my warmest and most grateful acknowledgments, and believe me

Faithfully yours,
OLIVER WENDELL HOLMES.

NAMES OF THE MEMBERS OF THE SATURDAY CLUB WHEN I USED TO ATTEND ITS MEETINGS.

Ralph Waldo Emerson,
Edwin P. Whipple,
Horatio Woodman,
John S. Dwight,
Samuel G. Ward,
R. H. Dana, Jr.,
Louis Agassiz,
Benjamin Pierce,
J. R. Lowell,
H. W. Longfellow,
J. L. Motley,
C. C. Felton,
O. W. Holmes,
E. R. Hoar,
William H. Prescott,
John G. Whittier,
Nathaniel Hawthorne,
T. G. Appleton,
J. M. Forbes,
Charles E. Norton
J. Elliot Cabot,
Samuel G. Howe,
Frederick H. Hedge,
Francis Parkman,
Alexander Agassiz,
R. H. Dana,
Wolcott Gibbs,
Horace Gray,
Edward N. Perkins,
Asa Gray,
W. D. Howells,
Edmund Quincy,
E. L. Godkin,
William B. Rogers,
William Amory,
James Freeman Clarke,
Phillips Brooks,
William W. Story,
George F. Hoar,
John Lowell,
O. W. Holmes, Jr.,
Theodore Lyman,
William James,
Francis A. Walker,
Charles F. Adams, Jr.,
F. L. Olmsted,

Estes Howe,
Charles Sumner,
Henry James,
Martin Brimmer,
James T. Fields,
S. W. Rowse,
John A. Andrew,
Jeffries Wyman,
E. W. Gurney,
W. M. Hunt,
Charles F. Adams, Sen.,
Charles W. Eliot,
Charles C. Perkins,

R. Pumpelly,
H. H. Richardson,
William Endicott, Jr.,
William C. Endicott,
William W. Goodwin,
John C. Gray,
Edward C. Pickering,
Thomas B. Aldrich,
Edward W. Emerson,
Walbridge A. Field,
Henry L. Higginson,
Edward W. Hooper,
Henry P. Walcott.

CHAPTER XXXII

THE WORCESTER FIRE SOCIETY

I HAVE been for fifty years a member of another club called the Worcester Fire Society, some of whose members have had a remarkable relation to important events in the history of the country, of which the story will be worth recording. The club was founded in 1793, before the days of fire-engines, so that if the house of any of the members caught fire, his associates might come to the rescue with buckets and bags and bed-keys and other apparatus to put out the fire and save the property. But it long since became a mere social club. It is limited to thirty members.

The elder Levi Lincoln, Mr. Jefferson's intimate friend, confidential correspondent and Attorney-General in his Cabinet, organizer of the political movement which built up Mr. Jefferson's power in New England in the beginning of the last century, was not, I believe, a member of the Society himself. But his sons were, and many of his descendants and connections by marriage, certainly twelve or fifteen in all. When the office of Justice of the Supreme Court of the United States became vacant, by reason of the death of Mr. Justice William Cushing of Massachusetts, September 13, 1809, Levi Lincoln the elder was appointed, confirmed by the Senate and commissioned to fill the vacancy. Mr. Jefferson earnestly desired and urged his appointment. President Madison accompanied the offer of the office with a letter urging Mr. Lincoln to accept it in spite of a malady of the eyes from which he was suffering. Mr. Madison says he had got along very well as Attorney-General and he thinks he would find less inconvenience in discharging the duties of Judge. But Mr. Lincoln declined the office. He lived until 1820, retaining his health and vigor, except for the trouble with his eyes.

He was a very able man. He argued the case in which it was decided by the Supreme Court of Massachusetts that slavery was abolished in that State by the Constitution, in 1780.

Judge Story was appointed in his place. If Mr. Lincoln had accepted, it is likely that the great judicial fame of Judge Story would be lacking from American jurisprudence. Story would have devoted himself, probably, to professional or political life. At any rate he would not have been appointed to the Bench before 1820.

There can be no doubt that if Lincoln had accepted the seat upon the Bench, he would have been a thorn in the flesh of Marshall. He doubtless shared Mr. Jefferson's dislike for the great Chief Justice. The case of Dartmouth College v. Woodward was decided in 1819. There was in fact but one dissent, but any person who reads Shirley's book on the history of that case will be inclined to believe that without Judge Story Dartmouth College v. Woodward would not have been decided as it was.

More interesting and important is the relation, to Mr. Webster's seat in the Senate, of the second Levi Lincoln, son of him of whom I have just spoken, himself a member of the Worcester Club that has been referred to. He was Governor of Massachusetts, Judge of the Supreme Court of Massachusetts, and a Member of the National House of Representatives. He was elected Senator of the United States by one branch of the Massachusetts Legislature when the term of Elijah H. Mills expired, March 3, 1827. There can be no doubt that if he had consented he would also have been elected by the other House. Mr. Webster was chosen at the next Session. But before he was elected he wrote very strongly urging Mr. Lincoln to accept the office. He said in his letter dated May 22, 1827:

"I beg to say that I see no way in which the public good can be so well promoted as by your consenting to go to the Senate. This is my own clear and decided opinion; it is the opinion, equally clear and decided, of intelligent and patriotic friends here, and I am able to add that it is also the decided opinion of all those friends elsewhere, whose judgment in such matters we should naturally regard. I believe I may say, without violating confidence, that it is the wish, entertained with some earnestness, of our friends at Washington, that you should consent to be Mr. Mills's successor. I need hardly add after what I have said that this is my own wish.''

Mr. Lincoln felt constrained to decline, although the office would doubtless have been very agreeable to him, by reason of some statements he had made when elected Governor that he should not be a candidate for the Senate. Mr. Lincoln might, without dishonor or even indelicacy, have accepted the office in spite of those utterances. It was quite clear that all the persons who might be supposed to have acted upon them, desired his election when the time came on. But he was a man of scrupulous honor and did not mean to leave any room for the imputation that he did not regard what is due to "consistency of character," to use his own phrase. Now if Mr. Lincoln had accepted the office it is likely that he would have held it until his death in 1868. At any rate it is quite certain that he would have held it until the political revolution of 1851.

It is quite clear to me that the office of Senator was at Mr. Lincoln's command. Observe that this was in 1827, and was the election for the term of six years, ending March 3, 1833. That includes the period of Jackson's great contest with Nullification, when Mr. Webster, with all his power, came to Jackson's support. It includes the time of the Reply to Hayne, and the great debate with Calhoun.

Daniel Webster, I need not say, would have been a great figure anywhere. But if Mr. Lincoln had acted otherwise, there would have been absent from our history and literature Webster's Reply to Hayne, the support of Jackson in the day of Nullification, the debate with Calhoun including the speech, "The Constitution not a Compact between Sovereign States," and the powerful attack on Jackson's assertion of power in the removal of the deposits. The speech on the President's Protest, with the wonderful passage describing the power of England, would not have been made.

If the sentiment of Patriotism, and love of Liberty and Union are to be dominant in this Republic, we cannot measure the value of the influence of Daniel Webster and the speech in reply to Hayne. I am not sure that, without Mr. Webster's powerful championship of the side which prevailed, Mr. Calhoun's theory would not have become established. At any rate, it was the fortune of Daniel Webster that the doctrine of National Unity, whenever it has prevailed in the hearts of his countrymen, has been supported by his argument and clothed in his language.

Another incident of the same kind, not of like importance to those of which I have told, but still of a good deal of interest and importance, happened more lately. I had a good deal to do with it myself.

When President Hayes entered upon office, there were but three members of the Senate of either party who were supporters of his Administration. I was one of them. The other two were my colleague, Mr. Dawes, and Stanley Matthews of Ohio. President Hayes was, in my opinion, a very wise and able and upright man. It was an admirable Administration. He had a strong and excellent Cabinet. But his nomination had disappointed the ambitions of some very influential men in his own party, and the powerful factions of which they were the leaders and candidates. The opposing party had not only felt the usual disappointment in defeat, but denied the lawfulness of his election. So I was more familiar than would ordinarily have been likely to have been the case with all the councils of his Administration. The Secretary of State was my near kinsman, and the Attorney-General had been my law partner.

When the vacancy occurred in the English mission by the resignation of Mr. John Welsh, I very strongly urged the appointment of Mr. Lowell. Mr. Evarts was quite unwilling to select Mr. Lowell, and in deference to his wishes, President Hayes offered the place to several other persons, including myself. The offer was communicated to me by Mr. Evarts who was, at that time, Secretary of State. But there were many good reasons why I could not accept it. The offer was then made to Governor Alexander H. Bullock, a member of the little society of which I have spoken. I was myself authorized by the President to communicate his desire to Governor Bullock. His answer, declining on account of the condition of his family, will be found in the life prefixed to the published volume of his speeches.

Now, if Governor Bullock had accepted the appointment, which was undoubtedly very attractive to him, what Mr. Lowell did in England would not have been done. He will doubtless go down in literature as a great poet. But it seems to me he is entitled to an equal rank among the prose writers of the country, and indeed among the prose writers of the English language of our time. His admirable address on Democracy, the delightful address as President of the Wordsworth Society, several estimates of the British poets, delivered by him on various occasions in England when he was Minister there, are among the very best examples of his work in prose.

APPENDIX I

It was upon Mr. Sherman's motion that the words, "Common Defence and General Welfare," which have played so important a part in the construction of the Constitution, were introduced into that instrument. He proposed to add to the taxing clause the words, "for the payment of said debts and for the defraying of expenses that shall be incurred for the defence and general welfare."

This proposition, according to Mr. Madison, was disagreed to as being unnecessary. It then obtained only the single vote of Connecticut. But three days afterward Mr. Sherman moved and obtained the appointment of a Committee, of which he was a member, to which this and several subjects were committed. That Committee reported the clause in the shape in which it now stands, and it was adopted unanimously.

Its adoption is an instance of Mr. Sherman's great tenacity, and his power to bring the body, of which he was a member, to his own way of thinking in the end, however unwilling in the beginning. This phrase has played not only an important but a decisive part in the great debate between a strict construction of the Constitution and the construction which has prevailed and made it the law of the being of a great National life.

This story is well told in Farrar's "Manual of the Constitution," pages 110, 309, 324.

APPENDIX II

ROGER MINOTT SHERMAN, son of Roger Sherman's brother Josiah, was born in Woburn, Mass., May 22, 1773. Mr. Sherman was much attached to him and defrayed the cost of his education. He was an inmate of his uncle's family while a student at Yale College. He was graduated in the year 1792. He was one of the ablest lawyers and advocates New England ever produced, probably having no equal at the Bar of New England except Jeremiah Mason and Daniel Webster. I attended a dinner of the Alumni of Yale College some years ago. President Woolsey sat on one side of me, and Dr. Leonard Bacon on the other; and right opposite at the table was Rev. Dr. Atwater, then I believe of Princeton, but formerly Mr. Sherman's pastor in Fairfield. President Woolsey said that Roger Minott Sherman came nearer his conception of Cicero than any other person he ever heard speak. They used frequently to invite him to deliver public addresses at the College. But he never would accept the invitation. After refusal, the invitation would be renewed again after a few years with like result.

To the above estimate of Mr. Sherman, Dr. Bacon and Mr. Atwater agreed.

When I was in the Law School at Harvard, Professor Simon Greenleaf told the class in one of his lectures that he was once travelling through Connecticut in a carriage on a summer journey, and came to a town, I think Fairfield, which was the county seat. He stopped to get his dinner and rest his horses. While the horses were being fed he went into the court-house, intending to stay only a few minutes, and found Roger Minott Sherman arguing a case before the Supreme Court with Judge Gould on the other side. He was much impressed by Mr. Sherman's clear and powerful argument. Mr. Sherman and Judge Gould were engaged on opposite sides in nearly all the cases. Professor Greenleaf was so much interested by what he heard that he remained and attended court during the entire week. I do not remember his exact language, but he, in substance, gave an estimate of Mr. Sherman as a profound lawyer and able advocate, not less exalted than President Woolsey had given of him as an orator.

Some slight account of Roger Minott Sherman will be found in Goodrich's "Recollections."

Mr. Evarts once told me that there was an important controversy, involving the title to a valuable cargo, in which a lawyer in Hartford was on one side, and a member of the Bar of the city of New York on the other. The New York lawyer went to Hartford to negotiate about the case. The Hartford lawyer had obtained the opinion of Roger Minott Sherman for his client and held it in his hand during the conversation, labelled on the outside, "Opinion of Roger Minott Sherman," and moved it about under the eye of his opponent. The opinion was in fact that the Hartford man's client had no case. But the New York lawyer supposed that if the man had got Roger Minott Sherman's opinion, and seemed to set so much store upon the document, it was favorable to the party who had consulted him. He was much alarmed and settled the case on favorable terms to his antagonist.

Mr. Sherman was famous for the quickness of his wit. A story went the rounds of the papers in my youth, which may or may not have any truth in it, but which I will record. It is said that he was once arguing a case against Nathan Smith, a very able but rather coarse lawyer. Mr. Smith had discussed the question of law with the subtilty for which he was distinguished. Mr. Sherman said to the court that he thought his brother Smith's metaphysics were out of place in that discussion; that he was not adverse to such refinement at a proper time, and would willingly, on a fit occasion, chop logic and split hairs with him. Smith pulled a hair out of his own head, and holding it up, said,—"Split that." Sherman replied, quick as lightning, "May it please your Honor, I didn't say bristles."

The following is the passage referred to from S. G. Goodrich's "Recollections of a Lifetime":

"Roger Minott Sherman was distinguished for acute logical powers and great elegance of diction,—words and sentences seemed to flow from his lips as if he were reading from the *Spectator*. He was a man of refined personal appearance and manners; tall, stooping a little in his walk; deliberate in his movements and speech, indicating circumspection, which was one of his characteristics. His countenance was pale and thoughtful, his eye remarkable for a keen penetrating expression. Though a man of grave general aspect, he was not destitute of humor. He was once travelling in western Virginia, and stopping at a small tavern, was beset with questions by the landlord, as to where he came from, whither he was going, etc. At last said Mr. Sherman, 'Sit down, sir, and I will tell you all about it.' The landlord sat down. 'Sir,' said he, 'I am from the Blue Light State of Connecticut.' The landlord stared. 'I am a deacon in a Calvinistic church.' The landlord was evidently shocked. 'I was a member of the Hartford Convention.' This was too much for the democratic nerves of the landlord; he speedily departed, and left his lodger to himself."

Gift of
W. H. Smith